Wordsworth Donisthorpe

Individualism

A System of Politics

Wordsworth Donisthorpe

Individualism
A System of Politics

ISBN/EAN: 9783337072872

Printed in Europe, USA, Canada, Australia, Japan

Cover: Foto ©Suzi / pixelio.de

More available books at **www.hansebooks.com**

INDIVIDUALISM

A SYSTEM OF POLITICS

BY

WORDSWORTH DONISTHORPE

BARRISTER-AT-LAW

AUTHOR OF 'PRINCIPLES OF PLUTOLOGY,' ETC.

London

MACMILLAN AND CO.

AND NEW YORK

1889

PREFACE

THE range of subjects dealt with in the present volume is doubtless a wide one; but it will be found, I trust, that all have been treated consistently from what may be called the individualist standpoint. The merit of formulating this theory of government, and thus of laying the rough foundations upon which a sound art of Politics may be based, undoubtedly belongs to Mr. Herbert Spencer, who has contributed more to the scientific study of society than any other thinker—not even excepting Auguste Comte or John Austin. It is therefore with the greater regret that I find myself unable to accept either the principles or the conclusions set forth in Mr. Spencer's most popular publication on the subject—*The Man v. the State.* Though this in no way lessens the great debt of gratitude which all seekers after truth in this field owe to him. And for myself I take this opportunity of acknowledging it.

One word as to the order of the following chapters. Had I followed my own inclination I should have placed them thus :—I, II, III, VIII, IX, XII, IV, X, V, VI, VII, XI, in which order I will briefly refer to them. But I was over-ruled by friendly criticism. It was urged that my readers would wish to know something of the practical bearing of

Individualism on everyday affairs before inquiring too closely into the philosophic basis of the theory.

Chapter I. deals with the nature, growth, and development of states or organised societies; Chapter II aims at forecasting the final structure of the State for governmental purposes; and Chapter III seeks for the true scope of its action in relation to the individual units of which it is composed, and the resulting limitation of the liberties of the citizen. The reader who then passes at once to Chapter VIII will there find the doctrine of individualism carried to its logical extreme as philosophic anarchy; while the necessary qualifications of this extreme view are set forth in Chapter IX. The latter originally appeared in the *Westminster Review* (July 1886), and is but slightly altered; the principal addition being the pages showing the twofold origin of Justice. This chapter also contains my reasons for dissenting from some of Mr. Spencer's conclusions; and Chapter XII carries the war against Absolutism into the domain occupied by Mr. Auberon Herbert, his ablest general. In Chapter IV, returning to inductive individualism, I analyse the conception *Property*, applying the definition reached to the solution of certain practical problems. Chapter X deals with the modern school of land-law reformers, whose views seem to me to be pretty clearly expressed in a lecture by Mr. C. A. Fyffe, afterwards endorsed by a cabinet minister who, though he has since passed out of public notice, well represented the neo-radical opinions of our day. Chapter V, by an inquiry into the true nature of Capital, lays the foundation of the system of labour capitalisation which is worked out in the two succeeding Chapters VI and VII. And Chapter XI treats of the only consistent system of politics which can be opposed to that of individualism, namely, socialism.

The doctrines of socialism are growing in popularity, not in this country only, but all over the civilised world ; and they are in my opinion the chief danger in the way of social progress. The apostles of this delusive gospel are legion, and inasmuch as they disagree among themselves to such an extent that it is difficult to fasten any particular teaching upon them as a body, I have adopted my usual plan of singling out one of the clearest and best among their writers, and treating his exposition to a searching examination.

In conclusion I would add that I have little reason to expect popularity for this work. It is written without any party sympathy whatever. And I have deliberately adopted a tone rather polemic than apologetic, in the belief that dull and mealy-mouthed disputation is less calculated to rivet the attention and impress the memory than a more vigorous and uncompromising style of criticism. And I have done this even when differing from those with whom I am, in the main, in accord.

WORDSWORTH DONISTHORPE.

CONTENTS

CHAPTER VIII

CHAPTER IX

CHAPTER X

CHAPTER XI

CHAPTER XII

CHAPTER I

THE STATE: ITS GROWTH AND EVOLUTION

"THE State is an organism." The words flow glibly from the tongue, but do we clearly know what we mean by the State? Among the lower forms of animal life we are at a loss to know whether to regard certain organisms, such, for example, as sponges, as individuals or as aggregations of individuals. But among the higher forms of life we have no difficulty. The animals best known to us are practically bounded by their skins, and it is very seldom that a question of individuation arises of any importance, though doubts have been expressed both in modern and ancient Courts of Justice as to whether the purchaser of a mare in foal is *ipso facto* the owner of the foal.

In the vegetable kingdom the difficulties of individuation are considerably greater; if the rose-tree is an individual, what shall we say to the rose? Consider the growth of the strawberry, and of the banyan, which sends down roots from its branches to strike into the ground and themselves become trunks. One such tree, if it can be called one tree, has been known to measure more than five hundred yards in circumference round the trunks. Some would call the growth a single tree, and others would describe it as a grove of trees.

Social organisms in this respect more nearly resemble vegetable than animal forms. It is difficult to define and demarcate the individual. Those who have not reflected upon this difficulty may readily realise it by trying to group the

B

following under the heads of individual states and parts of states—Canada, Egypt, Servia, Hungary, Ireland, Germany, Sweden, Ohio, Poland, Wales. But if, on the one hand, there is difficulty in deciding in certain cases, in other cases, on the other hand, there is no difficulty whatever. No one will pretend that Yorkshire and Lancashire are two different and separate states. We all know the meaning of France, though we might find some difficulty in defining even that very precisely about the eastern boundary. Now, without attempting to define exactly the term State, or to follow Austin in his exhaustive inquiry into the question, let us take it for granted that in the main we understand pretty clearly what we mean by the term. Just as we know, in spite of the puzzles of individuation, that there are such individual things as oak-trees, so we know that there are such individual things as states. And let us trace the natural history of states from their first appearance on the planet.

And first, as to their origin. The germ of the State must of course be looked for and found in that phase of social development known as complete savagery; and I would venture to say that the very first state which ever existed was a human family consisting of a mother and her offspring. With all deference to sociologists, the family is a state and the earliest form of state. By "state" I mean not a mere aggregation of men, but a growth, a social organism. The laws which govern the structure of the earliest form of state must be presocial and therefore biological. These are the laws which underlie all political laws, and from which all political laws take their origin. It may safely be said that all the laws, the complicated laws of civilised nations, conflicting as they seem to us at the present day, are the lineal descendants of filial obedience and parental affection.

And next, as to the growth of states. The family, as such, doubtless existed for a very long period without any tendency towards coalescence, but in course of time we find these families drawn together in little groups and loosely compounded under a single head. Whether this aggregation was originally due to conscious combination for purposes of mutual defence and other advantages, or whether it was simply a clannish extension of the family following upon paternal recognition of offspring, and the consequent continuation of the family life during the lifetime of the head of the family, is a question for which there is neither the time nor the need in this place. All that it behoves us to note here is that in process of time we find the family consisting, not as among the lower animals of the mother and her offspring alone, but of the father together with his wives and all their children, many of whom are themselves fathers of families. In addition to these members of the family there were others who for various reasons were admitted into it. Here again, interesting as the subject is, I must come to a halt and content myself with referring those who wish to look deeper into this question of the structure of the early patriarchal system to the learned and fascinating works of the late Sir Henry Maine. Later still, we find larger families whose original head is no longer living, though there is no doubt that the sub-families composing it are apparently and professedly connected by blood. Whether the paterfamilias was as a rule the head of the senior family, or, as appears to have certainly been the case in some places, the youngest son of the deceased patriarch, or whether it was some other person elected or nominated or otherwise fixed upon, does not concern us here. The compound family existed, and we may call it a Gens or a Curia, or by any other name for which there is any warrant. Whoever the paterfamilias might be, there is something artificial in obedience to a brother as compared with filial obedience, which goes far to show that the compounding and continued adhesion of these houses was a conscious and deliberate act of which the motive was the advantage (of one sort or another) derived from co-operation.

Finally, these families and houses are found aggregated into what is called a tribe. And still later, as we sail down the stream of history we see these tribes themselves beginning to confederate. The interests which the tribes had in common, though not so deep-rooted or important as those which were peculiar to the members of the several tribes, were nevertheless an ever-increasing quantity. Probably the earliest trustworthy records of intertribal action are the historical references to the Greek Amphictyonic Councils. These Amphictyones were

councils of the tribes and not of the states. The tribes, no
matter how great or how small their individual importance,
had all an equal vote. Not even Athens or Sparta counted for
more than one. And we see the same process going on in '
early Roman history. Whether the Comitia Curiata was originally anything more than a periodic gathering of the elders
under the old paternal roof (*curia*), or whether it was an
expressly invented institution for the management of tribal
affairs, cannot be positively stated (I incline to the former
view), but there can be no doubt from the name and from the
ceremonies associated with the institution that it dates back
from a period when the "Kurios" himself ruled the Gens,
and likely enough under that designation. Curiously enough,
the Amphictyones were concerned not only with the foreign
affairs of tribes federated for offensive or defensive alliance,
but also with the worship of the deceased common ancestor.
As time wore on, these somewhat loose federations became
more and more welded into a compact whole or *nation*. And
this is the highest social aggregate with which we are as yet
fully acquainted. Into the actual causes of these successive
compoundings and recompoundings we have no time to inquire
here. They are to be found set forth in Mr. H. Spencer's
Principles of Sociology.

Pari passu with this compounding and recompounding of
social groups a transformation necessarily takes place in judicial
procedure. The despotism of the *paterfamilias* continues to
obtain recognition inside the family, whereas transactions
between members of different families or between families *inter
se* are regulated in accordance with the laws of the *Gens.*
Similarly, when the Houses become federated, a higher system
of law governs the dealings between them. Some of the
differences in procedure survive to a very late period in history,
and prove a mystery and a stumbling-block to jurists and
historians. For example, the Romans recognised a distinction
between *res mancipi* and *res nec mancipi*, a distinction based
solely on the mode of transfer required by law. The line
of cleavage was in no wise coincident with the line of cleavage
between our real and personal property. Slaves, oxen, horses,
and certain other chattels, fall into the category of *res mancipi*,

together with land and houses. May not ploughs be added to the list ? Jurists have sought in vain to discover something common and peculiar to the members of this class, the true explanation being that whereas *res nec mancipi* were transferred according to the rules of the smaller group, *res mancipi*, on the other hand, were transferred by means of the process required by the law of the compound group. And for this reason : individual members of a family were in the habit of exchanging, bartering, and selling such things as spears, bows, shields, and the like, but not land and herds, which were held in common by the family, or by the head of the family, for the common good. Hence, when houses, acres, and flocks came to be the subject of dealings between family and family, it was necessary that the dealings should satisfy the requirements of the wider jurisprudence. Nor is it difficult to see that a more solemn and involved ceremonial would tend to develop itself in transfers from one family to another. Simple delivery in the presence of the patriarch or other responsible witnesses would be sufficient evidence as to the ownership of a shield or spear amongst members of the same family. The transaction would be sufficiently notorious. The thing would change hands, and words would be used indicative of the *animus* of the parties. But in the case of interfamily transactions much more would be needed. Not only are the things in which families would deal unfit for delivery from hand to hand (as, for example, a flock of sheep or a range of pasture), but, furthermore, the representative of the State (of the group-force) is not present embodied in a single person ready to take note of the transaction. It is necessary either to convene those who in assembly represent the will of the federated families, or to perform such ceremonies as can leave no room for doubt as to the fact and the nature of the transaction. In Rome these ceremonies took the form of mancipation. We ourselves can recall the beatings of boundaries and the thrashing of younger children, and sometimes of the parson, which took place at the chief landmarks.

Similarly, when tribes had already become welded into fairly homogeneous states, and were on the point of still further federating into larger nations, we find a new conflict of jurisdictions and of legal systems. Probably a like explanation may be given of the Roman division of law into "Jus personarum" and "Jus rerum," the former being the law of the smaller and earlier group, and the latter the law of the compound aggregate. It is unnecessary here to go into the history of the prætorian edict. It is sufficient to note that at the time of the remarkable integration known as the growth of the Roman Empire, the civil law was found unsuitable and inapplicable to the dealings between Roman citizens and members of surrounding states. Hence the "Jus Gentium" or law of the new federation, as opposed to the law of the chief component state. Whether this new jurisprudence came into existence through a process of extracting that which was common to the races and peoples making up the new aggregate ; or whether it was based (as some alleged) on the law of nature, *i.e.* abstract justice as it presented itself to the conscience of successive prætors; or whether it grew up in some other way, matters not here ; what is needful to be noted is this, that on the recompounding of the states, each with its own body of law, a new and more widely based legal system arose, which conflicted with and eventually tended to absorb the legal systems of the component states. The same process is at work amongst us at the present day. Nations and wide empires are themselves beginning loosely to aggregate and to become more or less federated. The legal systems of the several states are inapplicable to the dealings between members of such several states ; and the outcome of the striving after order and amicable arrangement is what is known as international private law. If any body of rules on the face of the earth presents the appearance of being based on equity pure and simple, surely it is this body of rules recognised by civilised nations as governing the dealings of members of different countries one with another. The principles underlying these laws will doubtless tend in time to swallow up the principles upon which are based the laws peculiar to the separate nations. Thus international law may be regarded as a foreshadowing of—

" The Parliament of man, the Federation of the world,
When the common sense of most shall hold a fretful realm in awe,
And the kindly earth shall slumber, lapt in universal law."

Thus the international private law of to-day bears the same relation to English or French law as the " Jus Gentium " of old bore to the Roman civil law or the Corpora Juris of Greek and African states ; the same relation again which the " Jus Gentilitium " bore to the patriarchal law which preceded it.

History presents a picture of ever-increasing political integration. First, the only political unit is the group consisting of a mother and her offspring; then on the recognition of paternity we enter upon the patriarchal stage, in which the unit consists of the descendants of a living male together with his wives and slaves ; the whole despotically governed by himself. Next we have clans or houses consisting of federated families descended from a common deceased ancestor, having a common name and worship and held together by common interests which tend to wax stronger and stronger. These *gentes* again tend to be recompounded in one or more degrees till we have the tribe and eventually the nation. Finally, nations are themselves showing signs of coalescence. At first the bonds which hold together the new federation are extremely slight and frail; but they tend to strengthen until the individuality of the component groups is almost, if not altogether, merged and lost. And concurrently with the political integration there necessarily goes a juridical integration.

Frequently the new federation has proved itself unstable and premature, and has rapidly or gradually disintegrated. Nature places a limit on the process. We have seen the Macedonian Empire no sooner built up than falling to pieces again. So too the Roman Empire, after some centuries of a cumbrous and elephantine existence, broke up into fragments which proved to have more vitality than the great whole from which they were detached. Clearly there is a limit to the size of a state ruled by a single government. Now what is the law of the limit of political integration ? In biology the limit of mass of any living organism depends on the power of co-ordination ; that is to say, any part of the body being affected the whole must respond ; otherwise it is not an organic whole, but a mere aggregate. The same holds good of social organisms. The size of such organism depends on its power of internal co-ordination. But as time wears on, the possibilities of integration are increased. We have better means of communication both in the way of locomotion and signalling. We have increased general knowledge, and more widely distributed information. And finally, we have the coming together of large masses of the population in towns. Hence, there has resulted a constant tendency towards increasing integration. Men can work together in larger numbers century by century. At the same time it behoves us to inquire whether the aggregations we see around us are themselves stable, or whether they are too large for equilibrium.

Since the break-up of the Roman Empire there has been a constantly increasing tendency towards the welding together of tribes and small states into larger wholes. Take the history of these Islands. About a thousand years ago this England of ours was divided into no less than seven (probably we may say eight) separate kingdoms. Ireland was divided into at least five kingdoms, and Scotland consisted of a larger number of independent states. Well, about the year 829, the states of the Heptarchy were rolled into one, to which was given by King Egbert the name of England. Two or three centuries later Wales was merged in the whole. Shortly after that Ireland was conquered, hardly merged perhaps, but conquered and annexed. Then in 1603 England and Scotland were united under one political head, and a century later, in 1707, their Parliaments became one. In the year 1801 the Act of Union brought the Irish representatives to Westminster, and so apparently consolidated and completed the political integration of the British Isles. So that here there has been a continuous tendency on the part of the smaller states to federate and finally to become welded into an organic whole. A similar process has been going on all over Europe.

In no preceding ages have the possibilities of integration been more enormously increased than in the present century. The wonderful applications of steam and of electricity to the satisfaction of man's wants, the immense strides made in the speculative sciences, and last, but not least, the bringing within reach of all classes of the people of the rich treasures of useful knowledge which were formerly the monopoly of the few; these and other causes have operated to stimulate political integration to an extent hitherto unattainable, not in this country only, but all over the civilised world. In our own day we have seen the unification of Italy; the unification of Germany; the gradual absorption of small states by larger states. Denmark is disappearing; Holland and Belgium have not many years of independent existence left to them. We have witnessed the most stupendous war this planet has yet seen, waged in America for the same great principle. In fine, the history of this century is the history of political integration. It is true that alongside of flourishing and growing social organisms we have others in a state of decay and dissolution; but even here, as in Turkey, signs are not wanting that the process of re-integration on a new basis is following close on the snapping of the old bonds. When, therefore, there is any question as to the wieldiness of an empire, the presumption at the present day is clearly in favour of a policy of integration rather than disruption, of increased rather than diminished mass. Above all, the British Empire, which before the development of the means of co-ordination above referred to supported an unprecedented mass, cannot now be suspected of inability to maintain its equilibrium without strong evidence to the contrary. A series of maps of Europe for the first year of each half century since the time of Justinian would well illustrate this tendency, and would at the same time demonstrate the folly and ignorance of those statesmen of all ages whose object was the maintenance of what they called "the balance of power." This view of foreign affairs is conservative in the worst sense of the word, and it is not yet quite extinct.

Among other means of co-ordination must be counted improved systems of political organisation. With the sifting and reduction of governmental duties, a corresponding adaptation of governmental organs has been effected. Much has been done in the way of division of labour, and every year the State learns a new lesson from the processes of individual enterprise. From a single despot or a chamber of notables, the ruling body has developed into a gigantic framework of departments, interdependent and actuated from a common centre.

In spite of the immense aids to empire-making, the enormous growth of "Greater Britain" within the last two centuries has put a considerable strain on the cohesive forces of Anglo-Saxondom. The most disastrous effect of this strain was the detachment of the American branch a hundred years ago. Nor until within the last few years (one might almost say months) has there been any very visible retendency towards imperial integration. The statesmen of England seem for two generations to have been smitten with the insular craze; though we should be careful not to express in psychological terms what is really a natural sociological accompaniment of rapidly-augmenting political mass. The agitation here and in the Colonies in favour of some kind of closer union between the mother country and her offspring is one of the healthiest signs of the times, and upon its eventual success or failure depends the future of the English social system.

The problem before us (though it is a problem which will eventually appear to solve itself without the assistance of individual cobblers) is the discovery and adoption of some increasing bond of union between England and her off-shoots and dependencies, such as shall admit of central action without weakening local liberty. And the solution is Integration with Decentralisation,—though this is, of course, merely a re-stating of the problem in fewer words. For what is the precise nature of the integration and decentralisation to be brought about ? Is not the freedom of the parts incompatible with the working of the aggregate as an organic whole ? Let us see. No sooner had Alfred the Great finally consolidated the union of the kingdoms of the Heptarchy, than he at once set to work, and re-subdivided the whole into counties. This interesting illustration throws light on the essential nature of true political integration. Local government *of some kind* is a necessary concomitant of political extension over a wide area, rather than antagonistic thereto. Integration must not be confounded with centralisation, nor must decentralisation be confounded with disruption. On the contrary, wide empire (or commonwealth, if Mr. Froude prefers the term) can be built and maintain its stability only on local liberty, on the freedom of the parts in all matters not affecting the whole.

The problem resolves itself into an inquiry as to the true limits of the imperial functions and the residual local functions, be they of large limbs or small. " Certain interests," writes De Tocqueville, " are common to all parts of a nation, such as the enactment of its general laws, and the maintenance of its foreign relations. Other interests are peculiar to certain parts of the nation, such as, for instance, the business of the several townships. . . . A centralised administration of local affairs is fit only to enervate the nations in which it exists, by incessantly diminishing their local spirit. It may ensure a victory in the hour of strife, but it gradually relaxes the sinews of strength." Thus by decentralisation is meant not local legislation, but local administration. So that no local enactment must contravene the law of the empire ; and although local authorities may lay down any rules they choose for the interpretation and administration of the general law, they must not be permitted to enact a conflicting law. And this is true of all local self-governing areas, from the largest colony to the smallest municipality. The principle upon which the functions of the one rest must equally apply to the functions of the other.

Hitherto this has been the guiding principle of local government in England, though there are signs of a tendency to run off the lines. In America, on the other hand, the reverse process is at work. The several states have exercised legislative privileges at variance with the proper functions of the central government; but the tendency at the present time is strongly in the direction of the absorption by the United States Government of the legislative powers of the several states. This is a healthy symptom and likely to become more pronounced.

What is the explanation of the lack of ardour shown by many of our colonists for some kind of Imperial Federation ? They are loyal enough ; and indeed the more loyal among them seem to regard the movement with the greater distrust. The answer is simple. They have unpleasant recollections of Downing Street. If England has neglected her maternal duties in many respects, she has made up for it by increased fussiness and arbitrariness in others. As might have been predicted, those colonies which she has treated with the most grandmotherly solicitude, like infants not fit to be trusted with the most ordinary duties of self-protection, have turned out the

least self-reliant, the least prosperous, and the most clamorous
for more help from home.   It is with nations as with individuals.   The more you let them alone, the better they thrive.
In illustration of this contention I cannot do better than quote
a paragraph from Mr. Froude's charming book *Occana*.   " From
the Cape to Australia—from intrigue and faction and the
perpetual interference of the Imperial Government, to a
country where politics are but differences of opinion, where the
hand of the Imperial Government is never felt, where the
people are busy with their own affairs, and the harbours are
crowded with ships, and the quays with loading-carts, and the
streets with men, where every one seems occupied, and every one
at least moderately contented—the change is great indeed.
The climate is the same.   The soil on the average is equal :
what Australia produces South Africa produces with equal
freedom.   In Australia, too, there is a mixture of races—
English, Germans, and Chinese.   Yet in one all is life, vigour,
and harmony ; the other lies blighted, and every effort for its
welfare fails.   What is the explanation of so vast a difference ?
One is a natural and healthy branch from the parent oak, left
to grow as nature prompts it, and bearing its leaves and acorns
at its own impulse.   No bands or ligaments impede the action
of the vital force.   The parent tree does not say to it, You
shall grow in this shape, and not in that ; but leaves it to
choose its own.   Thus it spreads and enlarges its girth, and
roots itself each year more firmly in the stem from which it
has sprung.   The Cape is a branch doing its best to thrive, but
withering from the point where it joins the trunk, as if at that
point some poison was infecting it."   This is a case of " doing
those things which we ought not to have done."   But England
is quite as guilty of " leaving undone those things which we
ought to have done."   While she has busied herself with
preaching and dictating to her own colonies, she has allowed
other nations to establish themselves in dangerous proximity to
them.   Colonial remonstrance has usually been in vain.
While our pioneering brethren across the Atlantic have acted
upon the Monroe doctrine in North America, we have allowed
French and Germans quietly to appropriate " unconsidered
trifles " in the way of harbours and islands from which at no

distant date they must be ejected, possibly not without trouble and expense. It is said that we may smile at these amateur invasions of New Guinea and the New Hebrides and Angra Pequena, etc. etc. Curiously enough, however, all the smiling is done at home. The Colonies do not join in the fun. They have suffered too much already in the process of "surviving" by way of proving that they are the fittest, and they prefer in future to take it for granted. If instead of bullying the Dutch in the Cape we had long ago proclaimed a sort of Monroe doctrine for South Africa and also for the islands of the Australasian Archipelago, we should have saved ourselves much complication. Again, regardless of the history of our Indian Empire, we have suppressed all private initiative like to that of the famous Company. Only recently a similar enterprise, on a scale the future limits of which could not be foreseen, was launched in Borneo, when the home government lost no time in throwing cold water upon it.

Too little consideration is paid to the necessities of the pioneers of Anglo-Saxondom on the borders of our straggling empire, and too much, far too much, to the sentiments of ignorant if well-meaning faddists at the centre. It is easy to sit at home and cant about the rights of the poor Indian to his hunting-grounds, but the struggling settler knows that a thousand human beings can be supported on those lands under cultivation for one who can find subsistence on it as a hunter: and he knows also what a wild beast is the native with whom he has to deal. "Aborigines protection" is a hobby which requires a consummate ignorance of aborigines generally and a plentiful infusion of fiction to render it a really fascinating pursuit. Yet England panders to the crotcheteer.

Thus, when the feasibility of the common government of two or more nations or areas is raised, there are two distinct questions to face. First, is the political integration of the two countries desirable and practicable? Second, if so, for what degree of decentralisation are the two or more component parts ripe? The questions are quite distinct and should be kept so Unfortunately there has been a marked tendency to confuse them.

In the light of the above reflections let us consider the

question of the government of Ireland. We have seen that as regards the total separation of Great Britain and Ireland, the presumption is against it. But presumption is not proof. Those who regard political integration most favourably, as calculated to remove the friction due to international barriers and jealousies, will hardly approve the action of the Fifth Monarchy Men, who, a couple of centuries ago, so far believed in the federation of mankind as to convene a meeting in London to weld all the nations of the world into one empire, and to proclaim Jesus Christ king. Surely this was carrying an abstract principle to an absurd length. But without going so far as that, history shows that it is quite possible to exceed the normal limits of a wise federation. It may be doubted whether Austria-Hungary is a stable combination. The kingdom of the Netherlands clearly was not; though many would have regarded it as quite as natural and politic as the union of Norway and Sweden or of Great Britain and Ireland. Hence the policy of the latter union is not altogether out of court, and must be considered on its merits as a practical question of political expediency. Disintegration, dismemberment, and disruption of the Empire are fine phrases, well calculated to split the ears of the groundlings; but the present application of a principle how good soever in theory is a question for the practical statesman.

Now, what are the grounds upon which the practical statesman must base his decision as to the expediency and opportuneness of a proposed union of two or more peoples or of a proposed discontinuance of any such existing union? Certainly not in accordance with phrases of general import. To demonstrate the folly of such a course it is only necessary to cite a few instances in which a decision was or might have been required. Will any one contend that, whether wise or unwise, the cession of the Ionian Islands to Greece was tantamount to the disruption of the British Empire? Then again the Transvaal was part of this Empire. When after an unsuccessful war, independence was conceded to the victors, did that amount to dismemberment? But to take an even less doubtful case. Not many years ago France nominally formed part of the dominions of the Kings of England; was the withdrawal of such claim a tribute to the principle of disintegration? Hundreds of other instances of varying degrees might be cited, but these suffice to show that before any case of separation, or admission of separation, can fairly be denounced as violating the principle of political integration, it must be clearly established that a true and natural union, as distinguished from an artificial or nominal union, antecedently existed. The actual point to be decided is whether the present time is opportune for tightening and strengthening the bonds which tend to weld the English and Irish into a homogeneous people, as the English and Welsh have long since been welded; or whether the circumstances are such that the bonds should be slackened, and an impetus given in the opposite direction; that is to say, towards the divergence of the two peoples.

I will venture to submit three reasons which at any time may be urged against the artificial union of peoples.

1st. Two nations cannot well be welded together when active co-ordination is difficult; as, for instance, when they are situated at a great distance apart and without rapid means of communication. Hence the natural disruption of the Spanish Empire in South America. Hence the probable transfer of the Dutch possessions in the East Indies either to England or to Germany at no very distant date. These are cases in which co-ordination with respect to a given centre is or was difficult, if not impossible. Of course no one will contend that this can be put forward as a valid reason against governing Ireland from Westminster. If the British Government is capable of ruling what are called the Crown Colonies at distances very much greater than from London to Dublin, it is obvious that this particular objection cannot hold.

2d. The second argument which may validly be urged against union or in favour of disunion, is that the two peoples in question are in different stages of social evolution. In such cases it is wellnigh impossible to weld the two into a single homogeneous state. Now this objection might fairly be urged againt the political union of the Anglo-Saxon people and the people of India. It is impossible to weld these two races into a homogeneous state, because they are in totally different

stages of social evolution. Institutions suitable to the one
people would ruin the other. The Hindus are somewhat back-
ward in civilisation, but will any one pretend that apart from
slight differences the English and the Irish are in different
phases of social development ? Are the Irish as *individuals*
vastly inferior to the English in any particular ? If so, what ?
Without enumerating their soldiers, poets, philosophers, artists,
and men of science, it is not necessary to go farther afield than
to Spain of a hundred years ago to meet the vulgar contention
that they are inferior as statesmen. In the middle of last
century, the Spanish Ambassador to the Court of St. James
was an Irishman, so was the Spanish Ambassador to the Court
of Stockholm ; so was the Spanish Ambassador to the Court of
Vienna ; the Prime Minister of Spain was himself an Irishman ;
so too was the organiser of the Spanish Army. In fine the
wisest and best government which Spain has ever known was
conducted by Irishmen. Surely without going into details or
naming names, this alone goes to show that the Irish are not
wanting in administrative ability. Thus the English and Irish
peoples can hardly be said to be in different stages of social
evolution. And the second argument against their permanent
union breaks down.

3d. The third reason which can be urged against the
union of races is that their claims upon the Government are
conflicting. Let me explain. So long as it is admitted by
both parties that it is the duty of the State to uphold the true
religion, clearly nations of different religions cannot well be
ruled by the same governing body. If the State is to take
sides in any degree in the matter of religion, it would be
difficult indeed for the same government to rule England and
Ireland. The Irish are of opinion that the Roman Catholic is
the best form of religion ; the English, for reasons known to
some of them, maintain that the Protestant form (or one of
them) is better. Now, if the Government is to decide between
these two, it must appear to side with one of the disputants ;
and the other will feel aggrieved and possibly rebellious.
Again, to take a kindred matter, the Irish have strong views
on the matter of the marriage-tie. The English are in favour
of permitting divorce under certain conditions. If the State

is expected to interfere in such matters, clearly the Union Government must offend one nation or the other. The English lean towards liberty; the Irish towards coercion. The State must choose between them. Conversely, the English favour coercion and the Irish liberty in the matter of tobacco culture. The reason is not far to seek. The climate and soil of Ireland are favourable to the growth of tobacco. In England it is otherwise. Thus by the prohibition of the growth of tobacco the revenue is increased without inflicting any injury on English farmers. The Union Government had to choose between them, and it elected to suppress tobacco culture in the British Isles. Again, England is a manufacturing people; Ireland is almost wholly an agricultural people. Hence freedom to buy in the cheapest markets (or the dearest if preferred) enables England to profit by purchasing her raw materials at the lowest figure, whilst the like liberty, besides being useless to Ireland, enables foreign competitors to undersell her sole produce in the home markets. Here again England favours liberty and Ireland coercion. If and so long as the State is expected by both parties alike to interfere in such matters at all, it is clear that the Union Government must favour one nation and aggrieve the other. Under such circumstances it is obvious that the union can be maintained only with difficulty and friction. It is also highly probable that where there is considerable disparity in the strength of the two nations, the Union Government will tend to lean toward the wishes of the stronger and the more numerously represented in the ruling body.

We see that while England favours coercion in some matters, Ireland favours coercion in other matters ; and not until the policy of non-interference by the State in *all* matters is recognised as a general rule, can the two peoples hope to flourish together under a common Government. At present this is not the case. Both parties clamour for State aid here and State control there, while they differ as to where the State should interfere and where it should not. Hence the third argument against the union seems to be at the present time a most valid one.

When Irish and English alike shall have learnt the great

lesson of history aright—the lesson of liberty—then, and not till then, will the time be thoroughly ripe for a happy union. Unfortunately, both parties in both countries—Liberals and Conservatives—are doing their utmost to inspire the people with blind faith in the omnipotence of the State. If the State is justified in transferring one-third of the property of one class of the citizens to another class, without compensation, it is difficult for the most highly instructed—it is impossible for the uninstructed—to understand why it cannot with consistency transfer two-thirds or even three-thirds, and an agitation is naturally set on foot with the very logical object of "freeing" the land. Why not? Englishmen of both parties have admitted the duty of the State to intervene between landlord and tenant, and the simple, unsophisticated folk of both countries push the principle to its logical extreme. Conservatives have vied with Liberals in voting the money of the British taxpayer for the purpose of pauperising the Irish in a hundred ways, and the logical reply of the British taxpayer is: If you want £150,000,000 for the Irish, let those contribute it who live in Ireland and may benefit by the expenditure, but do not take it out of the pockets of the English shopkeeper and farmer. The Government, with the approval of both parties, has constructed or subsidised railways, has built harbours and docks, has embanked rivers and made canals; it has provided the people with instruction at less than cost price; it has built houses and let them at less than the normal rent; it has fixed prices between buyer and seller, and frequently paid the difference out of public moneys. It has done all these things, and a thousand more, out of its own apparently bottomless purse, and the simple citizen cannot see why, with such a powerful machine, much more cannot be effected. Even now eminent financiers are gravely talking of regulating the value of silver. It has fallen, they say, too low. Let us enact that $16\frac{1}{2}$ ounces of silver shall for ever be worth one ounce of gold. Hey Presto! The thing is done. "And pray," asks Hodge, "why not while you are about it enact that the value of wheat shall again be sixty shillings a quarter? It will suit us agriculturists, and perhaps we are as deserving on the whole as retired Anglo-Indian pensioners." "Let us build houses for the poor," says Lord Salisbury; "at the expense of the landowner," adds Mr. Chamberlain; "and why not supply them with beef and bread?" replies Mr. Hyndman. And so the ball is kept rolling.

So long as the Irish pray for rain and the English pray for fine weather they had better supplicate different gods. When they are prepared to accept the weather as it comes, and to make the best of it, they can then worship in the same temple.

It is needless to observe that this alone does not solve the question of separation. There are other factors. Foremost among them is the reasonable doubt whether the *effective* majority in the area called Ireland is actually Irish. Apart from the mere question of numbers there is room for doubt whether the British element in that country is not as powerful as, if not more powerful than, the Irish. But whether this is so or not, in these days of rapid communication and stimulated intercourse, silent and unseen links are daily being forged which tend firmly to bind the two peoples together. No legislation will prevent the Saxon from bringing home an Irish bride, and if English beauty has not quite the same fascination for Irishmen there is a metallic attraction which seems to exercise a corresponding influence. Again, consider the large and increasing number of professional Irishmen who have made England their home, and the even larger number of English and Scotch traders and manufacturers who have settled in the rising towns in the North of Ireland and elsewhere. To make aliens of all these by a stroke of the pen would be a national calamity for both peoples, and more especially for the Irish.

Again, there is another consideration, which must nowadays be put forward with bated breath, and that is the predominant need of the superior race. For strategic reasons it might not be prudent for England to allow the western island to be under foreign government. If so, the argument of nations enters—the argument of force. In such cases it behoves the leaders in both countries to see that the paramount needs of race do not conflict with the just rights and liberties of individuals, no matter to what race they may belong. It must not be forgotten that it is the superior social organisation which tends to survive, and not necessarily that of the superior individual type of man. The latter may be absorbed and even eventually predominate, but it will be under the system of the better organised society.

Disruption and dismemberment are phrases, but if it can be shown that the repeal of the Union would be a step in the direction of breaking up what tends to become a *natural* integration, whether it is so now or not, then the cry stands condemned by history and by science. But why beat the air? English and Irish statesmen of all parties are now professedly unanimous in declaring that no such thing as separation is contemplated or even desired. The only question between them is as to the best form of local government, and here again we find complete unanimity in the view that increased decentralisation must be effected. In order to form a correct estimate of the direction which decentralisation should take in this particular instance it is necessary to consider the general question.

When wide areas come under a single government, certain powers must be delegated to local subordinate bodies, or the work cannot possibly be performed at all. The question for us to determine is, what functions should be delegated? and to whom should they be delegated? In scientific phraseology, what are the proper structures and functions of local governing bodies? How are the areas to be defined? How are the individuals within those areas to be represented? To what extent, if any, should they be permitted to act independently and arbitrarily.

It is customary for local government reformers to begin with the areas, and having determined these, and arranged a representative system, to fit out the authorities so constituted with suitable duties. This is not the method which science would prescribe. Rather let us first discover the matters which, while they must be accomplished somehow, cannot well fall within the province of the Imperial Government on the one hand, nor command the resources of private enterprise on the other. This can best be done, not by mapping out in theory

all the whole duty of society, and then distributing it on some
à priori plan, but by ascertaining what duties are actually
at the present day undertaken by the central authority in this
and other countries, and what by the local authorities.   By
comparing these with the functions of local governments in the
past we obtain a fair view of the field which history and
experience have marked out as the proper sphere of local
governmental action.   We find that many of such duties and
whole classes of them have long since passed out of the domain
of local government.   Some of them have been taken over by
the State, others have become obsolete, while others again have
been appropriated by private adventure.   On the other hand,
to compensate local authorities for the loss of these functions,
new ones have been freely conferred upon them in this country.
If the counties are no longer the custodians of the prisons,
they are compensated for the lost privilege by being entrusted
with the guardianship of the health of the cattle of the district.
The county is likewise empowered to keep an eye on billiard
players, ballet dancers, alcohol drinkers, and lunatics.   It is
entrusted with the carrying out of the Weights and Measures
Act and of the Adulteration Acts.   It supervises knackers'
yards, and grants conditional licenses to game dealers, to
pawnbrokers, to dynamite sellers, and some other traders.
The county also provides a section of the police, for which it
is in part responsible.   It is liable for the maintenance of
certain roads and of certain bridges, and of shire halls and
other semi-public buildings.

Besides the county we have in England several other areas
of local government of one sort and another.   There is the
Parish ; there is the Union ; there is the Municipal Borough ;
and there is the Local Government district, besides a number
of areas mapped out in accordance with special objects, such
as Highway Districts, Improvement Act Districts, etc.   The
functions of these authorities are very various.   They supple-
ment the work of the counties in providing police, in maintaining roads and bridges and lunatic asylums ; they are
concerned with the drainage of land and the prevention of
floods.   They comprise sanitation, education, registration, vaccination ; the provision of cemeteries, libraries, museums, wash-

houses, baths, playgrounds, etc.; the supply of gas, water, electricity, and certain conveyances; all these duties in addition to the great work of poor relief. Over and above these matters of more or less universal interest, there are special concerns proper to certain localities, such as the duties of fishery boards and the maintenance of docks, piers, harbours, and embankments.

This survey is, of course, very superficial and incomplete, but it is sufficient for the purpose of showing that the duties of local authorities do not seem of themselves to carve out areas in common; that is to say, there is no particular reason why the area requiring a separate authority to see to cattle disease should be the same area for which a highway board is required or separate provision for lunatics. The parish might be a suitable area for the registration of births and deaths, and at the same time most unsuitable for the construction of tramways. For the maintenance of main roads one would almost suppose the best area would be coextensive with the island. So the Romans thought. While for the purposes of gas or water supply the municipal borough would seem the most suitable. Police, prisons, paupers, and lunatics, again, appear to have no particular relation to any definite locality. The dispensation of justice is an imperial concern. The pauper has no claim on any locality; poor relief is not a forced tribute of pity from neighbours, but a sop to revolution, a bribe to those who would otherwise have the choice only between starvation and crime. Hence it is not a provincial concern. So the lunatic, like the criminal, is dangerous to the whole community, and like the criminal must be looked after for the general good.

Other areas, like the old acre, seem to be determined by the amount of work of a given kind that a busy man can get through in a given time. Such are the areas most suitable for registration, vaccination, and inspection. Others again are determined by nature, such as fishery boards and harbour authorities. The river basin would likewise seem to demarcate the area of drainage boards. For the purpose of churches, schools, libraries, museums, baths, wash-houses, parks, cemeteries, etc. etc., the area would naturally adjust itself to the amount of time required to get to them with convenience. People cannot be expected to walk four miles to a public wash-house, or ten miles to a park. Half a mile seems to be about the limit of the radius from the polling-booth beyond which the patriotism of the parliamentary voter is put to a considerable strain. Country churches and schools seem to draw for a radius of about two miles. But all such points can be ascertained only by that experience in each particular case which private enterprise alone seems able to supply.

One thing seems certain. The arbitrary creation of an area for no better reason than because it has a name, and the endowing of the authorities of such an area with duties, is opposed to all the teachings of nature and of science, and can lead to no better result than mischief and confusion. Rather than adopt such a system, let there be as many areas as there are functions; let them overlap over and over again. Why not? A gas company feels no inconvenience from the fact that its area of supply overlaps that of the neighbouring water company. Neither has a railway company ever been known to complain that the area to which its powers apply is not so coextensive with the county or counties in which it lies. What grounds are there for any such complaint? And yet when these and the like functions are undertaken, not by private individuals and companies, but by local authorities, there arises an outcry that the areas of exploitation should be identical. Why those persons whose common educational needs are peculiar to their district should also necessarily require peculiar railway accommodation, is a puzzle to all who are unacquainted with local authorities in general, and the raw material from which they are manufactured. If highway boards were composed of men peculiarly conversant with roads and road management, it is not likely they would claim to supply the inhabitants of the highway district with milk or with gas; but being, as they are, merely unqualified persons recruited from the ranks of the busybodies, and possessed of unbounded confidence in their own administrative abilities, they are accustomed to find themselves sitting together, not only on the highway board, but likewise on the school board, the board of guardians, and, perchance, round some other table of fussy officialism. Now why, they ask one another, cannot we transact all the public business in one place and at one time as they do in Parliament? Why, asks Smith, am I entrusted with the management of the affairs of the vestry, if I am not fit for a seat on the school board? It never occurs to him that he may have considerable acquaintance with the people of the parish and their requirements as to wash-houses and gas-lamps without possessing even the rudiments of a sound education, or any knowledge of educational needs. In fine, so far from being an evil, the overlapping of areas is natural, and, as will be seen, an unmixed good.

The localisation of government must always be in response to a distinctly seen demand. The reason for it must be apparent and easily explained. The area must be, as it were, self-determined, and not artificially carved out. Thus the Isle of Man should not form part of the same highway district as Cumberland or Wigtownshire. Why not? Because there is a sea voyage of some hours between them, and because the two regions have no roads in common. For like reasons a municipal borough is a natural self-defined area of self-government (so far as local administration can be called self-government); and the difficulty consists not so much in discovering that such a town, for instance, as Leeds, has peculiar interests which are not shared by Wakefield or Bradford, as in determining where the actual limits of Leeds should be drawn; where, that is to say, the suburban population seem to have more in common with the surrounding country than, by reason of their distance from the centre, they have with the town. That · because a region is called Nottinghamshire it should have a little Parliament of its own to which should be entrusted all conceivable local duties is the height of absurdity. If a county happened to be completely surrounded by a chain of mountains, or other barrier which cut it off from the adjacent country, there might be some reason in regarding it as for some purposes a suitable area for local government; but surely the accidental fact of its having been separated from the adjoining districts by an artificial line for some forgotten reason by a Saxon King is no ground at all. Voluntary combination should in all cases be the precursor of political

segregation.   Co-operation is coextensive with common needs.
People do not combine aimlessly, or because they live in the
same wapentake.   Indeed, there would be no reason for
granting local government at all, but for the trouble and
difficulty of interpreting and administering the general law on
every occasion from a distant centre.   Private enterprise can,
and will, affect all that is good and lawful for any local area
which is ripe for it.

There is only one thing which private enterprise cannot
do, or rather which it is prohibited from doing, and that is the
coercion of the minority—of the unwilling—of those who,
while they will not contribute towards the common end, yet
reap part of the advantage of it at the expense of the majority.
Clearly, if nearly all the inhabitants of a street determined to
light that street with gas, those who refused to contribute
would, nevertheless, have the benefit of a well-lit street.
Similarly with paving, draining, and many other things.   Left
to themselves, the majority in the locality would say to these
non-unionists, " You are unwilling to live among us on terms
of mutual assistance, and the common sharing of burdens and
advantages ; you had better go."   And go they would.   But
this is not tolerated by the larger majority outside.   The
minority in the locality is in the majority in the country in
this matter of freedom of combination.   Local anarchy would
solve the problem.   Instead of which a certain amount of
State socialism takes its place.   Compulsory co-operation is
sanctioned by the State under certain conditions which are
expressed in general terms.   The application of these laws to
the numerous special cases which arise in all parts of the
country requires either a very large and unwieldy central
machinery or some kind of local administration.   And herein
lies the folly of advocating local *legislation*.   If local authorities
are to be permitted to legislate independently, it is clear we
are brought back to the original position of local anarchy.   If
a majority can pass a law of a general nature, it can equally
well pass a law of a special nature, and order at once the
unwilling minority to quit.   Indeed, it needs but a little
thought to perceive clearly that local legislation is absurd.
The interpretation of State law may be left in the first instance

to local authorities; in fact, private enterprise already claims
that right; as, for instance, when a man removes a hurdle from
across a public footpath with his own hands. But if the
other party has no right of appeal, then we have again the
original situation, for the power of irresponsible interpretation
is virtually the power of independent legislation. Hence, it
appears, all so-called local legislation should be, in reality,
central legislation, administered either by State constituted
local authorities or by an association of private individuals.
If the law is exceeded, the local authorities have acted *ultra
vires*, and their action is invalidated. If the law is conformed
with, the private association has vindicated the law, and its
action will stand.

Thus the highest form of local government is one of
complete and unqualified private enterprise. If, for example,
the State considers that the laying down of private rails on the
public highway in the shape of tramways is really a public
good, it is justified in passing a general enactment to that effect,
subject to certain specified conditions, among which may be
the tacit consent of a given proportion of the inhabitants (or
certain of them) of the districts through which the line passes.
The tramway company under such a State law would then proceed to lay down its lines without necessarily asking the leave
of any one, and if no one could raise a valid objection, or, being
able, had not the energy or public spirit to do it, the company
would proceed with its business, to the great advantage of some
and the annoyance of others. If the people of a district have
not the combining instinct and the public spirit to associate
themselves together for common ends, the more they are left to
suffer for the defect and to develop the instinct the better for
themselves and the whole race. The thrusting of so-called self-
government upon people who do not claim it and exercise it
without external pressure is like sending Joachim to play to
the proverbial gentleman who cannot distinguish between " God
save the Queen " and " The Old Hundredth." It is not a
higher quality of article that he requires, but the faculty to
appreciate what he has at his door. The local authority,
whether State recognised or self-appointed, and the individual
with whom it is at issue, must be regarded as, in all respects,

upon an equal footing. Suppose Smith declines to pay the
demand made upon him by the municipality in respect of some
new water-works within whose circumscribed district he resides,
but from which he derives no benefit. The Court of Justice
(whether of first instance or of appeal) must decide whether
the conditions and circumstances are such as are declared by
implication in the Act of Parliament relating to the subject to
require the contribution of Smith. Unless such general enactment is beyond question, no arguments from local convenience
can override Smith's right to choose his own investments. If
local laws can of themselves operate to the detriment of any
individual in the district, then clearly they conflict with the
law of the land which guarantees that individual the full
enjoyment of all liberties which are not therein expressly
restricted. It is hardly necessary to add that I do not put
forward this doctrine of the Individualisation of Local Government as a system to be adopted all at once ; but merely as an
ideal to be kept in view and gradually approached. In its
entirety it is rather the system of the remote than of the near
future. It is probable that even England is hardly ripe for it
yet. As M. Léon Say has recently pointed out, " the proper
limit of State action cannot be laid down in the same way as
a boundary line on a map ; it is a boundary which alters in
accordance with the times, and the political, economic, and moral
condition of the people."

To apply some of these conclusions to practical questions
of the day : Local areas should be left to the natural delimita-
tion of voluntary combinations. And areas should overlap as
naturally as the areas of ordinary trade distribution. Above
all, the areas should not be carved out first and the functions
allotted after. Such a course is the very reverse of scientific.
The powers of local authorities should, *in no respect*, exceed those
of ordinary voluntary associations. Consequently, local bye-
laws cannot conflict with the law of the land. For the right
of the majority in a locality is not based on the superior force
of the majority in that locality, but on the superior force of the
effective majority in the country of which it is a part, which
force is *delegated* (for reasons which seem good to such effective
majority) to the numerical majority or other portion of the

inhabitants of the said district. This is an important fact not to be forgotten. Thus the local majority has no more right to act on its own initiative than the local minority ; or than the policeman who carries out the will of the State ; or than the private individual who interferes in the interest of law and justice in a row at a fair. They must all take the responsibility of their actions. It may be said, and truly, that if the State in its wisdom thinks fit to enact that the will of the majority in a given locality shall in all matters prevail, then the will of the majority in that locality is as supreme and as well based on ultimate force as the will of the effective majority in the country itself; being, in fact, based on the will of that majority. This is so. And the same is also true of any less general, though equally indefinite, delegation of State power to a local majority. Thus the indefinite power to do what it chooses in respect of such or such matters ; as, for instance, all matters relating to the trade in alcoholic liquors ; or to the hours of closing in retail shops ; or to the regulation of places of public amusement ; puts the local majority in respect of these matters in the same position that it would occupy if the locality were an independent one. The minority forfeit the liberty which belongs to them by virtue of being members of the larger community. The whole process is, to whatever extent it is carried, one of political disintegration.

And what is the remedy for all this ? Must we revert to a system of centralisation ? Not at all. Quite the reverse. Decentralise down to the unit itself, the individual. Does Smith find the house adjoining his own a source of annoyance to him ? Is there noise and singing there all night ? Is it the centre of attraction for disreputable persons whose presence is dangerous to him ? Let him prove the nuisance and suppress it, if he can. If not, let him betake himself elsewhere. If several persons in one street find a public-house in that street or near to it a continual source of drunkenness and of temptation to their servants, or otherwise obnoxious to them, let them prove the nuisance and suppress the house. If I keep a pig in my back garden and nobody feels injured by it, why should I alter my arrangements ? But if my neighbours or any of them find the smell objectionable, or fear the sanitary consequences, let them or any of them prove the nuisance and suppress my pig-stye. But it is asked, how is the nuisance to be proved? It is not enough in a Court of Justice to show that the neighbours or some of them, or even all of them, object to the thing complained of. That does not constitute it a nuisance. Your house may be painted in the worst possible taste, utterly hateful to the eyes of your neighbours, but they are powerless to compel you to alter it. The church bell next door may go near to distracting me, but I have no remedy by merely showing that I am subjected to great annoyance. But if the annoyance is caused not by a church bell but by my next door neighbour's organ, I may get the nuisance abated. Now unless the opinion of the majority of the locality is to be taken, how is the question of nuisance to be settled by the courts?

In reply to this the question may be asked, and how is it to be settled when the opinion of the majority is taken? The majority of whom? According as you carve out your localities into large or small areas, so you strengthen or render precarious the rights and liberties of individual citizens. Suppose a locality should decide to eject all persons professing religious opinions at variance with those held by the majority, would the State be justified in deserting the minority and leaving them to the tender mercies of a clique who might themselves be in a decided minority in the country, though locally in a majority? Suppose a majority of the inhabitants of Cork decided to prohibit the opening of a retail shop in that town by an Englishman, would the State be justified in permitting such an act of tyranny? Similarly, if the people of some obscure town should pronounce in favour of closing all houses for the sale of tobacco or cheese or alcoholic liquors, with or without compensation to the traders affected, could this be tolerated? With injustice and tyranny on the one side, and the effective force on the other, what conceivable reason can be adduced for putting up with the injustice? Of course if the effective majority in the country themselves choose to act unjustly, tyrannically, and foolishly, there is no power on earth to stop it. We have reached the ultimate source of power and it is poisoned. So much the worse. But when there is an appeal to a higher power, the surrender of such power into the hands of local majorities is nothing less than political suicide; it is voluntary political disintegration.

It is quite true that such is the nebulous state of the law regarding nuisances that almost any action brought by an individual for the suppression of anything objectionable to him is something like dipping his hand in the lucky-bag. But the remedy for this is a better induction from the numerous decisions in nuisance cases with a view to forming the nucleus of a code, a process which is in course of accomplishment, and which would be more rapidly effected but for disturbing causes. The very principles upon which the English law relating to nuisance is based are continually being called in question by the highest authorities; and probably the chief reason for the lack of attention given to the subject is the prevalent belief that the new legislation concerning local government will settle this and many other difficult problems. It will do nothing of the kind. Both parties at the present time seem pretty well agreed to take a step in the direction of the Commune; but it will only throw the difficulty a step farther back.

There can be no doubt that the belief in local legislation as distinguished from local administration is at the bottom of the present wave of feeling in favour of such moves as a separate parliament for Ireland, a secretary for Scotland, the disestablishment of the Church in Wales and the like. If the State Church is an advantage, why should the majority in Wales (a minority in the whole country) seek or be allowed to injure the Welsh minority? If, on the other hand, the State Church in any way injures either by taxation or unfair privileges and monopolies those who are not members of it, then the majority in Wales ought to be ashamed to desert their fellow-sufferers in England by getting rid of the evil where it is most felt and thereby weakening the feeling against it. Again, far too much respect has been paid to sentiment in the matter of certain fiscal and other privileges in the Isle of Man and the Channel Islands. Such anomalies should be swept away. Above all, the absurd custom of passing one act of Parliament for England, another for England and Ireland, and a third for Scotland is quite out of date. A vigorous effort should be made not to differentiate the laws of the three kingdoms or provinces, but to assimilate them.

We have but to look abroad to see how different has been the behaviour of foreign states. While we have been sleepily creating new difficulties for future statesmen and lawyers to remove, French and Prussian and | Italian statesmen and lawyers have been straining the resources of strong governments to assimilate the laws of the different provinces under their sway, with a view to removing all possible sources of dispute and envy, and to "maintaining and invigorating the principle of national unity."[1]   The object of the continental codes has been less the unification of the various legal systems obtaining in different parts of the country than the amalgamation of the political elements.   " In the case of the Prussian Code," writes Professor Amos, " it is less easy than in the case of the French Code to separate the object of promoting political unity from that of promoting legal unity among the heterogeneous elements of a newly-consolidated state, though the twofold object is quite as conspicuous here as it was in the French case." " The Italian Civil Code," writes the same author, " is a further specimen of the close connection existing in all the continental codes between consolidation of the laws on the one hand, and the necessity of riveting or promoting political and legal unity on the other.   This code is in fact a composite edition of the various codes prevalent in different parts of the whole newly-constituted Italian territories."[2]

This laxity on the part of Englishmen to accomplish what other nations in face of immeasurably greater obstacles have either effected or come near to effecting may perhaps be attributed to the comparative stability of England's internal economy, but the true explanation is the absorption of the national energy in the direction of increasing mass, at the expense of co-ordination, just as in the case of a growing child Nature applies herself with such zeal to growth as to neglect form and proportion.   When the full size has been approximately attained, then the awkward, gawky movements are less and less observable, and the limbs respond more smoothly, deftly, and gracefully to

[1] Preface to the *Italian Civil Code*, published in 1866.
[2] *An English Code*, by Sheldon Amos, M.A., 1873.

the stimulus from headquarters. The time has now arrived for England to pay less attention to the extension of her boundaries and more attention to the unification of her parts. It is for her to discover and perfect a political system workable over a world-wide area, avoiding centralisation on the one hand and disintegration on the other. This can be done only by a careful sifting of central and of local functions, whether the subordinate locality be a wide colony or a compact borough; whether it be situated at the Antipodes or on the banks of the Thames.

This is the great problem for the Anglo-Saxon people. I believe the mathematical genius who once demarcated London for certain fiscal purposes performed the operation with the aid of a map and a pair of compasses. Not far behind him in arbitrariness come those who would erect Wales into a separate province on the strength of a historic name, a half-dead language, and an annual Eisteddfod of sentimentalists. The Welsh are a fine people, but there are probably more of them in England than in Wales, and there are more people of English descent in Wales than there are of pure Welsh. Again, beyond the artificially bolstered-up system of Scotch law there is little or nothing to justify the drawing of a political boundary line between England and Scotland. Whether the Northumbrians are more akin to the Lowland Scotch or to the people of Devonshire or Kent is a question for ethnographers. If the Scotch law is in some respects, whether in substance or procedure, better than our own, why should we rest content with the inferior? And if in other respects English is better than Scotch law, clearly some persons in Scotland, if a minority, have a right to require that which deals justice. The case of Ireland, with the exception of certain recent legislation of a local and temporary character, presents fewer difficulties. Most of the English law, both common and statute, extends to Ireland, and if half the ingenuity which has been spent in differentiating the two legal systems had been expended on their assimilation, their unification would long since have been accomplished. The reckless way in which tiny dependencies like Gibraltar, Heligoland, the Channel Islands, and the Isle of Man have been permitted to make laws, not of a merely local effect, but conflicting with what should be the law of the whole empire, is remarkable. A like carelessness is noticeable in the United States of America (though to a diminishing extent). The New York Civil Code is a particularly feeble attempt at the codification of the English Common Law by utterly incompetent persons. But whether codification is desirable or practicable, or neither, in no way affects the importance of maintaining an identical legal system for the whole of Anglo-Saxondom. At the same time it is idle to pretend that this can be effected until some philosophical distinction has been drawn between matters which are in themselves local and matters which necessarily concern the whole empire. The application of the principles underlying this distinction is the great problem for the English-speaking peoples of to-day. Until this is done, all attempts at codification of the law are foredoomed to failure, all efforts, however benevolently conceived, towards the " conciliation " of discontented branches of the British Empire (whether in regions populated by Hindus, or by Dutch Boers, or by French Canadians, or by Scotch or Irish Celts, or by any of the numerous races of the world who for good or ill are destined to flourish or to perish under the Anglo-Saxon social system) are and will be vain and futile.

The art of government is making a new departure. A new day has dawned for humanity. The triumph of democracy is complete ; and imperial law must henceforth be based on individual and local liberty.

D

CHAPTER II

THE science of politics and the art of politics are two distinct branches of study, and should be kept so ; just as the science . of mechanics is a very different matter from the art of engineering. One may be an adept in the science, and yet utterly unskilled in the art—quite unable to apply the conclusions of the science to the art. So also we may be expert at an art, and yet be more ignorant than we should be of the science on which that art is based. For example, many an able mining-engineer is insufficiently acquainted with the truths of geology, while many an experienced geologist is altogether ignorant of the art of mining. At the same time, though it is very desirable to keep the two studies distinct, it is impossible for the practical man to carry on his work to the best advantage without some acquaintance with the underlying speculative science.

Now the science of politics, by whatever name known, is very little studied at the present day by our statesmen. They even affect to despise it. On the other hand men of science, or as they have been styled, " cloistered economists," are prone to imagine themselves capable of solving all kinds of political problems simply by the aid of scientific research, without any practical experience whatever of the facts and conditions of the situation. Let me give an illustration ; sociologists have reached the conclusion that the end towards which civilisation is moving, the goal which it bids fair to attain, is a system of self-government. In other words, self-government is the government of the future, and presumably therefore the best government. But it is for the practical statesman to decide when any particular nation is ripe for the application of the principle.

Few will deny that England has reached this stage of development; but when we look farther afield, when we pass even to India, where the people are indeed in a comparatively high degree of civilisation, we find grave doubts whether they are yet fit to exercise the functions of a self-governing nation. Certain doctrinaires in this country, but quite inexperienced in Indian affairs, are indeed anxious to thrust it upon them, but those who have more practical knowledge of the inhabitants are of a contrary opinion. And even those book-learned but inexperienced young statesmen would shrink from imposing free institutions on such races as the Zulus. We all remember the reception accorded by the Turks to Midhat's paper constitution. It remained a dead letter. Free institutions are no doubt good, but they are good only for peoples who demand them.

If this is true of uncivilised races, of semi-civilised races, and even of races which like the Hindu have reached a fairly high degree of civilisation, it follows that there must have been a time in our own course of development when we also were unripe for free institutions. When was that date passed ? Again, the same people is ready for one form of freedom before it is ripe for another. A nation is not suddenly transformed from a despotism into a free democracy ; it acquires its liberties one by one, and at dates separated by long intervals of time. Hence it is quite conceivable that there are some forms of freedom for which even the English people are not yet prepared. We are therefore compelled to qualify the general and too-sweeping proposition " Self-government is good " to this effect, " Self-government is good for those peoples which are ripe for it," or in other words, it is good for those for whom it is good. And for whom is it good ? To this question the cloistered economist has no answer. It is a question of experience, a question for the practical statesman.

Again, philosophical jurists have detected a distinct tendency in the laws of civilised nations towards individual ownership, in land as in other things. All forms of common ownership operate in restraint of transfer. And this is true not only of tribal and family ownership, but also in a less degree of what is called dual ownership, where the interests of the two parties are diverse. But, although the tendency towards separate ownership is strongly marked, it by no means follows that any particular people is ripe for it. In the case of Ireland, the English land system was thrust upon a nation which had not yet emerged from the stage of tribal ownership, and the effects of the shock have not yet spent themselves. The same thing was done again in Bengal a century ago. Lord Cornwallis's arguments in favour of his scheme of land reform are unimpeachable, the one flaw in them was this : basing his predictions as to the effect of the separate system in Bengal on his experience of the working of that system in his own country, he overlooked the extreme unlikeness between the two peoples. The immediate consequences were injury to the Zemindars, cruelty to the Ryots, and permanent loss of revenue to the Government. And at the present day the question seems to be whether it will not be deemed necessary to modify the arrangement, even at the cost of England's honour (no very high price they say nowadays). Here, again, is a problem for the practical statesman : must we refit the boot to the foot, or leave the foot to grow to the boot ? It is merely a question as to how far one or other process has been already in part effected. But the sociologist has said his last word, namely, the highest civilisation will adopt the system of separate or individual ownership.

I have dwelt at some length on the distinction between the art and the science of politics, because we are at the present moment exposed to two dangers—the one is the rule-of-thumb politician, who turns a deaf ear to all the teachings of science ; the other is the "professor," who hastens to apply the inductions of science to cases which do not supply the requisite conditions.

In order to understand political institutions, to track their general tendencies, and to predict their future we must study them from their origin, from the earliest times of which we have any records. The germs of all existing laws and institutions will be found far back in the days when our ancestors were in that stage of civilisation which is called the "patriarchal stage." In the archaic independent family all our modern complex institutions existed in embryo, just as the little acorn contains within itself all the potentialities of a spreading oak. The earliest form of the State is the family with its internal despotism and its external independence; for it must be remembered that the family was amenable to no law from without. Curiously enough, Austin, writing before any progress had been made in law-history, goes out of his way to refuse the title of political society to a single family. "Let us suppose," he says, "that a single family of savages lives in absolute estrangement from every other community. And let us suppose that the father, the chief of this insulated family, receives habitual obedience from the mother and children. Now without an application of the terms which would smack of the ridiculous, we could hardly style the society a society political and independent, the imperative father a monarch or sovereign, or the obedient mother and children subjects." He quotes Montesquieu in support of this view. Antiquarian research has thrown much light on the condition of society in its infancy, and the situation pictured by Austin is now known to have been a very accurate description of the condition of our ancestors. The father was king, priest, and judge, and the whole system was an absolute despotism. The early Hebrew records furnish us with pictures of these little independent nomad families, wandering about over the face of the earth at war with all mankind. It is from this period that the institution of monarchy dates.

But when these families came to group themselves together in clans and tribes for mutual protection and advantage there was a tendency for the heads of the families so compounded to claim an equal voice in the management of the general concerns. Thus resulted what is called an oligarchy, or, in the language of the rulers themselves, an aristocracy. It is true that there are forces at work which for a very long period tend to cause the reins of government to pass into the hands of some member of the ruling body—some man of great force of character or natural superior power. The point to note now is that from the date at which families first began to compound themselves into houses or "gentes," we have the possibility of aristocratic government. As we have seen, these houses or clans again recompound themselves into tribes, which in process of time aggregate into the larger group called the nation.

A tendency has been observed by historians for the government of the nation to gravitate steadily into the hands of larger and larger numbers of the people, till the ruling body comes to comprise all the individual members of the community. It is not urged that this state has ever yet been reached, but that such is the observable tendency. This tendency has been styled democratic. There are many forces in society operating in a contrary direction, but as social development proceeds, the forces acting in the direction of democracy increasingly prevail. This is a well-based political induction. We are not now concerned with the causes of this tendency—the fact is patent. No doubt the increase of knowledge, and its diffusion among all classes of society, together with increased facilities for communication between the masses and their classes, and the increasing power of organisation, will together have the effect of rendering the rule of the few for the good of the few distasteful to the many, while at the same time supplying the populace with the means of rectifying the anomaly.

Having recognised the truth that civilised nations have tended, are tending, and will continue to tend in a democratic direction, let us proceed to ask the question, Is the tendency a good one? Is it a tendency to be desired or merely one to be put up with as a necessary evil? I believe the very best friends of democracy have admitted its inherent weakness and vices. Not to multiply authorities, let me cite one who is universally admitted to have been a staunch Liberal and a true friend of the people. Lord Brougham writes :—" The democratic form has some virtues of a high order. The defects, however, are equal to the excellences. The supreme power is placed in wholly irresponsible hands. The tyranny of the multitude is intolerable, because it pervades the whole community searchingly, and oppresses the humblest as well as the highest. Faction is even more predominant than in aristocracies on certain subjects, and always the most important. Anything like free discussion is impossible. The administration of justice is constantly interfered with, especially of criminàl justice. There is no security for steady and consistent policy, either in foreign or domestic affairs ; a risk of entire and violent change attends the administration and even the constitution ; and the peace of the country as well abroad as at home is in perpetual and imminent danger."

Few will deny that there is at least a considerable amount of truth in this impeachment. The practical question for us all is whether, in spite of its inherent faults, we are to accept the principle of democracy, or to fall back on some system of aristocracy or monarchy, or as Lord Brougham himself advocates, on some mixed system ? Seeing that to democracy applies the old proverb, " Too many cooks spoil the broth," seeing that divided counsels result in delay and sometimes in disaster, seeing that democratic government is wanting in continuity of purpose, is shifty and inconstant, swayed by sudden gusts of popular impulse, and above all, that it embodies the will rather of the ignorant than of the wise : admitting all these charges, shall we in despair look elsewhere for the form of government of the future, or shall we rather seek to discover the several causes of these observed diseases, and if possible the cure ?

I hardly feel called upon to furnish illustrations of these observed vices of popular government. Those who care to see them fully exposed may be referred to the late Sir Henry Maine's very able work on the subject. But to take one very recent instance : I do not say that the Conservative Government was wrong some few years ago to commence laying down the Quetta Railway with a view to improving our defences against the threatened Russian advance upon Afghanistan. And I do not here say that the Liberals were wrong to pull it up again ; but I do say most emphatically that the country was wrong which permitted such a piece of extravagant fooling as the combination of the two acts. What would be thought of an employer of labour who set one gang of men to dig a hole and another gang to fill it up again ? As we should regard this man, so the other civilised countries of Europe probably regard us. And are they not justified ?

Instances might be cited in which democracies have gone nigh to committing political suicide, as for example where carried away by temporary enthusiasm or heró-worship they have voluntarily abdicated in favour of a dictator; arming him with sufficient powers to enable him to defy the quickly-repentant will of the people. Both Cicero and Tacitus, who knew something of democratic impulsiveness and instability, have been cited in favour of a mixed form of government: "Statuo esse," writes the former, "optime constitutam rempublicam quæ ex tribus generibus illis, regali, optimo et populari, modice confusa." Similarly Tacitus hints that such a mixed form is almost too good to be hoped for. "Cunctas nationes et urbes, populus aut primores aut singuli regunt. Delecta ex his et constituta reipublicæ forma laudari facilius quam evenire." We have attained to that laudable constitution, and we ought, therefore, in the opinion of Lord Brougham, to rest and be thankful. Either he fails to see, or he wilfully shuts his eyes to the price that must necessarily be paid for this complex arrangement. In order to perpetuate what he would call our present mixed form of democratic monarchy we must be prepared to stereotype what is left of caste among our people, we must respect hereditary privilege, we must arrest the growing tendency in the direction of civil equality. No; the advantages may be great, but the price is too high for an Englishman.

I have said that the strongest argument of all against pure democracy is the apparent absurdity of putting the reins of government into the hands of the most ignorant classes of the community. Is it expedient, feasible, or even safe to place the inexperienced masses (no fault of theirs) at the helm of the State? Recently we have extended the franchise to the agricultural labourer, and I ask any unprejudiced person whether he is honestly of opinion that Hodge is really qualified to make laws either immediately or vicariously? Would he accept Hodge's ruling on a delicate question of morals? Is he prepared to lend a wistful and a wondering ear to the inspired utterances of the modern Elisha? "Vox populi vox Dei." Good; but the voice of the people is not necessarily the howl of the numerical majority. Apart from all false sentiment, apart from mob flattery (the maudlin foible of the day), apart from democratic bias, everybody knows, and honest men admit, that Hodge's several views on things in general are not of the most enlightened character. And I for one positively decline to submit passively to his dictation in all the numerous concerns of life which are usually regarded as falling within the province of the law-giver. Let us face this problem fairly and squarely. Not on the one hand by falling back in dismay into the arms of a doomed class despotism, nor on the other hand by falsely attributing to the uneducated or half-educated untold faculties of intuition which in our inmost hearts we know well they do not possess.

The art of legislation is a very difficult and complicated study; much more so than farming or boot-making for example. And yet, as has been remarked with amazement by thinkers of the weight of Socrates, Shakespeare, and Spencer, whereas a lifetime is required for the mastery of the humblest handicrafts, almost any ignorant busybody is credited with intuitively understanding that most intricate art legislation. The sole qualifications of a past master seem to be noisy self-assertion, burning class-envy, and fanatical faith in some social nostrum. Were I to walk into an engine-room and point out to the engineer the intolerable waste of steam entailed by a hole in the boiler, and urge him promptly to stop it, he might turn upon me with some such reply as this: "Sir, that hole is called the safety-valve; if you would bring your mighty brain-power to bear on some subject with which previous study has qualified you to deal, without making an ass of yourself, you might be doing more good to the community and less harm to me. Good morning." And yet this same engineer will walk into the great legislative laboratory where the complex parts of the machinery of State are forged, and with the serenest self-confidence take off his coat and set to work. What is the explanation of this anomalous state of things?

The functions of the legislator are twofold. Under a democratic system therefore the functions of the citizen are twofold; for every citizen is by hypothesis a legislator. The first is that of making laws; the second is that of safeguarding liberties. These are clearly two different functions. And I am at once prepared to admit and to contend that every citizen is not only morally justified but also morally bound to take his share in legislation so far as this duty of safeguarding his own liberty is concerned. The process of breaking his own fetters is a very different process from that of forging shackles for his neighbours. I am aware that the two are usually confounded and spoken of as though they were one and the same thing. But a very little reflection is required to see that they are two very different things. It does not need a bootmaker to find out where the shoe pinches; the wearer is competent to do that. It takes a bootmaker to make a boot that will not pinch. Hence every citizen has a clear right to a voice in the legislature, if by that is meant the right to safeguard his own liberty against all law-makers—to see that no law is passed which infringes upon his own rights and liberties. And under a representative system it is the duty of the representative to see that no law is passed which infringes upon the rights of his constituents. That is his duty. Hodge, therefore, has as good a right as any other citizen to watch the course of legislation on his own behalf, and to move for the repeal of any existing law which unduly interferes with his freedom of action. This is surely a very different matter from worrying and harassing other people.

And here is another argument for democracy. The end, aim, and test of all government—such is human nature—is the welfare of the ruling class. All history proves it. Human nature is such that it is absolutely impossible to provide against it. Hence aristocracies always have made laws for the good of the aristocratic class, and only indirectly and mediately for the good of the whole people. When the whole people has the making of the laws, then the test of the laws is necessarily the welfare of the whole people. Bad laws may of course be passed, but they will tend to fall into abeyance and finally to perish. The welfare of the whole people being the object of those who have the making of the laws, a defective system has a tendency to readjust itself. Good institutions will survive; bad institutions will die. By a bad institution is meant bad for the ruling class—the law-making class. And that is the reason why it tends to perish. Little by little those who suffer from it come consciously to see or unconsciously to feel the true cause of the mischief, and to uproot it accordingly; just as our own upper-class rulers have learnt the harmfulness to their own order of many early laws of their own creation, and have, during the last five or six centuries, made great strides in the direction of freedom by removing many State restrictions which impeded their own liberty of action. These reforms have also incidentally benefited the whole people in many instances; but such was not, in truth, the end and cause of reform. As evidence of this it can be shown that that which is good for the aristocratic class is not always good for the people; but that so long as the ruling class actually does benefit by it as a class, so long it will continue to survive. And this constitutes a real danger for the people. A protective duty on corn did undoubtedly benefit the landowners, and its reimposition would undoubtedly benefit them now; and although the repeal of the corn-laws has been an unmixed blessing to the people, we may safely say that it would never have been brought about but for the swamping of the land-owning vote by the Reform Act of 1832. The country might have suffered for years, but the stimulus to remove the evil did not exist in the class which then ruled the land.

If this reasoning be sound we have reached the conclusion that the democratic form of government is not only defensible, but also highly desirable, and even essential to social evolution; but the doctrine is subject to this qualification—that the function of the citizen is the safeguarding of his own liberties, and not the manufacture of restraints on the liberty of his fellows.

Each new layer added to the electorate seems to have to learn the lesson *de novo* that sweet as it is to bully others, it is sweeter still not to be bullied oneself. About thirty years ago the more powerful section of the ruling body had learnt the lesson thoroughly, or nearly so; but since then we have had two extensions of the franchise, and in each case it has become increasingly manifest that the lesson has been unlearnt by the new recruits. This we may regret; but it is a comfort to reflect that they are of the same metal as their predecessors, and will doubtless show an equal aptitude for self-government. They will speedily learn the great lesson of liberty. It is only an abundant faith in the destiny of the race, the fullest confidence in the stuff of which this people is made, and a reasoned conviction of the truth of the democratic principle, that can buoy any honest and thoughtful person up at the present time to help forward the popular movement. Indeed, some of the proposals emanating from the new contingent are so wild, so dishonest, so silly, and withal so impracticable, that it is no wonder if some of even the faithful begin to waver. Fortunately, in the conflict of opposing interests lies the salvation of liberty. The principle of true Liberalism is, in the words of Mr. Gladstone, "trust in the people, qualified by prudence; the principle of Conservatism is mistrust of the people, qualified by fear." This is the true spirit of enlightened democratism. It is because of faith in the destiny of our race that we may look without dread on its temporary aberrations. We see that hitherto they have marched steadily forward, not without turnings and even backslidings, it is true, but still, in the long run, forward on the path of progress. Clinging to this faith we may look not with fear but with confidence to the indefinite extension of the franchise, in the belief that whatever may be the temptations held out to them by place-seekers and dishonest demagogues, there is ingrained in the inmost nature of Englishmen an inherited love of justice and a consuming zeal for freedom which, in the long run, must prevail.

There seem to be but three reasons which any one is justified in adducing for not accepting the democratic principle: 1. Because he does not know what is meant by the term. 2. Because he lacks faith in the destiny of his own people. 3. Because he is consciously actuated by class interest, and is a traitor to his country.

There is one warning which all good Democrats must take to heart: Beware of mistaking a sham democracy for a real one. Government by a class is not democracy. Democracy is the government of the people by the people—the whole people. Government by a class, even though that class be the largest class in the country, is not democracy. Indeed it is a question whether the despotism of a large class is not, in many respects, worse than the despotism of a small class or a single individual. It is less amenable to the ordinary resources of revolution. And here it should be pointed out that the doctrine of the Divine Right of the Majority, or, in secular phraseology, the doctrine of " counting heads to save the trouble of breaking them," can be carried, and is carried, a great deal too far. There are two principal qualifications of the doctrine which are usually lost sight of. Upon these it is important to lay stress, because modern democratic State socialism is based upon their non-recognition. Firstly the units of society are *not* equal. Under a system of adult suffrage it is quite conceivable that on a question of family law nearly all the women might be found voting on one side, and nearly all the men on the other. In such a case it is absurd to pretend that counting heads would be a peaceful substitute for fighting it out. Similarly at the present day, in all democratic countries under a very extended franchise, apart from sentiment, ten rich men count for more, *as a fact*, than a thousand wage-receivers. It is merely a foolish fiction to pretend that the majority vote is a test of the will of the people ; because the will of a people (like the will of an individual animal) is the resultant of forces operating in various directions. That which the doctrine presumes we want to ascertain is, What would be the result if each question were fought out ? And the answer is certainly not always to be found by counting heads *pro* and *con.*

The second flaw in the doctrine is the false assumption that every one is prepared to fight for that which he desires to obtain—that the desire is uniformly urgent. This is not true. A big dog will seldom attack a little dog in possession of a bone. He desires the bone. So does the little dog. But their motives are not equally urgent. In a state of unorganised anarchy—anarchy as it is pictured by those who do not understand it—if two unequally-matched men meet over a prize coveted by both, they do not, as a fact, take each other's measure and decide the question accordingly. The stronger man may be actuated by a weaker desire. He may be less hungry or more averse to trouble and pain. And in any case it is probably, on the average, the best economy from his own point of view to buy off the weaker man by making a division of the prize—not necessarily an equal division, but one satisfactory to the weaker man in view of his inferiority. To apply this consideration to practical politics it may be true that the majority in this country are favourable, say, to universal vaccination. It does not follow that a compulsory law embodies the will of the people, because every man who is opposed to that law is at least ten times more anxious to gain his end than his adversaries are to gain theirs. He is ready to make far greater sacrifices to attain it. One man rather wishes for what he regards as a slight sanitary safeguard; the other is determined not to submit to a gross violation of his liberty. How differently the two are actuated! One man is willing to pay a farthing in the pound for a desirable object; the other is ready to risk property, and perhaps life, to defeat that object. In such cases as this it is sheer folly to pretend that counting heads is a fair indication of the forces behind.

Majorities for their own sakes would do well not to bring the minorities to bay. The result may be either painful or humiliating—painful, as when the minority (in heads, in riches, and in organisation) withstood the tyranny of the Stuarts; humiliating, as when England bowed down before the determined Boers of the Transvaal. It is not wise to threaten what you do not mean to perform. Minorities mean action; majorities, as a rule, do not.

Having reached the conclusion that all history shows an increasing tendency towards a democratic form of government, and, moreover, that democracy is not only inevitable but desirable in all respects, we come now to consider by what means the government of the people can be best effected.

To begin with, all those who have a voice in the legislature can assemble in some large and convenient place, and there and then discuss and settle the affairs of State. This was the case in ancient Athens, where, at times of great excitement, the Ecclesia convened in the Agora would number many thousands of voters. The sense of the meeting was taken by a show of hands, and as might be expected, even in so small a state as Athens, the proceedings were often of a noisy and tumultuous description. Another great disadvantage of the arrangement was that, when only ordinary affairs of State had to be transacted, and no burning questions were to the front, there seems to have been great difficulty in getting together the requisite quorum of five or six thousand persons. Every citizen (male) over twenty years of age and unconvicted of any serious offence, having a right to a seat, so to speak, in Parliament, there was no particular dignity associated with the function, and it was found necessary not only to pay the members a small sum for each separate attendance, but also to fine those who absented themselves. We have in England a functionary called the party whip, whose business it is to make a good muster of his party when any measure of importance is before the House; but in Athens the whips were not metaphorically so called. Certain public slaves sallied forth armed with ropes previously steeped in cold vermilion, and any stray members encountered were gently rope-ended, and so branded with red, like sheep, as evidence against them.

Again, the duties of the Ecclesia were not only very wide, but also very indefinite, and instead of becoming more and more specialised, the functions undertaken by it seem to have grown increasingly multifarious as the power of the aristocratic body dwindled away. Of the Boulé, of the Areiopagus, of the Ephetæ, etc., it is not necessary here to speak in detail, it is enough to say that they were not bodies expressly created by the all-powerful popular body for the purpose of helping and checking and otherwise conducing to the smooth working of that central body, like the Senate of the United States of America, or the Privy Council of this country ; on the contrary, they dated from further back than the democratic régime, and like our House of Lords they were found ready-made, and were used for purposes for which they were neither intended nor fitted.

Nearly everything of a general character which has been said of the Athenian Ecclesia is true *mutatis mutandis* of the Roman Comitia Curiata. Whatever may have been the original nature of the Comitia, howsoever the vote may have been taken in its earlier days ; whether each paterfamilias counted for one, or whether each gens or each curia counted for one, and the heads of families voted within their own curia as to what should be the vote of that curia—all these questions though interesting, do not concern us here—the point is that the Comitia was the assembly of the populus, and that the individual citizens took a direct part in its deliberations. The struggle between the democracy and the oligarchy is, in plain words, the struggle for a voice in the government between the adult males in the State on the one hand, and the heads of the clans of which the State is composed on the other. The heads of houses would naturally resist the growing tendency of democracy to disintegrate the family and to reintegrate its constituents as units in a homogeneous state. Of course those in whom the authority of the Curia was originally vested would see their interest in resisting this tendency. The grandfathers, the elders, the venerable "fogies," who composed the Senate of Rome, the Boulé of Athens, and the Gerusia of Sparta, would lean towards the old law rather than the new, and consequently their power would tend to pass from them and be arrogated by the popular and progressive body.

But even Rome, though considerably larger than Athens, was small in comparison with any modern self-governing state ; strata of the population are now included among the citizens which were then taken no account of, and if, even in those days, the processes of legislation were unwieldy and discontinuous, what would they be now if our five millions of voters had to be convened for the transaction of public business ? This has been the problem for modern Europe to solve. Either the size of independent states must be kept down within very narrow limits, or the poorer strata of the population must be disfranchised, or else some other system of self-government must be invented.

First, there has been suggested and tried, that modern imitation of the plebiscitum so far adapted to modern requirements as to admit of the local publication and discussion of the question before the country, and the taking of the general opinion piecemeal in the several localities. This system was adopted by the late Emperor of the French. But this very illustration brings to light a great danger in the process. To avoid the constant friction and expense of polling the constituencies, the plan readily suggests itself of putting the question to be decided in a very general form. Instead of asking the people, "Will you have this law?" and then a few days after, "Will you have this?" what can be simpler than to ask them once for all, "Will you have any law which I, the head of the Executive, may propose, till further notice?" The thing is done; the further notice never comes; it is nobody's business to take the opinion of the people; the head of the Executive knows better than to risk his position; and from an independent democracy, we have suddenly converted the Government into an absolute autocracy.

A less dangerous plan has been proposed and tried (with some success at the present day in Switzerland). It is known as the Referendum! The main objection to the Referendum, apart from the friction and expense, is the principle implied, to the effect that every citizen is capable, without any previous instruction, not only of knowing where bad legislation pinches him, but also what sort of legislation is good for other classes besides his own. This is in itself a fatal objection to the plan.

The only other method which presents itself is that known as "representative government." The whole machinery of representation is a complex growth, and by no means so simple an arrangement as some might be disposed to think. The germ of the idea lies in the system of voting by proxy. A busy man in a distant province is unable to find time or money to journey up to the metropolis to take part in the national deliberations; but a rich and leisured man of his neighbourhood is going up, and he empowers him to vote for both. Others hear of the arrangement, and being anxious to record their votes but unable to afford it, they also club together in batches according to their political views and send up one man to represent each batch. Representative government is a comparatively modern invention, for it is a mistake to suppose that the so-called delegates sent up to the Amphictyonic Councils to represent the tribes were, properly speaking, delegates at all. They attended in their own right, like the members of our House of Lords, as heads of the senior family or gens of the tribe.

The principle of legislation by proxy having once obtained recognition, a regular system for carrying out the arrangement would soon establish itself. And here we have the germ of the assembly of popular representatives in which

E

each citizen, as such, counts for one, apart from all tribal considerations. The simplicity of the system and the greatly-reduced friction of the governmental machine would naturally have the effect, and, as a matter of history, did have the effect, of stimulating legislation. It would tend, and did tend, to become more searching, more detailed, and far more complex. The qualifications of the representative would be higher. It would require a man of more than the average culture to master the existing law, and to draw the line between the mere defence of the liberties of his constituents and the imposition of restraints on other members of the community. Hence the custom naturally arose of electing a deputy to go up to Parliament, not only to speak but also to think for those whom he represented. Where the line should be drawn is still an unsolved problem. The principles by which we must decide where the liberty of one man becomes tyranny over another man have nowhere yet been clearly formulated. It is sufficient here to show that the difficulty would be early felt, and the effect would be the election of representatives empowered to think and act for those who sent them, and not to serve merely as mouthpieces or messengers. This discovery, and the complicated representative institutions erected upon it in all modern democratic states, must never be lost sight of in proposals for reform and further advance on the democratic path. It is forgetfulness of this principle which explains the favour with which the Referendum is regarded in certain quarters where anything like sympathy with class rule would have been least looked for.

Perhaps the foregoing considerations will enable us to lay down with confidence certain principles (or what Brougham called " canons " [1]) of representative government.

1. The first principle I would submit is that the vote is a right and not a trust. Every man has a right, a moral right, to see that his own liberty is not infringed upon by his neighbours under the pretence of safeguarding their liberties. Any attempt of the sort he is morally justified in resisting by force if necessary. He is not bound to submit by any contract, actual

---

[1] I confess I am not in love with the word "canons." It savours too much to my mind of blind dogma, of rules based on authority rather than reason.

or tacit, or otherwise than by fear of the brute force of those who are opposed to him. The bearing of this principle on the question of bribery and corruption is interesting, but this is not the place to discuss it.

2. By logical implication the suffrage must be universal, and here let me recall what I have already said ; namely, that although science may and does point to this consummation as the end and goal towards which we are tending, it by no means necessarily follows that this or any other nation is ripe for it at the present time. This is a question for the practical statesman. My own opinion for what it is worth is, that we are in this country ready for universal suffrage, male and female. Nay more, I fail to see why even the paupers should be denied this right. Have they not a claim to see that their liberties, microscopic though they may be, are not trampled upon ? Either they have no right to State support, or they have a clear right to see that what State support they receive is not less than that which they have a legal claim to.

3. Thirdly, we are driven to the conclusion that no qualifications can be required either of the voter or of the deputy. It used to be contended that the property qualification was a guarantee that respectable persons should be returned to the House of Commons. But in the first place, property and respectability do not necessarily go together ; secondly, it is a simple matter and was a common practice to convey property to the candidate before the election and to have it reconveyed immediately after he had taken his seat, so that the supposed security was a farce ; and thirdly, there seems to be no particular reason why a parliamentary representative should be what is called respectable, so long as he is chosen and trusted by his fellow-men to watch over their interests in the legislature.

4. This brings us to the fourth " canon " ; for if one class of persons in the community has no right to prescribe rules for another class as to what manner of representative they must elect, it follows that Parliament itself should not be permitted through the vote of the majority to exclude any duly-elected member who has been returned by an independent constituency.

The admission of such a claim on the part of the majority is
out of harmony with all the principles of democracy, and is
nothing less than class despotism.

5. The fifth principle which I will submit has already
been touched upon. Though essential to the sound working
of democratic institutions, it is not likely just now to meet
with very general approval.   It is, that a parliamentary deputy
must be a representative, and not a mere delegate.   Let me
distinctly define my position : I admit the right of the constituency to control the acts of its deputy in all things down
to the minutest particulars, but I dispute the wisdom; and I
denounce the practice as calculated to impair the process of
legislation.   I have a perfect right to choose my own bootmaker, and, if I think proper, to stand over him and dictate
the mode of his working ; but I should be a fool for my pains.
Similarly if I want some one to look after my interests in
Parliament, I am justified in choosing my man for the purpose,
and I shall show my sense in choosing some one who has knowledge and experience of that kind of work ; but having chosen
him, I must send him unpledged, unfettered, and free to adopt
such methods as he may think fit.   By all means let me ask him
questions and sound him on all points of interest to me ; let
me thoroughly cross-examine him and " heckle " him ; let me
choose the candidate most in accord with my own views, but
having taken these precautions let me send to Parliament not
a telephone but a *man.* -

6. The next principle is even more important than the
last.   The end and object of parliamentary institutions is, as
we have seen, the representation of the various and conflicting
interests in the country.   Suppose we desired to learn the
general wishes of the animal kingdom, we should ask each
species to send a representative, or perhaps a proportionate
number of representatives ; we certainly should not map the
surface of the earth out in parallelograms, and get a representative from each parallelogram.   Indeed, there is practically
nothing whatever in common between the inhabitants of a
given area.   The consequence of territorial representation is
similar to that of multiple election ; interests are hardly represented at all.   Each deputy is a sort of miniature parlia-

ment in himself; a colourless, insipid, fasciculus of negations
without a definite program, or even a definite idea. To begin
with, as we all know, the aim of a candidate is to say as
little as he possibly can before the election, for fear of giving
offence to one or other of the groups in his constituency. If
he says a word in favour of temperance, the licensed victuallers
look askance at him; if he ventures to suggest that a poor
man has as good a right to his Sunday pint as a rich man to
his Sunday bottle of port, the teetotallers gather together and
talk ominously about the sons of Belial. If he dares to say
more about the State church than that the question has not
yet come within the domain of practical politics, a thousand
tongues are instantly set in motion about the godlessness of
advanced politicians. That an enemy can do more harm than
a friend can do good, is well known by all who are conversant
with electioneering; and the consequence is that every candidate confines himself as much as possible to the merest
generalities. He is going to do something great, but no one
can learn exactly what; he is in favour of everything which is
calculated to benefit the people; he has the interests of his
constituents at heart; and so forth. It is impossible to declare
his opinions boldly and frankly.

Such are some of the effects of the representation of areas.
Its results are plainly visible in the invertebrate condition of
the present House of Commons. The remedy for this state of
things is the alternative system of the representation of interests,
or what is usually described as the representation of minorities,
though that is only an incidental advantage of its adoption.
No matter how small a minority may be, it can, under this
system of representation, secure a voice in the management of
national affairs, provided that scattered all over the country it
can count enough votes to obtain a single seat. The number
requisite for this purpose is of course the quotient obtained by
dividing the whole number of the electorate by the number of .
seats in the people's house. It is hardly needful to point out
how many important interests are at the present moment
utterly disfranchised owing to the accidental fact of their not
being huddled together within a circumscribed district. The
retirement of Mr. Leonard Courtney from the Government of

which he was a member because of the strength of his convictions on this point will not be lost upon his countrymen.   The
sixth canon, then, is that interests must be directly represented
in Parliament, and not mere geographical areas.

7. The next point to be referred to was one of the points of
the Charter.   All the other points except short Parliaments
have already been carried ; it relates to the payment of members.
It is really difficult to see why one class of work is not as
much entitled to remuneration as any other class of work, provided it is useful work.   I do not say that in many cases it is
worth paying for.   If it is worth having, it is worth paying for.
I know we have many members of Parliament whose services
would be dear at any figure that has ever been suggested as
a reasonable salary.   And this throws some light on the further
question, Out of what fund should the remuneration come ?

The objections to payment at all are—first, that it would
lower the tone of the House to pay the members ; secondly,
that it is never wise to pay for that which can be had for
nothing, however useful it may be, as in the case of air and
water, for example.   Now, the reply to the first objection is
that we do not want "tone" in Parliament, we want representation.   The reply to the second objection is, though it is
true that we get members of Parliament for nothing, what sort
of members do we get ?   Out of over six hundred and fifty
persons in the House of Commons how many represent any
class or interest, except the uninteresting class which is
nervously ambitious to obtain a seat in Parliament and to keep
it ?   Can honesty, sincerity, and courage be expected of such
men ?

From what fund, then, must remuneration come ?   There
are three possible sources.   From the rates ?   But as a rate-
payer it would be very much against my grain to be forced to
contribute towards the support of one who did not represent
my views ; in other words, to pay for the privilege of being
misrepresented.   If my own candidate got in I should not
object ; but there must always be a minority, and it is surely
hard upon the minority to compel it to join in the maintenance
of one who may be working against their interests.

It is also suggested that payment should be made out of

the public treasury.   Well, the difficulty here would be to assess the value of the services of the several members ; it would certainly be absurdly unfair to pay them all equally.   To pay the same sum to an old, experienced, and tried statesman, and to a fledgling squire fresh from college, whose sole claim to the confidence of the constituency is his father's wealth and local standing, would be about as sensible a proceeding as to pay equal sums to the skilled cabinetmaker and the joiner's apprentice.   The notion is preposterous and ridiculous.   And yet if members are to be paid out of the public treasury it will be necessary to strike an average and pay them all alike, about £300 a year, as has been proposed.   The services of some members may be worth some £3000 a year, and the services of others less than threepence.

The third alternative is that each member should be paid by his own constituents ; those who want him should pay for him, and those who do not want him should be allowed to make a better use of their money.   There are two objections to this course : the first is that it would be necessary to ascertain who *are* his constituents ; and in order to know this it would be necessary to repeal the Ballot Act.   We shall come to that presently.   The second is that the system would be tantamount to a tax on the franchise.   But this is more in appearance than in reality.   Payment on either of the other two systems amounts to the same thing, except that in these cases the tax is compulsory instead of voluntary.   Moreover, if it is worth a voter's while to have his interests looked to in Parliament, he must expect to have to pay something for it.   The work costs money, and cannot really be got for nothing ; and who so fit a person to pay for it as the person who reaps the benefit of it ?   The last method therefore, namely, payment of members by their constituents, seems to be open to the fewest or the least objections.

8. Let us revert to the question of the Ballot.   This again is a question for the practical statesman.   Personally I am strongly in favour of abolishing secret voting as soon as we are ripe for open voting ; as soon, that is to say, as every voter feels independent, and ceases to stand in dread of undue indirect influence.   When practical statesmen see that this condi-

tion is reached, the sooner the Ballot is done away with the better. It is a standing admission of serfdom. It is notorious that when the Act was passed the Ballot for its own sake had not a single friend ; not one who did not admit that it was good only as a temporary expedient—the lesser of two evils ; and only to be tolerated so long as unfair influence was exercised over a certain class of the voters. Both Mill and Brougham were strongly opposed to it. Surely it is important that every man should have the right not only of exercising the franchise, but also of doing so openly ; he should not be deprived of the pleasure and pride of expressing his convictions, of stating on which side he is voting and the grounds of his vote, without the fear of any evil consequences before his eyes. Truth is infectious. And perhaps the best that can be said for the Ballot (except as a temporary expedient) is in the words of Cicero, that it gives men an open countenance, while it cloaks their minds.[1] The eighth rule of representative government is that voting should be open and above board.

9. The duration of Parliaments should be natural and not artificial. The old Chartist cry for short Parliaments is no longer heard, because we have arrived at a stage at which we see that no arbitrary limitation of the length of their duration is called for. We have the seven years' rule ; but as a matter of fact no Parliaments ever succeed in living out that spell. They die a natural death, I suppose, about every five years. In America they have a presidential election every four years ; whereas here in England we change our President (our Prime Minister) practically every five years ; the change being brought about naturally instead of artificially. Under the sound system of the democracy of the future, no doubt a Parliament will die a natural death as soon as it ceases to represent the feeling of the country.

10. One of the strongest arguments against democratic government is that drawn from the delay due to divided counsels. If in trade, for example, all the shareholders of a joint-stock company had to be consulted before the board of directors or the

---

[1] " Grata populo est Tabella, quæ frontes aperit hominum, mentes tegit, datque eam libertatem ut quid volunt faciant."

managing director could accept an offer or complete a purchase, the whole state of the market would have changed and the transaction would be almost impracticable. So the difficulty and delay in settling urgent matters of foreign policy in a Parliament of over a thousand members are wellnigh insuperable; the system is suicidal; and even modified as it now is, it places England at a great disadvantage with respect to autocratically governed states like Russia and Germany. Whether foreign policy could not be altogether removed from the domain of party, is a question deserving of all the consideration that can be bestowed upon it; how far such matters might be left to a permanent mixed Committee is a question for practical statesmen; but whatever the course eventually adopted may be, it is certain that the democracy must learn the lesson taught in the industrial arena, namely, the need for an independent Executive. I am not going to discuss the interpretation to be put upon the existing law by which the prerogative of the Executive is supposed to be limited in this country; I am merely insisting on the absolute necessity for specialised administration. The Executive must have full power to declare war, and perform many other important functions without first appealing to Parliament. The function must be delegated; but the delegate must be temporarily independent. Freedom to take the initiative, with an obligation to obtain indemnity afterwards, will create a sufficient ministerial responsibility.

11. It has been admitted that the democracy is impulsive; this also must be counteracted. All free peoples have spontaneously provided for the mature deliberation of important and disputed questions of State. Even in our Courts of Justice we find it necessary to guard against haste and insufficient examination of the question at issue. We have Courts of Appeal. So all free peoples have furnished themselves with a Second Chamber which has certain powers of veto on the proposals of the First. Even within the last few years we have seen a sudden wave of popular impulse which went nigh to sending our armies to the Crimea again. A year later, and those who had identified themselves with this impulse were swept from office. I am not contending that we have to thank

the House of Lords for this, or for averting any other evil consequences of popular impulse. Neither do I deny that it may have done some good in this way. All I am contending for is, that there should be a Second Chamber which should have the power of appealing from the First Chamber to the people, the verdict of the General Election to be of course final. Much evil would thereby be averted, and the only possible harm which could come of it would be the delay of a few months in passing some useful and popular measure. We must not forget that with a Second Chamber properly constituted there would be as great a likelihood of the action of the " senators " being in accord with the feeling of the people as of the reverse. We must not confound the principle of a Second Chamber with the admission of the hereditary principle. Let me again insist that there is no particular need for hurry. The change is coming of its own accord without any call for violence or discontinuity. It is a question for the practical statesman to say what gradual reforms in the constitution of the House of Lords are required in order to convert it into a suitable legislative court of reflection, deliberation, and possibly delay ; but by no means of obstruction.

12. The last canon upon which I propose to lay stress, is that democratic government should be worked on the system of Party. Party government is the key to steady democratic progress. In our Courts of Justice we find it is not enough to have a thoroughly pure and indefatigable judge to sit down, consider the evidence, and adjudicate accordingly. That is not found to be the best system. There is counsel for the one side and counsel for the other. In the heat of the forensic duel many truths are elicited, many arguments adduced, which would be overlooked by the impartial judge ; and the result is a nearer approximation to justice than would otherwise accrue. The same rule holds good in Parliament. One party is counsel for the one side, the other party is counsel for the other side, and the country has to judge between them. In the heat of party strife not a stone is left unturned, not an argument lost sight of, by which the country is enabled to decide the issue.

But there is one condition essential to the safe working of

the party system, and that is that the principle upon which the two parties are divided, the distinction upon which the classification is based, must be the deepest and most general principle underlying all the chief political questions of the hour. For instance, when the great question of the day was whether the government of the country should be carried on by the many or the few, when all minor measures were considered from the point of view of the effect they would have in putting power into the hands of the people ;—in those days Parliament and the country were properly divided into two parties called Tories and Liberals, of which one consistently advocated all measures tending to consolidate the power in the hands of the upper classes, and the other as naturally worked and voted in the opposite direction. At the present day there is no question of the kind before the country. It has been settled long ago. As a political power, Toryism is utterly extinct. So also the occupation of the old Liberal party is gone. And yet the shells remain in which men aggregate, and the aggregates dub themselves Tories and Liberals. There is no vitality in them. The only points which members of a party nowadays have in common are a party name, personal attachments, and in some cases an old political tradition handed down from an age when the party cry was something more than a shibboleth.

The question of to-day is, What ought the Government to *do ?* and the flabby and unwholesome condition of public opinion on the subject is due to the fact that the opposite views on this important point are not represented as they should be by two great parties in the State. Whatever the form of the Government may be, the question still remains to be answered, What are its duties ? Are we to adopt Socialism ? or are we to adopt Individualism ? Statesmen must class themselves in accordance with their answer to this question.

If we will but bear these twelve rules or canons of representative government in mind, we shall, I think, find ourselves in a position to rebut any of the arguments usually adduced against a democratic form of government, although at first sight they are, I admit, sufficiently formidable.

CHAPTER III

WHEN we examine the numerous questions which exercise the minds of those who take an intelligent interest in politics, we find that they fall into two distinct classes : one class relating to the structure or constitution of government ; the other to the function or duty of government. These two fundamental questions, " What is the State ? " and " What does the State ? " though standing clearly apart, are usually confounded and treated together. Now, although they may be equally vital, that is no reason for assuming that those who agree upon the one point must necessarily hold identical views on the other. With respect to structure, politicians fall at once into two large and nearly equal parties, namely, those who are satisfied with the existing constitution just as it is, and those who contend that it ought to be more or less modified. Doubtless, the members of this latter class differ also among themselves as to the kind and amount of change desirable, from the red republican, through all shades of radicalism, to the most timid trimmer that adorns the Liberal benches. Their opponents are of opinion that changes are dangerous, or that at all events, if they must occur, it is best to let them come of themselves, and to retard rather than hasten them on. This party also contains many shades of Toryism, from the old-fashioned worshipper of antiquity, who would fain, if possible, reverse the tide of history and undo the evil of modern days, to the so-called Liberal-Conservative, who deems it wise to bend to circumstances and to float passively on the stream, though not to swim with it.

Turn now to the other great question, " What ought the

Government, however constituted, to do ? " " What are the duties of the State, be it monarchical, republican, or mixed ?" And here again politicians may be split up into two great parties. There are those who maintain the greatest possible liberty of the individual citizen compatible with the equal liberty of his fellows, and who disapprove, therefore, of all meddlesome legislation. They would restrict the functions of the State to the administration of justice, the maintenance of order, the defence of the country against foreign antagonism, and the collection and management of revenue for these purposes ; and leave other matters to take care of themselves. On the other hand, there are those who believe that a well-organised body like the State is, or might be made, the most highly-efficient machine for the carrying out of many great and noble schemes for the improvement of the people and the amelioration of their lot. Such are the persons who support State education, State charities, State museums and galleries, State railways and telegraphs, State banks, State post-offices, and even State censors and spies. Such are the persons who would close the public-house at ten o'clock or altogether, and who would convert drunkards by force, who would and do force their medical nostrums upon unbelievers, and imprison those who resist. Such *were* the persons who took into the general charge the eternal welfare of their fellow-creatures, and founded inquisitions to keep them in the right path. All these and a thousand other matters say they, can be best regulated and managed by the State.

Diametrically opposed as these two parties are, and fundamental as the issue between them undoubtedly is, it is a remarkable fact that they enjoy at present no distinctive appellations ; and it is entirely upon difference of opinion concerning State structure that the existing party divisions are based. Indeed, some persons (even experienced statesmen) appear to be so far carried away by zeal for structural change or resistance to it, as never to give the equally if not more vital question of function a thought. Others, again, care little for the form of government so long as it is easy to live happily and freely under it—

> " For forms of government let fools contest,
> Whate'er is best administered is best ; "

or as the old but less refined saw hath it, "A good horse is never a bad colour."

Men of this stamp have during the last fifty years kept themselves in the background. The battle for equality, the struggles for parliamentary reform, for a redistribution of seats, for extension of the suffrage, for the enfranchisement of women, for the reconstruction of the House of Lords, and for the endless other constitutional reforms and changes, must be fought out when liberty is not in danger. But the very structural changes accomplished since the framing of the first Reform Bill have produced unforeseen effects upon the views of the ultimate governing body with respect to the duties of the State, which effects have been quickened since some two decades ago Mr. Disraeli threw open the floodgates still wider to the torrent of democracy. Speaking at the inaugural meeting of the Liberty and Property Defence League, Mr. Pleydell Bouverie, said—

"One sees proposals of even eminent men nowadays which, by looking into the history of this country, you will find are strictly allied to the old sumptuary laws, and laws for the regulation of labour, and for settling what men are to earn, eat, and drink, which are to be found in the statute book four hundred years ago. We thought these notions had been exploded as hurtful and foolish, but they are coming to the front again, and I think it is due to the fact that a large amount of political power is now wielded by the comparatively uneducated and ignorant classes. The very mistakes and fallacies which were not recognised to be such by the educated classes four hundred years ago, and which influenced their legislation, are again influencing the classes which have recently acquired political power. They are for emulating those old-fashioned Acts of Parliament ; unreasonable and impossible expectations are indulged in ; and there is a great desire for ridiculous interference by Act of Parliament, which will again have to be exploded by the good sense of those who agree with the gentlemen here."

Agitations for constitutional reform in harmony with the principle of equality are giving place to agitations for restrictions on the liberty of one class for the benefit of another, and the liberty of the individual for the supposed benefit of the public. This tendency brings politics home to the doors of those who take but a lukewarm interest in the "levelling" process, and a very keen interest in their own freedom.

Before we are competent to define the proper sphere of
State action with any degree of accuracy we must survey the
whole field covered by officialism at the present day, in this
country and in other countries, and in past times.   By the use
of the comparative method we shall possibly be enabled to
detect permanent tendencies which will guide us in predicting
the probable limitations of State action among civilised communities of the future.   This work has not yet been done, or
even begun, and it is needless to say I do not presume to
attempt it here.   At the same time it may be some help to
those who are seriously considering this most important of all
political questions of the day, if we cast our eye over the
province of governmental interference in our own country, and
point out what substitutes for such action have in the several
departments been suggested, and how far they are feasible.   From
a condition of tribal socialism Englishmen have taken many
centuries to attain their present degree of civil liberty, and it
is admitted that considerable remnants of the old patriarchal
socialism still remain, and are likely to remain (though possibly
in diminishing quantities) for many years, decades, and perhaps
centuries to come.   In so far as such socialism is necessary
because we are not yet ripe for absolute individualism, we are
bound to regard it as " beneficent socialism."   It is none the
less socialism.   It must be understood then that in the following review of existing State interferences I am at present
offering no opinion on their goodness or badness, but merely
pointing out the fact.
    Although there is no particular order in which State
functions need be considered, it may be well to begin with
those which are admitted by most people to be normal functions,
and to pass on to those which are condemned by larger and
larger numbers, till we come to those which even socialists
would hardly defend.   First, then, we find that the State undertakes the defence of the country against foreign aggression.   It
maintains at the general expense a costly army and navy.   It
builds forts and ships, and supplies itself with all the requirements in connection therewith.   Some persons contend that it
should not make its own guns and ammunition ; that it should
not build its own ships, or construct its own military railways,

that it should not even erect its own fortifications ; but that it should purchase all such things and services from private persons under suitable contracts regulated by competition. Apart from the defence of the country, the State goes farther, it follows the trade of its citizens to the uttermost parts of the earth, and for their protection it keeps up lines of communication along the water highways. It holds other peoples in subjection, partly for their own good, but chiefly for the commercial advantage of Englishmen. Some persons think that traders should be left to take care of themselves, to raise and maintain their own armies and fleets, as the East India Company did last century.

The next State function of which the large majority approve is the maintenance at home of law and order ; that is to say, the defence of every citizen against the aggression of other citizens, and the enforcement of promises of a certain kind (contracts). With the exception of Anarchists none dispute the propriety of this State work. The performance of it requires the maintenance of Courts of Justice and an army of police. The extent to which the State should go in *preventing* crime is keenly disputed. Some, for instance, would prohibit the carrying of firearms ; others would allow the storing of dynamite in private houses, leaving the consequences to private responsibility. Recourse has been had recently to spies and informers ; some consider this bad, others maintain that it is defensible.

The next State function which very few persons deprecate is the levying of the necessary means for carrying out the above and other Government work. The raising of revenue by some kind of taxation is denounced by Mr. Auberon Herbert, but he seems on this point to be in a minority of one, though I have no wish here to beg the question.

We now come to matters of State interference which excite a considerable amount of opposition—rightly or wrongly. The State holds itself responsible for the qualification of certain private workers. Persons who wish to practise medicine and surgery, to sell drugs, to lend money on pledges, to deal in second-hand metals, to sell alcoholic liquors, tobacco, or " game," to plead in the Courts, to mind engines, to carry on a variety of other occupations, must satisfy the State that they are properly qualified by education or respectability, or both. Some think that if the Bar, for example, were thrown open, the public would easily judge for itself as to the competency of the competitors, just as it now does in spite of the Government certificate. The same argument is applied to medicine. Due responsibility for culpable negligence would, it is said, suffice.

And the State carries on many works also on its own account. It carries letters and sends telegrams and parcels. Some point to the fact that the telephone companies, which are private, are much more cheaply worked than the telegraphs, and deduce the natural conclusion from the observation. Others point to the high charges which private carriers made for letter-distributing before the State took up the work and claimed the monopoly. But the State examines poetry and chooses the best poet as the Laureate. It studies astronomy on its own account and appoints an Astronomer Royal. It undertakes scientific expeditions and (some ten or twenty years after) publishes reports of them. It vies with private enterprise in its efforts to get to the North Pole. It collects pictures and books and objects of antiquarian and scientific interest, and stores them in national museums and galleries. It keeps up botanical gardens, and also gardens for simple recreation. All these things may be regarded as national, and not calculated to benefit any particular class of persons at the expense of the others. In some quarters it is objected that these matters would be attended to by private enterprise if it were not for State competition, and better managed. It is pointed out that the Polaris Expedition effected more than the British Expedition under Captain Nares at less than a tenth of the cost ; and that the report of the *Challenger* is only still very far from complete. On the other hand, it is contended that no private library can compare in any respect with that of the British Museum. Similarly, it is said, that private individuals could never have kept such recreation grounds as Hyde Park out of the hands of the builders for the good of the public health.

We have surveyed the field of modern State action, and

F

passed in review certain institutions intended to benefit the nation as a whole. But beyond these national institutions the State undertakes to provide others which benefit one class at the expense of the remainder : it maintains local baths and wash-houses, free libraries and free or half-free schools, and it builds dwelling-houses for certain classes of persons. It is contended by the advocates of these State institutions that, although one class is primarily benefited, the whole community derives indirect advantage from them. Individualists, on the other hand, urge that private enterprise will, in the absence of Government competition, supply enough to meet the demand, and that more than this is detrimental to the public welfare. It is also said that the quality of the supply is thus stereotyped and private initiative crippled. The State is asked by some to distribute the population in accordance with the fertility of the soil and the production of the district, by what is called State emigration or State-aided colonisation. This is strongly opposed by the majority, which maintains that population distributes itself most economically when left to itself. But the same majority approves of so distributing wealth that those who have shall contribute something towards the maintenance of the utterly destitute. Some contend that the levying of a poor-rate is in response to a legal and moral claim on the part of the poorest section of the community —a *right* to live. Others say it is a tribute to the national sentiment, the offspring of pity, and in the same category with the laws against cruelty to animals ; while others again defend the poor law as a safety-valve against revolution, and without any other justification. Again the question has been keenly debated whether the State is warranted in stepping in between a citizen and his own animals in the interest of humanity. Some say these matters may safely be left to the social sanction.

Other State interferences may be classified under the heads of Sanitation, Morality, Religion, and Justice. Whether individuals should be allowed to dispose of their sewage as they think fit, or should be compelled to adopt some general and approved system ; whether they should be forced to adopt certain medical precautions in the general interest, such as those required by quarantine laws, Vaccination Acts, Contagious Diseases Acts, notification and compulsory removal laws and the like; whether they should be allowed to build according to demand, or according to rules like those contained in the Metropolitan Buildings Acts; whether such matters as smoke-abatement should be treated as questions of mere private nuisance; whether the dead should be disposed of according to the fancies of their surviving relations, or on some State-ordained system; whether private persons should be permitted to use and also to abuse public waters by polluting them until such time as they see the necessity of combining to keep them pure; whether the makers and vendors of foods, drugs, beverages, etc., should be untrammelled by any other law than the maxim *caveat emptor*, or whether the State should analyse these commodities and punish adulterators; upon all these questions of sanitation, and a hundred others of the same kind, opinions differ.

In the interests of Morality some contend (an enormous majority) that the State should punish bigamy and practices inimical to monogamy, and should prescribe between whom marriages should lawfully be sanctioned. Some of those who admit this, contend that the State is needlessly strict in its prohibitions, *e.g.* in the case of marriage with the sister of a deceased wife. Some of those who would allow young girls, against their inclinations, to be sacrificed to the greed or ambition of parents or guardians, provided the contract is one of marriage, deny the sufficiency of parental responsibility in the case of similar contracts of a temporary character, even when the young person is a consenting party. Opinions widely differ as to how far the State is warranted in sharing the responsibility with parents, and in standing *in loco parentis* with respect to orphans. It is also debated whether the suppression of brothels other than disorderly houses is, properly speaking, a State duty; and the same difference extends to the question of public-houses, where drunkenness may (or may not) result in disorder and nuisance. In the interest of morality the State exercises censorship of plays, though it has not till the other day been deemed necessary to continue the precaution in the case of light literature. In the matter of gambling, opinions widely differ, and the State seems to comply with them all.   It prohibits some kinds of betting and lotteries under heavy penalties.   Other kinds, such as betting on race-courses, it tolerates, but refuses to sanction; and other kinds, again, it recognises and sanctions, such as Stock Exchange speculations.   Probably it may be said that according to the spirit of Scotch jurisprudence a fair bet should be enforced like any other contract, whereas English law would consistently refuse to sanction it.   As to which is the best course for the State to adopt, having regard to the general welfare, opinions again differ.

Coming to State action in the interest of Religion, there is great diversity of view.   The tendency has clearly been in the direction of diminished Government interference in such matters.   People are no longer burned for heresy.   Whether heretics should be burnt is still a debated question, but the "Noes" have it.   Not so, however, with regard to Sabbath observance, Sunday trading, Sunday amusements, etc.   On these points, and on the maintenance of a Church Estab-lishment, public opinion seems to be pretty evenly balanced. There still remain on the Statute-books certain laws relating to oaths, and others relating to blasphemy, which imply that the State considers itself bound to punish offences against what may be called the national religion.

In this very brief survey of existing State functions in England we have necessarily omitted all reference to whole classes of Government action, and notably to that coming under the head Justice.   And we have passed over the whole field of municipal functions, such as road-making, maintaining, paving, and cleaning; lighting, bridge-building; the laying of sewers and drains, water supply, fire extinction, the regulation of cemeteries, markets, and fairs, etc. etc.   In spite of all these omissions the area surveyed is wide enough to call up doubts in the minds of both parties—Individualists and Socialists— as to whether the happy mean has in all cases been yet hit by the State.

The spirit of the individualist movement is one of resistance to any overstepping by the legislature of its normal boundaries. It is the embodiment of the absolute principle of civil liberty,

or the greatest possible liberty of each. compatible with the
equal liberty of all.   Of those who have faith in State action
it is probable that none follow up the principle to its extreme
logical conclusion, and look forward to the time when every
man in the land shall have his own inspector to follow him
about, to carry his goloshes, and to see that he puts them on
before crossing the road; to take notes of what he says; to
correct his grammar and his religious opinions when out of
harmony with authorised usage; to see that he drinks what
is good for him, and no more; to put out his candle at nine
at night, and to accompany him twice to church every Sunday.
Consistency wavers before such a prospect—an age when there
shall be no crime, no drunkenness, no wrangling, not even
difference of opinion, and we shall be an orderly people, doing
that which is right in the eyes of the majority—the supreme,
allwise, and serenely disinterested majority!   But if the State
socialists shrink from this outcome of State idolatry, so also
do their opponents shrink from carrying the principle of
non-interference to extreme lengths.   Probably if they are
prepared to accept any working principle at all as to the
expediency of any proposed legislation, it is that the. *onus
probandi* lies on those who would limit the freedom of the
citizen.   "The old-fashioned presumption was always that in
the case of any interference with liberty, its reasonableness
should be demonstrated before it should be adopted; but
nowadays it seems to be the notion that the presumption is
the other way, and the burden of proof is on those who have
to defend liberty instead of on those who insist upon interference."   Yes, till the sweets of bondage are proved, it is
better to remain free.

The need for such a movement was never more urgent than
it is to-day, for, blink the matter as we may, there is no
denying that a new departure has of late been made by the
Conservative party, the outcome of which it is impossible to
foresee.   In an apparent bid for socialist support, opposed
though it is to Conservative traditions and practice, there is
nothing actually inconsistent with Conservative theory.   Be
this as it may, the die is cast.   The Conservative party have
thrown in their lot with State socialism.   The gloomy and

unheeded forebodings of Lord Wemyss, in 1883, are already fulfilled.

"Whereas in commerce freedom of contract is the very breath of its nostrils, the soul of its being ; and whereas the commercial transactions in land—that is, the bargains between landlord and tenant—are in the aggregate greater than those of any two or three of the other largest British commercial interests ; these bargains are not only to be forbidden in the future, but broken in the past. This is what the two great parties in the State affirmed when, with grateful hearts and cheerful countenances, they with delightful unanimity passed the second reading of the Government Agricultural Holdings Bill. Contracts, not in 'exceptional' Ireland, but here in law-abiding, free, commercial England and Scotland—forbidden in the future and broken in the past ! And why ? Solely because—disguise the truth as they may under specious phrases, bury it no matter how deep under agricultural commissioners' reports—Liberals and Conservatives have cast principle and sound economic doctrine aside, and are playing a game of grab for the farmers' vote."

The result of the game will, of course, depend on the answer to the question, Who holds the trump card ? And the trump card is not nationalisation of land only, but nationalisation of all wealth. That is the trump card in the game. Hitherto, the part of the Conservative has been to throw obstacles in the path of the Radical charioteer, while the Whig has taken his seat on the box and hampered the driver's movements, endeavouring all the while to damp his ardour with prudent counsel. It now remains to be seen whether the old party of progress with liberty can any longer continue to play the role of unheeded mentor to the new party of communism and spoliation. If those Liberals who, anxious not to impede the process of structural reform, have up to the present silently tolerated much over-legislation of which they secretly disapprove, rather than seem to join hands with those who would bolster up effete institutions, do not now come forward and speak out boldly for the ancient rights and liberties of all classes on the time-honoured lines of property and freedom, to whom shall the country look ?

Now that the masses have tasted power they will strive for more, and it will be a wise precaution to guard democracy from its own defects by limiting the powers of the State, however constituted, and to enact, while yet it is day, that all interference of Government in matters outside its normal duties shall be a violation of the constitution. So long as the people see us arbitrarily shutting up their clubs, while our own are left open; forcing their children to learn what we were taught instead of what their fathers were taught, namely, their handicraft; closing their places of business on specified days; taxing them for the support of our museums, picture galleries, and scientific expeditions; in fine, acting as though by our mere fiat we could shower luxuries upon them or doom them to starvation —is it very wonderful they should wish to wield this power which can effect so much for good or for evil? If, ask they, we can reduce their working hours to ten, why not to eight? If we can build schools for their children, why not cottages for them? If we can afford to protect them gratis from smallpox, why cannot we pay the doctor's bill when they do catch it? Naturally they argue that capital is better paid than labour, because the labourer is not well represented in the House of Commons, and not at all in the House of Lords. When they obtain the reins, then, say they, it will be the labourer's turn. And who shall blame them? They are only taking a leaf out of our book. It cannot be honestly denied that recourse has been had to class legislation for the benefit of the upper classes at the expense of the lower. Have not wages been kept down by law? Has not the price of bread been kept up by law for the benefit of a class? What have shipowners to say about the old navigation laws? But it is not necessary to assign instances when there are hundreds in the recollection of all. Something more than mortal, then, will these new masters be, if, for any nobler motive than enlightened self-interest, they can be induced, with victory within their grasp, to forego the luxury of revenge and the plunder of their quondam taskmasters.

Nor can we lay the blame of this evil example of overlegislation at the door of either party in the State. Both are alike culpable, though, for reasons which are apparent, the Radical party chiefly has been made the tool of the rising socialism. Unless, therefore, it can be shown to the satisfaction of the working classes that class legislation worked in their own interest cannot in the long run be of advantage to them,

but rather the reverse, we must prepare for a long period of
sullen uniformity and mob despotism, such as has never been
known before. And yet individualism has no easy task before
it. The enemy is overwhelming in numbers and strongly
entrenched. With the old Anglo-Saxon love of liberty and
self-dependence on the one side; ranged against it are the not
yet extinct class hatred, a thirst for retaliation, and, above and
before all, sympathy with suffering. Not that it is necessary
to overcome the sympathy, but to convince those who sympathise, that the best medicine for all social ills is liberty;
optima medicina est non uti medicina. This is in many cases
no light matter. Try and convince the recipient of outdoor
relief that such relief is inexpedient. Have you seen whole
families during the famines in Ireland or India literally starving
to death on land from which its owner or usufructuary draws
thousands a year? Demonstrate to them that it would be
neither wise nor kind to abolish by law the payment of rent.
Have you hopelessly watched a crew of stalwart fellows go
down on some rotten craft within sight of port? Convince
Mr. Plimsoll, and those who think with him, that the seaworthiness of ships is best left to the shipowners. Have you
known little children of nine and ten sent down into the pit
to toil in solitude, in danger, and in darkness for the livelong
day? If so, are you sure that the law relating to mines and
prohibiting such cruelty is altogether unjustifiable? Is it
true that £80,000,000 is anually spent in intoxicating drink
in this country? If so, shall we blame those who would do
their utmost, by legislation, to extirpate the national curse?
Again, it is not pleasant to see the little ones of the people
growing up in ignorance of much that is useful and beautiful
for the want of elementary teaching. Surely men will not be
found capable of banding themselves together for the express
purpose of resisting all these noble efforts for the amelioration
of poverty and weakness.

Now this question brings us to the remarkable misconcep-
tion that has somehow got afloat as to the views of individualists with respect to rules and regulations in general. It seems
to be supposed that anything of the nature of a rule is in their
eyes anathema. The Radical papers teem with questions

calculated to bring ridicule upon those who oppose State interference in general. It seems to be forgotten that other bodies can make laws besides the State. The Stock Exchange and the Jockey Club at once present themselves as instances of private bodies making laws which are virtually accepted by the whole country. The customs of the Lancashire cotton trade are the finest example of commercial law in the world. Every club, every society and association, makes its own laws, which are sufficiently sanctioned to meet with respect and obedience, quite as uniformly as the laws of the land. And yet the prevailing impression seems to be that only the State can make laws having any binding effect—that without such State rules and regulations everything would be topsy-turvy. Mine-owners and miners would conspire to blow up the mines ; shipowners would scuttle their ships, drown their crews, get up a glorious reputation for going to the bottom, and pay double insurance ; cabmen would charge at least a guinea a mile ; bankers would smother the country with worthless paper ; railway companies would smash up passengers and goods, charge prohibitive fares, and ruin their shareholders ; theatrical managers would drive all the respectable and monied classes away from the theatres by exhibitions of bad taste ; publicans would sit up all night in order to sell a pint of ale ; pawnbrokers would charge 60 per cent a month, and receive stolen goods with alacrity ; landlords would keep their farms unlet and uncultivated ; farmers would pay more in rent than they could recoup in profit ; and everybody would work to death without taking a holiday ; in fine, society is accredited with suicidal mania and must be kept in a strait-waistcoat.

The first question asked is, "What! would you allow a thoughtless collier to light his pipe in the workings ?" or, "Would you let the railway companies charge what they like ?" or, "Would you have all the land thrown out of cultivation ?" or, "Would you have all the crops devoured by vermin ?" or something equally irrelevant. Now the answer to all these and similar questions is, that it is not the expediency or appropriateness of this or that regulation with which individualism concerns itself. It may be an excellent provision that passenger trains should not run at more than sixty miles an hour, or it may not; if it is, let the companies make such a rule, or let the public refrain from travelling by lines which have no such rule; but let not Parliament interfere in the matter. Again, as to the naked lights in a coalpit, is it really believed that colliers are so absurdly reckless of their own lives as to imperil them for the sake of a whiff of tobacco? And even granting that there are a few such dangerous lunatics in the pits, as out of them, is the mineowner so anxious himself for a meeting with his creditors as to allow such doings if they can possibly be prevented? The plain fact is, apart from theory, that before the passing of any Acts relating to mines, the most stringent regulations were in force concerning the use of lights and lamps in the workings —rules not so much imposed by the masters, as agreed to alike by owners, managers, and men, for the common safety. It is the ability to make such rules, to obey them, and to enforce them, which makes the Anglo-Saxon race what it is—a colonising people, a people fit for self-government. And it is the weakening and supplanting of these contractual rules by rules emanating from a central legislature which will some day, if persisted in, reduce the Englishman to the level of his continental neighbours. It is not from any horror of law and order, of method and regulation in all things, that individualism is opposed to State interference; on the contrary, it is rather the reverse; it is because it attaches so high a value to these things, and because it fears to see the habits of self-rule crushed out by the enervating effects of grandmotherly government.

In one respect there is no comparison at all between the contractual regulations made by those chiefly interested and the State regulations made, so to speak, by outsiders; and that is, in point of economy, the true balance of advantage. It is doubtless more or less dangerous to go into a pit at all; but a law to prohibit coal-mining would be to sacrifice too much for the sake of safety. Again, a safety lamp costs more than a naked candle; but to tolerate the candle would be to sacrifice too little for the sake of safety. There is always a happy medium, and the legislature is not likely to find it.

Take shipping—seaworthiness is a matter of degree; if absolute, unquestionable seaworthiness is insisted upon, the lower-class seaman is ruined; if the cranky craft is allowed, foul deeds for the sake of insurance are rendered possible. Where the line should be drawn is a nice question, and must be settled between the shipowner and the sailor; it certainly cannot be settled by the State without the certainty of a false economy. " To the seafaring population," writes Mr. Crofts, " the character of each ship and ship's captain are as well known as the performances of every racehorse to the betting fraternity. If a sailor takes employment on a rotten and overladen ship, with a drunken skipper, to whom astronomical reckonings are as Greek, it is in most cases not because he does not know any better, but because he cannot do any better. Able-bodied seamen with good recommendations and habits naturally monopolise the forecastles of the best ships, where bad characters and Lascars are at a discount. If these latter want to go to sea, their evil reputation does not permit of their being over-fastidious in the choice of accommodation and masters; and the question for them is frequently one of going afloat with a chance of living, or staying ashore with a certainty of starving."

I have no desire to impugn the motives of those simple-minded philanthropists, who, filled with sympathy for suffering humanity, struggle to mitigate the laws of nature by Act of Parliament. It is not with these men we need quarrel; they are possibly intelligent men of little knowledge, and open to conviction when the truth is stated to them simply; but it is their subtler allies that are to be feared, imposters who trade on the nobler instincts of their fellow-workers for the sake of place, popularity, or pelf. Such men are beneath conviction; frequently they know the futility of their own proposals, but it suits them to pose as philanthropists. Let us name no names, but there are well-known legislators who speak with unction of the rights and wrongs of labour, and who grind down their own work-people with an iron heel. There is such a thing as Brummagem philanthropy; these are the impostors who form the extreme sect of what Mr. Gladstone once called " Political quacks."

But the lovers of civil liberty are not without questionable allies, men who are open to the charge of protesting against State interference with the industry in which they are themselves interested, lest such interference should favour their weaker fellow-workers. When we see men whose whole political lives have been spent in plotting against the liberties of the people, suddenly cry out for liberty, more liberty, as soon as their own pockets are threatened, we may know how far to trust such men, and what their alliance is worth. Poor Jack must not be allowed to drink rum; it is bad for him physically and morally, but he may drown, for am I not a shipowner? The wretched miner must be wrapped up in cotton wool and work no more than four hours a day, but as for the peasant he may rot on my threshold, for am I not a landlord? Let the poverty-stricken be defended against the rapacity of the merciless pawnbroker; but it is preposterous to tolerate the claim of the helpless widow and children whom a railway accident has left destitute, for be it known that I am a railway king. One can hardly blame those demagogues who stigmatise individualism as selfishness. Sympathy with suffering quickens the zeal of these scribblers for quixotic legislation, while their knowledge of political philosophy is too defective to permit of their seeing its futility.

It is unfortunately too true that a consistent individualist must combine knowledge of principles and the courage of his opinions with a certain surgeon-like imperturbability in the presence of the inevitable: he must know how to withhold the iced drink from the parched fever patient; he must be prepared to be accused of selfishness and greed, of hardness of heart and indifference to the sufferings of others, and of hypocrisy in appealing to the lofty principles of liberty for the sinister purpose of bolstering up unjust privileges and monopolies. These charges must be met and disproved, not only in general but in detail.

Between socialism and liberalism there is no necessary bond, neither, as we shall see, is conservatism uniformly individualistic. After passing in view some of the more prominent pieces of proposed legislation of a semi-socialistic character, which are even now within the range of practical

politics, judged by the rate at which we have been travelling of
late in this direction, Mr. Fawcett concluded one of his latest
pamphlets in these remarkable words: " In endeavouring to
explain some of the consequences which their adoption would
involve, we should greatly regret to do any injustice to the
motives of those by whom they are advocated. Mischievous as
we believe many of these schemes would prove to be, the great
majority of those by whom they are advocated are undoubtedly
prompted by no other desire than to promote social, moral, and
material advancement. The conclusion above all others which
we desire to enforce is, that any scheme, however well-intentioned it may be, will indefinitely increase every evil it seeks
to alleviate if it lessens individual responsibility by encouraging
the people to rely less upon themselves and more upon the
State."

Again, Mr. Thorold Rogers, in a lecture on " Some Aspects
of Laissez-faire and Control," has treated the question historically. But, as he will himself admit, the trustworthiness
of the results of a study of tendencies to a very great extent
depends on the length of time during which those tendencies
can be shown to have been in operation. Mr. Rogers's conclusion that the general consensus is distinctly favourable
to increased State interference is probably correct for the
present time, and it coincides with what has been already
said about the recent rapid advance of State socialism; but
to infer from proof of such present tendency that increased
Government action is a concomitant of civilisation would or
would not be justifiable according as the tendency can be
shown to be a persistent one, or at least an increasing one
throughout the whole range of history. Any shorter period of
observation is apt to be delusive; the present prevalence of
socialistic opinions in this and other countries can no more be
pointed to as part of a universal development than could
the equally remarkable advance of the extreme doctrine of
" let-be " thirty or forty years ago. Almost as philosophically
might the marked revival of that doctrine during a recent
period in England be cited in support of the doctrine of
individualism. Now, if we take English constitutional history as the subject of our examination, we shall find that

so far from being on the increase, State interference with individual liberty has been a constantly-diminishing quantity. We have but to cast our eyes down the statutes of the Plantagenet period to discover in what numberless private concerns the State intruded, with which no modern Government would dream of meddling. The price of corn, the wages of labourers, the importation of coin, the manufacture of beer, the rate of interest on loans, attendance at divine service, and a thousand other matters, were carefully supervised by the State. A statute of Henry VIII. goes so far as to forbid the use of machinery in the manufacture of broadcloth, a law which drove a good deal of the woollen trade to Holland, where the "divers devilish contrivances" were under no ban. Why, there are actually early English laws setting forth with what amount of energy and thoroughness the ploughman shall plough each furrow. Further illustrations are unnecessary, for it will be admitted by any candid reader of history that, on the whole, the tendency to State interference diminishes with the evolution of societies. The slight reaction observable in our own day seems to be satisfactorily explained by the sudden inclusion within the electorate of two new layers of citizens with limited political experience. The evil will disappear only when the newly-enfranchised classes perceive not only that they will themselves suffer from restrictions on free action, but that they will be the first and the worst sufferers. When Mr. Rogers descends to the particular instances of what may be called modern socialistic legislation, he seems to be anxious and able to find some special justification for each in its turn. Mr. Rogers is quite incapable of prostituting science to the defence of party, and yet any one might be forgiven for thinking otherwise to whom Mr. Rogers's writings were previously unknown. The Factory Acts are good, he says, because they result in the restraint of waste. It might easily be shown that the economy of labour has been indefinitely postponed by the operation of the Factory Acts. "The doctrine of *laissez-faire* is absolute in the case of contracts for the use of labour, *except in cases where*—" and then comes a string of exceptions apparently cast in general language for the purpose of justifying the Acts just named, the Truck Acts, the Act of 1883 for prohibiting the payment of wages in public-houses, and other similar interferences with individual freedom.

I am not going to defend the tally-shop, though many a poor wife has cursed the day since when her husband's wages, instead of being paid in groceries and household stores, were paid in cash to be spent in drink. What is of more importance to note is, that where workmen as a class were thrifty and steady, as in the mining districts of Durham and Northumberland, the truck system died a natural death without any need for State intervention. Similarly, the fishermen in several of the east-coast ports have put a stop to the system of paying wages in the public-house in a very simple manner; by steadily refusing to order liquor, or even to drink it at the expense of another, they have made it unprofitable to the publican to give the use of his premises for the purpose. Men who have not the strength of mind to act thus will not be made more self-reliant or more fit to wrestle with the many temptations of the world by being put into leading-strings and kept out of sight of beer. With respect to the free choice of a calling, Mr. Rogers agrees " that the aggregate of industry sorts itself best in the interests of all when the process is left to perfectly free action." But this excellent generalisation goes too far for him ; it condemns much recent legislation ; consequently a qualifying clause must be introduced to justify it, so that the rule now reads, " The aggregate of industry sorts itself best in the interest of all when, *certain obvious conditions being satisfied, and precautions taken,* the process is left to perfectly free action." One of these precautions seems to be the State examination of everybody in order that " adequate evidence should be given of professional competence." " The impulse," says Mr. Rogers, " is towards the creation of new professions with special tests of proficiency ; this is the case with the art of the dispensing druggist, of the surveyor, of the elementary schoolmaster," and he might have added, of the skipper and second hand of fishing-boats. The enforcement of professional responsibility by law is a totally distinct question, and rests on the answer given to a deeper question than that concerning the demarkation of State functions. When we come to the railways, Mr. Rogers seems to have some difficulty in finding any sound or even specious reason for making them an exception to the general rule. "The case of these *adventurers* is most peculiar," he says. "The directors and shareholders of the existing companies vote in Parliament against rival lines without pretending to consider the public good." I believe the brewers as a class do not support local-option bills; it is hinted that the bishops are somewhat biassed in favour of the Established Church ; and landowners are not always agitating for a heavy land-tax ; but the charge against the railway directors appears to be, not so much that they consider the interests of their own class first, after the manner of others, but that they have not the decency to *pretend* to put the interests of plasterers, tanners, physicians, etc. etc., before their own. So the railways are to be brought under increased State control, the so-called Cheap Trains Act is only an instalment in the direction of this control. Reasons are also forthcoming for the violation of the "let-be" principle in the matter of agricultural holdings, of homes for the poor, of places of entertainment and refreshment, of education, and of sanitary arrangements. With respect to education, Mr. Rogers is candid enough and paradoxical enough to admit that "it is of no material or economical benefit to the recipient ; " and since we force it upon others solely for our own benefit, at some loss and inconvenience to themselves, we have no right to charge them anything for it. Many people will agree that if education is to be compulsory, it should certainly be free, but they will underline the word "if."

But conservatism also dallies with socialism.

"Some persons," writes Lord Salisbury, on the subject of artisans' dwellings, " may be disposed to inquire at the outset whether it is right that Parliament should interfere at all. I see a statement in the newspaper that the Liberty and Property Defence League are preparing to denounce any such interference as unsound in principle. I have the greatest respect for the League. They preach a wholesome doctrine, and necessary for these times. But if this account of their views is a true one, I think they have in this instance gone farther than sound reasoning and the *precedents of our legislation* will justify. At present no proposal has been made, as far as I know, to give assistance for this purpose except by way of loan, and surely it cannot be maintained that loans for public objects are against the *practice* of this

country because their first effects may be to promote the interest of individuals. Without entering upon disputable ground by quoting Ireland
and the West Indies, it is sufficient to recall the advances made by
various Governments, but especially by that of Sir Robert Peel, for the
extension of drainage in this country. A very large sum was advanced
to landlords at an interest which secured the State from loss, but lower
than their own credit would have obtained. It was duly paid after
having done its work. That work was in the first instance to increase
the rental of the land, and, in the second, undoubtedly it served the useful purpose of giving employment under the agricultural depression caused
by the repeal of the corn-laws, and of increasing the general production
of the country. In the case before us also the loan would be justified by
imperious considerations of public policy, even if all thoughts of humanity
were cast aside. These overcrowded centres of population are also centres
of disease, and successive discoveries of biologists tell us more and more
clearly that there is in this matter an indissoluble partnership among all
human beings breathing in the same vicinity. If the causes of disease
were inanimate, no one would hesitate about employing advances of public
money to render them innocuous. Why should the expenditure become
illegitimate because the causes happen to be human beings ? But this
unhappy population has a special claim on any assistance that Parliament
can give. The evil has in a great measure been created by Parliament
itself. If London had been allowed to go on as it was half a century ago,
many benefits of vast importance would have been lost, but the intense
competition for house room would not exist and the reformation of
'rookeries' would have been a much less arduous task. But improvements on a vast scale have been made, and those improvements in too
many cases have only meant packing the people tighter. New streets,
railways, viaducts, law courts and other public buildings, made compulsory
under the authority of Parliament, have swept away the dwellings of thousands of the poor, and in that proportion have made the competition more
intense for those that remain. Many tenements have let for a high price,
which, if artificial compression had not been used, would have found no
tenant. Under these circumstances it is no violation, even of the most
scrupulous principles, to ask Parliament to give what relief it can.
Laissez-faire is an admirable doctrine, but it must be applied upon both
sides."

Whether loans for public objects are, or are not, against
the *practice* of this country is hardly relevant when we are
discussing the wisdom of the plan. This country, like most
other countries, is occasionally guilty of foolish practices, and
what we want to know is, not what the State has been in the
habit of doing in the past but what it ought to do in the
future. As to the advances made under Sir Robert Peel to
landlords for drainage purposes at a lower rate of interest than

G

their own credit would have obtained, the question is, Was this effected without loss to the country? That the State was duly repaid with interest in full may be quite true, and yet the country may have lost heavily by the transaction. The interest on State loans has to be paid for out of taxation; and the question is, Would the money intercepted by the State for these purposes have found its way into more remunerative channels than the three per cents or not? And in any case, would the wealth so intercepted have fructified at a greater rate in the hands of the people than on the fields of the landlords? There is at least this to be said, the capital which is invested by the private enterprise of the people does, as a fact, on the average realise over three per cent per annum, whereas the investment on drainage was after all nothing less than a speculation which was justified only by success. It might have been a colossal failure. Perhaps the worst that can be said of this speculation is, that its good luck has elevated it into a very dangerous precedent. The amount of risk involved in it was accurately measured by the interest which the landlords would have had to pay if they had borrowed the money on their own credit. "If," said the late Mr. Fawcett, "the State makes loans in cases where they cannot be obtained from ordinary commercial sources, it is clear that, in the judgment of those best qualified to form an opinion, the State is running a risk of loss." As to the useful purposes of giving employment, could a more dangerous doctrine be formulated?

Lord Salisbury's chief argument for State interference in this direction is based on a complete misapprehension of the position of the "let-be" school. It amounts in effect to this. These London slums are *foci* of pestilence; if similar dangers were due solely to inanimate causes, you would not hesitate to spend the public money in their prompt removal. Why, then, should you refrain from doing so merely lest one wretched class of the community should be accidentally benefited at the expense of the remainder? Why, indeed? But that is not the reason for objecting to the expenditure. Lord Salisbury is mistaken when he says "that no one would hesitate if the causes of disease were inanimate." They would and do hesitate ; they strongly protest. But their reason is the most profound distrust in the efficiency of State machinery for these and all similar purposes—absolute disbelief in the power of the State to effect the desired object. There is no doubt whatever that Parliament has already done much in the way of aggravating the evil, and in making "improvements which in too many cases have only meant packing the people tighter." Therefore, although it may be "no violation of the most scrupulous principles to ask Parliament to give what relief it can," it is nevertheless permissible to doubt if Parliament can give any, and to protest against throwing good money after bad. The problem to be solved is, How to build and fit out a £75 tenement for £30 or £40 ; and we have only to look deep enough into all the schemes propounded with a view to its solution to find that the key to every one of them is plunder more or less disguised. The promoters of the urban scheme would continue to compel the ratepayers to buy land at a guinea a foot, and to sell it to the philanthropists for five shillings. The friends of the suburban scheme have more respect for the pockets of the ratepayers ; they would organise "a system of cheap trains"; in other words, they would compel the railway companies to carry certain classes of passengers at a dead loss. Whether this is done after the manner of Dick Turpin, or on the model of the so-called Cheap Trains Act matters little. Whether shareholders are to be robbed in the old-fashioned style, or tricked out of their rights by a dishonest Act of Parliament, is a question for those whose policy is spoliation with decency. The passenger duty has been condemned by all parties on grounds of justice and expediency, and the companies had been given distinctly to understand that the tax would be abolished as soon as the state of the revenue justified the sacrifice. On the faith of this understanding the companies refrained from further agitation in the matter, until they were informed that they were at last to receive part of their admitted rights *on condition* of their carrying a certain class of persons over their lines at an unremunerative rate. There are many other schemes before the public, but of this we may rest assured, that plunder underlies them all. If anything was wanted to demonstrate the utter hopelessness of any attempt to improve the dwellings of the poor by State help, that want was met by Lord Salisbury's own very able analysis of the position. The difficulty to be overcome is summed up in these words, " Until their wages rise they cannot pay for the bare cost of decent lodging such as existing agencies can offer."

Lord Pembroke's pamphlet on "Liberty and Socialism" begins with an analysis of the causes which have led to the rapid decline in popular favour of the doctrine of *laissez-faire* during the last two or three decades. " A few years ago the doctrine of non-interference seemed to be paramount in English politics, and any one who ventured to prophesy that there would be a reversal of public opinion before the end of the century was ridiculed as a crotcheteer and an alarmist." And yet only recently the *Times* is found maintaining that "the doctrine of *laissez-faire* is as dead as the worship of Osiris." "Among other things that helped to bring about the reaction," says Lord Pembroke, " was the fact that it had been an era of continual political reform. Laws and institutions that the country had outgrown had to be removed ; restrictions that our wiser knowledge had shown us the folly of had to be swept away. One would hardly have supposed that this process could have been favourable to a belief in the efficacy of interference. But, however strange and unreasonable, it is undoubtedly true, that in many minds this purely liberative and destructive course of legislation has given rise to the notion that perpetual meddling by Act of Parliament is necessary to prevent stagnation — that unless our legislators keep stirring up things progress will stop ; that what is called on platforms ' beneficial legislation ' is a kind of stimulating manure indispensable to the national growth. To those who hold this profoundly foolish, but by no means uncommon view, the very name *laissez-faire* implies dereliction of duty, and thereby stands condemned." Who cannot bear testimony to this strange confusion of ideas ? Because repealing or undoing Acts of Parliament are themselves called legislation, they are frequently adduced as proofs of the efficacy of legislation. Should the question be asked at a public meeting, " What good has ever come of legislation yet ? " some one is sure to

reply, "Look at the repeal of the corn-laws." It is more
than probable that the expression *laissez-faire* is still commonly
understood in its oldest sense to mean: Let things alone, let
them drift, let that which is filthy be filthy still. There is no
doubt that this is the sense in which it was used by the
French Minister of State who first gave the phrase political
currency. And this may be another cause of its present
unpopularity. Another vulgar notion, which is thoroughly
disposed of in Mr. Herbert Spencer's *Over-Legislation*, is the
erroneous one that if the maxim is carried out the duties of
the State will necessarily be reduced to nil, and there will be
no further use for a legislature. To those who are acquainted
with the chaotic state of the English law and its ponderous
procedure this mistaken notion will not require disproof. The
reform, completion, and codification of the law will supply
material for many an abler Parliament than any we have yet
sent to Westminster.

Lord Pembroke makes search for a simple principle which
shall "limit the rights of society against the individual, and of
the individual against society—a principle which if it cannot,
owing to the limitation of human knowledge, completely solve
all difficulties, will at least prove a true guide in all cases in
which we can see correctly how to apply it." The search is
fruitless and the discovery is pronounced impossible. " I can
no more imagine a principle that would tell us in every case
the limits of individual and State rights, than one that would
tell us in every case whether the dictates of egoism or altruism
are to be obeyed." The principle attributed to the school of
Spencer and Von Humboldt, viz. " absolute freedom for each,
limited only by the like freedom for others," is examined and
discarded as only " an undue straining of language." " If by
any effort of ingenuity it be stretched wide enough to be made
the true rule in all known stages of human progress, it is
evident that its width of interpretation would make it quite
worthless as a practical guide to us. If, on the other hand, it
is admitted that it could not apply as a wise practical rule to
all these phases, or even to any one of them that has yet been
known—and it is only claimed that it is an ideal principle
towards which progress is constantly tending, and which may

become of universal application when men are very different
from what they are now—its equal uselessness to us in the
present day as a practical guide or test is no less plain." And,
as a test of its value as a practical guide, the writer asks those
who hold it to consider how they propose to apply it to the
law of marriage. "Are they prepared to abrogate this greatest
of all interferences with freedom of contract, and do they hold
that such a reform would bring a preponderance of benefit in
our present state of civilisation ? If, on the other hand, they
declare that the principle of absolute freedom for each, limited
only by the like freedom of all, does not condemn such a law,
I am puzzled to guess what form of State regulation it is
capable of defending us against. We must not loosen or
tighten its interpretation to suit our convenience." The writer
reverts to this awkward question of marriage : " I think," he
says, "we have a right to ask those who regard this as an
infallible practical rule whether they are prepared to adhere
to it in this instance ? If they answer in the affirmative, as
Von Humboldt did, most people will have a strong opinion
about the soundness and wisdom of the principle." Now,
without in the least disputing Lord Pembroke's right to ask this
crucial question, the extreme individualist may with equal right
decline to answer it. Clearly he must either admit that the
marriage law is an exception, which upsets the trustworthiness
of his principle, or else he must express the contrary view ;
in which case there can be no doubt that "most people
will have a strong opinion," not only about the soundness
of his principle, but also about the desirableness of his
acquaintance. And unless he is prepared to pose as a
martyr to his political doctrines, he had better keep his
mouth shut. His interrogator may, from that, possibly
infer his inner admission, but it is surely cruel to demand
an answer to such a question in the market - place.
Perhaps Lord Pembroke's own opinion upon this point
would be interesting, and since he will admit that we
"have a right to demand it," he will doubtless favour us
with it on the occasion of his promised return to this
subject.

When Lord Pembroke confidently asks, " Yet will any one

contend that the abolition of prescribed cab fares would be an improvement ?" I may venture to point out, not only that the suggestion has been seriously made, but that it has actually been carried out in practice in the city of Liverpool, and succeeded remarkably well. We cannot follow the writer through his extremely interesting and profound examination of the application to the concrete of Mr. Spencer's division of State action into negatively-regulative and positively-regulative ; but I am quite ready to admit that until this part of the essay has been carefully considered and fairly answered, individualists of the absolutist school, of whom Mr. Auberon Herbert is the able, albeit somewhat Quixotic chief in this country, must rest content to sit in the cool shades of speculative philosophy, and leave the field of practical politics to others. " Experience and observation will enable us to frame rules and principles that will become wider and more general with the advance of political science ; and if in this science the first principles should be the last things to be discovered, we should remember that it will prove no exception to the general rule." This is the outcome of Lord Pembroke's study, and it is in complete harmony with the teachings of inductive philosophy.

Let me cite one more authority on this great question. Mr. Goschen is known rather as a shrewd and observant statesman than as a student of abstract science, and it is gratifying to find him warning the public against the dangers of modern State socialism. " The dangers in the road of social reconstruction under Government control are so grave that they can scarcely be exaggerated ; dangers arising not only from the serious chance of inefficiency in the methods chosen, but from the transfer of responsibilities by the establishment of national law in the place of individual duty ; from the withdrawal of confidence in the qualities of men in order to bestow it on the merits of administrations ; from the growing tendency to invoke the aid of the State, and the declining belief in individual power." Mr. Goschen appears to derive some comfort from the reflection that *pari passu* with an increased demand for State interference goes an increased tendency towards decentralisation. " The transfer of work in

the way of interference from the central body to local
authorities diminishes the extension of central power and
patronage, which is a most undesirable accompaniment of
increased Government action; it reduces the number of the
army of men whom the central authority are compelled to
employ; it eases the work of the Government; it imposes
public functions on different classes of citizens; it interests an
additional stratum of society in public business; and lastly, it
provides to some extent a safety-valve against possible tyranny
on the part of an all-powerful class. *If* the extended demand
for Government interference is to be progressively satisfied, it
is earnestly to be hoped that we may proceed *pari passu* on
the lines of decentralisation." I fail to see that decentralisation can be an antidote to democratic despotism. What
is the use of reducing the number of central officials if ten
times the number is to be maintained by the local authorities ?
Why ease the work of a government which will only make use
of its increased opportunities to devise new mischief, simply in
order that local bodies may help to do it ? Why impose
public functions on new strata of society, when those functions
are abnormal and despotic ? If we are to have a despot,
myriad-headed or otherwise, the more central, cumbrous, and
unwieldy the machinery through which it has to obtain its
ends, the better for its victims. The tyranny of the Sultan is
as nothing to the tyranny of the pashas. The larger the area
from which the central body is drawn, the greater the number
of conflicting interests which it is necessary to reconcile before
the desired policy can be carried out, and the better the
chance of its being emasculated during the process. Local
despotism is the worst despotism. Decentralisation cannot go
farther than the family; and what kind of local government is
more loathsome than the unchecked rule of a brutal paterfamilias ? Local option, in regard to liquor and to other
matters, is part and parcel of a system of decentralisation
which, for the trampling underfoot of private liberty and the
crushing out of individuality, has no equal among modern forms
of government. When the normal functions of the central
legislature, and of provincial legislatures down to the municipality, have been defined and approximately adapted to the

age, then, and then only, is decentralisation compatible with civil liberty.

"How," asked Mr. Gladstone, "is the time of the House of Commons to be economised?" The answer is simple : Let the House of Commons mind its own business—thoroughly and exclusively.

CHAPTER IV

" PROPERTY," says Proudhon, " is theft." Very likely: we must not dismiss this opinion with a sneer. Proudhon was unquestionably one of the clearest thinkers of his time. The institution of property is described by Jeremy Bentham as " the noblest triumph of humanity over itself." Good again ! But the two propositions do not quite tally. Let us take an Italian opinion: "The right of property," says Beccaria,[1] the great Italian jurist, " is a terrible right, which perhaps is not necessary." If we inquire of the poets we get something of this kind—

> " O property ! what art thou but a weight
> To crush all soul, and paralyse all strength,
> And grind all heart and action out of man ? "

But poets are not always meant to be taken seriously. Here is the opinion of the most serious and respectable of theologians, the worthy Dr. Paley : " Property communicates a charm to whatever is the object of it. It is the first of our abstract ideas. It cleaves to us the closest and the longest. It endears to the child its plaything, to the peasant his cottage, to the landholder his estate. It supplies the place of prospect and of scenery. Instead of coveting the beauty of distant situations, it teaches every man to find it in his own. It gives boldness and grandeur to plains and fens, tinge and colouring to clays and fallows." At any rate, property seems to be a remarkable institution. It inspires the intensest reverence and the profoundest abhorrence.

Perhaps it will be said that I have cited extreme

[1] Quoted from Bentham's *Theory of Legislation.*

authorities. Then I will appeal to an authority who ranks above them all, one who knew more about the conception in its essence than all put together—John Austin. Surely from him we shall learn whether property is a divine or a diabolical creation. Here is his definition : " By property I mean every right over a thing which is indefinite in point of user." There it is. There is nothing very terrible in it, nothing very sublime. It is tame enough, but it is true. It is the meaning which every one must wish to convey, if he knows what he is talking about, and if he wishes to be clearly understood by others. But it requires explanation.

A right over a thing is a power to use or enjoy the thing somehow or other. Otherwise it is not worth having or talking about. The moon may be solemnly conveyed to me by the State in consideration of my public services. I am grateful for nothing. But not every power to use or enjoy a thing is a right. The cat which has caught a sparrow has the power to eat the sparrow, but we do not speak of the cat's proprietary right. A right is a power sanctioned by the State. Rights over specific things are but species of rights in general, and proprietary rights again are but varieties of rights over things.

Rights in general (by which term I mean to denote all those liberties which are recognised and sanctioned by the State) may be divided into two classes—rights which are expressed in terms of things, and rights which do not relate to things. In Russia a citizen may not quit the country without a State permit. In England we enjoy that liberty. This is a right which is not a right over a thing. In France a married man with a family cannot bequeath all his goods to any one he chooses. In England he can do so. This is a right over things. Let us dismiss all those liberties which are not rights over things, or more correctly speaking, which are not liberties expressed in terms of things, and consider this latter class alone.

We shall find that rights over things may be subdivided into two great classes—rights to Use and rights to Value. I let my house to John Smith, and I mortgage it to Tom Jones. Smith has a right to the *Use* of the house ; Jones has a right only to part of its *Value*. Now according to Austin's definition of property, rights to value are not proprietary rights. It is true that Blackstone and the lawyers speak of lien as a " special qualified property ; " but this is only a learned way of saying that they do not know what it is ; we may pass it by. It reminds one of the celebrated definition of a metaphysician as a person talking about what he does not understand to one who does not understand him. Nor are all rights to *Use* proprietary. But Property is a species of the genus Use. Let us see whether we cannot clearly distinguish between those Uses which are properly called Property and those which are not.

Before doing this, it may be as well to note that not only ordinary people but also lawyers and jurists employ the term *Property* in two very different senses—a wide and a narrow sense. Hence the extraordinary confusion. In the wider and improper sense it is used to denote all rights to exclusive use ; available against anybody and everybody, or as the jurists say " against the world at large." Then we have Blackstone and the Fog school trying to use the word in two senses at once, and introducing such muddy, meaningless expressions as that just quoted. No wonder we have such divergent views of the institution. The definition given by the French Code is about as useless as any definition well could be. It defines nothing. " Property is the right of enjoying and disposing of a thing in the most absolute manner, provided the owner does not make any use of it which is prohibited by law." It is obvious that we all have proprietary rights over anything whatever if this definition is correct. I have a right to use your house or your horse in any way which is not contrary to law.

Whether property is a good or a bad thing clearly depends on the answer to. the question, What is property ? The same thing is true of liberty. As I have said, property after all is only a species of liberty. What is true of liberty in general is also true of that kind of liberty which we choose to call property. " There is no such thing as natural property," said Bentham ; " it is entirely the work of law." But law, we are told, is contrary to liberty. It therefore behoves us to inquire a little more carefully concerning this more general expression, *Liberty.* Let us follow Bentham :—

" The proposition that every law is contrary to liberty, though as clear as evidence can make it, is not generally acknowledged. On the contrary, those among the friends of liberty who are more ardent than enlightened make it a duty of conscience to combat this truth. How they pervert language! They refuse to employ the word liberty in its common acceptation; they speak a tongue peculiar to themselves. This is the definition they give of liberty : ' Liberty consists in the right of doing everything which is not injurious to another.' But is this the ordinary sense of the word ? Is not the liberty to do evil liberty ? If not, what is it ? What word can we use in speaking of it ? Do we not say that it is neces- sary to take away liberty from idiots and bad men because they abuse it ?"

Bentham is right. Nothing can be clearer than that law restricts liberty. But at the same time we ought not to lose sight of the fact that law also widens liberty. For example, if it gives me a right to do what I should be powerless to do without the sanction of the State, it is clear that my liberties are widened at the same time that the liberties of all other persons are restricted proportionately. And here I will venture to state a proposition. Law creates more liberty than it destroys. Any law which fails to do this in the long run is destined to perish. This truth is nowhere more forcibly ex- emplified than it is in the case of those liberties which we call proprietary rights. We hear people talk about the sacred- ness of property, as if it were more sacred than any other right. So far from being primordial, property arose with law, and could not exist without it. As Bentham puts it : " The savage who has killed a deer may hope to keep it for himself so long as his cave is undiscovered, so long as he watches to defend it and is stronger than his rivals, but that is all. If we suppose the least agreement among savages to respect the acquisitions of each other, we see the introduction of a prin- ciple to which no name can be given but that of *Law.*"

It is sometimes, though vulgarly, supposed that property is the right to do whatever you like with your own. True, it often does amount to that; but this is quite accidental. On the other hand, frequently enough the proprietor enjoys fewer and less rights over the thing owned than some others enjoy. For example, the owners of land held under the old tenure of *emphyteusis* exercised hardly any right whatever over his own property ; so little, that at last the prætor came to regard the *emphyteuta* (*i.e.* the tenant) as the true proprietor, or, as we should say, the equitable owner. Not only was a grantee entitled to possess the lands, to reap the fruits, under the burden of annual payment, but he could make changes in the substance by reclaiming waste land, building, planting, and other operations, provided he did not deteriorate the subject. He could sell his right and it descended to his heirs. In case of a sale the proprietor had, it is true, the privilege of pre-emption if he was anxious to purchase the subject on his own account, and willing to pay the price offered for it; and for every alienation to a stranger he was entitled to exact a fine of about two per cent on the price. The *emphyteuta's* right was forfeited and reverted to the proprietor if he deteriorated the subject or neglected to pay the annual rent for a period of three years. The right might also be extinguished by consent of parties, by total destruction of subject, by expiry of term (if any), and by the death of grantee without leaving lawful heirs.

A very similar real right was called " superficies "; a landed proprietor conceded to any person an area of ground for erecting a building upon it, but without parting with the ownership of the soil. The property of the building remained with the proprietor of the land, but the grantee acquired a real right to the full possession and enjoyment of the edifice, either for a definite period or in perpetuity; and this right was transferable during life, and it descended to heirs. It was regulated by contract, and might be granted either for a price down or for an annual rent. " In many respects," says Lord Mackenzie, " this *jus superficiarium* bears a strong re-semblance to the long building leases granted by landowners in England in consideration of a rent, and under reservation of the ownership of the soil."[1]

In our own country the holders of very long leases, though not regarded as proprietors, certainly enjoy rights over the property quite out of proportion to those exercised by the freeholder. Probably it is from a feeling of the truth of this that there is at the present time a very strong desire on the part of many to convert the leaseholder into the proprietor, or, at least, to give him every facility for becoming the proprietor in cases where the lease is a long one. I do not wish in this place to offer any opinion on the merits of this political

[1] See Lord Mackenzie's *Studies in Roman Law*

question, but I may point out that the proposed change in its essence is rather one of juridical classification than anything else. I do not say that much injustice might not result from what may appear to be nothing more than a mistaken classification, just in the same way as much injustice was done, and still is done nearly every day owing to the action of the law, in accordance with the accepted definitions of such words as partnership, use, lien, etc. All I desire to affirm is, that unjust action need not necessarily result from bad juridical definitions.

After this digression we will return to the distinction between property and other rights to use things. I suppose most of us think, in spite of legal jargon and of the sophistries of jurisprudence, that we know pretty well what property is. Let us see. Who is the proprietor of a mortgaged estate? The person who holds the land, so to speak, as security for his loan? or the original owner? Who is the owner of a pawned watch? The pawnbroker, or he who pawned it? These are two very simple cases, and yet the more we look at them the more difficult does the answer become. Of course we know what view of the matter the Courts will take in this and other countries; but that is not the question I am asking. Believing that the term proprietor has a meaning, I ask, Who is the true proprietor? not, Who is regarded by the English law as the proprietor? I suppose there can be no two opinions as to who is the owner of a hired horse; yet, if we generalise and say that it is easy to declare who is the owner of any hired thing, we shall find ourselves at once in a difficulty. If the article lent be a horse or a plough, there is no difficulty about the matter. But if *A* lends a hundred sovereigns to *B*, who then is the owner of those gold pieces? Or if a testator leaves a house and a cellar of wine to his widow for life, with remainder to his children, who is the owner of the house, who of the wine? Now, apart from legal technicalities, we may say that the widow is not the owner of the house, but that she is the owner of the wine. Who is the owner of a watch which has been stolen and sold by the thief to a *bonâ fide* purchaser? Is it the original owner of the watch, who has never voluntarily parted with it? Or is it the man who has paid for it *bonâ fide*, not knowing it to have been stolen?

Here again we know what is the view acted upon in the English Courts. We also know how the law of ancient Rome regarded the matter ; and we might ascertain, if we cared to do so, who is the owner according to the French, Prussian, or Italian codes, and who is treated as the owner by the Mahommedan or Hindoo law. But what we want to come at is, Who is really the owner of the watch ? Who is the owner of a piece of prairie land which has been imperfectly fenced in by some pioneer of civilisation ? Who is the owner of a newly-discovered island ? Suppose a draper deposits a certain amount of cloth with a tailor with instructions to make it up into clothing, and the tailor does it, who is the owner of the clothing ? Is it the draper who was originally the owner of the cloth ? or is it the tailor who converted the cloth into wearing apparel ? In Rome, if an artist painted a picture on canvas or board belonging to another man, the picture belonged to the painter and not to the owner of the canvas or board. " For it would be ridiculous," says Justinian, " that a work by Apelles or Parrhasius should go as an accession to a wretched tablet." But if a poet wrote verses on another man's parchment the finished article belonged to the owner of the parchment. If a workman made clothing out of cloth or skins, or a table out of wood belonging to another, the new goods belonged to the workman, and the original owner of the material had only a lien upon them to the extent of its original value. But even here there was an exception where the product could be retransformed into its original state, as in the case of silversmith's work, which could be melted again into bullion. In this case the original owner of the silver was the owner of the plate, and the workman had only the lien. If there is to be found any general principle underlying these apparently contradictory rules, it is, I think, the principle that the property or dominion should belong to him whose just share in the finished article is of the greater value ; and the lien to him whose share is less. Thus, as a rule, a picture is worth a good deal more than double the value of the canvas on which it is painted, whereas the value of parchment was in Roman times greater than the cost of clerk work upon it. The poet could get his poem copied out again at less than the price of the parchment. So, as a rule, the larger part of the value of plate is the value of the precious metal of which it is made. When wine was made from grapes it could not be restored to its original form, and moreover it was worth far more than double the value of the original grapes, and it was held to be the property of the wine-maker.

All this may seem of very slight consideration, but in truth it is of the utmost importance. Upon the answers given to these very simple questions depend the future of the land question, the future of the Church question, and, more important than either, the future of the labour question.

We have seen that not all rights over things are proprietary rights. For example, I have a right to ride on a horse which I have hired from a livery stable-keeper. That right may or may not be available against all the world; but in neither case can it be regarded as a proprietary right. There is no particular reason why a right to the use of a hired thing should not avail against all the world, beyond the fact that in England and most other countries it does not. Once upon a time[1] a canal company granted to a person of the name of Hill the exclusive right of putting pleasure-boats on their canal. Hill very naturally thought that, under these circumstances, he had a right to prevent any one else from doing so. Consequently when, nevertheless, another person did put pleasure-boats on the canal, he instantly sued him; but the Court decided against him. "A grantor," it was held, "may bind himself by covenant to allow any right he pleases over his property, but he cannot annex to it a new incident, so as to enable the grantee to sue in his own name for an infringement of such a limited right as that now claimed." This may be good law, but it is shockingly bad policy.

But are we any nearer the discovery of the distinction between rights over things which are correctly styled proprietary rights and other kinds of rights over things? It is true we have seen that so far from being a "right to do what you like with your own," property is sometimes almost an infinitesimal right over the thing owned. What is the most noticeable difference between the rights of one who lets a horse out for hire, and the rights of one who hires the horse? Suppose you

[1] *Hill* v. *Tupper*, 2 H. and C. 121.

H

hire a horse for a ride on the roads, and you proceed to hunt him across country, under the ancient Roman law you were guilty of *furtum*; you had misappropriated a use of the horse to which you had no title.   There are a thousand liberties which the hirer may *not* take with the thing hired, compared with one or two which he may take.   He may not clip or singe the horse, he may not dock his mane or tail; if he should feed the horse, he must do it at his own risk in case the food should disagree.   But it would take a week to enumerate all the things that he must *not* do.   What he may do is distinctly known and defined.   Not so in the case of the proprietor; he may clip the horse, paint the horse, kill the horse, eat the horse, sell the horse—in short, he may do just those thousand and one things with the horse which the hirer must *not* do.   Thus the most marked distinction between the rights of the hirer and of the proprietor is one of definiteness. The rights of the proprietor are indefinite.   He may do just whatever he pleases with his own, with one important class of exceptions.   He must not infringe upon the definite rights of others.   What he may do is indefinite, what he may not do is defined and clearly set forth.   It is precisely the other way about in the case of the hirer.   Here, that which he may do is clearly defined, that which he may not do is undefined.

We may now define property as all those undefined uses over a thing which remain over after the definite and specific uses of others have been deducted.   These defined uses may be few or many, of greater or less value than the residue of proprietary rights.   They may vest in one or more individuals or in the whole State; for the nation reserves the very definite right of purchasing anything whatever in this country at its market value from the proprietor when required for purposes of public utility.   That definite right must be deducted from the whole bundle of rights inhering in the proprietor.   In nine cases out of ten there are several other rights to deduct before we are in a position to define negatively the rights of the proprietor.

In the light of these reflections I now propose to take two forms of property, and to inquire rather minutely into the arguments which are to-day put forward, not without heat, for and against their recognition by the State.   I take these two forms

because they are in every way typical. They are Land ownership and Tithe ownership. They are of course of very different
importance ; but each in its way illustrates the true definition
of the term " property " in a marked degree. As to the thing
owned, land is said to be peculiar in many respects. And as
to the person owning, tithes are a peculiar form of property.
It is held by many (by no means shallow thinkers) that land
ought not to be held by private owners. And it is held by
others that tithe ownership is wrong, if not indeed absurd.

Take land first :—Absolute, unlimited right to the land is
of course an utter absurdity. It is not usual even to speak
of a proprietor of land. We speak of an estate in land, though
there would be nothing improper in describing the landowner's
rights as proprietary, provided we bear in mind that such a
thing as an *absolute* right to land has never been recognised in
this country. Thus in order to ascertain what are the rights
of the landowner, we must first deduct the State right to expropriate the landowner, whenever it shall appear desirable in
the common interest to do so. The landowner cannot say it
is unjust, illegal, contrary to usage, because it is not. The
practice has been recognised from time immemorial.

Vattel defines *dominium eminens* to be " the right which
belongs to the society or the sovereign of disposing in case of
necessity and for the public safety of all the wealth contained
in the State."

And Chancellor Walworth says: " All separate interests
of individuals in property are held of the Government, and notwithstanding the grant to individuals, the *eminent domain*, the
highest and most exact idea of property, remains in the Government, or in the aggregate body of the people in their sovereign
capacity, and they have a right to resume the possession of the
property in the manner directed by the constitution and laws
of the State whenever the public interest requires it. This
right of resumption may be exercised not only where the safety,
but also where the interest, or even the expediency of the State
is concerned ; as where the land of the individual is wanted
for a road, canal, or other public improvement."

No landowner has ever been in a position in this country to
raise the plea that it is illegal to dispossess him of property in

the land for purposes of public utility, because it is not. He
simply has the indefinite rights which remain after deducting the
definite rights vested in other people inclusive of the State. We
know that these rights have been exercised over and over again of
late years. In the case of railway concessions, the landowner
receives full compensation for his interest in the land ; beyond
this he has no claim whatever. It is his misfortune if his
ancient memories and family associations are ruthlessly
sacrificed in the public interest ; and there the matter ends.
He holds his land subject to the liability to be turned out
whenever it shall be to the public interest to turn him out.
The accident has come about which renders it desirable to
make public property of his land, and he has no more ground
of complaint than he would have if a flash of lightning sent
his chimney-stack through his roof.

Next to this definite State right come public rights of way
and other uses which have been always admitted as customary
These public rights over the land of the landowner are perfectly
definite. Again, there are frequently private easements to
deduct. That is to say, a neighbour has a right of way across
the land, or a right to the support of his house, or a negative
right to the stream which flows through the land ; a right to forbid the landowner from molesting or spoiling or diverting such
stream. Sometimes, as in the case of copyhold, the right of dig-
ging under the surface for coal or iron is vested in some one who
is not, strictly speaking, the landowner. Finally, the owner must
so exercise his indefinite residual rights as not to injure others.
He must not become, or allow his property to become, a nuisance.
But when we have deducted all these definite rights vested in
others, there is still left a residuum—a large fasciculus—of
undefined rights, which are properly described as proprietary.

With these qualifications what conceivable objection can
be raised to property in land ? When we see that property
simply means the indefinite rights which cannot be enumerated
simply because they are so indefinite, is there any serious and
valid reason why these rights, whether over land or anything
else, should not be vested in some one individual ? For my
part I not only see no reasonable objection to this course, but,
furthermore, I observe that in this and in other countries, and

also throughout all history, property in land has done more to
stimulate exertion on that land than any other system whatever.
We see what miracles have been wrought in certain parts of
France and Belgium by the system of peasant proprietorship.
I do not say that these peasant proprietors are altogether happy
or prosperous. The contrary is probably attributable to the
absurd laws interfering with freedom of bequest in those
countries. So far as the soil itself is concerned, there can be
no doubt that its fertility has been enormously stimulated by
the system of land property. The peasant owner of a plot of
one acre will produce from that acre more than three labourers
can produce from an equal area belonging to somebody else.
So it is said. Surely, in itself, this is a strong argument in
favour of separate ownership of land ; and probably those who
call themselves land nationalisationists, and who run a tilt against
private property in land, are doing more harm, or would do
more if they could,than any other class of socialists in the country.

I admit at once that many valid objections can be urged
against the system of property in land as it is at present
regulated. Let us examine one or two of these objections
carefully. First, it is alleged that the landowner exercises too
much influence over his tenants, that his power is hardly
compatible with the perfect freedom of those who hold under
him. Certainly this has been the case in many parts of the
country, but it was much more marked some years ago than it
is now, and what was called landlord tyranny is almost a thing
of the past. But, apart from the undoubted influence which
his position seems to give him, it is said that the contracts
which are entered into between landlord and tenant are, as a
rule, unfair to the tenant. Well, if this is so—and I for one
do not believe that in the majority of cases there is any
foundation for the contention—still, if it is true even in a
great many cases, this is no argument against the system of
private property in land. It simply goes to show that the
farmers of England are not yet as well advanced in organisation
as the artizans of the towns. If the farmer finds himself
unable, individually, to provide for entering into a sound and
fair contract, he ought to have recourse to the ordinary
resources of free men, that is to say, union. It is folly to

apply to the legislature to upset an existing and beneficial order of things in order to give the farmer some slight advantage in entering into a contract.

The second objection to the land system is, that land tends to accumulate in single hands. This is said to be a very strong objection. The land does tend to accumulate in single hands. That is true ; but what is the reason of it ? It is not because we allow of private ownership. Separate or private ownership is recognised and encouraged on the Continent in countries where we see the peasants in complete ownership of the soil. What then is the reason that in this country the soil is held to the extent of tens of thousands of acres in single hands, and that in the opinion of some these vast accumulations tend to grow rather than to dwindle ? It is not because of the system of separate ownership. It does not happen in the case of other kinds of fixed capital. We do not see mills, factories, and furnaces held in unworkable quantities in single hands ; and if we see this anomaly in the case of land, it is simply because we have been the victims of socialistic legislation. One of the worst forms of this kind of law-making is embodied in the legislation of this country relating to what are called trusts. The State practically acts as a trustee, and interferes with the liberties of private persons in the interest of persons long since dead and gone, of non-existent persons, and of indeterminate persons. The system of settlements permitted in this country is a flagrant instance of socialistic legislation. The power which a living man exercises, and is allowed to exercise, of so settling his land that when he is dead he shall still have a say in its disposition and in the conditions subject to which it shall be enjoyed by the occupier, would be impossible but for the help of the State, which practically prolongs the life of a dead man by enforcing obedience to his commands.

Thirdly, it is urged that under the present system of land-tenure, capital is divorced from the soil. This is perfectly true, but why is it so ? and why is it not so in other departments of industry, where capital finds its way to the most productive channels? Not because of private ownership, but chiefly because of the cost and difficulty of transfer, which is entirely due to the law.

There are three objects in an ordinary deed of conveyance, and there are only three which have to be taken into consideration when land is transferred from one person to another; and those same objects must be held in view when any other kind of property is to be transferred. The first is, that the transaction shall be sufficiently solemn to preclude the probability of haste, inadvertence, or impulse. More importance was attached to this precaution in ancient times under the Roman law than we seem to think necessary to-day. Possibly we English are not so impulsive a race as the Romans. The next object to be kept in view is, that the evidence of the transaction shall be unimpeachable. And lastly, it is necessary that third persons shall be made aware of the change of ownership. These three objects having been attained, and more especially the last two, nothing more remains to be done. There is no conceivable reason why land should not be transferred as quickly, as easily, and as cheaply as any other kind of property whatever. We know well that English lawyers and conveyancers are in the habit of shrugging their shoulders when this statement is made, and of attributing to those who make it absolute ignorance of the whole subject. They make no attempt to show why there should be any difference; they are content to take refuge behind the intricacies of the subject, *Beati possidentes!* It is in vain to point out that in the English Colonies this is done: that it is done in some of the old countries of Europe, as well as in the younger civilisations of America. The reply is, that it cannot be worked in England, and that it is of no use talking. The thing is impossible, and there is an end to it. But, in truth, the lawyer knows in his heart that there is no difficulty whatever. The transfer of land could and should be effected in this country as readily and simply as the transfer of a horse or of a steam-engine.

It is a singular fact that in England the law fails to recognise the advance which has taken place in the education of the people. We alone, of European nations, are still apparently ignorant of the fact that people can read and write. In other countries, in France, in America, and in our own Colonies, land can be transferred in the simplest possible

manner by the instrumentality of registration. The Lord
Chancellor, in presenting the Land Transfer Bill, 1887,
defended it against the charge of State interference. The Land
Act of 1875 had failed mainly because it made registration
optional. The new Bill proposed to make it compulsory. " It
is untrue," said the Lord Chancellor, "that the compulsory
registration of land is an interference with the liberty of the
subject ; it is the creation of a system of land-tenure, and it
would be as correct to describe the 'Statute of Frauds' as an
interference with liberty, as to make that complaint about this
measure." This is perfectly true. Land registration will not
meet with the opposition of individualists on the ground that
compulsory registration curtails freedom, and substitutes State
action for individual action. The interference comes in when
the State enforces a contract at all. It is a normal State
function ; provided it is safeguarded against fraud. Hence the
State cannot undertake to enforce all promises ; it must limit
the enforcement of contract in several ways. In some cases it
is satisfied with sufficient verbal evidence of the fact of the
promise, in other cases the promise must be in writing, in
others again writing is not enough, it must be in the form of a
deed (a form which originally amounted to a public notification),
and in those cases where no writing is required, it must have
proof of consideration. It will not undertake to sanction a
nude pact. Now surely all these carefully-balanced conditions
are the very bulwarks of liberty. They are the outcome of
ages of experience, the very progeny of individualism. There
is no reason whatever why a one-sided promise should not be
enforced by the State *if* such promise was made. *Omne verbum
de ore fideli cadit in debitum.* Yes, but was the promise made ?
What is the evidence which the State ought to accept ? That
is the question. Is a little hard swearing to ruin a man ? Or
is it not better to insist upon certain simple precautions which
in no way trench upon the freedom of a citizen, and which
safeguard the alleged promisor against false evidence, if not also
against his own hastiness ? No one is aggrieved. If writing
is required, let the promisee get the agreement in writing. If
this gives the other party time to think better of the bargain,
so much the better.

But there is a stronger reason even than this in favour of what is unfortunately mis-called compulsory registration. Registration is undoubtedly in modern times the simplest and most perfect form of public notification. Third parties are frequently, nay almost invariably, interested in the transfer of land. How are these third parties to be apprised of the intended transfer by which their own rights may be seriously affected? The old formalities of emancipation with the scales and the balance, the *libripens* and the five witnesses, made a sufficient noise in a place the size of ancient Rome. So the formalities which accompanied livery of seisin, the number and importance of the persons present, the solemnity of the words and gestures of the feoffor, all contributed to render the transfer notorious in the neighbourhood. In Justinian's time, when *res mancipi* had been absorbed by *res nec mancipi* and when *traditio* sufficed to transfer ownership; and now in England, where a deed can be executed in a cupboard without the knowledge of interested persons who possibly reside in remote parts of the country ; the door is open to fraud. We cannot come back to the beating of boundaries, the blowing of trumpets, and the thrashing of boys and priests at the landmarks ; but we can make use of a louder trumpet than any known to our forefathers—the public register, supported by the public press. With such an instrument in our hands, it is simply criminal to neglect it. A Bill for withdrawing State recognition from unregistered land-transfers should speedily become law, and so increase the liberty of Englishmen.

Fourthly, it is alleged by the opponents of a separate system of land ownership that the landowner pockets—what ? The unearned increment ? Surely this phrase expresses the most extraordinary piece of illogical confusion that could well have been palmed off upon a semi-intelligent public by so honest and clear-headed a thinker as John Stuart Mill. How he could have brought himself to talk about unearned increment as he did, is one of those riddles with which Genius every now and then puzzles us. Unearned increment simply means the reward of successful risk. Two men invest a sum of money each in a piece of land. *A* in this, and *B* in that. One plot turns out a success and the other a failure ; you turn to the man who has success on his side and you tell him that he sat down and did nothing while the land brought him in unearned increment. He might have put out his money into consols or into railway stock with a similar result; he would then have pocketed his unearned increment in peace. Then the unlucky speculator *B* has suffered the unearned *decrement ;* but does any one propose that the State should make his loss good ? Why not ? Every kind of investment looks for a reward in proportion to the risk run. If you invest in consols you get something under 3 per cent, in railways about 4 per cent—you might get 8 or 15 or 2, but the average profit on all the investments throughout the country is somewhere about 3 per cent. If you invest in a worsted factory, you may perhaps not be satisfied unless you get over 10 per cent. Every industry has its own average rate of profit—agriculture like any other. If you invest in agricultural land you may think yourself lucky if you get $2\frac{1}{2}$ per cent. In town property the risk is greater and the profits expected are consequently higher. But to single out the owner of land, whether agricultural or urban, and to charge him with pocketing unearned increment indicates utter ignorance of the economics of trade.

The fifth objection urged against our present system is that unworthy families are artificially bolstered up. In other businesses if a son is not worthy of his father, if he be an intemperate, dissipated, good-for-nothing fellow, he goes to the wall and is lost sight of. There is an end of him and of the matter ; but in the case of land proprietors the generation is tided over, the land is entailed and the family kept up, and we have a deteriorated breed. This is perfectly true ; but why should we revolutionise the whole system in order to meet this objection ? When the tenant for life is treated as the absolute owner, he will be able to disencumber himself of his land as rapidly as he now can and does of his money and chattels. The son will reap the reward of the father's folly, and will be compelled to commence life *de novo*, without the artificial support of the State.

Thus we see that none of the objections popularly urged against the system of property in land touch the roots of the

matter. Some of the more childish objections would apply
with equal force to private property of all kinds. I have
heard agitators ask whether the people of England are going
any longer to tolerate a system which would enable the
wealthy and malevolent speculator to buy up a strip of land
extending across Great Britain and to forbid the rest of the
nation from passing to and fro across it. I have heard them
ask whether a system can be good which would admit of a
large landowner in time of dearth making a bonfire of the
produce of tens of thousands of acres. It is clear from what
I have said as to the true meaning of the word property, that
no speculator could prevent the people from making any use
they thought fit of his slip of land. It is also clear that the
second objection is applicable to property in anything whatever. Suppose a wealthy Vandal should buy up all the extant
works of Reynolds, Hogarth, and Turner with a view to
making a bonfire of the lot, would the English people think it
necessary to abolish the institution of private property? Or
would they not rather find some rough and ready method of
dealing with such a misanthropic maniac?

Mr. Bradlaugh not long since introduced a Bill into the
House of Commons for the purpose of bringing pressure to bear
upon owners of uncultivated land. He was accused of adopting
socialistic remedies for the cure of admitted evils. I do not
think the charge a fair one. The State has reserved the right
to buy up any land whatever for purposes of public utility,
whether such land is uncultivated or not. It is conceivable
that, in case supplies from abroad ran short, it might be
deemed necessary to stimulate production in this country, in
which case no individual could reasonably object to the expropriation of a landowner who neglected to turn his land to the
best account. The question is whether the public would be
gainers by the course proposed by Mr. Bradlaugh. It is
probable that the effect of his measure might be to induce
some careless landlords to bring land under cultivation which
has hitherto been devoted to sport. But we must not forget
that the value of land devoted to sport must not be measured
by the rents paid by the squatters and commoners who glean
whatever may be left after sport has been provided for. So

that in taking a seven years' average (as is done by the Bill) of the rents received from such land, it would be necessary in all justice to estimate the rental which the landlord virtually pays to himself for the use of his land for sporting purposes, and it seems to me that even if an actual rent was required it would be very easy for landowners to evade the law by renting each other's lands at their proper valuation for sporting purposes. We are driven to inquire whether Mr. Bradlaugh proposes to forbid the use of land by the owner for this purpose, or for any other purpose than that of food-producing. Whenever land is left in the natural state, because in the opinion of its owner it would be unprofitable to cultivate it, we may be sure that even if the State got it for nothing at all it would incur a dangerous risk in bringing it under cultivation. In ninety-nine cases out of a hundred the landowner is a better judge of his land than the general public, and he is also more anxious to get the most he can out of it ; and therefore, although in one or two exceptional instances some little good might result from these compulsory purchases, in the great majority of cases the nation would be a loser, and food if raised at all on such land would be sold at a loss. At the same time it should be pointed out, that between the aim of this Bill and the aim of nationalisationists there is a fundamental difference of principle.

I do not know whether it is worth while to criticise in detail the arguments of this school. I am not sure that there are any arguments common to them all or to a majority of them. The truth is that "land nationalisationist" is a term applied to a great many very different classes of doctrinaires, some of whom have definite notions of what they want, whilst others have no clear aim beyond that of upsetting the existing system and, if possible, transferring wealth from the pockets of landowners into their own. Probably this is the leading idea in the minds of nine-tenths of those who dub themselves by this appellation. On the other hand, I should be the last to affirm, because the majority of any party are dishonest or illogical or both, that therefore the thinkers and leaders of that party are equally dishonest or illogical. I know there are men who sincerely believe that State ownership of the land

would be for the public benefit. These are not the men who
would dismiss the landlords without compensation on the
ground that they are no better than robbers; they recognise
the great difficulty of transferring the land from its present
owner to the State without doing injustice on the one hand,
or crippling the national resources on the other. I am disposed to agree with them thus far, that if their ultimate
object were desirable, the process might be effected without
either of the two evils dreaded. But we disagree as to the
desirability of the end, no matter how brought about. I
contend that even if the landowners of this country presented
their acres to the people as a free gift, one of two things would
happen. The gift would turn out a white elephant and would
cost the State untold millions, or a new race of proprietors
would take the place of those who had retired. State ownership of land, in the sense in which ownership is properly understood, has never worked satisfactorily yet, and it never will.
If by ownership we choose to mean something different from
what we usually mean by the term, there is no particular
reason why we should not reply that the State is already the
owner of the land. What I here mean by property and also
by ownership is the bundle of indefinite rights over anything
after all definite rights have been deducted; and it is these
indefinite rights which individuals know how to enjoy and how
to turn to account, and which the State would necessarily
either waste or abuse.

There is one argument vulgarly used against what is called
landlordism which deserves notice for no other reason than that
it is frequently employed by dishonest agitators in addressing the
working classes in this country. It is said that the land is
held by those whose ancestors came by it unjustly. Some
estates are still held, as they point out, by those whose
ancestors won them by the sword; others by those whose
ancestors received them as favours · from the king; others
again are said to have been purchased with ill-gotten wealth
wrung from the oppressed tax-payers. It is further urged that
these present landowners can have no just title to land acquired
in this way. Highly-coloured pictures of the wrongs inflicted
upon the people by the ancestors of landlords are drawn in

order to excite the passions of the audience, and there is just
enough of historic truth in the allegations to command the assent
and appeal to the imagination of uneducated persons; though
it must be admitted that the shrewd common-sense of the
English public is as a rule proof against this kind of flimsy
sophistry.   Still the argument, for what it is worth, must be
met, like Bombastes, face to face, and with a like result.
Let us grant that some large estate is still in the hands of the
successors of one who originally acquired it by force.   Let us
pretend that it was wrested by a fierce Norman baron from
some good kind Saxon occupier, whose only aim was to cultivate his land and live at peace with all men; is this a
sufficient reason for dispossessing the present owner without
compensation ?   Again, suppose that some swindler, well known
to history, long ago contrived to amass a large fortune and to
invest it in Government securities; will it be contended that
his descendants of a century later should be compelled to dis-
gorge ?   Or to take a wider view; even admitting that Englishmen appropriated the land of Ireland by conquest, wrongfully
dispossessing the then owners, is that a valid reason for ex-
propriating the successors of the conquerors, three, five, or
seven centuries later ?   The Welsh, we are told by these
spouters, are the " natural owners " of Wales, whatever that
may mean.   But who are the Welsh ? how did they come by
Wales ?   We shall soon find, if we are consistent, that we
English have no rightful footing in this country.   England
belonged to the Welsh before the existence of the English
people ; and further back still, there are traces of a Celtic conquest.   It is known that a race of men inhabited this island
before Irish, Gael, or Welsh had crossed the eastern waters.
Where are the descendants of these men, to whom we should
justly hand over the British Isles ?   Some say their descendants are still to be found in the valleys of the Pyrenees.
Even if there is any doubt, the Basques have a better title,
by reason of the very doubt, than either Saxon, Celt, or
Norman ; and the sooner we hand over our ill-gotten territories
to the most probable rightful owner, the better.

    It is a pity such twaddle as this should have to be talked ;
but, so long as certain metaphysical notions of right and

justice prevail, it will be necessary to combat the most whim-
sical theories by the method of *reductio ad absurdum.*

I have dealt thus at length with property in land because
there is a very strong feeling among even the most powerful
thinkers, that a fundamental difference exists between property
in the soil and property in movables. Mr. Herbert Spencer
has gone so far as to furnish arguments in support of this contention.

" How," he asks, " did possession of land become individualised ?
There can be little doubt as to the general nature of the answer. Force
in one form or other is the sole cause adequate to make the members of
a society yield up their combined claims to the area they inhabit. Such
force may be that of an external aggressor, of that of an internal
aggressor, but in either case it implies militant activity." He goes on
to say, " It seems possible that the primitive ownership of land by the
community, which, with the development of coercive institutions lapsed
in large measure or wholly into private ownership, will be revived as
industrialism further develops. . . . In legal theory landowners are
directly or indirectly tenants of the Crown (which in our day is equivalent to the State, or, in other words, the community). The community,
from time to time, resumes possession after making due compensation.
Perhaps the right of the community to the land thus tacitly asserted
will in time to come be overtly asserted and acted upon after making
full allowance for the accumulated value artificially given."

Now I cannot admit that aggression is the cause of private
property in land, any more than in anything else. Force, of
course, it is ; but so also force is at the back of every contract.
It is that kind of force which is employed by and with the
previous consent of the coerced party ; and which, while in
one direction it restricts liberty, in another direction enlarges
it to an even greater extent. The one kind of property has
sprung into existence for the same reason as other kinds ;
namely, because the race has been benefited by the institution
of property. When Mr. Spencer looks forward to the time at
which the community will openly assert what it now (in his
opinion) only tacitly asserts, he seems to be drawing a distinction without a difference ; for the community at the present
day not only tacitly but overtly claims the right of dispossessing the owners of land whenever the welfare of the State
requires it. There is nothing tacit or hidden in the claim of
the State to construct roads or railways through the land of a

citizen without any other consideration for his feelings than the allowance of full compensation.

Even the orthodox Blackstone himself seems to have some misgiving as to the natural justice of the institution of property.

" Pleased as we are," says he, " with the possession, we seem afraid to look back to the means by which it was acquired, as if fearful of some defect in our title ; or at best we rest satisfied with the decision of the laws in our favour without examining the reason or authority upon which those laws have been built. We think it enough that our title is derived by the grant of the former proprietor by descent from our ancestors or by the last will and testament of the dying owner ; not caring to reflect that there is no foundation in nature or in natural law why a set of words upon parchment should convey the dominion of lands ; why the son should have a right to exclude his fellow creatures from a determinate spot of ground because his father had done so before him ; or why the occupier of a particular field or of a jewel, when lying on his deathbed, and no longer able to maintain possession, should be entitled to tell the rest of the world which of them should enjoy it after him. These inquiries, it must be owned, would be useless and even troublesome in common life. It is well if the mass of mankind will obey the laws when made, without scrutinising too nicely the reasons of making them."

He then tries to find some adequate justification for the institution of private property, and he finally adopts, as the best and strongest, the theory of Grotius. I do not know whether it has been pointed out that Blackstone's explanation of the origin of property is borrowed bodily from the *De jure belli et pacis* without a word of acknowledgment, but those who compare the two will see that it is. He adopts Grotius's theory of an original title from the Creator as recorded in the first chapter of Genesis ; he makes the same statement as to primitive institutions ; the same reference to the manners of the semi-civilised races of America ; and the very same quotation from Justinian—" erant omnia communia et indivisa omnibus, veluti unum cunctis patrimonium esset."

Turning to Grotius himself we find that he also had his doubts as to the unholy origin of the institution. He says : " There we learn what was the cause why men departed from the community of things, first of movables, then of immovables ; namely, because when they were not content to feed on spontaneous produce, to dwell in caves, to go naked, or clothed

in bark or in skins, but had sought a more exquisite kind of
living, there was need of industry which particular persons
might employ on particular things. And as to the common
use of the fruits of the earth, it was prevented by the disper-
sion of men into different localities and by the *want of justice*
and kindness which interfered with a *fair* division of labour
and sustenance, and thus we learn how things became
property."

While views like these can be entertained by men whom
it would be an impertinence even to compare with the talkers
self-styled land nationalisationists, it is fair to admit that the
arguments of the latter receive material support from the
writings of these recognised authorities. But it should also
be pointed out that while these arguments are deemed sufficient
to warrant the most positive dogmatism on the part of shallow
politicians, Mr. Spencer himself draws from them the most
hesitating and doubting conclusions. "It may be doubted,"
says he, "whether the final stage is at present reached."
Again, speaking of the assimilation of real and personal property, he says, " the assimilation may eventually be denied ;"
and again he suggests that " at a stage still more advanced, *it
may be* that private ownership of land will disappear," and he
concludes, in a passage already quoted, that the revival of primitive ownership of land by the community " seems possible."
The whole of the chapter forecasting the future of property
in land bristles with such qualifying expressions as " perhaps,"
" it may be," " it seems possible," " it may be doubted," and such-
like admissions of hesitation and uncertainty. The chapter on
Property in his volume *Political Institutions* concludes thus :

" There is reason to suspect that while private possession of things
produced by labour will grow even more definite and sacred than at
present, the inhabited area which cannot be produced by labour will
eventually be distinguished as something which may not be privately
possessed. As the individual, primitively owner of himself, partially or
wholly loses ownership of himself during the militant régime, but gradually resumes it as the industrial régime develops, so possibly the communal proprietorship of land, partially or wholly merged in the ownership
of dominant men during evolution of the militant type, will be resumed
as the industrial type becomes fully evolved."

I have said before, and I say now, that in my opinion

all this doubt and difficulty would have disappeared from Mr. Spencer's mind if he had thoroughly appreciated the definition of property given by Austin as the result of his profound analysis of the term.

The very notion of property involves, as I have said, the distinct contemplation of two factors—a thing owned, and a person owning. I have hitherto dealt with differences in the nature of things owned. We will now look at the subject from the other point of view.

To begin with, the owner must either be one, or more than one. If more than one, the persons owning must be determinate persons, that is to say, persons who can be singled out and pointed to. If this cannot be done the question arises, Who are the owners ? and who is to forbid third persons from exercising the rights of proprietorship ? For example, who are the owners of what is usually described as the property of the Church of England ? Does it belong to any determinate persons ? Can they be singled out ? No one supposes that the mere officials of that body can be regarded as the owners, but if the bishops and clergy are not the owners, who are ? Writing upon this subject John Stuart Mill says:

"Would you rob the Church ? it is asked, and at the sound of these words rise up images of rapine, violence, plunder ; and every sentiment of repugnance which would be excited by a proposal to take away from an individual the earnings of his toil, or the inheritance of his fathers, comes heightened in the particular case by the added idea of sacrilege. But the Church ! Who is the Church ? Who is it that we desire to rob ? Who are the persons whose property, whose rights, we are proposing to take away ? Not the clergy ; from them we do not propose to take anything. To every man who now benefits by the endowments we would leave his entire income. But if not the clergy, surely we are not proposing to rob the laity ; we are exhorting the laity to claim their property out of the hands of the clergy who are not the Church, but only the managing members of the association."

Clearly, unless there are definite persons to vindicate the rights of ownership, there is nothing to prevent any other persons from exercising such rights, except the State itself. But what is the ground for State interference, unless it be that the State regards itself as the owner, or acts as the defender of the rights of certain determinate citizens ? That the

Church is a corporate body, with rights as well defined as those of other corporate bodies, seems to be an exploded idea, even amongst its supporters. The fundamental conception of the Church of England which is constantly put forward by the advocates of disestablishment, says Lord Selborne, "is that of a State church—a political creation—a church called into existence by the State, and deriving from the State the essential law of its being." "But," says the author of the learned but unsatisfactory *Defence of the Church of England*, "I do not and cannot take my stand upon any mystical view, such *e.g.* as that the Church is a person with a corporate conscience cognisant of matters of religion." Lord Selborne's own view of the Church is a singularly inadequate one. He says: "The Church is a society placed by its divine Founder *in* the world, though the spirit by which it is or ought to be actuated is not *of* the world." I do not propose to follow him through his elaborate argument to prove the identity of the Church before and after the Reformation. I do not care whether it was the Church of Rome or the Church of England of which the rights and liberties were declared to be inviolable by King John's great Charter, confirmed by Henry III. I care nothing at all for the decretals ascribed to Isidore, Archbishop of Seville, upon which the entire edifice of mediæval and modern papal supremacy was built up. I care no more for the *origin* of Church property, than I do for the *origin* of the Irish landowner's property. The question for us is a present-day question. If we are asked to respect the proprietary rights of the Church of England, we have nothing to do with ancient history, or with titles buried in oblivion; all we have to do is to find out, who, if any, are the persons claiming the property. The difficulty is only removed one step farther back by the modern churchman's device of disclaiming proprietary rights on behalf of the Church as a whole, and reclaiming them on behalf of limbs and branches of the Church in local areas. "In regard to all land endowments," says Dean Plumptree, "the facts are so plain that he who runs may read them. They were given or bequeathed by the Crown, or individual proprietors, not to the Church at large, for the Church at large has never been a corporate society capable of holding property, but to abbeys or cathedrals which were corporate bodies with that capacity, or to the rectors and vicars of parishes as corporations sole." Again, Professor Freeman says : " People talk as if the Church property was the property of one vast corporation called the Church. In truth, it is simply the property of several local churches, the ecclesiastical corporations sole and aggregate, bishops, chapters, rectors, and vicars, or any other. The Church of England, as a single body, has no property ; the property belongs to the Church of Canterbury, the Church of Westminster, the Church of Little Pedlington, or any other. These local bodies, forming corporations sole or aggregate, hold estates which have been acquired at sundry times and in divers manners from the first preaching of Christianity to the English till now." As I have said, this only goes to shift the question a step farther back. Who and what is the rector or vicar or other corporation sole ? In what sense can such a corporation hold property, or vindicate his proprietary rights against the invasion of third persons ? Nobody pretends that the Rev. John Smith is really the owner of the property vested in the rector, even though the Rev. John Smith himself happens to be the rector. Then to whom does the property really and truly belong ? To his parishioners ? Certainly not. Churchmen are the first to deny that the parishioners, as such, have any claim. " It is only," say they, " those of the parishioners who are members of the Church of England," and so we are driven back to the original question, Who are the members of the Church of England ? Those who having begun life as members of that religious body have since joined other denominations, or thrown off allegiance to religion in any of its forms ? Those who regularly accept the ministrations of the Church— possibly, in many cases, with a view to business and credit ? Those who profess the Creed and are ready to subscribe the Thirty-nine Articles of the Church, either fully, or " to a certain limited extent " ? But it is useless to ask any further questions ; everybody knows that it is practically impossible to point out any determinate persons who constitute the Church of England as a whole, or the Church of Canterbury, of Westminster, or of Little Pedlington in particular.

It is no solution of the problem to say that the Church
property is held in trust. The further question at once arises,
Who are the beneficiaries? Let us look into the title of the
Church to one particular kind of property which is claimed on
its behalf, namely, tithes. This will reduce the scope of our
inquiry to within reasonable limits. I confess that the habit
of seeking for the origin of titles in antedeluvian or prehistoric
times seems to me both unsatisfactory and mischievous.
Those who defend the claim of the Church to this kind of
property usually begin their defence with a reference to
Leviticus, " If a man will at all redeem aught of his tithes, he
shall add thereto the fifth part thereof." Then follows a
terrible denunciation of those who would abolish tithes, or who
would attempt to curtail them. " Will a man rob God? Yet
ye have robbed me. But ye say, Wherein have we robbed
thee? In tithes and offerings. Ye are cursed with a curse: for
ye have robbed me, even this whole nation." As a recent writer
naïvely remarks, these words of Malachi " are rather serious in
this matter." He goes on to wonder whether we in England
are not under the curse. Says he: " Whether it has ever
occurred to the grumblers of the present day, in the period of
agricultural depression, that some of this depression is a little
owing to the outcry against tithes, we will not now stop to
inquire." From Malachi we are brought *per saltum* to
Edmund, King of England, who levied a church-rent of corn.
Then Ethelred made laws in a jumble of Latin and Anglo-
Saxon which it is not easy to construe. But one decree stands
clearly out, " Let every man pay his tithes justly." But what
is justly? Next comes a copy of the laws of Edward the
Confessor, which specify the subjects of tithes—corn, foals,
calves, cheese, lambs, wool, butter, pigs, honey, " moreover of
woods, meadows, waters, mills, parks, warrens, fishings, coppices,
orchards, and negotiations, and all things which the Lord hath
given." This law, which was successively confirmed by
William I., Henry I., Henry II., and Henry III., is really
important as showing conclusively that it was originally
intended in this country to levy tithes on commerce, as well as
on agricultural produce. " Negotiations " do not seem to count
for much against the long list of farm and forest produce, but

for what they were worth, there they are. Why, asks the farmer, should our produce be the only kind which has been unable to shake off this encumbrance? There was nothing unjust, nothing wrong, nothing inexpedient in thus taxing the people for what was then thought to be their spiritual welfare. Those who would not voluntarily give their share of the cost of a public necessary were compelled to do so. So long as tenths were paid to the State Church or Church State (for they were one and indivisible) no fault can be found with the arrangement. The evil began when benefices became appropriated to particular abbeys, priories, etc. From this step there was no natural halting-place till lay impropriators appeared on the scenes. Thus was a tax with a specific object gradually converted into a species of private property. When the monasteries were suppressed, the tithes, of course, passed to the State (the king) who, from time to time, made infendation of them into lay hands, and the thing was done. The question for us to-day is, Are tithes taxes, or are they private property? Are tithe-owners, like zemindars, to be regarded as persons having real rights in the soil, or as mere collectors of taxes for a given purpose?

If we regard them as tax-collectors, then I cannot agree with those who contend that tithe commutation is justified by events, both from a moral and an economic point of view. The clergy say they have been rendered more independent of their flocks and are no longer brought so much into collision with them in ascertaining the amount of their demands. Surely this is precisely what is *not* wanted. To render one's servants independent of oneself is but a poor policy. The removal of the friction of collection simply means the removal of the knowledge of the impost. The objection to indirect taxation applies here also. If the people do not feel the tax, they begin to forget it. When the object of the tax is gone or is no longer needed they forget to demand its remission. This is an unhealthy state of the public mind. The evil of a tax should be distinctly felt, and willingly borne for the sake of the good which is seen to result from it. Looking at tithes from the opposite standpoint, that is to say, as private property, it is clear that the corporations sole in whom the

rent-charge is vested would be justified at any time in ceasing
their ministrations and in sitting down in the full enjoyment
of their income. And why should they not? If these corporations actually own property, it is no business of yours or
of mine to dictate how it shall be used. A's ancestor held
land from his lord on condition that he would supply men and
arms on occasion, and perform other military services. B's
ancestor held land on condition that he would minister to the
spiritual welfare of the neighbourhood, and see after the poor
and destitute. A's successors now hold the same land
unconditionally, and why should not B's successors do the
same? The only answer forthcoming is, Because they don't;
and the rejoinder is, Perhaps they may come to do so. There
is no middle course between these two. No one can doubt
that originally tithes were a species of tax. Difference of
opinion enters in when the question is asked, whether they
have since at any time hardened into a species of private
property. This was actually the case with the land-tax in
Bengal and in many other Eastern countries. It was the case
in England when, after the suppression of the monasteries,
certain tithes passed into the hands of the predecessors of the
present lay impropriators. Here again we cannot go into
ancient titles; we have nothing to do with the right or wrong
of Henry VIII.'s policy. The lay impropriators of the present
day, as a juridical fact, have an indisputable claim to their
tithe rent-charge against all the world; a real right which
cannot be questioned or curtailed without flagrant injustice
and spoliation. Their title is as good and valid as that of any
other person having a first charge on the land, and as their
property is held unconditionally, and in no respect *ex contractu*,
the lay impropriator's claim is not contingent on the performance of duties. His rights are on all-fours with the
rights of the landowner himself, and his cause is but
weakened by binding it up with the cause of the ecclesiastical
tithe-owner. In short, there can be no doubt whatever that in
their case what was once a tax on agriculture and commerce
has become hardened and consolidated by time into uncon-
ditioned private property. This process might also have been
completed in the case of clerical tithe-owners, but it has not.

The conditions still hold, and the State or public still claims
the right to certain services (definable from time to time by
the State) in consideration of the tithe rent-charge. This
claim has been reaffirmed over and over again in our own
day. If the public needed to reconsider the nature of the
services to be required, it is quite possible that the ecclesiastical tithe rent-charge might fall into other keeping. It
is also conceivable that these charges might eventually harden
into private property if left unmolested; but it is difficult to
see how this is to be effected unless certain indeterminate bodies
come to be identified, defined, and determined. They can
never become capable otherwise of holding property. It is
opposed to the juridical principles of all law.

There is a simple explanation of the difficulty which most
people seem to labour under in recognising that tithes are a
species of tax. Tithes are levied on a particular class of
property and expended on a particular public object; whereas
most taxes are expended, as occasion requires, on any public
object. The reason why this tax is levied on a particular kind
of property is, that there was originally hardly any other kind
of property to tax, at least none worth taxing—although, as I
have said, commerce was actually included at first under the
head of negotiations; but "negotiators" soon gave the priest
the slip. Not so the farmer, rooted as he was to the soil. It
was the gradually increasing independence of the Church in
Plantagenet times which brought about the specific allocation
of this tax. Tithes originally resembled the land-tax collected
by the zemindars of Bengal and the Turkish tax-farmers—a
tax levied for the welfare of the people, but collected by
special officials to whom the particular function was entrusted
by the State. Like all taxes of this class it necessarily tended
to harden into the private property of the tax-gatherer. Such
is the natural and inevitable consequence of adopting this
mode of raising revenue. In the case of the zemindars and of
the English lay impropriators the process, as I have said, has
long ago been completed and the State must recognise
accomplished facts. It would be a gross breach of faith to
question the proprietary rights of these classes; but clerical
tithes have never been hardened into property. The con-

tractual nature of the clerical tithe-owners' claim is patent to all; it is not even a transferable right, it is simply a payment for current services rendered. Moreover, no determinate person, individual or corporate, can be pointed to as the owner. Except for services rendered, tithes are not even claimed by the so-called tithe-owner. As to the services required they are not sufficiently definite, but there is one feature in them worth noting; they have been defined and modified by the legislature and may be again. Then it must be admitted that the people might without injustice turn to the ecclesiastics and say, " We no longer require the kind of services you have hitherto rendered us," just as they might say and do say to the dockyard labourers. " We shall," they might add, " either devote the proceeds of the tax to some other object, or, as is usual when the object of a tax or rate ceases to be an object, remit it altogether." A war tax of twopence in the pound on incomes is remitted if there is no war, and no one says, Why not spend it on the schools? However this is a question of policy into which we need not enter here. The one point I wish to emphasise is, that the position of the ecclesiastical tithe-owner in no respect resembles that of the lay impropriator. They had, it is true, the same origin, but they have become completely differentiated, and have now little left in common beyond a common origin. If we rashly proceed to act upon a view of the Church's position based on ancient title-deeds, we must not be surprised if our nationalisationist friends likewise claim to dip into ancient history for a justification of the proprietory rights of landowners. Our business is to examine the present position juridically, and to leave the origin of all rights to the antiquarian and to the historian. Let us beware of confounding together rights which, though bearing similar names and having similar origins, fall, when juridically analysed, into very different classes.

I do not wish to be understood as offering any opinion whatever on the policy of the Bills which have recently been introduced into Parliament dealing with tithes. I am inclined to think that the proposed change in the system of tithe-collection is calculated to perpetuate what are called the rights of the Church rather than to safeguard in their integrity the rights of the clergy. The Church is *to the jurist*, as we have seen, a myth; a figment of the imagination; a name and nothing more. But the clergy are real and substantial beings, with rights and duties like other mortals, and any tampering with their reasonable expectations, as guaranteed by the laws and customs of this realm, would be a gross injustice and a national disgrace. Notice to the present clerical tithe-receiver that he will have no successor could injure nobody. He has himself worked and invested capital in qualifying for the post of spiritual teacher, and cannot be robbed of his reward by any honest means. Even if tithes were altogether remitted it would be as necessary to make full compensation as it was when purchase was abolished in the army. Vested interests may perhaps be defined as rights based not upon contract but upon custom. Even when the State has expressly repudiated the permanent obligation of paying certain salaries, it has found itself morally compelled to make compensation to those who have been deprived of livelihood by the abolition of offices which had come to be generally regarded as permanent.

But if we are justified by ancient custom in recognising rights which have no basis in law, it may be contended that we are justified in recognising obligations similarly based on immemorial custom. Agriculturists who have paid tithes for over a thousand years may be said to have a vested obligation to continue those payments, and it is no hardship upon farmers or upon landowners, who have come into their present position with their eyes open, to ask them to continue their contributions to the public Treasury. It may be urged that so far as the tithe-payer is concerned, it would not be actually unjust to go on levying tithes, and that it would not be unjust to remit them. This is true of all taxation. Putting the Church as a fictitious person altogether out of view, the existing clergy as individuals have a right either to the continuance of their offices for their lifetime or to full compensation. This claim might be met, and a considerable reduction simultaneously made, in the tax called tithes, whereby no human being would be mulcted. The pressure on agriculture would be temporarily relieved, and justice would be done all round. I have entered thus fully into the tithe question because it illustrates the doctrine of property in relation to the person owning. From this point of view the several kinds of Church property stand in the same position.

Even admitting that the independence of personal belief from State interference is the final outcome of social evolution, admitting that this nation is already ripe for the advance, I think many persons calling themselves liberationists are apt to lose sight of the main conditions of its achievement. It cannot be laid down too early or too emphatically that in carrying out the work, true proprietary rights must be held absolutely inviolate. Your pound of flesh, but not one drop of blood. Nothing can be more unreasonable or more unjust than to protest against the application of public monies to improper purposes, and at the same time to clamour for the expropriation of a certain class of citizens. Those who protest against taxation for spiritual purposes on the ground that it is wrong to rob an individual even for the public good are for ever barred from demanding the confiscation of the incomes of a class, even for the public good. If disendowment is to be brought about, it must be done without rendering one single member of the Established Church a penny the poorer. That is a *sine quâ non*. Perhaps the strongest argument for postponing the practical consideration of the question for some time is that the true definition of property has not yet come to be recognised by our laws.

The consequence is, that much misunderstanding exists as to what is corporate property. Cases of bequests to indeterminate persons abound, and a careful examination of the various and conflicting decisions of our judges goes to show that English jurisprudence is hardly yet equal to the task of dealing with this great question without doing moral injustice. Mill, who could not withhold a tribute of admiration for the great individualist Turgot, somewhat immodestly apologises for him for opposing foundations. " Notwithstanding our deep reverence for this illustrious man," he writes, " and the great weight which is due to his sentiments on all subjects which he had maturely considered, we must regard his opinion on this subject as one of what it is now allowable to call the prejudices of his age." It might have been allowable fifty years ago (Mill wrote on Church Property in 1833), but to-day the best thinkers are in line with Turgot, and are inclined to apologise for Mill, whose opinion on this subject, at least, may clearly be set down as due to the prejudice of the age in which *he* wrote. " Turgot and his friends," said he, " seem to have conceived the perfection of political society to be reached, if man could but be compelled to abstain from injuring man, not considering that men need help as well as forbearance, and that nature is to the greater number a severer taskmaster, even than man is to man. They left each individual to fight his own battle against fate and necessity with little aid from his fellow-men, save what he might purchase in open market and pay for." Could the individualists' position be more clearly defined to-day so far as the perfection of *political* society is concerned ? Mill's notion of a state which should help the individual to " fight against necessity " is a little out of harmony with the scientific thought of our day. His famous article on *Corporation and Church Property* is doubtless an able contribution to the discussion, but its weakness is its embodiment of socialist principles in reaction from the apparently hard individualism of Turgot.

In applying the principle of let-be to practical politics it is necessary to make a thorough and searching analysis of juridical terms, and of these the chief is the term Property. When this has been done, we shall, I think, without impugning the probity of such thinkers as Proudhon, find ourselves in harmony with the views expressed by Bastiat in his celebrated vindication of proprietary rights.

" Men of property and leisure ! Whence come the fears which have seized upon you ! The perfumed but poisoned breath of Utopia menaces your existence. You are loudly told that the fortune you have amassed for the purpose of securing a little repose in your old age, and food, instruction, and a start in life for your children, has been acquired by you at the expense of your brethren ; that you have placed yourselves between the gifts of nature and the poor ; that, like greedy tax-gatherers, you have levied a tribute on these gifts, under the names of property, interest, and rent. You are called upon for restitution ; and what augments your terror is, that your advocates in conducting your defence feel themselves too often compelled to avow that your usurpation is flagrant but that it is necessary. Such accusations I meet with a direct and emphatic negative. You have not intercepted the gifts of nature.

You have received them, it is true, at the hands of nature, but you have also transferred them to your brethren without receiving anything. What you have received is simply a recompense for your efforts and by no means the price of the gifts of nature. Such property is legitimate and unassailable ; no Utopia can prevail against it, for it enters into the very constitution of our being. No theory can ever succeed in blighting it, or in shaking it.

"Men of toil and privation! you cannot shut your eyes to the truth that the primitive condition of the race is that of a perfect equality of poverty and ignorance ; man redeems himself from this state by the sweat of his brow, and directs his course towards another equality, that of material prosperity, knowledge, and moral dignity. The progress of men is unequal indeed, and you could not complain even though the rapid march of the vanguard were in some measure to retard your own advances. But, in truth, it is quite the reverse. No ray of light penetrates a single mind without in some degree enlightening yours. No step of progress, even though prompted by the conscious striving for property, but it is a step of progress for you. No wealth is created which does not tend to enrich you ; no property is acquired which does not tend to enlarge your own liberties. For the order of things is so arranged that no man can work honestly for himself without at the same time working for all.

"Men of philanthropy! Lovers of equality! Blind defenders of the suffering classes! You who look forward to the reign of community in this world, why in your pride do you seek to subjugate men's wills and bring them under the yoke of your own inventions? Do you not see that this community after which you sigh has been already attained and provided for by nature? Has nature need either of your conceptions or of your violence? Do you not see that this community is being realised day by day, in virtue of its admirable decrees ; that the execution of these decrees has not been entrusted to your hap-hazard services and puerile tinkerings nor even to the increasing sympathy manifested in charity ; but that it has been entrusted to the most personal, the most permanent of all our energies—self-interest, a principle embedded in our inmost nature, which never flags and which never rests. Study then the social mechanism and you will find that it testifies to a universal harmony which far outstrips your dreams and chimeras. Instead of presumptuously offering to reconstruct the workmanship of nature, you will then, I trust, be content humbly to admire and to bless it."

I have dwelt thus at length on land ownership and tithe ownership because these two forms of property may be said to be typical ; each of them indicating the limits by which any clear and logical definition is necessarily bounded. Thus the rights over the thing owned are not unlimited, and the person or persons owning must be determinate. Unfortunately these considerations are not always borne in mind even by lawyers. "Property," says Lord Mackenzie, "though naturally unlimited, is susceptible of important restrictions." To begin with, it never is unlimited ; and if it were, what ground have we for supposing that this is its *natural* form—whatever that may mean ? This confusion results from mistaking the indefinite for the limitless.

Austin avoided this mistake, but perhaps in defining *property* as "a right over a determinate thing, indefinite in point of user, unrestricted in point of disposition, and unlimited in point of duration," we may doubt whether the two last qualifications are not necessary accidentals in ninety-nine cases out of a hundred, rather than essentially connoted by the term. If I have the use of a pound of tea for six months, it is precious little that your reversion will be worth at the end of that period. If the tenant for life of a painting includes amongst his rights over it the right of burning it, we may just as well admit his right to be unlimited in point of time. And yet this is a mere accident. On the whole, Austin's maturer conclusion is that which I am inclined to adopt when he says, "I mean by *property* every right over a thing which is indefinite in point of user." And there he stops. This is the outcome of his analysis of property as the institution exists at the present day. History endorses this view. Savigny says that property is founded upon adverse possession ripened by prescription. Very likely ; it matters little what it was founded upon ; the question is, What is it when it has been founded ? Speaking of its origin Sir Henry Maine oddly says : "What mankind did in the primitive state may not be a hopeless subject of inquiry, but of their motives for doing it, it is impossible to know anything." Again he says : "It is not surprising that the first proprietor should have been the strong man armed who kept his goods in peace. But *why* it was that lapse of time created a sentiment of respect for his possession, which is the exact source of the universal reverence of mankind for that which has for a long period *de facto* existed, is a question really deserving the profoundest examination, but lying far beyond the boundary of our present inquiries." I cannot admit that the motives of our early ancestors are inscrutable, but I quite agree that the inquiry falls quite outside the province of the lawyer. Let land nationalisationists and antiquarians and meta-

physicians and " agitators " argue out such questions as whether
Adam's *dominion* over all the beasts of the field was a *jus in rem*
or merely a *jus ad rem acquirendam*; whether Malachi was
inspired when he denounced those who neglected to pay their
tithes ; whether the land of Great Britain originally belonged
to the dolichocephalic troglodytes or to lake-dwellers with skulls
like the Neanderthal specimen; whether Colonel North of
Leeds has an absolute right to pull down Kirkstall Abbey
without the consent of the people of Leeds, or of Yorkshire, or
of England, or of the British Empire.   All these questions will
continue to amuse and to enrage countless hosts of " thinkers "
for years to come.   The lawyer and the statesman and the
jurist have nothing to do with them.   And since, after all, the
permanent laws of all countries are made by the wise men in
those countries, perhaps the best thing common-sense people
can do at the present time is to clear their heads and make
up their minds what it is which they mean by property before
shouting themselves hoarse with the Beccarias and Proudhons
on the one side, or the Benthams and Bastiats on the other.

CHAPTER V

WHAT is Capital ? Surely many will complain that the conception is clearly defined already, or that the whole science of
political economy must be rotten from the very foundation.
"If the nature of capital be thoroughly understood," wrote Mr.
John Macdonnel (*Survey of Political Economy*, 1871) "political
economy is known almost to the bottom ; almost all purely
economical questions may be solved, and the greater part of
future discussions consists of drawing deductions from the
fundamental properties of capital. Its momentousness must,
in the first place, be impressed upon the mind of every student
of political economy. Man without capital is as purely a
fiction of the imagination as a line without breadth or a
point without magnitude. It is as essential to the continuance
of life as air. It is the breath of industry."

If the term Capital conveys no definite meaning, of what a
jargon must nearly all the problems and theorems of the so-
called science consist ! In Mill's own words : " A branch may
be diseased and all the rest healthy ; but unsoundness at the
root diffuses unhealthiness through the whole tree." And it is
in speaking of capital that this apt illustration is called forth.
Consequently it behoves us to ascertain, first, whether the term
really has one clear meaning, and secondly, whether it is used
in the same sense by those whose works on the subject are
studied. And in order to answer these questions let us begin
by laying side by side two or three definitions of capital
extracted from well-known works. In the *Principles of
Political Economy*, by J. S. Mill, we find the following not

very concise definition : " What capital does for production is to afford the shelter, protection, tools, and materials which the work requires, and to feed and otherwise maintain the labourers during the process. Whatever things are destined for this use —destined to supply productive labour with these various pre-requisites—are capital."

In the *Manual of Political Economy*, by Professor H. Fawcett, 1865, the following is the definition given : " The wealth which has been accumulated with the object of assisting production is termed capital ; and therefore the capital of the country is the wealth which is not immediately consumed unproductively, and which may, consequently, be devoted to assist the further production of wealth." This statement has not been materially altered in later editions.

In a work entitled *Political Economy for Plain People*, by Mr. G. P. Scrope, 1873, it is written : " We should therefore define capital as *that portion of movable stock which is employed or reserved for employment in production ;* to which we would add (in order to avoid ambiguity as far as possible), *with a view to profit by the sale of its produce.*"

Mill's definition may be translated into a single proposition thus : " Whatever things are destined to supply productive labour with the shelter, protection, tools, and materials which the work requires, and to feed and otherwise maintain the labourers during the process, are capital." Scrope's definition already fulfils this desideratum, if the italics, which are his own, be read separately. But Fawcett's definition, though, to use his own words, " it is a wide defini- tion," will be found on closer inspection to be two wide definitions, of which the second embraces some things and excludes others not embraced and excluded by the first, although they are connected by the form used to indicate identical propositions. According to the first the intention of the accumulator constitutes an essential factor in the concep- tion. In the second the possible destiny of the wealth takes the place of the accumulator's intention. There is much wealth, which, though not accumulated with the *object* of assisting production, nevertheless *may* be devoted to that purpose. Such wealth is capital according to the second

K

definition, but *not* capital according to the first. No doubt
Fawcett was led to perpetrate this extraordinary *non sequitur*
by the laudable desire to eliminate from the conception of
capital that element of destiny which is so prominent in the
definition of the great logician. We are enabled, he no doubt
said to himself, with this clue to look back and declare pretty
accurately what *was* capital so many years ago, and in
so many years to come we shall be similarly able to decide
what is capital to-day; but by what conceivable process can
we point to the things around us and say which are capital and
which are not, if that depends entirely upon their destiny?
The eventual destiny of a thing is not necessarily coincident
with the present intention of its possessor or of any one else;
but as the latter is ascertainable and the former is not, it shall
be taken as the true test of capital. And then, perchance,
after coming to this determination, there arose before the
professor a vision of an old nobleman on the verge of the tomb,
feeding his hunters on the oats that should make porridge for
his labourers, with a thrifty son and heir looking on and
biding his time; and the object of the accumulator seemed a
too nice distinction between capital and non-capital and so
was superimposed the second not exactly complementary but
rather optional mark. Now since it is quite possible and easy
to say whether a given article may or may not by possibility
be devoted to production, we have by means of these optional
definitions really eliminated the metaphysical factor of destiny
or fatality from the conception. And this is, we admit, very
satisfactory, when lo! here comes G. Poulett Scrope and spoils the
whole design, bringing back destiny in disguise. Disgusted
with the professor's canny trick of producing one or other of
his two definitions from his pocket as suits his convenience,
under pretence that they are equivalent, Scrope rolls the
two into one. Instead of this class *or* that class, he says
both this class *and* that class are capital, both those things
which are *reserved* for employment in production, and also those
things which, whether so reserved or not, actually are so
employed. It is almost a pity he did not substitute "may by
possibility be employed " for " are employed." We should so
have bid farewell for ever to destiny. But alas! what means

that which *is* employed? Of what particular thing can we say that it *is* employed in production? Certainly not of any kind of so-called circulating capital. Here is a sack of oats. It certainly has not been employed in production, or it would not be oats, and as to whether it is to be so employed or not, it is impossible to predict with certainty: after all, it is again a question of destiny.

So that, on the one hand, the wealth which, though intended for the purchase of luxury, is eventually rescued from destruction by some accident, such as the death of its possessor, and on the other hand, that which, though intended to assist the further production of wealth, stands an equal chance of being wasted, are both included under the head of capital. Heads I win, tails you lose; in either case Poulett Scrope smiles on the wealth around him and dubs it capital.

Concerning this factor intention, Courcelle Seneuil writes (*Traite d'Economie Politique*, 1867, p. 49): "Comme notre définition du mot 'capital' diffère de celle qui est généralement admise, et qui a été accréditée par les auteurs les plus respectables, il est nécessaire de donner à ce sujet une courte explication. La plupart des économistes comprennent sous le nom commun de capital cette parti seulement des richesses existantes que ses possesseurs ont *l'intention*, de conserver ou de reproduire par l'industrie. Ainsi tel objet compté entre les richesses serait ou ne serait pas capital selon l'intention de son possesseur et acquerrait ou perdrait la qualité de capital selon les changements que subirait cette intention. Une telle classification a le défaut de ne s'attacher à aucun fait matériel sensible; le même objet deviendrait ou cesserait d'être capital en changeant de propriétaire; un pain, par exemple, serait capital dans la boutique du boulanger, mais une fois acquis par le consommateur, il ne serait plus un capital. Qui ne voit tout se qu'une telle classification a de conventionel et d'arbitraire? Mieux vaut ramener le mot capital à son acception vulgaire, d'après laquelle il désigne une somme de richesses, d'utilités existantes créés par un travail antérieur."

This popular definition is almost identical with the one

adopted by J. B. Say, though it is only fair to the latter to say that he distinguished between *capital productif* and *capital improductif*, denoting by the first what is commonly denominated capital by the English economists, namely, in Bastiat's rough categories, "tools, materials, provisions." Though heartily admitting the force of Courcelle Seneuil's critical arguments against the current acceptation of the term, I cannot find that he makes any use, in his two cumbrous and erudite volumes, of the popular conception. I concur rather with Mr. Macdonnel in regretting that a useful term should be wasted. "J. B. Say seems to have needlessly spoiled a term which fitted a well-defined idea," or rather, a very vague idea, which deserves to be well defined.

M'Culloch's definition agrees with what we must call Professor Fawcett's second definition: "The capital of a country consists of those portions of the produce of industry existing in it which are DIRECTLY available either for the support of human beings or the facilitating of production." When Mr. Macdonnel says that "whatever wealth, labour excluded, is devoted to help to form new wealth is capital," we must interpret "devoted" in the sense of "already applied" or of "intended to be applied" to the said purpose, to either of which senses my objections apply.

On the whole, then, after comparison, I think we must give the preference to Mill's definition. And no doubt it is the most representative of the generally-accepted usage of the term. So for the purposes of this analysis we may mainly confine ourselves to the condensed form of it given above, namely : "Whatever things are destined to supply productive labour with the shelter, protection, tools, and materials which the work requires, and to feed and otherwise maintain the labourers during the process, are capital."

Now, passing over the objectionable factor destiny, and assuming for the present that the destination of an article may be approximately coincident with the present intention of its possessor, even then the definition is merely one of enumeration. What is a quadruped ? A quadruped is a horse, or a rat, or an elephant, or a pig, etc., without any reference to the distinctive attributes of the class. Of what conceivable use is

such a definition ?   You may walk through a forest, and every
now and then mark a tree with chalk.   When you have done,
no doubt a certain class does exist, viz. the chalked trees.
But, so far as scientific utility is concerned, the classification
might just as well never have been made.   If the enumeration
be exhaustive we may have a very distinct idea of the various
things *denoted* by capital, but what we want is an equally
distinct idea of the attributes *connoted* by the term.

Until we have found the connotation of a term it cannot
be said to have been defined, though it may have been translated into other words.

But the connotation of a term is often implied before it is
expressed, because it is often felt before it is seen.   Even in
the case of the chalked trees the grouping may be of use
provided you were guided in your selection by some clearly or
dimly recognised features common to all the trees chalked and
peculiar to them.   And so it is with capital.   That there is an
actual something approximately common and peculiar to all
the groups of things enumerated in Mill's definition of capital
we cannot deny.   On the contrary, it is this vaguely conceived connotation which has enabled economists to do so
much work with such a classification ; just as a chemist may
do good work with an ill understood or impure chemical.   And
it is this something which I propose to bring into the light
of day shorn of its imperfections and denuded of the fog
which has hitherto surrounded it.   Like tainted water in the
kitchen, it has been mixed with all our food, doing more harm
in some quarters than in others, and, on the whole, sufficing
better than no water at all.   What classes have suffered most
from the pollution I shall point out in the next chapter.

The best recipe for exposing the weakness of a so-called
definition by enumeration is to hunt it down through all the
groups said to be comprised within it, and by selecting extreme
examples of each to show how they are at variance with the
vaguely implied connotation as interpreted by common sense.
This we will now proceed to do.

First example.—Here is a cotton-mill, with machinery, coal,
cotton, oil, an organised body of workpeople, and every other
evidence of being devoted to production.   It is burnt down.

Was it capital ?   Common sense, guided by a vague perception of the connotation of the term, answers, It was capital : but the definition says No ; it was not destined to assist production, and therefore it was not capital.

Second example.—A Scotch nobleman has a hundred sacks of oats intended to be consumed by his hunters ; he dies, and his thrifty heir converts the oats into porridge for his workpeople.   Were the oats capital ?   Mill says, Yes, and common sense thinks so too, while Professor Fawcett first says No, and then says Yes.

Third example.—A thousand colliers on the eve of a monster meeting eat their suppers, not knowing whether a strike will commence on the morrow or not.   Is their supper capital ?   Mill gives it up, so does Scrope, and so does Fawcett till, on second thoughts, he says it may possibly be devoted to production, and therefore it is capital.   Common sense feels that it is capital.

Quitting destiny, the next factor that merits attention is productive labour.   The commodity in question may be destined to supply labour with the shelter, production, tools, or materials which the work requires, but unless that labour be *productive* labour the article is not capital.   And now arises the question : What is productive labour ?   Half a dozen different answers are at once forthcoming.   J. B. Say confers that title upon all labour which results in utilities or, in other words, gives pleasure to others.   M'Culloch goes one step farther, and includes all labour which gives pleasure even to the labourer, such as eating turtle   or   blowing bubbles ; Mill rejects all utilities that are not capable of being embodied mediately or immediately in material objects other than human, while the stricter sect exclude all that cannot at once be carried off : for example, Mill regards as productive labour the work of the schoolmaster, because eventually the country will be the richer for it materially ; but not until the country is the richer for it will Professors Scrope and Fawcett pay any regard to it ; and even then, if it comes through the medium of the skill of labourers, as it needs must, the former refuses to class the new increment as due to capital, but rather as due to labour.   We will, however, as heretofore, follow Mill.   Accord-

ing to him productive labour includes "only those kinds of
exertion which produce utilities embodied in material objects"
as the direct or the ultimate result. Lest I should appear to
some wilfully to misunderstand Mill's exact meaning, and to
complicate purposely this definition within a definition, I shall
do well to quote him on this point in full. "I shall . . .
understand . . . by productive labour only those kinds of
exertion which produce utilities embodied in material objects.
But in limiting myself to this sense of the word I mean to
avail myself of the full extent of that restricted acceptation,
and I shall not refuse the appellation productive to labour
which yields no material profit as its direct result, provided
that an increase of material products is its ultimate consequence." As examples of this indirectly or mediately productive labour, he cites the labour expended in the acquisition
of manufacturing skill, and the labour of officers of Government
in affording the protection which is indispensable to the
prosperity of industry.

Now the only objection I have to offer to this definition
is, that it can have no conceivable application. It is clearly
impossible to draw a line, even a rough line, between labour
that will eventually conduce to material wealth and labour
that will not. We have already admitted the labour of the
educator and the Government officer, and it will be hard to
exclude the soldier and the tragedian if one will but think of
the ultimate results of their work. To avoid the indefinite extension of the class, Mill had recourse to a new boundary line ;
he again falls back on the intention of the labourer and worker.
Concerning the labour of the musical performer, actor, and
showman, he observes : "Some good may, no doubt, be produced beyond the moment upon the feelings and disposition
or general state of enjoyment of the spectators ; or, instead of
good there may be harm ; but neither the one nor the other is
the effect intended, is the result for which the exhibitor works
and the spectator pays : nothing but the immediate pleasure."
Surely this sudden change of front is lamentable—is inadmissible.
We follow tediously the consequences of a given action through
several generations down to the final embodiment of its resulting utility in a material object, and we triumphantly claim for

the said action the title of productive labour, when to our
chagrin we are met by the very prescriber of the requisite qualifications with the objection that such embodiment was not the
original object of the worker. May we not safely retort that
such is not the aim of anything like half the labourers whose
work has been styled productive; of the soldier, for instance,
or the clergyman? Nor should we better ourselves by accepting any other economist's definition of productive labour in
preference to Mill's.

We must, however, take things as we find them, and
having obtained the value of productive labour in known terms,
substitute them in the original equation; and we have
the following: "Whatever things are destined to supply
those kinds of exertion which produce utilities immediately or
mediately embodied, and intended to be embodied, in material
objects, with the shelter, etc. etc., are capital."

In order to apply the term to any given article we have
to ascertain not only what it is destined to be devoted to, but
also whether the utility possibly resulting from it is ever
destined to be embodied in material objects, and further
whether, if so, such embodiment was the intention of its
original employer.

We are still on the threshold of our inquiry. We now
come to the consideration of the separate groups of things
which alone, even under the above-mentioned circumstances,
can be classed as capital. And the first of these is shelter.
It will be remembered that Scrope was careful to reject
everything as capital that is not movable. But shelter is
usually afforded by something immovable, such as a roof and·
walls. The warehouse that protects the finished goods is to
be rejected; the light shed that protects the machinery is also
to be rejected. The tarpaulin that protects the waggons in
the yard is or is not included according to the nature of the
fastenings by which it is connected with the poles in the earth;
while the umbrella, beneath whose grateful shelter the foreman
inspects the works and the workers, is unmistakably capital of
the first water, being very movable.

Surely political economy had its origin long prior to the
days of Adam Smith, in the brains of the ancient lawyers, who

distinguished real from personal property, on the grounds that
no man, be he never so feloniously disposed, can run away
with an acre of land. I lay stress on this movable qualification, because, though not expressly contained in Mill's
definition, it is throughout his work assumed to be so contained, and everywhere land and its appurtenances are excluded from the category of capital.

The next station at which we shall stop is called
" protection." Does this include the high wall that wards off
the thief; the iron bars in front of the jeweller's window ; the
policeman who watches the premises ; the law that protects
the property of citizens ? All, any, or none of these ? Mill's
definition would, I suppose, include all : but in practice, as
we have seen, he excludes all things attached to the soil.
Professors Fawcett and Scrope would exclude also the policeman and the law, except in so far as the latter is embodied in
material statute-books, more or less movable. Let not the
reader smile at these divisions and differences. Even the
most frivolous of them has its origin in philosophical distinctions
more or less profound.

Nor does the term " tools " convey any clearer meaning.
Is the anvil a tool as well as the hammer ? the chimney as
well as the bellows ? the stream as well as the water-wheel ?
The steam as well as the piston ? the coal as well as the boiler ?
It would be hard to draw the line between them ; yet would
any of the above-named economists call the wind that fills the
sail capital ? And similarly with materials. We do not seem
to emerge from the fog as we advance. What, in the name of
clear conception, are materials ? There is a branch of them
known as raw materials. Here is a piece of undyed cloth.
It is the dyer's raw material, and therefore, by definition,
capital. Again, here is a plastered house, destined to be
painted custard colour, according to the genius of the English
people. Evidently it is precisely in the situation of the
undyed cloth, and therefore it must be regarded as the
painter's capital. Is it so regarded ? Everything, in short,
destined to be improved, repaired, touched up, is capital ; and
hence the greater the quantity of unfinished articles in a
country the greater its potential capital. So that we may

create capital by scratching the paint off a neighbour's door, because the door will probably soon become raw material in the hands of the painter. The fog thickens.

We need not push "materials" any farther, but after noting that the shelter, protection, tools, and materials must not only be devoted to but actually required by the work in order to merit the title of capital, we will proceed to consider the next group of commodities included under Mill's definition. Whatever things are destined to feed and otherwise maintain the labourers during the process are also capital. Farther on Mill admits that not all the food, but only so much as is absolutely requisite to enable the labourers to perform their share of the work, is capital. Now, unless we are prepared to show how much of John's beer, bread, and beef goes to the repair of John's muscles and motor nerves, and to what extent the latter are actually confined to the work he has to do, I cannot perceive of what use the term capital can be to science. How can we compare profits with capital, quantitatively—that is, find the ratio of profits to capital—unless we can measure both ? Again, one bootmaker, devouring in one week fifty shillings' worth of turtle, venison, and old port, works hard and turns out six pair of boots ; are the sources of his strength to be deemed all capital ? It may be that a smaller quantity of the same stuff would not have sufficed to support him, any more than a reduction could have been made in the amount of beer, beef, and bread consumed by another bootmaker at a cost of fifteen shillings, who turns out an equal number of similar boots. There is no stipulation in the definition as to the kind of food that may be called capital, but only that the quantity must not exceed that which is actually converted into labour. Mr. Macdonnel handles this question in rather a remarkable and amusing manner. After putting the question whether a bottle of champagne is or is not capital, he answers that it depends on circumstances. If consumed by one who produces nothing valuable it is not capital (but *was* it ?). If by one who produces something valuable, then it is capital ; " or, to be accurate, so much of the value of it as would have bought equal nourishment forms capital, the rest being purely unproductive expenditure."

So that not the champagne, or even part of it, which would not have sufficed to afford the requisite stimulus, but part of the value of the whole of the champagne, is capital. The value, not the matter, is capital. This recalls the definition of J. B. Say: "Le valeur de toutes ces choses" (before enumerated) "compose ce qu'on appelle un capital productif."

Laughable as this shuffle appears, it is paralleled, and indeed eclipsed, by the feats of legerdemain performed by Mill himself and his whole army of disciples, which have yet to be exposed.

As to those things which otherwise maintain the labourers, no doubt clothes, fuel, and shelter are meant, but so dense is the mist already surrounding us that even this cloud adds little or nothing to the darkness.

And so, having at last groped our way to the end of our journey, we confess with disappointment that the currently accepted and best definition of capital, apparently clear and definite enough when seen at a distance, on nearer and closer scrutiny " dissolves, and, like the baseless fabric of th' air vision, leaves not a rack behind."

Enough of this sort of analysis is as good as a feast. In fact, some people have no sympathy with us in such work, and indeed get very angry when we attempt it.

" In political economy," says Scrope, " much labour has been expended in vain, and great confusion introduced where all is really plain enough, by over-*refining*, and by ill-judged endeavours to give a mathematical accuracy to definitions and propositions which, from the nature of their subject, can pretend to no more than the grouping of phenomena according to their most striking general characters." But what are the most striking general characters of those things which are grouped together under the head of capital ? That is precisely what we want to get at—the connotation of the term.

However, let us lay aside our dissecting-knife and assume that, to all practical intents and purposes, our political economists mean roughly to comprise in the class just what Bastiat groups together as " tools, materials, provisions," and that the variance between them is due to a desire to be more exact— one regarding this feature, another that, as most requiring elucidation or qualification; let us grant that all these various and elaborate definitions do but testify to a consciousness of the imperfection of the original proposition, embodied in so many qualifying clauses. Be it so. Tools, materials, provisions; this is what is meant in plain words by capital. We will ask no questions about anvils and chimneys; we will ask no questions about raw materials and painted houses; we will ask no questions about venison and beef, beer and port wine. After all, honest folk know what they are talking about when they speak of tools, of materials, and of provisions. Like good children, we will not ask troublesome questions.

Now may we not say we know what capital is? at least roughly? Not a bit of it. Just as we begin to try and accommodate ourselves to loose forms of speech, and to rest content with tolerably clear ideas of things, all our limits are suddenly swept away by the intrusion of two new elements into the conception, both wholly subversive of our newly-found interpretation of the term.

In two extraordinary propositions we are informed, firstly, that anything of value whatsoever which can be exchanged for capital (as defined) is itself capital, by which we must understand anything of value whatsoever, for the value of a thing means that it can be exchanged for other things; secondly, that there is no such thing at all as capital in an absolute sense, but that an article may be *capital* in relation to one person, *not capital* in relation to another person.

These statements seem so remarkable that they must be borne out by suitable quotations from the works of our representative economist Mill. Speaking of a man's capital on p. 69 of the *Principles* he says: " What, then, is his capital? Precisely that part of his possessions which is to constitute his fund for carrying on fresh production. It is of no consequence that a part or even the whole of it is in a form in which it cannot directly supply the wants of the labourers." Again, on p. 71: " Whether all these values are in a shape directly applicable to productive use makes no difference. Their shape, however it may be, is a temporary accident, but once destined for production they do not fail to find a way of transforming themselves into things capable of being applied to it."

To some minds it would appear almost desirable to employ
two technical terms—one to designate the group of articles
hitherto classed together as capital, and another to designate
whatever of value is destined to be exchanged for such
capital. But as neither term would be of any conceivable
use to exact science, I shall not waste space in converting
one bad tool into two not much better. Let us rather prepare
ourselves for the second revelation, to the effect that, after all,
there is no such thing as capital *per se.* Speaking of a
particular instance, Mill, on p. 74 of the *Principles*, writes :
" In the present instance that which is virtually capital to
the individual is or is not capital to the nation according as
the fund which, by the supposition, he has not dissipated, has
or has not been dissipated by somebody else." In other words,
wealth which is capital to an individual may be not-capital
to the nation or another individual or group of individuals.
The same article is capital to *A*, not-capital to *B ;* and capital
is, therefore, merely a relative term, *i.e.* implies a particular
relation between a particular person and a particular thing.

Our original definition, to be more accurate, requires to be
so expanded as to embody these two new important factors
somehow or other. I submit the following :—

" Whatever things are destined to supply those kinds of
exertion which produce utilities immediately or mediately
embodied (and originally intended to be embodied) in material
objects with the shelter, protection, tools, and materials which
the work requires, and to feed and otherwise maintain the
labourers during the process, or whatever things are capable
of being and destined to be exchanged for such, are, in relation
to some person or persons according to circumstances not
specified, capital." Or, to adopt Bastiat's abbreviated form, as
we have consented to do, " Tools, materials, provisions, and
whatsoever is intended or destined to be exchanged for such,
are capital with respect to somebody."

Our determination to look at things kindly, and, as
Scrope advises us, with our eyes half-closed, has, I fear,
landed us in a quagmire not much better than that in which
our method of analysis terminated.

If we really wish to know what the term capital means

we *must* have recourse to the comparative method, and by extracting that which is common and peculiar to all forms of so-called capital that we can bring together within our field of vision, finally discover the true connotation, instead of barely enumerating the more convenient forms, and averting our gaze from the ugly borderland specimens, the ornithorhynchuses and pterodactyluses of our kingdom.

Let us commence operations by colligating the following cases drawn together from various points of the compass :—

The above-mentioned factory in working order before it is burnt down.

The hundred sacks of oats intended for his hunters by the above-mentioned old nobleman.

The slaves on a sugar-plantation.

The tall chimney which causes the strong draught in a boiler-house.

An acre of plough land in Middlessex.

An acre of land on the banks of Lake Tanganyika.

A casket of diamonds cut and polished.

I shall assume that common sense, or rather the opinion of all those whose vague idea of capital is sufficiently clear to cause them to desire a term or name for the conception, will admit that of this group of cases the first five are capital and the last two are not capital. What we have to do is to find out what is common to the five and not common to the last two.

And, first of all, we see that the element of destiny is excluded by the factory, which by supposition is not destined to produce new wealth. Next we see that the intention of the possessor does not affect the question, for although the oats are intended to be unproductively consumed, yet they are regarded as capital.

The case of the slaves disposes of the allegation that man is not capital, " but only that for which capital exists."

The tall chimney excludes the factor movability, which, but for high authorities, I should hardly have considered worthy of express exclusion.

And land may or may not be capital according to circumstances, for in Middlesex we regard it as such, but not on the banks of Tanganyika.

Lastly, value is not a sufficient mark, for the diamonds are not capital, though no one will dispute their value.

Up to the present we can see only two factors common to the five examples of capital. Firstly, they all possess value ; and secondly, they are all originally fit or suitable for the production of wealth. They contain a possibility of helping to form new capital.

But value is already excluded because it is not only common to the forms of capital but also to the casket of diamonds. Nor are we more fortunate with our potentiality, for there is that in the acre of land on the shores of the African lake which would enable it to assist in the production of new wealth, viz. a fertile soil. Moreover, the wind that turns the mill-sails and drives the ship contributes most unmistakably to the creation of wealth, and yet it is not capital.

To what straits, then, are we driven !

It seems as though there were no attribute at once common to all forms of wealth properly called capital and yet peculiar to them. Nor does any amount of search and scrutiny serve to throw any light on the position. If we increase the number of cases we are no better off. Have we not tried everything, and in vain ? Must we after all give it up ? One more attempt. Value is common to all, and fitness to assist in the creation of new wealth is also common to all. Yet neither of these attributes is peculiar to capital. May it be that the combination of the two is the required connotation ? We feel we are getting nearer. The wind that helps to create wealth has no value, and the diamonds that have great value help to create no wealth. Alas ! consider these bananas at Covent Garden. They are sold for threepence each, and are therefore very valuable. Humboldt calculated their productiveness as compared with that of wheat as 133 to 1 ; and in many parts of India and the West Indies they form the chief food of labourers. Yet as we look at them we feel they are not capital in this country. Again, this fibrous variety of actinolite, called asbestos from its incombustibility, has been utilised, and would be in a hundred ways in the shape of incombustible cloth (for its fibres are as fine as flax) but for its high value.

Suddenly the truth flashes in upon us. The connotation of capital rends its veil of mist and gloom and comes forth clear, sharply-defined, and brilliant as a crystal. Once seen there is no mistaking it.

"Capital is that the value of which is *due* to the value of its products."

It is not long, it is not vague, but pithy, transparent, and to the point. Anything which owes its value to the demand, not for itself, as calculated to afford immediate gratification to the consumer, but for some other commodity into the creation of which it enters as an element, whether as raw material, as tool or machine, as worker, brute or human—such a thing is capital.

If the value of a commodity partly consumed for its own sake, partly in the manufacture of other articles (as coals, for example), varies with the value of the goods manufactured by means of it, it is clearly capital, whether or no the portion of it under consideration be or be not destined for immediate consumption.

With this key we at once and easily unlock all difficulties. Take the piece of undyed cloth. Is it capital in the hands of the dyer? In order to answer this question we first inquire whether the value of the said cloth is due to the demand for it in the dyed state. If so, if the immediate consumer does not offer so high a price for the undyed material as the dyer can afford to do, then it is capital. Take the diamonds, supposing them to be of a fair size. Are they capital? Clearly the polisher or glass-cutter cannot afford to buy them for the purposes of his trade at the value their unassisted pleasure-giving power can command in the market as ornaments; their value is not affected by his demand, hence they are not capital.

Is venison capital? Certainly not. Because its value is due, not to the demand for the products into which it may enter (as labourers, for instance), but to its intrinsic power of affording immediate gratification.

Is bread capital in England? In order to answer this question we must ascertain whether an extended demand for any commodity into which bread enters as an element causes a rise in the value of bread. Unquestionably an extended demand for labourers (or, as is commonly said, for labour) is

followed by a rise in the value of bread, other things equal.
Hence bread is capital in England. And so on with any
commodity that may be proposed for consideration.

Both land and labourers must now be reinstated under
the head of capital, for clearly the value of labourers is
entirely due to the value of their productions, and not to
the gratification obtainable from them immediately, except
in a few cases, such as singers, dancers, actors, and the
like, who in the exercise of their functions cause direct satisfaction.

Labourers in general, commonly so called—that is to
say, human beings engaged in the creation of new and valuable *matter*, whether by manual exertion or as managers,
superintendents, co-ordinators, or inventors—are capital.
There is nothing new in this. It has been admitted, for
various insufficient reasons, by some of our shrewdest
economists.

M‘Culloch (*Principles*, p. 116) writes :—

" However extended the sense previously attached to the term capital
may at first sight appear, we are inclined to think that it should be interpreted still more comprehensively. Instead of understanding by capital all
that portion of the produce of industry *extrinsic* to man which may be made
applicable to his support and to the facilitating of production, there does
not seem to be any good reason why man himself should not, and very
many why he should, be considered as forming a part of the national
capital. Man is as much the produce of previous outlays of wealth
expended on his sustenance, education, etc., as any of the instruments constructed by his agency ; and it would seem that in those inquiries which
regard only his mechanical operations and do not involve the consideration
of his higher and nobler powers, he should be regarded in precisely the
same point of view. Every individual who has arrived at maturity,
though he may not be instructed in any particular art or profession, may
yet with perfect propriety be viewed in relation to his natural powers as
a machine which it has cost twenty years of assiduous attention and the
expenditure of a considerable capital to construct. And if a further sum
be expended in qualifying him for the exercise of a business or profession
requiring unusual skill, his value will be proportionally increased, and he
will be entitled to a greater reward for his exertions, as a machine becomes
more valuable when it acquires new powers by the expenditure of
additional capital or labour in its construction. Adam Smith has fully
admitted the justice of this principle, though he has not reasoned consistently from it. He states that the acquired and useful talents of the
inhabitants should be considered as forming a portion of the national

capital. ' The acquisition of such talents,' he justly observes, ' during the education, study, or apprenticeship of the acquirer, always costs a real expense, which is a capital fixed and realised, as it were, in his person.' "

Unfortunately M'Culloch finds himself just as unable to cope with his new principle as Smith did before him, not because it was a false one, but because it was based by both on a false reasoning, a rotten foundation.

Nor is it by any means new to comprehend land under the head of capital, though we are in a minority in so doing.   Mr. Macdonnel passes this criticism on the English economists, after comprising land under materials or tools, and therefore under capital: " This is indeed contrary to the usage of English economists, who put land, the representative of all other natural agents, in a category by itself.   But two reasons, I think, warrant a deviation.   In the first place, the classification of English economists with regard to this point involves an inconsistency ; for though laying it down—to take Mr. Fawcett as their spokesman—' that capital is all that wealth, in whatever shape or form it may exist, which is set aside to assist future production,' and though of course viewing land as a portion of wealth, they exclude land from the kinds of wealth included under capital."

However, without troubling ourselves to examine authorities on this point further, we perceive that under capital fall both land and labourers—not labour, which is a mere metaphysical entity, or, what comes to the same thing, no entity at all, but labourers.   Strange to say, this confusion of materials with forces is made by all the leading economists without exception, including even the great logician and philosopher, J. S. Mill, who says : " The human being himself I do not class as wealth. He is the purpose for which wealth exists."   And then he proceeds to class his ability to work under the head of labour.   " But his acquired capacities, which exist only as means, and have been called into existence by labour, fall rightly, as it seems to me, within that designation."

A weak objection to classing labour under the head of capital is offered by Scrope in the form of a criticism on M'Culloch's opinion just quoted.

"We need hardly observe," he says, "that things which

are identical can have no reciprocal action on each other "—
from which we are to conclude that if land and labour be capital, disquisitions on the reciprocal influence of land, labour,
and other kinds of capital, of rent, wages, and other kinds of
profits, must needs be vain delusions and absurdities. We
may reply that species of one genus may differ considerably
amongst themselves, and may act and react one upon another
to any extent, notwithstanding the fact that they have attributes in common.

Nor is it disputed that there are well-marked species or
sub-classes of capital which are approximately coincident with
the old so-called genera, land and labourers, and it is this fact
which gives value to the problems and theorems contained in
works which are based upon an erroneous view of the term
capital. Were it not so the whole tree would indeed be rotten
because of the disease at the root.

But no one denies that, of all kinds of capital, human
beings alone have this peculiarity, that they are the cause of
values as well as the part cause of valuables. No wonder
labourers are a very marked and distinct sub - class of
capital !

Land, too, has most important peculiarities, into which we
need not enter here.[1] Rarities are often classed together and
distinguished by a class-mark. For instance, we talk of monopoly prices in speaking of coal, of the works of old masters,
and the like. Then there is the well-known division of capital
into fixed and circulating, which we will now proceed briefly
to consider ; and at the same time we must observe that this
division testifies to a real but vaguely-discerned distinction
which underlies the flimsy one commonly alleged. We are
told (Mill's *Principles,* p. 114): " Of the capital engaged in
the production of any commodity there is a part which, after
being once used, exists no longer as capital, is no longer capable of rendering service to production, or at least not the same
service, nor to the same sort of production. . . . . Capital
which in this manner fulfils the whole of its office in the production in which it is engaged, by a single use, is called
circulating capital . . . Another large portion of capital, how-

---

[1] See chapter on " Property."

ever, consists in instruments of production of a more or
less permanent character, which produce their effect, not by
being parted with, but by being kept, and the efficacy of which
is not exhausted by a single use. . . . Capital which exists in
any of these durable shapes, and the return to which is spread
over a period of corresponding duration, is called fixed capital."

So that the distinction appears to consist in the number of
times a given commodity may be employed in the same
process, those which can be employed only once being called
circulating, those which can be employed more than once, fixed.

Now to me it seems that, although in ninety-nine cases out
of a hundred fixed capital suffices for more than one process,
and circulating capital for only one, yet these are but accidental
and not the essential characteristics of the two classes.

The real distinction lies deeper. It is this : those things
the eventual consumption of which is essential to the creation
of the required compound or new product form one class,
vaguely indicated by the term *circulating ;* those things the
eventual consumption of which is not essential, but only
accidental, to the creation of the required compound, form
another class—*fixed* capital. No doubt all capital is consumed,
but so is everything else ; the iron ladle required to stir this
molten metal soon wears out and must be renewed. If it wore
out in one use, as the wick of a candle is destroyed as fast as
the tallow, Mill would call it circulating capital. So with a
quill pen. One day's use destroys it. Yet the ladle,
the wick, and the pen are all (so far as they are
capital at all) fixed capital. Why ? Because, if they
never wore out at all, even after a million processes, so
far from being less useful, they would not only not impair
the product to which they contribute, but rather render it more
pure. The gold pen with which this is written has been in
use for many years and is in no wise worse than when it was new.
And so with a permanent wick in an oil-lamp, but not so with
the oil or tallow. If that were not changed, consumed, the
lamp or candle would give no light, the sempstress would not
see to work, and the product, shirt, or dress, would not be made.

The number of processes for which an article will serve is
quite immaterial to science ; it is a mere question of degree of

durability, and we can base upon it no such valuable philosophical classification as can be based upon the distinction between essentially and accidentally consumed capital. And here I may point out that this very distinction is the one which underlies the division of capital into *tools* and *materials*. Tools are exactly what I have defined as fixed or accidentally consumed capital. Materials are our circulating or essentially consumed capital. This discovery of identity, and the conception upon which the classes have hitherto been instinctively based, are of immense importance in the study of Plutology.

And now, in conclusion, we may here review, and, with the aid of our new light, with advantage scrutinise, Mill's four theorems concerning capital.

The first is that industry is limited by capital. Now if this means that the creation of new wealth is limited by the quantity of the materials which enter into its constitution, the so-called theorem is merely a truism. But if it means that it is limited by the quantity of capital *other than human* (which it evidently must do consistently with Mill's doctrines) it amounts to saying generally that where one of the elements is wanting the compound containing it cannot be produced: also a truism. However, it so happens that there are such compounds as combinations of labourers and not-capital, as, for example, a stone statue. Sculpture, provided the material used be not valuable, is an industry not limited by any capital other than labourers. According to Mill's own notion of capital, therefore, his first theorem is false.

The second theorem is that capital is the result of saving. Now in what conceivable sense can it be said of a new and useful invention that it is the result of saving? And yet it may be, and usually is, capital in the highest degree. Or how is a newly-found oil well the result of saving? And yet it is unquestionably capital. No doubt, in so far as articles capable of affording immediate gratification are by preference combined with others for the purpose of producing more valuable products these products are the result of saving ; and it is also true that most products do contain such saved elements. But we do not want half truths or accidental truths to stand for general or necessary truths ; and so judged the second theorem is false.

The third theorem is that capital is consumed. This proposition we have already discussed in treating of the division
into fixed and circulating capital. I have shown that it is
not of the essence of fixed capital to be consumed. All things
are ever changing of course. But it is no more essential to fixed
capital to wear out than it is to a silver teapot to contain a
small quantity of lead, indisputable though the fact may be as
a merely accidental fact. So that here we have a universal but
accidental proposition standing for an essential truth.

The fourth theorem is that a demand for commodities is
not a demand for labour. It is difficult to translate this into
scientific language, but, so far as it is intelligible, it seems to
be either a truism or misleading. Consider the two following
statements : A demand for iron ore is not a demand for limestone and coal. A demand for grapes is not a demand for
apples. There is a wide difference between the two negations,
for in the first case a demand for iron ore is accompanied by
a demand for limestone and coal invariably, and it may
roughly be said that a demand for the one is a demand for the
other two. To say that it is not so is to state a truism of the
weakest order, being based simply on the literal meaning of the
words. But in the case of the grapes the negation is of
a different character. A demand for grapes is not accompanied by a demand for apples, which is in nowise affected
thereby. If we criticise Mill's theorem in the first sense
then we have a miserable truism to deal with. A demand
for one thing is not, and cannot be, a demand for another.
But if we regard it in the second sense, and inquire
whether a demand for commodities is or is not invariably
accompanied by a demand for labourers, I contend that it
depends, in any given case, upon the answer to the question,
whether the commodities demanded are or are not capital
requiring the assistance of labourers in order to become capable
of affording gratification. If they are such capital, then
a demand for them *is* virtually a demand for labourers. If
they are not such capital, then a demand for them is *not*
a demand for labourers. We must condemn this theorem as
being either a truism or misleading.

There cannot be stronger testimony to the harmfulness of

loose thought and corresponding phraseology than is afforded
by the spectacle of a great logician like Mill propounding four
fundamental theorems as the basis of his work, of which it must
be said that the first is false, the second is false, the
third non-essential, and the fourth either a truism or
misleading.

CHAPTER VI

" CAN'T you let things alone ? " asks the comfortable capitalist in his easy-chair. " Let sleeping dogs lie. All is fairly well, if only reformers would but sit still." No ! there is a time for rest and a time for action. When the social forces are gradually shaping themselves, and their eventual tendency is undiscernible, the social tinker is out of place. His suggestions for change, though frequently prompted by kindly feeling, are all based on rule of thumb. He would amend the laws of nature on superior principles evolved from his own inner consciousness. Sometimes he labours in vain. His efforts end in naught. Sometimes he is successful in his immediate aims, and then his efforts end in untold mischief.

But when the body politic is in unstable equilibrium— when the fabric of society is shaken to its foundations ; when all the signs of the times point to imminent change, for better or for worse—then the true statesman is he who, before the inevitable crash comes, can so forecast the resultant of apparently conflicting forces as to be able to guide them at once and without unnecessary waste of energy and time into their destined channel. The navigator cannot make the wind, and the statesman cannot create the social current, but both can so utilise the force supplied by nature as to make for salvation rather than wreck. To-day presents such an occasion. To sit still and " wish for the day " means ruin. All over the civilised world he that hath ears to hear may listen to the mutterings of the coming storm. Riots in America; riots in Belgium;

riots in France; riots in Holland; riots even in tranquil
London,—all originating not with the scum and refuse of society,
but with honest, despairing workers clamouring for bread and
for work, and not knowing whither to turn; depression in trade
(despite the rose-coloured reports of Royal Commissions) of an
intensity and duration unprecedented in the history of
industrialism: here a strike, brought to a close by the slow
starvation of the strikers, only to be followed by another due
to impossible wages; there a lock-out, rendered necessary by
vanishing profits; everywhere discontent and wretchedness,
aggravated by class envy and glaring inequalities of distribution;
all these and a hundred other signs bode revolution. It must
come. It is for us to decide whether it shall be short, sharp,
and bloody, or peaceful and thorough. There is no alternative, and now that the people have taken the tiller into
their own hands, it is upon the people that the responsibility
must lie.

Probably the first thing in this country to strike an
observer, unused all his life to the strange phenomenon, would
be the spectacle of a large majority of human beings toiling all
day long and every day of their dreary existence in order that
a small minority may enjoy the proceeds of their work—
toiling, too, at wages avowedly based on a calculation of the
cost of "keeping body and soul together." Surely, if it were
not so tragical, the situation would be almost comical. Yet we
are asked to tremble at the approach of the revolution. Of
whom? Of those who tamely submit, almost without protest,
to this anomalous, this monstrous system of wagedom? Of
men who stand passively by to see the lives of their wives and
mothers and sisters crushed out of them beneath the car wheels
of Juggernaut Plutax? And this, too, is an age of cheap
literature, of gratis education, of rapid communication, and of
free meeting? Is it that the Englishman of to-day has too
much sense and too little pluck for revolution of the "blood and
iron" type? Or is it that he has hopes of a peaceful revolution and courage to wait for it? Perhaps.

But, first, what is the explanation of this singular economic
system? In accordance with what principle of justice does one
of two partners take all the profits and the other none? It

was many years ago pointed out by Ricardo, and has long been a well-established doctrine of political economy, that under the competitive system of trade, wages have a tendency to gravitate down to a certain limit which may be called the cost of subsistence. No sooner has a temporary rise taken place than it is immediately swallowed up by the increase of population. In short, population is limited by the demand for wage labour, and therefore it is absurd to suppose that average wages can for any considerable period of time exceed their normal amount. That amount, to be perfectly accurate, is simply this: the amount requisite to keep the workman in *sufficient* health, plus enough to enable him to rear up children to take his place when he is used up; and by "sufficient health" is meant, not enough for happiness, but enough to enable him to go through the average task required of him and the like of him. As Mill himself admits, "when by improvements in agriculture, the repeal of the corn-laws, or other such causes, the necessaries of life are cheapened . . . wages will fall at last, so as to leave the labourers no better off than before." So that whatever a workman may suppose himself to be saving and putting away over and above his cost of living must not be mistaken for profit. It is merely the refunding of the money spent on his own youth and training, or a sinking fund to pay for the unremunerative youth and training of his children, from whichever point of view we choose to regard it. In neither case can it be regarded as profit. He has no more to call his own at the end of the process than he had at the beginning. He has his own body for what it is worth; but so also the capitalist has his engine and fixed capital. True, he has been fed and kept during the process, but so has the engine been kept in repair and supplied with fuel. Again, if the capitalist is wise he has written off a certain sum—say ten per cent—for wear and tear of the engine, *i.e.* as a sinking fund wherewith to buy a new one when it is worn out. In all respects the economic position of the two is identical. The labourer and the engine are treated precisely alike. Then in what respect is the free labourer better off than the slave ? Let us face this question honestly. If we do not, posterity will. The truth is that economically the free labourer is no better off than a slave.

The *whole* of the profits of his contribution to production are
appropriated by the capitalist. The fruits of labour do not,
under the existing system, pass to the wage receiver. Moreover,
in one respect he is worse off than the slaves or even than the
horses of his employer. In the case of costly slaves on a sugar
plantation, and in the case of an English capitalist's horses, it
is found more economical to keep them in good condition and
to get a moderate amount of work out of them, rather than to
overwork and underfeed them and buy new ones when they are
worn out. With free men in an over-stocked labour market
this is not the case, or at least it is not believed to be the case
by the majority of employers, and the consequence is the
workers are usually worse treated than if they had to be bought
and sold outright.

Of course it is not necessary to remind English workers
that in spite of all this, wagedom is a great advance upon
slavery. Liberty is worth not only fighting for, but suffering
for. And after all, the European worker can choose his own
work and his own employer, and can in comparatively rare
cases even break the fetters of wagedom and himself become
an employer. Indeed, as will be seen, wagedom is a necessary
and beneficent transitional system between the serfdom of the
past and the freedom of the future. The history of the con-
version of the serf into the wage receiver is a proud chapter in
the story of civilisation.

But though a necessary state, wagedom is not a permanent
state. Signs of a new order of industrialism are already
apparent on all sides. The workers are chafing under the
unfair distribution of wealth which clearly results from the
present arrangement. Even the orthodox economists are
trying hard to explain it away, while a few independent thinkers
are busy seeking for the foundations of the new order.

And what is it which the orthodox school have discovered
as a palliative for the "iron law of wages"? They have
established the beautiful doctrine of the "standard of comfort."
This bewitching tribute to sentiment is one of the master-
pieces of modern economics. According to this soothing
theory each class of workers tends to fix on some standard of
living below which it will not condescend to exist. Rather

than live at a lower scale of luxury individual members of the class will pass out of existence altogether, or, at least, they will cease to increase and multiply.

The observation on which the doctrine is supposed to be based is that certain classes of workers appear to exercise this self-restraint. Medical men, lawyers, engineers, bankers, etc., do not allow competition so to swell their ranks that their incomes are driven down to the cost of subsistence, or, as a class, anywhere near it. Now, if this is so with highly skilled workers such as those named, it must be so, it is urged, in a less noticeable degree with workers of less skilled grades.

It does not occur to these academic writers that there is a simpler explanation of the observed fact than that of a tacit class-determination not to sink beneath a fixed standard of luxury. A very little reflection will suffice to satisfy us that the main reason why the competition between, say, railway contractors is not keen enough to reduce the whole class to starvation pay is that only persons with a very large reserve of capital to start with can compete at all. The same remark applies to bankers and merchants, and as for lawyers and medical men, quite apart from their State-guaranteed monopoly, a considerable initial outlay is necessary before any one is in a position to enter the lists of competitors, and that initial outlay means sunk capital, so that that which keeps up their average remuneration is not any fixed resolve on the part of these classes of workers to prevent competition from lowering their standard of comfort, but the inability of those not already enjoying such standard to swell the roll of competitors.

When we come down to that class of work which does not at present require the possession of any capital (beyond the worker's own body) the case is very different. The mere exercise of a little imagination might have saved the professors from falling into this absurd fallacy. Let us suppose that wool-sorters (for example) form the excellent resolution not to allow their wages to fall below five shillings a day. What happens? Trade is depressed; wages fall; wool-sorters are obstinate. Men out of work troop in and offer their services at four-and-six. It is clear there are more sorters than there is wool to be sorted. Now, are we asked to suppose that

those who are out of work are to starve rather than to lower
the wage of their class ? or that those who have work are to
retire and starve in their stead ? or that both are to stand out
solid for the old wage or go on strike ? This is only the
dream of the unionist, not the fact of real life. But, says the
economist, so long as wages remain below five shillings the
sorters must refrain from marriage, so as to keep down their
numbers. Can he really believe that this is done by any class
of men, any particular class of workers ? and if it were—if
the wages of wool-sorters could be maintained at a higher rate
than the wages of those occupied in kindred pursuits—does he
suppose that there would be no flow from the ranks of outsiders into an occupation better paid and requiring no more
skill than their own ?

The more we examine this sublimated hypothesis the
clearer it becomes that in order to give it a shadow of
credibility we must at least include the whole of the unskilled
workers in a single class, and even hesitate to place in a
different class those whose work requires but little skill
or original outlay ; but when this is done the doctrine falls
to the ground. Facts are all against it. And even regarded
as a bit of good advice it is simply disgusting in its cruel
cynicism.

One of the most pitiful spectacles in the labour controversy is that presented by certain economists who are constantly piling figures on figures to show that the lot of the
working classes has materially improved within the last forty
years. They seldom choose a shorter period, and never choose
a longer. Whoever presents these periodic budgets, they are
invariably received by a delighted circle of capitalists with a
willing conviction. Vainly do the workers protest that they
cannot see it, that the memory of the oldest amongst them
fails to bear out the contention ; vainly do the socialists and
others point out that the improvement is more in appearance
than in reality—that three shoddy coats of to-day last no
longer than one of the olden times, that rents are higher and
meat dearer. The late Mr. Lloyd Jones may knock the whole
fabric of " evidence " into a cocked hat, as he did at the
Industrial Remuneration Conference of 1885. No matter ;

on the next occasion up comes the brazen image and down go the worshippers in adoration before it, and even trade unionists cry Amen.

It is useless to point out to them that even if their statements were true of the last forty years their conclusion would not be warranted. The immense strides in the applied sciences, and more especially in the means of locomotion, of quickly-distributed information, and of world-wide commerce, are alone sufficient to account for any observed temporary aberration from the Ricardian law during the period chosen. Let these disturbing causes disappear and the effects must disappear with them. Water is not always level, but when the storm has passed away, and the atmospheric disturbances abated, the waves settle down again into the old plane. Then, again, these theorists forget to compare the wages of the whole working population of to-day with those of forty years ago. They single out a few trades, and those chiefly in which machinery has wrought great and sudden changes. And they forget also to take into account the perquisites and privileges which pertain to the state of decaying serfdom. These are not to be mourned for, because they savour of slavery, but they had their economic value.

But the best answer to the allegation that wages are better than they were, and tend permanently to become so, is this : it is à *priori* impossible. The mathematical enthusiast who sits up night after night measuring disc after disc, plate after plate, hoop after hoop, in the vain endeavour to square the circle by exhaustive induction, receives his fair share of ridicule. It has been proved à *priori* that the ratio of the circumference to the radius of a circle is incommensurable, and there the matter ends.

Similarly the tendency of wages to sink to the subsistence level has been demonstrated à *priori*, and those who seek to disprove it by an appeal to experiment or observation are precisely in the foolish position of the squarer of the circle. They deserve an equal share of derision. To refuse to listen to argument is a dangerous habit of mind, and we should be slow to give way to it, but surely when a man gravely undertakes to prove that the earth is flat, or that two and two make five, or that the ratio of circumference to diameter is exactly 3·14159, or that he himself is Noah and remembers building the Ark, in such cases it is a saving of time to laugh him out of Court, especially if his " proof " extends through some folios of statistics and volumes of calculations based on unverifiable estimates and groundless assumptions.

But not only are workers kicking against the wage system ; not only are our " economists " ashamed of it, and reduced to weaving moonbeams to clothe its hideousness ; not only are philanthropists trying to devise some new and better system as a substitute for it, but even men of business and employers of labour are themselves beginning to admit, in deed if not in word, that the present arrangement is not quite all that it should be. Employers as well as employed seem to allow to a certain extent that wages should somehow vary with the rate of profits. This admission, opposed though it is to the fundamental doctrine on which the existing system is based, seems to be nearly universal. Arbitrations between masters and men are invariably conducted on the assumption that if profits are higher wages should be higher also. The sliding scale by which wages are made to vary with the price of the product is another instance of the admission of this new principle. So also are the co-operative societies that are springing up on all sides. In fine, there seems to be floating in the air, as it were, a notion (it can hardly be called a theory) that labour payment should somehow vary with profits. The notion is vague, it owns no parentage, it is associated with no great name ; it is perhaps the spontaneous outgrowth of an intuitively far-seeing public opinion, which is so often the precursor of the eventually accepted philosophical theory.

Now, one of two things : either this new principle is unsound, vicious, and arbitrary, or else the whole modern system of wagedom is rotten. There is no alternative. Ricardo's position is unassailable. Wages must and always will gravitate to the inevitable limit in spite of all the temporary tinkerings of trade unions and of the legislature. As well try to elude the tendency of water to find its level as that of wages to oscillate about the Ricardian limit. Let us therefore make up our minds to look forward to the eternal

semi-starvation of the great majority of our fellow-countrymen
as the necessary consequence of the laws of nature, or else set
to work to discover some substitute for wagedom.

Ferdinand Lassalle and some others of Ricardo's more
intelligent disciples, finding themselves upon the horns of this
dilemma, broke away from the orthodox school and proposed
to solve the great problem by abolishing property in the agents
of production altogether.   This is the socialistic solution.
English Radicals have proposed and carried out a number of
legislative measures calculated or intended to relieve much of
the temporary ill effects of keen competition — measures
regulating the hours of labour, the ages at which children
may perform certain tasks, the modes of carrying on some
trades, the seasons of general holiday-making, etc.   A strong
impulse has also been given in this country (but more
especially in France) to the system of "profit-sharing," as
it is styled.   Again, co-operative production societies indicate
another solution, and finally, there is the "capitalisation
of labour" to be explained in these pages.   Let us examine
these proposed measures of reform in their order, bearing
in mind that all alike assume the instability of the existing
order, and the necessity for some change in the relation
subsisting between the so-called "employer and employed,"
that is to say, between the manual workers and the captains
or organisers of industry.

And first, what is the remedy put forward by socialism ?
and what are the grounds on which it is based ?   It is impossible to go thoroughly into this great question in the space
which can here be allotted to it, but in order that there may
be no appearance of misrepresentation it may be well to accept
the words and arguments of a well-known English exponent
of the doctrine.   "Socialism,"[1] in the opinion of this writer,
"founds part of its disapproval of the present industrial system
on the very facts pointed out by orthodox economists.   It
accepts Ricardo's iron law of wages, and recognising that wages
tend to fall to the minimum on which the labourer can exist,
it declares against the system of the hiring of workers for a

---

[1] "The Socialist Movement," by Annie Besant, *Westminster Review*, July
1886.

fixed wage, and the appropriation of their produce by the hirer."

So far the socialist and the individualist reformer are at one. But the former draws an inference which the latter is unable to accept :—

"Socialism declares that natural agents ought not to be private property, and that no idle class should be permitted to stand between land and labour and demand payment of a tax before it will permit the production of wealth. . . . What, then, is the remedy proposed by socialism ? It is to deal with capital as it deals with land ; to abolish the capitalist as well as the landlord, and to bring the means of production as well as the natural agents on which they are used under the control of the community. . . . Interest on capital has no place in socialism."

This is plain speaking. Socialists differ among themselves as to the precise nature of the end to be aimed at, and still more as to the means to be adopted for the attainment of that end, but the above summary clearly states that which they may be said to hold in common.

It is but just to socialists to admit that if there are any fallacies lurking beneath the arguments on which their creed is founded, those fallacies are shared and were formulated by the orthodox economists themselves, with whose fundamental principles, as the reviewer admits, socialism does not quarrel. Are there any such fallacies ? and if so, what are they ? I think there are several.

One is, that the present social system (in so far as it is individualistic) recognises absolute proprietary right as something higher than the *salus populi*. "The whole nation is at the mercy of a comparatively small class so long as it consents to admit that this class has *a right* to own the ground on which the nation lives." But the nation consents to nothing of the kind, and never has so consented. The institution of private property (in land and in everything else) is merely maintained as being the best-known arrangement for ensuring the most desirable and equitable distribution of wealth which is possible to humanity. Nor is private property regarded as absolute right. To begin with, land ownership is unknown to English law, and in practice the wishes of so-called landowners are not allowed to stand between the land and the

M

general welfare, whether a street is to be cut through a congested district, or a railway through an insufficiently opened up part of the country. All that individualism claims for the landowner or the chattelowner is, that after deducting all national claims—when the true, highest interests of the community have all been considered—the residual powers over land and over chattels shall be vested in some person called the proprietor. By this plan it is believed, after an experience of ages, that more utility will be squeezed out of the thing so "owned" than could be extracted from it under any known form of communal holding. I think it was Dr. Siemens who said that if he found an invention in the gutter he would give it to some one, he would grant him a patent for it, in the certainty that by so doing, by making it private property, it would have a better chance of coming to perfection and benefiting the community than if it were left to such community in common. And the same argument has since been applied to land ownership by Lord Bramwell. How many of the greatest inventions of modern times would have been perfected if there had been no patent law ? Whenever anything whatever is owned by two or more persons having diverse interest in it, some of its utilities instead of being enjoyed by all are actually enjoyed by none. Every one's experience must bear witness to this.

It is not only the individualist who holds this view. Some of the most advanced statesmen in this and other countries contend that property in land stimulates the energies of the workers and increases enormously the productivity of the soil. " Peasant proprietorship " has been the cry of the most zealous land reformers of the century, of whom J. S. Mill was chief. Occupying ownership is now the cure put forward for the incurable by both political parties in Ireland. Socialists consistently denounce it. But even Mr. Henry George protests against any further land nationalisation than a heavy land-tax, for the same reason, viz. that separate ownership in land stimulates production. In fine, rent is the cheapest form in which payment for certain necessary services can be made by the community. Any other mode of obtaining those services would be comparatively extravagant. And the same observation applies in part to the payment of interest on capital of other kinds. It would be impossible for authors to prove an "abstract right" to a monopoly of the copy of their works. All they can show is, that the community gains more than it loses by granting them what is called "copyright." The hostility of socialists towards absolute rights which have no existence reveals a weak place in their philosophy.

Another socialistic fallacy (though it is not shared by all socialists) is that co-operation is socialistic. It is nothing of the sort, by their own definitions. Co-operation is the origin and sustaining cause of civilisation. There are two kinds, voluntary and compulsory. The latter only is socialistic. In voluntary co-operation there is nothing whatever of socialism. Trade unionism as such is not socialistic. It has frequently adopted socialistic methods, and even now in this country supports socialistic measures, but in itself it is merely voluntary co-operation. This mistake is so commonly made that it is necessary to expose it at every turn.

One of the chief of the socialistic fallacies is that *all* wealth is the result of labour. It is further held that the value of everything is proportionate to the labour that has been bestowed on it (two contradictory propositions) and that *therefore* the labourers have a moral right to all existing wealth, an inference which betrays an amount of logical ineptitude hardly to be expected of serious thinkers.

These three remarkable contentions may be considered together. To begin with, *all* wealth is not the result of labour. Wealth is everything which is useful to man. Thus air and water are wealth. But it is unfair to impose a definition. Clearly by "wealth" socialists mean that which is useful and *also valuable* (that is, rare enough to be the subject of contention). So that we have only to add the quality of rarity or difficulty of attainment to any useful thing and straightway it becomes a product of labour. Some defenders of this article of faith seem to consider their case proved if they can show that some slight amount of exertion was necessary to the creation of the thing cited, or even to its enjoyment. If valuable timber is washed down a swollen river it has to be dragged out of the water and cut up before it is useful. If a savage gathers a ripe peach he must reach out his hand, or walk to the tree and open his mouth, and so on. If a large diamond is found by a digger on his first day at the fields, we are told not only that he has to pick it up, but also that we must remember how many other diggers have been toiling for weeks and found nothing.

Of course, apart from all this rubbish, the truth is that a large proportion of valuable things contain a large element of labour in their composition, and almost always some small element of original wealth. A ruby ring contains much original wealth and comparatively little labour. A violin contains much labour and very little original wealth. Other things vary in their composition.

But this abstract theory, baseless though it is, would not deserve mention were it not, firstly, that it is a legacy (a veritable *damnosa hereditas*) from Ricardo, and, secondly, that it has been made the foundation of the ridiculous practical contention in connection with which it is always mentioned, to wit, that all wealth being the result of labour, and labour only, the manual workers of to-day have a moral claim to all wealth.

Now, if we admit that by far the greater portion of wealth contains a vastly predominant proportion of labour element, which is the fact—nay, if we go so far as to admit that all wealth is entirely composed of the labour element, which is *not* the fact—how does this affect the practical inference ? A century ago, let us suppose, there were two workmen, Smith and Brown. Smith was a good, steady, and industrious worker ; Brown was an idle fellow. Smith managed to put by a little money and to leave his son enough to set himself up as an employer. Smith the second inherits his father's good qualities, and converts his competency into a fortune. Brown leaves nothing, and Brown the second follows in his father's footsteps. Now comes the third generation. Smith the third begins life as a wealthy man. He has no occasion to work with his hands. The labour of his ancestors enables him to live in idleness if he chooses, instead of which he applies himself to the study of the sciences, or the fine arts, or politics. He invents an ingenious labour-saving machine, or makes discoveries in astronomy or chemistry which add to the world's stock of knowledge; or he composes a fine epic or a grand oratorio; or he takes a seat in Parliament and labours for the freedom and elevation of his fellow-countrymen. Brown the third begins life as an unskilled labourer; he digs and wheels and carries. Suddenly up springs the socialist. "This won't do," says he; "you, Brown, have a right to Smith's wealth; it is all the result of labour, and you are a labourer, while he is not; this anomaly must be put right." Could any contention be more absurd or more unjust? The fallacy consists in concluding that, because the creator of wealth has a right to the fruits of his labour, therefore existing labourers have a right to the fruits of past labour. Now, the missing link in the chain of this reasoning has not altogether escaped the attention of some of the more logical thinkers of the school. "We admit," say some of them, "that if Smith the first had gone on living and working for a century, and had himself amassed the whole of the fortune, he would have been justified in resting on his oars and enjoying the fruits of his work; but instead of that, this fortune has come into the hands of Smith the third, who has never done a stitch of bread-winning work in his life. This is unjust to society, upon whom he relies for sustenance."

It is clear that this further contention strikes at the root of gift and bequest. According to this view it logically follows that no man has the right to enjoy the fruits of another man's labour even with the consent and by the desire of that other, not even though the two men are father and son; and the reason alleged is that a man who appears to be living on his capital is in reality living on the labour of those around him. At this point socialists are divided in counsel. Some would (most illogically) permit gift but prohibit bequest. They fail to see the impossibility of distinguishing in practice between the two. Of *donatio mortis causa* they have probably never heard, nor of the numerous devices by which legacy and succession duty have been eluded. But perhaps these questions are a little too practical for the bulk of that

somewhat dreamy school.[1]   However this may be, those who
would prohibit either gift or bequest, or both, base their action
on what may be styled *the* socialist fallacy *par excellence,*
viz. that interest is necessarily paid out of the fruits of the
labour of to-day.   On this point I must be pardoned for again
quoting from our Westminster reviewer :—

   " If a man possesses three or four thousand pounds he can
invest them, and live all his life long on the interest without
ever doing a stroke of honest work, and can then bequeath to
some one else the right to live in idleness, and so on in
perpetuity.   Money in the capitalist system is like the
miraculous oil in the widow's cruse—it can always be spent
and never exhausted.   A man in sixty years will have
received in interest at five per cent three times his original
fortune, and although he may have spent the interest, and thus
have spent every penny of his fortune three times over, he will
yet possess his fortune as large as it was when he began.   He
has consumed in commodities three times the sum originally
owned, and yet is not one penny the worse.   Other people
have laboured for him, fed him, clothed him, housed him, and
he has done nothing in exchange."

   Here truly we have the socialist fallacy in a nut-shell.
The illustration is a good one.   Capital is compared to the oil
in the widow's cruse in the story.   A truer comparison could
not be found.   Capital fructifies.   A man who lives on the
interest on his capital costs nobody else anything whatever.
If he and his capital were annihilated to-day nobody would be
any the richer to-morrow.   If he lived on half the interest on his
capital his wealth would go on increasing year by year at no
cost to any one.   It is not true that " it can *only* be increased
by other people's labour being left unpaid for while he is paid
twice over for his."   It is not true that it can only be
increased by other people's labour being left even *partly*
unpaid for.   It grows of itself like a tree.

   Again, I find myself at issue not only with socialists, but
with our " orthodox political economists."   When the socialist

---

[1] I do not wish to be too sweeping in these charges.   I have read some very
ingenious suggestions on this subject published by the Fabian Society, but though
ingenious they are to my mind highly unsatisfactory and impracticable.

triumphantly asserts that "capital always has been, and always must be, obtained by the partial confiscation of the results of labour," there is not a single economist living or dead who can be called to refute the statement. All their writings without exception, from Adam Smith downwards, either imply the conclusion or express the premises from which the conclusion must logically follow. There is no escape. The reasoning is faultless. Marx has strung the links together in a chain without a flaw. Yet what is the consequence of accepting the proposition? Two courses of action only are open to us. We may go on on our present lines, recognising the fact that capitalists are robbers living on the extorted toil of others, that *le propriété c'est le vol*, or we may abolish property. Political economists, which shall we do? You leave us no alternative. All capital you tell us is the result of labour and abstinence. Now, abstinence cannot create ; it can leave unconsumed, but it cannot increase what exists. *Therefore* all capital whatever, on your own showing, must be the result of labour. If so, clearly the increment of capital which results from a successful industrial operation, and which you are pleased to call profits, must really be the result of labour *alone.* Capital left to accumulate at interest must increase, on your own arguments, by having laid upon it layer after layer of the fruits of labour—the labour not of the owner of the capital, but of *other people.*

Leaving our orthodox friends to get out of the mess as best they can, let us pass at once to the true solution.

Capital fructifies. On the average in this country the total wealth employed in production (not counting the value of the thirty millions of workers at slave prices) increases annually by about three per cent. In order that wealth may increase it is necessary that, instead of being enjoyed, it should be destroyed—that each portion should be thrown into the crucible, so to speak, together with other portions. The compound resulting from the synthesis is worth either more or less than the original elements. If less, the process is not likely to be often repeated ; if more, the increment of value is called profit. One of the elements cast into the melting-pot, not without *risk*, is labour force. The proportion of this element is sometimes large and sometimes small. Whoever undertakes the risk of casting bread upon the waters must suffer the loss, if there is a loss, and must pocket the profit if there is a profit. This seems just, and its expediency is demonstrated by experience. Naturally profiting by experience, cautious men engage in those processes which have heretofore resulted in a profit, and therefore the balance on all the operations in the year is a favourable one. *On the average* every £100 worth of wealth employed, in production rather than consumption comes out worth about £103.[1] Clearly, if it were a mere "toss-up" whether profit or loss would accrue, the average would be nil : wealth would be stationary ; capital would not be invested ; and the national consumption would destroy the whole of it within a few years.

Now, if an idle man, not caring to take even the trouble to look into the chances of his investments, were to divide his capital up into as many fractions as there are industries (a hypothetical supposition, of course), and to invest one fraction in each industry, he would lose on some ventures and gain on others ; on the balance, the chances are that he would gain about three per cent on the whole lot, taking good and bad together. Now this operation of investing *without risk* (*i.e.* with no greater risk than is involved in trusting to the national sanity) is called "putting out at interest." By investing on what is called absolute security we are really investing at average national profit. Economic interest is average profit—average profit after the elimination of the element of *risk*.

Any increased gain over and above interest on capital is the reward of, not abstinence, but risk. Business men as a rule write off a certain part of gross profits as interest, because they well know that such portion does not represent the reward of risk or of skill in planning the investment, but merely the normal average *growth of capital*. This custom of business men has led political economists to invent the most fantastic and

---

[1] I assume for the sake of simplicity that the operation lasts a year, like most agricultural processes. When the operation is quicker the average profit is proportionately smaller, and when the operation is lengthier the profit is proportionately higher. Average profits, however, in the several well-tried processes vary for other reasons which need not be gone into here—v. *Wealth of Nations*.

misleading definitions and explanations of interest. No wonder
our captains of industry make common cause with the working
classes in denouncing and despising the methods and conclusions
of this pseudo-science. Practical men have long since ceased to
attach any importance to the slip-shod twaddle of those who
pose as the theorists of the art of wealth-producing ; but, oddly
enough, the socialists have hastened to detect and take advantage of their convenient and suitable vapourings and sententious
dogmas. Amongst other handy weapons they have seized upon
the "orthodox" definition of capital. "What is capital ? "
asks the socialist reviewer, "and how has it come into existence ? " The answer is supplied at once by the "orthodox."
" Capital is any wealth which is employed for profit. On this
there is no dispute." Is there not ? A glance at the conflicting
definitions of a dozen of the chief representatives of political
economy would somewhat shatter this comfortable faith. Why,
Mill, Say, Fawcett, M'Culloch, Bastiat, and a whole crowd of
other accepted authorities all give definitions, and *no two are
alike.* I refer not to the wording but to the sense and meaning. However, Senior is chosen, and he says, " Economists are
agreed that *whatever* gives a profit is called capital." In the
first place they are not agreed, and in the second it would not
matter if they were, as the proposition is unintelligible. What
does he mean by "gives a profit " ? Does he mean to say that
those particular things which, having been employed for the
purpose of production, actually have resulted in a profit, were
or might have been called capital, while similar things employed
in a losing speculation were not capital ? Or does he mean
that certain general classes of things which are *fit* to be employed in production are capital ? Or does he (with Fawcett)
mean that things which are *intended* to be devoted to production, whether suitable or not, by being exchanged for suitable
things, are capital ? Or does he mean anything at all ? I
suppose the wind that propels the ship or drives the mill-sail
"gives a profit." Is it capital ? Money spent in sinking a
shaft in the expectation of finding coal, and finding none, gives
no profit. Is it capital ? The time spent in analysing such
" definitions " as this and the like of it certainly gives no profit.
I must be pardoned therefore for stating dogmatically what I

have shown in the foregoing chapter that capital is all that wealth whose value is due to the demand for it as an element of production, and not for the purposes of direct consumption. It follows that labourers (or labour force, if preferred) are themselves capital, and every labourer is himself a capitalist to the extent of possessing a valuable machine whose market value is due to the demand for workers as agents of production.

This effectually disposes of one logical objection to supplanting wage payment by any form of profit-sharing. "Capital and labour being two distinct and, in a sense, opposed agents of production, there must be something wrong about a practical plan which confounds them together in respect of their remuneration." And if we admit the truth of the premiss we cannot well refuse to accept the inference. If capital and labour actually are distinct agents of production, as political economists assure us, then there is something unphilosophical in classing them together for the purpose of apportioning their respective shares in the new product. In that case labour must be content with its wages, and capital must take the whole of the profits, and the situation resulting is the one we all see before us, and which is so graphically described by Mrs. Besant.

"Here is this unpropertied class, this naked proletariat, face to face with landlord and capitalist, who hold in their grip the means of subsistence. It must reach those means of subsistence or starve. The terms laid down for its acceptance are clear and decisive : 'We will place within your hands the means of existence if you will produce sufficient to support us as well as yourselves, and if you will consent that the whole of your produce, over that which is sufficient to support you in a hardy, frugal life, shall be the property of us and of our children. If you are very thrifty, very self-denying, and very lucky, you may be able to save enough out of your small share of your produce to feed yourself in your old age, and so avoid falling back on us. Your children will tread the same mill-round, and we hope you will remain contented with the position in which Providence has placed you, and not envy those born to a higher lot.' Needless to say, the terms are accepted by a proletariat ignorant of its own strength, and the way to profit is open to landlord and capitalist."

Having examined the socialist remedy and the arguments on which it is based, let us now turn to the neo-radical remedy.

The neo-radical is of the thoroughly English type of thinker who never accepts any principle except " to a certain limited extent, don't you know." He is always pointing out that " a line must be drawn somewhere," but *where* he never seems to know or care, so that it is drawn somewhere. He believes in self-help and *laissez-faire* " to a certain limited extent." He also believes in State interference and socialism " to a certain limited extent." He is the incarnation of the spirit of compromise, even where compromise is impossible. But being the resultant, so to speak, of robust English common sense and of crass ignorance and lopsided education, he naturally finds himself in an increasing majority in the country along with the successive passing of the three great Reform Acts. Consequently we have to deal with the neo-radical remedy not as the consistent and well-thought-out nostrum of doctrinaires, but as the half-hammered-out jumble of conflicting schemes and " dodges " of practical politicians. Of course, if these were confined to paper, no one would give them so much as a passing glance. One would as soon think of catechising Hodge as to his theory of the Cosmos, as of inquiring into the political *principles* of the neo-radical, the muddle-headed, knee-deep State socialist. He has none, of course ; but he has succeeded in carrying into effect what we must, I suppose, call his ideas. We have had some half century of increasing State socialism, not in the form of a creed to addle the brains of fanatics, but in the form of actual operative legislation—of practical politics. Perhaps on a survey of all these odds and ends of " beneficent legislation " one is able to extract something like a pervading notion, viz. the principle of attacking evil on the spot wherever it shows itself, whether in the form of want, of misery, of crime, of discontent, or of sin. If a hole appears fill it up; if an excrescence shows itself cut it off. Direct local application, as opposed to general hygienic treatment, is the neo-radical's watchword. " Are you suffering from headache ? " he asks, " then have a pick-me-up." " Is that a wart ? Cut it off." " There is a rash on your chest. A cold douche will throw it in and cause it to disappear." And so on. He never inquires whether you are suffering from bad diet or unhealthy habits of life, or whether all your ailments may not be effects of the

same cause.   He has assumed the name of Radical on the
lucus a non lucendo principle, because he never goes to the
roots of the malady.   With him to arrest the symptoms is to
cure the disease.   If some parents send their little ones too
young into the dark mines and clattering factories, he sends
inspectors to turn them out again.   It never occurs to him to
inquire what dire necessities have concurred to drive parents
to such cruel extremities, or whether, if due to sheer hard-
heartedness, the demoralisation of the workers may not be
attributed to some deep-seated social disorder.   If parental
love is not strong enough to ensure the welfare of the children
he has no hesitation in substituting State love for it.   The
effects of weakening the family affections are unknown to him
as recorded in the history of the past.   He has probably never
even heard of Sparta.   As to its probable effects in the future
they do not present themselves to his frigid imagination.
Naturally, if he is not afraid to meddle with the delicate framework of family life, it is not likely that he will keep his hands
off the somewhat rougher systems of industrial co-operation.
Every trade has some screw loose ; growing organisations take
time and experience to attain to perfection.   But the neo-
radical has no patience to wait ; he will cure the defects at
once himself.   Are sailors occasionally drowned at sea ?   It is
clearly due to overlading.   He will cure all that, so he takes
his bit of chalk and draws his load-line.   " Now," says he to
the ship-owner, " you may not load above that."   A few years
elapse ; the new legislation has been in full working order all
the time, and lo ! the number of seamen lost at sea has increased.
What is to be done ?   Oh ! it is all as plain as a pike-staff to
our neo-radical : it is over-insurance that does it.   We must
pass a short Act of Parliament to stop that.   It is a noteworthy
fact that if the matter to be dealt with is shipping, it is sure
to be taken in hand by some one (perhaps a Derbyshire coal-
owner) who has never seen the sea in his life.   If factories
want looking to, the work is undertaken by some noble earl
whose experience of factory work is limited to being " shown
round the premises," as Catherine of Russia was shown round
the happy village greens during the famine.   If shop hours
want regulating the proper neo-radical for the job is some

barrister out of work. The education of the people falls to the
care of some self-made lace manufacturer, whose own education
reflects more credit on himself than on his teachers. I well
remember that the demand for more mines regulation legislation was most strenuously advocated by a London journeyman
tailor ; while most of the happy ideas for reforming agricultural
relations emanate from *Birmingham.*

The reason for this strange allotment of duties is obvious.
The man who knows most about the business to be reformed,
knows too well the difficulties to be overcome and the impossibility of effecting the end aimed at. The young subaltern, who
bungles his theodolite and votes fortification stultification,
would undertake the conquest of China with a light heart.
Have you never heard a little boy of ten summers say what he
would do if he found himself surrounded in a wood by a gang
of robbers ? If not, ask one, and you will find the germ of
neo-radicalism : it is a compound of self-confidence and blissful
ignorance.

It is usually taken for granted that neo-radical legislation,
whether good or bad for the country as a whole, is at least an
unqualified boon to the wage receivers. Without inquiring
into the general results of such measures, let us see how the
working classes are affected by them. To begin with the
Poor Law, apart from its possible utility as a safety-valve against
revolution, there can be no doubt that nothing operates
with so deadening effect upon charity as compulsion ; and,
after all, true charity is sometimes good for both giver and
receiver.

But neither should the demoralising effects of State charity
upon its recipients be lost sight of. In the present state of
the Poor Law these effects are somewhat toned down, and
for a vivid and unmistakable illustration of the consequences of pauperisation we should refer to the times when
the principle was carried out consistently, that is to say,
before 1834.

The famous 43d of Elizabeth had been amplified by the
passing of East's Act in 1815, under which relief was granted
by the justices as a matter of course on the mere application
of the pauper or professing pauper. " The administration and

operation of the state of the law thus established quickly
absorbed so large and so increasing a part of the public resources, and brought about so prevailing an amount of idleness, improvidence, insolence, turbulence, and vice, that nine-
teen years from the passing of East's Act it was found
necessary to pass a large remedial measure in order to prevent
the destruction of landed property, the diversion of capital
from the cultivation of the land, and the utter demoralisation
and pauperisation of the great mass of the population—to
prevent, in short, national ruin." [1]

The same writer expresses the opinion that the Report of
the Poor Law Inquiry Commission, together with the evidence
appended, deserves to be read by every one who wishes to
learn the manner in which a law of compulsory relief affects
the material and social welfare of the poorer classes. In the
words of the Report, " It appears to the pauper that Government
has undertaken to repeal in his favour the ordinary laws of
nature ; to enact that children shall not suffer for the mis-
conduct of their parents; that no one shall lose the means of
comfortable subsistence, whatever be his indolence, prodigality,
or vice ; in short, that the penalty which after all must be
paid by *some one* for idleness and improvidence is to fall, not
on the guilty party or on his family, but on the ratepayers."

Nor does all this apply only to a time when the principle
of compulsory charity was carried to an inordinate extreme.
" Still," to follow Mr. Pretyman, " the man who might find
employment if he felt that it were necessary to his subsistence,
or the man who is reduced to want by self-indulgence, can tax
the public for his support. Still the woman who has parted
with her virtue can cast upon the ratepayers the burden of
maintaining her offspring. Still men who are in receipt of
permanent parish relief marry with the result that child after
child is born and reared in a state of pauperism, and frequently
to an inheritance of disease. Still is early and improvident
marriage encouraged by the law. Still the husband can, by
deserting his wife and children, throw their maintenance upon
the public."

Next in importance to the State supply of the necessaries

[1] *Dispauperisation*, by J. R. Pretyman, M.A., Longmans, Green, and Co.

of life to those who are individually in a state of absolute
destitution comes the supply at less than cost price of certain
necessaries and commodities, and even luxuries, to the poor as
a whole class.   It is a fact, for instance, that in some poor
neighbourhoods like the East End of London, water is supplied
at less than cost price.   It is obvious that the water companies
are compelled to charge their other customers more than they
otherwise would in order to cover this loss.   The argument put
forward in defence of this course is a very strong one, whether
we regard it as sufficient or not.   It is said that if the poor
have to pay for water *ad valorem* they naturally economise
as much as possible, and more than is consistent with the
sanitary condition of the neighbourhood.   If so, it may possibly
be a wise insurance on the part of society to supply the water
at less than the cost of delivery.   But the inhabitants of these
poor localities must not suppose that they obtain any pecuniary
gain by the arrangement.

Similarly with cheap trains and cheap dwellings, which
may be considered together.   Whenever the optimists begin to
glory over enhanced wages " during the last forty years," the
workers (especially London workers) very properly reply : Yes,
but look at the enhanced rents.   It ought to be obvious to the
workers that if an employer wants hands at a particular spot
he must pay such wages as will enable his workpeople to pay
the rent demanded at or near that spot, or else to pay the railway fare from a more distant and cheaper locality.   If rents in
the neighbourhood come down, down come wages.   If by competition, or improvements in mechanical knowledge, or by compulsory Cheap Trains Acts, or any other cause, railway travelling to and from the spot is rendered cheaper, down go wages.
That neo-radicals should offer Artisans' Dwellings Acts to the
people is intelligible enough, but that they should be backed
up by intelligent socialists who accept the " iron law of wages,"
and who therefore must know that the employer will necessarily
gobble up all that his workpeople may appear to gain from low
rents or cheap trains, passes all understanding.   However, so
it is.   To the workman himself who will but consider the
question in the light of common sense it must appear abun-
dantly evident that so long as the manual workers put up with

the wage system, all neo-radical sops of this nature are the merest mockery. To be plain, the employer of labour, who votes for measures of this character in the House of Commons, while he is offering fine phrases to his victims with his tongue in his cheek, is in reality merely offering himself a handsome present at the expense of the nation. But if he thus pleases the working-class voters, and puts money into his pocket at the same time without incurring the censure of any one, who shall find fault with him ? He is asked for bread and he gives a stone ; he is asked for an egg and he gives a scorpion ; but he gets the donce's best thanks for his generosity, and pockets a round sum into the bargain. Verily make to yourselves friends of the mammon of unrighteousness, for they know on which side their bread is buttered.

When we come to what may be called State-doled luxuries the advantage to the working classes becomes still less apparent. Free libraries, free picture galleries, free museums, all paid for out of the State treasury or out of the rates, are probably a boon to those who have time and leisure to make ample use of them. But whether the Northumbrian miner or the Galway peasant ever receives his *quid pro quo* for the hundreds of thousands of pounds raised by taxation and spent on " pictures of national interest " is a question which the miner and the peasant must answer for themselves. It may be that membership of a community which possesses such treasures, even without the hope of ever catching a glimpse of them, is in itself a sufficient reward.

I forget how much over eighty thousand pounds was spent by this nation, with its million paupers, on the fiasco expedition to the North Pole a few years ago under Captain Nares. But all-important as scientific exploration and experiment undoubtedly are, it is a question whether,—if those who have had the necessary educational opportunities to interest themselves in these matters are not numerous enough or public-spirited enough to find the sinews of war out of their own pockets without exacting a contribution from those who are struggling to put bread into their children's mouths,—it might not be as well to let such inquiries stand over till the rich are in a position to dispense with the assistance of the poor.

Apart from these considerations it may, I think, be affirmed that an artificial supply—that is, a supply which is not in response to a natural demand—has a tendency to induce a morbid appetite. For example, " in nearly all the free public libraries prose fiction is in most demand, religion in least."[1] The latter part of the indictment is serious or not, according as the people of whom it is true is a professedly religious people or not ; but in any case it seems a sad waste of public money to provide the lazy with a mental pabulum which, in the words of Sir Theodore Martin, " brings creeping paralysis upon their brains, by steeping them in the trivialities of flimsy magazines and catch-penny novels that grow up and perish like the summer fly."

Our picture galleries have hardly yet come so far under the like influences as to become depraved by pandering to the tastes of the listless, but the time cannot be far distant. As for free museums, one might almost as correctly speak of free out-door winter midnight services. They are *not* popular. As a frequent visitor to the Natural History Museum at South Kensington I am bound to say that, considering its rich and varied treasures, and the care which has been bestowed upon them, the emptiness of its well-arranged galleries is simply deplorable.

In favour of public State-aided baths and wash-houses the same argument applies which is urged on behalf of cheap water —water under cost price—namely, that they are safeguards against dirt and disease. This may be so, but the time will come in which the respectable poor will resent the implication that, unless they are washed at the expense of their richer neighbours, they will remain dirty. Similarly their self-respect will rebel against such degrading charity as Cheap Trains Acts and Education Acts confer. Clearly, if certain third-class passengers are carried at less than the normal profit on railway investments, the remaining passengers must pay the balance— not the shareholders and not the nation. The indirect effect may be to restrict the operations of the company, but directly the only effect is to compel one class to pay part of the fares of the other class.

[1] *Westminster Review*, July 1886.

N

What are the arguments for State education ? The first is that education is good, which is true or not according to the meaning of the word " education." If it means teaching Greek to a child who will soon want to know something of agriculture, or teaching plumbing to one who is going to be a solicitor's clerk, or any similar substitution of that which is good for that which is better, then I should say decidedly that education is a bad thing. Whether the School Boards provide the suitable or the unsuitable at the present time may be an open question, but we must remember that the State department as now constituted is young and fresh, and like all new brooms it ought *primâ facie* to sweep clean. The very worst quality of razor shaves well at first. Time only discloses its inferiority. At present in line with the more advanced thinkers, what will it be in a hundred years, when, like all State institutions, it has fallen behind the age—when it has been fastened upon by parasitic officialism, and represents the " authorised " creed of a bygone generation ? Have we forgotten that the State has undertaken the education of the people before ? that a tax of one-tenth of the produce of the land was imposed for that purpose? that the education provided was "free and compulsory," just as hanging is at the present day for all who are duly qualified ? No doubt in the days of Charlemagne and Alfred such education was up to the level of the age, but whether it still fulfils all the requirements of an educational curriculum is a question which is answered by the establishment of a new and improved national organ.

The second argument for State education is, that the supply of the desired quality through independent channels is not forthcoming ; that the instruction administered to the children in the voluntary schools was unduly admixed with effete matter. There is much truth in this, but the neo-radical action based on the observation was hasty and ill-considered. The mind of the country was steadily expanding, and this well-meant attempt at compulsory evolution will probably in the end operate rather as a check than as an impetus.

But a third contention implied in State education is that even when supplied in good condition the demand for education is restricted. Having artificially created a supply, the neo-

radical proceeds to create an artificial demand.   When provided
by the State, the "lower orders" will not purchase it at cost
price.   Such is the weakness of parental love that parents will
not confer upon their children what kind neo-radicals consider
good for them.   What is to be done now ?   Clearly State love
must be substituted for parental love.   Parents must be coerced
to supply their little ones with the approved mental food.
Education is made "compulsory."   A little experience soon
convinces our philanthropists that it is not so much a lack of
parental love as a lack of parental funds that stands between
the children and the good things provided for them.   Education
must be free, that is to say, everybody must be educated for
nothing, which means, being interpreted, that everybody must
pay for everybody else's education and get his own gratis.

When education has been "free and compulsory" for a few
years it will be found that a large number of persons do not want
it at any price.   They will rebel against compulsory attendance
just as they now rebel against compulsory fees.   They can in
many cases provide a better and more suitable education for
their children from their own point of view than is provided by
the State schools, and they will prefer to bring them up as well-
trained agriculturists, or plumbers, or farriers, rather than to
have them trained as clerks in the Government mould with the
ignominious condition imposed of accepting compulsory alms.
The strongest argument in favour of all these forms of State
charity is that if the classes thus insultingly pauperised do not
see the insult, the act loses its contumely and becomes a mere
act of patronage.   It is sometimes a relief when the respectable
man whom one has diffidently "tipped," pockets the tip
and the insult, touches his hat, and expresses his thanks.

The next class of neo-radical State interferences, ostensibly
in favour of the wage receivers (though they glide imperceptibly
one into the other) embraces compulsory rest, compulsory
insurance, and compulsory security.   The first is provided for
by a number of Acts relating to Factories, Bank Holidays, Shop
Hours Regulation, Sunday Closing, Lord's Day Observance, and
the like : the effect of which is to prescribe fixed limits to the
working hours of women, children, and young persons, at all
times and in all occupations ; and in the case of men, on

specified days and in certain occupations.   Indirectly, of course, the Factory Acts have the effect, by turning out the female hands, of compelling owners to close their factories, and so to force the full-grown men to rest, if not to be thankful. Whether they have cause to be thankful must depend on the financial position of the worker.   As a specimen of the light in which workmen as a class regard compulsory idleness (or say rest) I will quote one letter written by a dock labourer to the Editor of a Radical newspaper :—

"SIR—In your 'Topics of the Day' of last week you refer to the closing of the banks at two on Saturdays, and make some remarks about the bank employés, in which I quite agree ; but what I want to call your attention to is another class of employés, and that is dock labourers, and how it may affect them.   I remind you that the docks are under the control of the Customs, and I am told that it is being mooted to extend the favour to the Customs.   If they get it, how will it affect tens of thousands of poor dock labourers ?   It is only the permanent staff in the docks that get paid for holidays, which does not amount to more than 5 per cent, the other 95 being paid by the hour.   At the present time eight hours per day is the time for work, but after this month seven hours per day for the next four months. It may seem a small matter, but is a great matter to those concerned in it.   If a man is fortunate enough to get a day's work in the winter, he gets 2s. 11d., and should the docks close at two o'clock, he will only get 2s. 1d., so that it will affect the whole of the dock labourers (extra men) of the country.

And now I will say a word as to how Bank Holidays affect dock labourers.   In the past the Act of Parliament got it for the banks first, after which it was extended to the Customs, and *so closed the docks, and closed the dock labourers' mouths*—for it is little they get to put in them on those days.   And while I am writing I will mention the extra holiday the Customs have, viz. the Queen's Birthday, which is supposed to be a day of rejoicing, but I can assure you that it is a day of moaning and cursing amongst the class I am speaking about, and to which I belong.   I hope this will meet the eye of some of your M.P.'s, and that they will give us a little consideration.

I am, Sir, yours, etc.   A DOCK LABOURER."[1]

The writer naturally makes the mistake of supposing that the 5 per cent of employés on the permanent staff "get paid for holidays."   This is a common error.   Work is paid according to its value ; and if fifty days in the year are added

[1] *Weekly Dispatch*, October 10, 1886.

to the compulsory holidays, one-seventh is struck off the pay of the workers.

It seems hard that in a country where an owner of dumb animals can be prosecuted for overworking them, a parent or an employer should be allowed to overwork human beings. And this is of some force in defending these Acts so far as children and young persons are concerned; though the implication must be distinctly borne in mind that working-class parents are cruel enough for the sake of gain to overwork their children. I do not believe it. The class as a class, so long as wagedom lasts, is bound, parent and child, to do more work, or rather to work for a longer time, than is good for health of mind or body; but I deny that the working classes, as a rule, allow their children to be overworked from the standpoint of their permanent necessities. In any case, to remove the care of the children from the shoulders of parents on to the shoulders of the State is to still further weaken the parental sense of responsibility. A little good may possibly accrue to the rising generation, but the ultimate and permanent effect must be to demoralise and degrade the race.

There are certain other indirect evil consequences of this kind of legislation which the neo-radical has clearly overlooked. It is often pointed out that if the working hours of English operatives are shortened, the foreigner will have an immense advantage in competition. To which the reply always is, that the labour question is an international one, and that if all civilised nations put a compulsory limit on the hours of work no one would lose. Meantime, apart from the untruth of this last statement, while the neo-radical is in a hurry, other nations are in no hurry, and the consequence is that whether the labour question should be international or not, the foreigner is at present taking advantage of the short hours of the British workman. I have already pointed out that I regard even those hours as too long, but I maintain that they cannot be shortened wisely under a system of labour payment which offers no inducement to make up in intensity for what is lost in time. A free English workman under a system of capitalisation could do in six hours more than a foreign wage-slave would do in twelve. Meantime he works in the same way, and the country pays a hundred millions a year for his extra two hours' rest a day.

Why, again, in these days of electric lighting should capital rest in the night time ? Journalists, actors, some cab-drivers, railway servants, postmen, policemen, and hundreds of others do the major portion of their work when the rest of the world is snoring. Why not some factory operatives ? In the mines and the furnaces where there are no women, and where consequently the Factory Acts do not apply, we have a succession of shifts. It is not proposed that the hands should work twenty-four hours a day, but there should be three shifts of eight hours each ; by which the dream of the rhyming workman would be realised :—

> " Eight hours' work, eight hours' play,
> Eight hours' sleep, and eight bob a day."

This consummation (with the exception of the last item) has actually been reached in benighted and despotic Russia, where no foolish kindly-intentioned Factory Acts interfere with private enterprise.

Again, are the following suggestions worth a little reflection ? I have no intention of entering into a theological controversy, but I suppose few persons have conceived the idea of calculating the cost in pounds, shillings, and pence of Sunday, as it is at present observed in this country. Such a calculation is not a very difficult one, while it presents several features of interest.

Before coming to figures, however, let us pave the way by an inquiry into the nature and foundation of our English institution of Sunday observance. Two reasons are commonly alleged. The first is, of course, the religious one that to rest on the seventh day is a divine ordinance ; the second is that workers of all classes are all the better for a rest or holiday once a week. With respect to the first, every one knows that according to the authority the day appointed to be kept holy is the Saturday or Jewish Sabbath ; nor is there any passage in the Testaments which can be adduced in support of the substitution of the first for the seventh day.

Without going farther into this part of the question

probably most enlightened Christians will admit that what is
required is that every person shall set apart one day in the
week as a holiday, into the mode of spending which there may
be differences of opinion. Some persons will go farther, and
contend that one day in the week is too little for some kinds
of work and too much for other kinds. For the present
purpose I may accept the uniform system of one day in seven.
Now if it is immaterial, even from a Christian point of view,
upon which particular day of the week we fix, it is clearly
of equal unimportance whether all of us fix upon the same day
or upon different days.

   With respect to the second or hygienic reason above
referred to, these observations apply with even greater force,
for it obviously cannot signify whether we rest on the first,
fourth, or seventh day, provided we get the amount of recreation required.

   Now what again, if any, would accrue from the establishment of seven Sabbaths in the week ? in other words, from a
division of the days of the week among the labouring classes
in suchwise that one-seventh of our workers are always
enjoying a holiday. Some would have the Mondays, others the
Tuesdays, others the Wednesdays, and so on throughout the
week. It may seem at first sight that such an arrangement
would make no difference to the work done or to the value of
the work, but this is a mistake. It is true that no more
hours' work would be performed than now, but the labour
would be both better paid and more productive. And the
reason is this. Under the present system we give our
labourers a weekly holiday, and we also give our capital a
weekly holiday—our engines, our warehouses, our stock our
plant, etc. This is pure waste. Not even the most scrupulous
Sabbatarian will maintain that an engine ought to rest for one
whole day in the week. Now, roughly speaking, capital may
be said to contribute two-thirds towards production against
one-third contributed by labour (in more correct parlance, the
non-human capital contributes about twice as much as the
human). The immediate effect of depriving this non-human
capital of its rest-day would be virtually to increase its quantity
by one-seventh. Thus, the present proportion between the

values of the two elements of production would be modified. By the law of value relating to co-elements we see that this would bring about a considerable rise in the price of labour. The law is as follows: Other things equal, a rise in the value of one co-element is followed by a *fall* in the values of all the other co-elements, and a fall by a rise, but not necessarily at the same rate. Now, labourers and machinery, etc., are co-elements; the old theory of rivalry has been long ago exploded. Hence, together with a cheapening of production all along the line, we should have the equally satisfactory concomitant of a rise in wages. This stimulated demand would eventually call into existence an increase of population equal to about one-seventh of the number of the labouring class. A more immediate result would be an increase in production, equal to about two-thirds of one-seventh of the present amount, in round numbers an increase of one-tenth, or over a hundred million pounds a year—a sum sufficient to provide the whole of the revenue without any taxation whatever. England can therefore at any moment virtually abolish taxation by the simple expedient of distributing the Sabbath all over the week. We may here mention an incidental advantage of this reform. It would reconcile the possibilities of our modern civilisation with the absoluteness and rigidity of the old institution. At present it is matter of common observation that Sunday is a holiday rather in name than in fact to large sections of the community. Postmen, railway officials, policemen, hotel servants and domestics generally, with many more, can hardly boast of fulfilling the letter of the law. But under the proposed system all members of all classes would be enabled to enjoy a complete holiday once a week, without in the least inconveniencing the remainder of the population. We should be able to send and receive our letters as usual in the metropolis without misgivings as to the postman's sufferings. We should not be left in ignorance of accidents and the dying wishes of distant friends, for want of telegraph accommodation on the Sunday; nor would the trite argument continue to apply against opening museums and galleries on the Sunday, based on sympathy with overworked officials. To sum up, the new arrangement would perfect our holidays and render them of universal application; would raise the price of labour throughout the country, and would pay the whole sum now annually levied by taxation.

But if the people cannot be trusted to take sufficient rest for health how can they be trusted to insure themselves against misfortune? Hence an Employers' Liability Act must be passed, and a Bill brought in to make life assurance compulsory. The agitation for the latter object is fortunately as yet unsuccessful, but the former became law some few years ago. The principle of it is simple enough. Wages cannot be forced up by legislation however cunningly conceived: that is now generally admitted. In case of accident to a workman under the old system the loss came out of savings from past wages or a draft on future wages. The *average* wage necessarily covered the loss from accidents, and prudent workmen contributed towards an accident insurance fund. By the Act the burden of providing against accidents (of certain kinds) is now cast on the employer. The insurance fund is no longer needed. In other words, the employer *keeps back* (as by law compelled) that small portion of the wage which went to cover the average risk of accident. This he virtually puts into an accident insurance fund, from which from time to time he pays out what he is called upon to pay by law. The consequence is that the improvident man is obliged to insure. The annual premium is extorted from him by force. Of course, this is a good thing, if we take it for granted that human nature is organically improvident, and that not even by the experience of generations is providence to be hoped for. Unless we assume this, the effect of the Act must be to counteract the teachings of nature by disturbing the sequence of cause and effect. But not only are the provident and the improvident thrust together into one boat; the same thing is done for the careless and the cautious. The ungainly lout, who stumbles over any unusual object in his way, is as well provided for, at as little cost to himself, as the careful man who keeps his eyes open. Under the individualist system of old the latter could put away a smaller sum per annum than the former to form a fund to meet possible accidents. His own habit of caution lessened the risk. This habit was good for himself, good for his employer, and good for the community. The Act tends, of course, to weaken the habit. A workman nowadays almost feels that he has a *right* to an accident. Why should a set of careless fellows draw pounds and pounds for doing nothing while he, just because he examines ropes and rungs before trusting them, has his wages reduced to cover his employer's loss ?

The best excuse for the ignorant promoters of this Act is that they really did not know that it must have the effect of lowering wages by exactly the amount required to cover the employer's liability.

A large number of workmen have already discovered what their legislating benefactors fail to see, and the consequence is that they have contracted with their employers " out of the Act." To meet this difficulty the neo-radicals now propose to render such contract void. The workman is to be permitted to accept a contribution from his employer towards the accident fund in consideration of foregoing any claim which at any future time may arise under the Act, and then, when the claim has arisen, to snap his fingers at the other party to the bargain and demand full compensation. In other words, he is to be allowed to receive compensation twice over for the same injury, once by contract and once by fraud.

It is unnecessary to go into the demoralising effects of this so-called Employers' Liability Act *Amendment* Bill. All Bills which contain the dishonourable clause enabling a man to enter into a binding engagement to-day and to break it with impunity and advantage to-morrow—a clause which is but too frequently met with in these days—are the unmistakable offspring of neo-radicalism.

Individualists know full well that the cost of labour under the wage system includes the risk of the work to be performed. Wages necessarily vary with the risk. Adam Smith pointed that out over a hundred years ago. Consequently they have never condemned the original Act of 1881 on the ground that it taxed the employer. They know that it merely compels him to undertake the functions of an accident insurance company. The law compels him to compel his workpeople to insure against accidents.

The Act is condemned because it puts on an equal footing the provident and the improvident, the careful and the careless, and because it removes the incentives to constant watchfulness and prudence which tend, if let alone, to become hardened into congenital habits. The Amendment Bill, on the other hand, they condemn as a contemptible and immoral proposal.

In addition to compulsory rest and compulsory insurance, the neo-radical hastens to confer compulsory security upon the workers of the country. We have seen the effect of his efforts in the first two directions: how far has he been successful in the third? Ships are to be absolutely sea-worthy; mines are to be ventilated, and explosions rendered impossible; machinery in factories is to be fenced round; workshops are to be kept in perfect sanitary condition; railway trains are to adopt the block system and the automatic continuous brake; and level crossings are to be abolished. The men in the whitelead works are to wear suitable clothing, and to drink suitable squashes; bakers are no longer to carry on their calling in a basement; dogs are all to be put into muzzles; acrobats are not to perform on the trapeze without proper neo-radical precautions; and, doubtless, in a few years, hunting, cricket, and football will be forbidden as too dangerous to life and limb.

Meantime, what is the result of all this striving after security? The Mines' Regulation Act was passed in 1872. It is alleged, on the high authority of its friends and admirers, that it has been the means of saving a few dozen lives a year, which is more than doubtful. Well, that is important: lives are valuable, and cannot be evaluated in terms of £ s. d. But look on the debit side of the account. For the five years following that in which the Act came into operation, over 12,000 workers were on an average each year thrown out of employment in the branch of industry affected, so that at the end of five years over 62,000 persons had been thrown out of work—cast on to an overstocked labour market, to compete in other departments of trade at a disadvantage, and, if the whole truth could be told, to perish of slow starvation. Sixty persons saved from a miner's grave—60,000 starved to death by the Act![1]

[1] The Act came into force in 1873. In 1874 there were employed in and

And the same disproportion between the direct good and the indirect evil· wrought by neo-radical legislation of this character holds throughout. The little benefit conferred is a prominent and noticeable little benefit, while the immense mischief done is remote and not always easily traceable to its true cause. It may be doubted whether anything has tended to undermine England's industrial superiority so much as the Factory Legislation of the last fifty years. Perhaps it is malicious to unearth the forgotten motives which brought them into existence. But that they were the progeny of the mean revengefulness of the landed classes for the liberal reforms of the day is proved beyond doubt by Roebuck, who pointed out that the division list on Feilden's Act of 1847 coincided almost exactly with the division list on the Repeal of the Corn-Laws in 1846. Nearly every member of Parliament who voted for State interference with factories voted also *against* the cheap loaf. This opinion is confirmed by a letter from Mr. Bright himself, which appeared in the *Times* much more recently. " A large section of Tories," says he, " voted for the Factory Bill to revenge themselves upon the manufacturers, who were opposing the Corn-Laws." This is significant. It entirely precludes the theory of the philanthropic origin of these measures, and helps to explain the anomaly of a Tory saint bringing in a popular measure, to be resisted tooth and nail by the best friend of the people. The effects of the Acts have fully justified Mr. Bright's opposition. Mr. Bright, in opposing Feilden's Ten Hours' Bill, predicted that "it must promote that depression which has for many years prevailed in the great interests of the country ; and was calculated to destroy the manufacturing supremacy of the country. . . . That instead of conferring a benefit on the working classes, as

about the coal mines, 538,829 persons. Five years later, in 1879, the mining population had decreased to 476,810, showing a loss of no less than 62,019 persons. Where did they go ? The other markets were all overstocked. These poor people understood mining operations, but probably were but ill-fitted to compete in other branches of industry. Let us not blink matters. They were slowly but surely *murdered* by Act of Parliament—starved to death ! Meantime the decrease in fatal accidents in the mines during the same period is fixed by the same authority at 83. These figures are taken from the Report of the Royal Commission on Accidents in Mines. 1881.

they supposed, it would cause a greater evil to them than perhaps any measure which that House had ever passed."[1] He described the Bill as "a delusion practised on the working classes," and as "one of the worst measures ever passed." Some half-dozen years before the passing of the first Factory Act,[2] trade unionism was showing such strength that it had been deemed necessary by the anti-popular party to pass a very rigorous measure directed against it.[3] "If you want any change," this Act virtually said to the proletariat, "apply to us, the aristocracy and your friends, and we will bring pressure to bear on your masters; but do not dare to put forward demands in your own name, or we will join your masters in crushing you."

And just as democracies, torn asunder by faction, will sometimes entrust their liberties to the guardianship of a military dictator ; just as the down-trodden peasants of Russia pray for protection against the greed of the landowner to the holy Czar ; so in a weak moment the workpeople of England delegated their own growing power to the non-progressive party, to be used ostensibly against the employers of labour, but really against the free-traders.   The originator of this hypocritical and dishonest piece of statecraft has been apotheosised by the people ; and the laying of the first stone of the fabric of State socialism in this country is nowadays commemorated by both parties as an epoch in the history of civilisation.[4]

The consequences of the surrender of the workers of their right of initiation into the hands of their self-appointed patrons were manifold.   Instead of relying on combination and on direct compromise with their employers—a system which was already beginning to bear fruits, as the Act of 1826 shows— they have ever since turned their eyes toward the supposed fountain of favours—Parliament.   The very trade unionists themselves at their annual congresses deliberate on, not what they shall do for themselves, but what Parliament shall be

[1] *Hansard*, vol. lxxxix., p. 486.
[2] Lord Ashley's Act, passed in 1833.
[3] 6 Geo. IV., c. 129.
[4] The new street which has been named after the father of the Factory Acts is fairly emblematic of the tortuous gait of party spite in the guise of philanthropy. Why cannot our streets and statesmen be straight ?

asked to do for them.   If the sight of a glass of beer is too
tempting to be resisted by those who receive their wages in
a public-house, instead of advising their followers to band themselves together and refuse to accept their wages in such places,
as the east-coast fishermen did, these leaders of labour go
down on their knees to the legislature for a " Payment of Wages
in Public-houses Prohibition Bill."

But the poor helpless creatures who cannot toddle on without clinging to the petticoats of the great national nurse
must not expect to be trusted even to look after their own
private affairs.   Like babies they must be protected against
themselves.   If they do not go to Church on Sunday there is
an old Act on the Statute-book which subjects them to a fine
of five shillings—an Act which many are thirsting to put in
force.   And they must not go to museums or picture galleries
on Sunday.   Mr. Broadhurst tells the goody-goodies who gave
him his under-secretaryship that they do not desire it.   Well, if
not, they need not go ; but both those who do (Mr. Broadhurst
will admit that there are three or four) and those who do not
might be allowed to express their views by the simple process
of going or staying away, without calling upon Mr. Broadhurst
for an opinion, or upon the saints who have the legislature in
leading-strings.   Again, the shiftless wage receiver may not
have a glass of beer before such an hour, or after such an hour,
or on such a day, without a certificate in the form of a railway
ticket, or a lie on his tongue.   The particular hour fixed varies
with the ebb and flow of saintly influence in the House of
Commons.   Then the " people " must not assemble in the
streets to talk politics obnoxious to their rulers.   They may
cant and sing, but if they talk politics they are " obstructing
the thoroughfare " and must go to prison for two months.
Places of amusement may be opened on all days *except* the poor
man's weekly holiday.   The " classes " may drink and play
billiards all night long in Pall Mall, but the " masses " must go
to bed at regulation hour, or drink water and play " solitaire "
at home.   Such is the final consummation of neo-radicalism ;
the people dubbed " the masses " and treated as masses—all,
without regard to their individuality, run in one mould, and
branded with one brand.

The net result of the patchings and tinkerings, the meddlings and muddlings of this well-meaning set of incapables is just what might have been expected of it. By nibbling at the liberties first of one class and then of another; by violating all those rules of government the soundness of which have been demonstrated by the experience of ages; by increasing and entangling all the duties of Parliament and the Executive; by loading the Statute-book with long, tedious, and stupid Acts of Parliament, too prolix and heterogeneous for even trained lawyers to digest; by multiplying policemen and inspectors and examiners and State-officials of one sort and another, till no man can take a pinch of snuff without being asked to show his license, or chop faggots without a Government certificate; by this, that, and the other readjustment of the order of nature by rule of thumb, a state of things has been brought about in which the workers of England, without being made one whit the healthier or the happier, have been reduced to the last degree of inefficiency, poverty, and dependence.

Fortunately the beliefs of these semi-socialists sit lightly on them. If their first scheme is a failure it is thrown overboard without remorse; a clean sweep is made and a fresh start. They are amenable to reason if it is brought home to them through the channel of personal experience; and consequently it may be predicted that when the country has been brought to the brink of ruin, and when they themselves have tasted the bitter fruit of their own fooling, they will wheel round and set briskly to work to undo it. Even now there are signs of this reaction.

But while the neo-radical would be a comparatively harmless creature but for his unparalleled opportunities for mischief, and while, like the bull in the china shop, he is not in himself a dangerous or vicious animal, there is a certain sect of genuine and consistent socialists who regard the attainment of their Utopia as possible only on constitutional lines, and who see in neo-radicalism the thin end of their own peculiar wedge being steadily driven home by the huge force of national thick-headedness. And these theorists find themselves aided not only by the milk-and-water socialists of the neo-radical school, but even more effectually by a third and more reprehensible set of politicians, dishonest, self-seeking demagogues, who without either faith in the methods, or interest in the ultimate effects of the doctrine they preach, trade on the credulity of their fellow-countrymen, for their own mean personal aggrandisement, posing as philanthropists and friends of the people for the sake of popularity and its rewards—place and pelf. Such are the men who aspire to lead the credulous and ignorant in order that they may some day barter their delegated power and betray their followers to the enemy for an under-secretaryship or a snug berth as county-court judge. There is no need to name names. Those who have been found out are well known, and if I were to name some of those who have not yet been found out, their poor trusty supporters would disbelieve and denounce me—yet a little while. Meanwhile neo-radicalism is triumphant, trade ;is stagnant, and the workers work and work and die, and their children take their places, without hope or opportunity of betterment.

But there is a bright side to even neo-radicalism. It is by no means an unmixed evil. It serves as the safety-valve for the forces of ignorant rebellion, which would otherwise be pent up and attain a dangerous and explosive degree of intensity. It owes its existence partly, as I have said, to the common sense as distinguished from the severe logicality of Englishmen. In France if there is such a safety-valve it is always out of order ; it will not act. It jammed in 1789 ; it jammed in 1848 ; and it jammed in 1870. It is never to be depended on. In England revolutionary forces were stronger in the days of the Chartist movement than they have ever been in France. The love of justice and liberty has always been stronger on this side of the channel. But the great Radical leaders of the day got control of the boiler and let off the steam in dribblets. Rebellion fizzled out in neo-radical legislation which, beyond lowering the pressure of the forces of discontent, did no good to any one. (Yet, surely, this in itself was a great good !) Socialists who look with favour on neo-radicalism mistake the blowing off of steam for the effective exercise of motive power. While the socialists are getting up steam they forget to sit on the safety-valve. It is true some of the wiser heads among them are beginning to look askance at neo-radicalism.   Individualists do the same, but for another reason: they believe that the " subterranean forces " of society might be turned to better account than making discordant noises. Both parties are agreed in lamenting the waste of power ; but while socialists would burst the boiler, individualists would get the engine in motion along the lines of civilisation.   Semi-socialists are content to pile on fuel with one hand " to a certain limited extent, don't you know," and to let off steam with the other, also " to a certain limited extent."   However, perhaps we may trust these trimmers to thwart the aims and disappoint the expectations of their more consistent brethren.

"Just as the French workers have already nearly captured the municipal management of Paris, so it is our duty to leave no stone unturned in order to obtain control of either the reformed or unreformed municipal bodies of London. We see how much we could do to help on the socialist cause if we had only a determined and persistent minority, as the French socialists have, upon the municipal council."

So writes the editor of the organ of social democracy in London, and he ventures to predict the outcome of his policy in these words :—

"When next the people marshal themselves in battle array against their oppressors, London will help Paris and Paris London to begin and carry on in earnest the world-wide international revolution. The memories of the great Civil War and the Chartist movement on this side of the Channel will be blended with those of '89 and the Commune on the other as the two greatest cities of the civilised world combine their forces in one final effort." [1]

Never! Long before that, the neo-radicals of the day will blow off steam enough to reduce the pressure far below bursting point. Even neo-radicals, to use a teleological metaphor, were not created without a purpose.

Under the head of neo-radicalism must on no account be included the radicalism of the old Manchester school, which was merely advanced Liberalism. Indeed the old and the new Radical are more widely separated by principle than the Conservative and Liberal. They stand at opposite poles. The old Radical was all for freedom and was opposed to State

[1] *Justice*, September 4, 1886.

O

interference ; the new Radical is for despotism and Government control in everything. Just as in Protestant countries
the Roman Catholics preach religious liberty and equality,
while in Catholic countries they practise religious intolerance,
so those renegades who have passed over into the new camp
never loved liberty for its own sake, but merely because they
were themselves in a minority : and now that the reins are in
their own hands they are as ready as the most selfish tyrant
to impose their own despotic yoke on their fellow-countrymen.
Let-be was an excellent ladder on which to mount to power,
but now they have got there, they are the first to kick it
down. Not a single word of what I have written about the
new school (if an academy of ignorance can fairly be called a
school) is intended to apply to those champions of freedom
who fought for civil equality and for civil liberty, who abolished
religious disqualifications and gave us free trade.

Unfortunately the race is wellnigh extinct. Mr. Bright
is gone and his coadjutors of the Anti-Corn Law League
have most of them passed away, and with them the spirit
which inspired them. The League itself, it is true, has
been resuscitated under a new title and with a wider
aim, but the names of the Liberal leaders of to-day do
not appear on the roll of its members. Among modern
Radicals one solitary figure stands out as an advocate of
true freedom. To his honour be it said, Mr. Bradlaugh has
never stooped to promise prosperity to the incompetent and
luxury to the lazy. So strong is the temptation in these
democratic days to offer political bribes to the voter, that one
has need of great popularity, of considerable self-restraint, and
of singular political honesty to steer clear of class privilege on
the one hand and majority despotism on the other. "To my
mind,"[1] said the member for Northampton to his constituents,
" to my mind the great danger, especially to the democracies
of Europe—I hope not to the democracy of America—is to look
to the State to do things for you. The State is only you. It is
often less than you, and it can never be more than you. . . .
Democracies should leave as little as possible for the State to do.
Every citizen should prevent, as much as possible, any control

---

[1] The *Northamptonshire Guardian,* September 4, 1886.

over individual energy." How many Liberal members dare
say ditto to that in presence of their own constituents ?

It is a relief to turn to a third remedy for the
present unjust system of distribution. What is called the
system of "profit-sharing" is advocated by men who are
actuated by a sense of justice and sympathy, and whose
suggestions are based on experiment and observation. The
advocates of "profit-sharing" accept the principle which I
have described as floating in the air—that somehow wages
should vary with profits, that when the employer is making
large gains, his workpeople ought to enjoy a corresponding
prosperity. But the method they propose is this : the employer
should be persuaded to put by a certain percentage of his trade
profits for division by way of bonus among his employees in
proportion to their ordinary wages. In this way the workers
will be in a position to save if they are thrifty, and so in good
time to become themselves capitalists. But why *should* he,
the employer asks, rob himself of his proper profits in order to
enrich his workmen ? Might he not as well give a tithe of his
income to the poor-box ? To which the "profit-sharers" answer.
"No : it is true that the workers have no claim upon you,
either moral or economic, for a share ; but you will find that
if you *give* them such bonus as we suggest they will work
harder and make the total net profits so much larger that
you will not lose but rather gain by the process. They will
perceive that the harder and better they work the more they
will get, and so while they toil for their own good they will
necessarily at the same time toil for yours." As to what
percentage should be divided among the "hands," profit-sharers
differ in opinion. Nearly all agree that the share should be
small : and it is clear that according to the principles of the
system only the net profits, after payment of wages and
interest, can be devoted to the purpose.

There is no doubt that a great deal can be said for profit-
sharing. It has a decided tendency to allay the spirit of
hostile rivalry between employers and employed. It seems to
exercise a salutary influence in preventing strikes and trade
disputes. It certainly stimulates the workers to greater and
better work. The hands are more careful to guard against

mistakes, and that the interest taken in the business by the hands is much increased is shown, says M. Godin, the founder of the "Familistère," by the constant new inventions and improvements made by the men. "Since they were made partners" (not true partners?), says he, "a great number of patents have been taken out by the Familistère."

Again, as Mr. Egerton [1] tells us, "those working for a share of the profits rarely ask for a Monday holiday, as do most other (French) workmen. Thus their houses are able to execute orders with greater rapidity. When there was a strike amongst the painters, the workmen at M. Leclaire's worked fourteen and even more hours per day without the slightest complaint."

Again, writing of these same men, he says: "The idea of equality of pay would be looked upon by them (Leclaire's men) as ridiculous."

M. Laroche Joubert, who founded the profit-sharing paper mills in Angoulême, is so enthusiastic with regard to the system that he brought a Bill into the Chamber to make it compulsory upon all who tendered for public works. According to his own account, his house has made profits even in the worst of times. M. Joubert contends that his business is not liable to strikes, and that there is great zeal displayed by the hands, who *rarely leave the house.* But the practical commercial success of such profit-sharing houses as those of Leclaire, of M. Godin, and of M. Joubert no more justify us in eulogising the system as such, than do the failures of Herr Borchert justify us in condemning it. All alike were based on an arrangement arbitrary, paternal, and in all respects characteristically continental.

Let us see what there is to be urged against it. In the first place it is demoralising to the workpeople. They become the recipients of the employer's generosity. "The graduated divisions of profits are conferred as favours, not as rights." In the second place it begs the question as to the true and rightful ownership of the profits of industry: and in the third place so long as the percentage to be divided remains arbitrary and is left to the discretion of the master, the inevitable result of competition (under the law of population) will be to bring wages and bonus together down to the subsistence

[1] Government Report on Co-operation in Foreign Countries.

level. As Herr Borchert, who has had fifteen years' practical experience of it, says, " it cannot but retain the character of an exceptional measure, being at best a mere experiment among a number of others that crop up and disappear with every fresh turn of the social problem." If the bonus increases . in any one trade the wages will correspondingly diminish. I speak of the time when the system shall have been adopted not only by kind-hearted and large-minded men, like those who have already tried it, but by the general run of cheese-paring capitalists. When competition is keen—when trade is bad—when profits are small—when a hungry population is clamouring for work and bread—then the strain will come. Those who try to give more than the old wage in any form will have to close their works or forego the normal reward of risk. The more selfish (or, say, prudent) among them will prefer to invest their money on absolute security rather than at great risk for an equal return. Why spin cotton for 3 per cent with a prospect of less or even of loss when the like amount can be obtained from consols without any anxiety whatever ? Again, when the workman's share of the bonus is small compared with his wage the stimulus to increased exertion is not so great as might be supposed, and it is doubtful whether 5 or 10 per cent of the net profits all along the line, even if wages remained the same, would have any appreciable effect on production ; and if it had not, the system could not be permanent or even of long duration. Lastly, the ownership by the labourers of no matter how small a share in the employer's fixed capital (and that is how most profit-sharers insist on the workman's share being invested) forms a bond between the two which places the small and compulsory share-holder in a position of dependence on the large and free share-holder.[1] The resulting system, as was clearly shown in the *Maison Leclaire*, is one of a patriarchal character. The employer becomes a little monarch, a bureaucracy develops itself, laws are made affecting the workers such as no free man should submit to, and the rights of the several parties become increasingly difficult of demarcation. When disputes arise it is found that the rules have been drafted in the interest

---

[1] *E.g.* it is compulsory in the Familistère.

rather of the lion than of the fox and the ass, and in case of litigation the latter go to the wall. In fact these establishments are despotic little industrial communes, and as such are quite unfitted for acclimatisation in the hardy soil of British freedom.[1]

Between the theory of profit-sharing and the theory of co-operation there is this fundamental difference: the former regards the whole of the profits of industry as morally and economically the property of the capitalist; the latter regards the whole of the profits (as such) as morally the property of the manual workers. Consequently it is not surprising that all profit-sharing businesses have been founded by employers, mostly with philanthropic intentions, while co-operative factories have been mostly started by the men themselves without any aid *ab extra*. Again, the men in profit-sharing houses are usually of a pronounced conservative type, while " co-operators" are notorious for their aggressive radicalism. (I do not use these terms in the party sense.) Thus Lord Vivian, writing from Belgium, says: " The Vooruit and all the Ghent societies have been established by the working classes alone, all attempts to found such associations on the invitation or with the assistance of the employers having failed. This is probably due in great part to the action of the Belgian socialists, who maintain that the working classes can only rely on themselves to obtain their rights and improve their condition, and that these societies must therefore consist exclusively of working men. The last socialist program lays down that ' the enfranchisement of labour should be the work of the working classes themselves; since the other classes of society cannot seriously help on this object, the working men's party should always work separately.'"[2]

In treating of co-operation we must not fail to distinguish between co-operative distribution and co-operative production. Beyond the fact that they are known by the name of co-operation these two systems have little or nothing in common. The principles on which they are based differ, the objects with which they originated differ, and they are justified (if at all) on

[1] Those who wish to see the results of profit-sharing in actual working order should read Mr. Sedley Taylor's writings on the subject.

[2] Report on Co-operation in Foreign Countries—Belgium.

quite different grounds. And yet such is the confusion produced by mere names that those persons who approve of the one almost always express approval of the other.

"How is it," it is asked, "that, while co-operative distribution has made such amazing strides, co-operative production is nearly stationary?" But for this accidental confusion it would have been unnecessary to have referred to co-operative distribution in this place at all. As it is, however, it may be as well to say a word or two on the subject of co-operation, as vulgarly understood, before proceeding to consider co-operation in its more accurate sense.

Co-operative distribution is based on the principle of rolling . into one, consumer and worker, demander and supplier—a principle which traverses the law of the division of labour. A deal of cackling has been done over some of the earlier co-operative societies, and doubtless the stores of to-day in England are a remarkable and an interesting study. Monster mushroom growths of sudden and luxuriant expansion, their existence goes to show that there is a screw loose somewhere, and that the present system of retail trade is out of equilibrium with society. And that this is so might have been seen beforehand. The enormous advances made in the art of transport during the last generation have defeated all the calculations of the retail traders. One can telegraph to Constantinople for a few pounds of Turkish tobacco, and get it for hardly more than the cost of an equal amount at the nearest tobacconist's, and with a better chance of obtaining the precise article required. It is no uncommon thing for people in the provinces to obtain the whole of their groceries from London instead of from the retail grocer hard by. The very existence of small retailers is threatened. The value of the service they render is not equal to their cost of living and the rent of their business premises. Clearly, retailing on a gigantic scale tends, like large farming on corn-growing and pasture lands, to elbow out the small people. There is an enormous saving in cost of staff, and a still greater in carriage, and there is a smaller proportion of surplus stock. Small traders finding themselves thus hard pressed by a rival organisation, which began with the wage-receiving classes and rapidly extended upwards to the

" upmost " classes, had recourse to various expedients for keeping
and gaining custom, of which one was the obvious one of giving
long credits. And they· developed the carrying branch of
their business very considerably. But when orders were called
for, goods left at the required hour, and a year's credit given,
it was not to be expected that apparent prices could remain
the same. The price of the article must cover the interest on
the accounts and also the resulting bad debts, and the services
of the extra hands required; and the difference between
retailers' prices and store prices would become daily accentuated.
Of course if the consumer imagines that by foregoing the
interest on his domestic expenditure, and by putting his
shoulder to the wheel and carrying his own parcels, he is really
getting his things cheaper, it is a happy delusion which does no
one much harm, but it is not a delusion on which stores can
thrive for ever. The old lady who bought a herring for a
farthing and engaged a cab to carry it home, would probably
discover the flaw in her household economy after a dozen or so
of experiments. For a time, no doubt, aggregations of men,
working on new and improved principles, may beat the representatives of the *ancien régime* out of the field, but meantime they must act through some form of organisation, and the
men who do the organising part of the business are mortal—a
fact which co-operationists (like socialists) appear to forget.
Other things equal, the private trader *must* have a considerable
advantage over a company of associated traders, still more over
a motley crew of ignorant persons whose affairs are in the
hands of paid officials.

The abolition of long credits by retail traders, and the improvements taking place in the independent systems of small
parcels delivery,[1] together with the more general recognition of
the doctrine of " small profits and quick returns," will soon more
than equalise the conditions. Retail traders will many of them
be killed out, but others who carry on business in the large
way required by modern social arrangements will sooner or
later outstrip the co-operative societies, beat them on their
own ground, and compel them to wind up their affairs. Even
now it is only necessary to compare the prices and quality of

---

[1] An improvement too likely to be retarded by recent Government competition.

goods supplied by the Civil Service or Army and Navy Stores with similar goods supplied by Whiteley, or other large retail provider, to discover that the system of co-operative distribution, having drawn attention to a real defect in retail trade organisation, is wellnigh played out.   Five or ten years hence no such amateur bazaars as those now flourishing in Victoria Street and the Haymarket will remain to excite the envy and hatred of the retailer.   They will die a natural death.

But since the object was originally to dispense with the costly services of the " middleman " or " retailer," the movement was clearly justified by success.   Beginning with workmen, the contagion rapidly spread to the ranks of the capitalists and all classes of society, and from one country to another, and it still continues to vindicate its existence.   In one sense, no doubt, co-operation as here understood can be extended to production, as indeed it was by the Rochdale pioneers, who ground their own flour and made their own bread.   The same thing was done by several of the French co-operative bakeries, and so long as the co-operators made only for their own consumption, so as to evade the miller's profits, the principle was the same as that on which co-operative distribution rests.   But the justification was wanting.   While the small and numerous local retailers were and are a useless anachronism, the manufacturer is nothing of the kind.   I am not aware that any association has supplied its own members exclusively with boots, or pianos, or chairs, so that the appearance of co-operative societies of piano-makers and the like brings us face to face with the other form of co-operation, in which members are not regarded as demanders.

Co-operative production, in this sense, is a very different matter.   It has a separate origin, a separate object, and a separate justification.   It is based on the observed fact that ͺ the contributor of capital (so-called) walks off, not only with the profits of capital but also with the profits of labour.   This is so, and some of the more clear-sighted among the working classes see that it is so.   Furthermore, they cannot see why the capitalist should take any profit at all.   His contribution, they say, being dead matter, cannot add to the value of the new product ; whatever is so added is the result of labour, and of labour alone. So they argue. Thus if the workers could only scrape together enough wealth to make a start, the profits could be divided in proportion to the *labour* contributed ; or if capital must for some invisible reason have a reward, then it should take the form of interest on value lent. It is unnecessary to point out that this reasoning involves the socialist fallacy that dead capital cannot yield a profit. In fine, the systems of co-operative production which have been started in this country are all based on an avowed recognition of this mistaken doctrine, the effect of which is simply to put the boot on the other leg. Under the present system of wagedom the capitalist takes the whole of the profits and the contributor of labour none. Under the proposed system of co-operation the labourer takes the whole of the profits and the contributor of dead capital none. One arrangement is as unfair and as inexpedient as the other. Each should properly take profits in proportion to the value of his original contribution. The borrowing of capital at a fixed interest is open to many of the objections which can be urged against paying the workman a fixed wage.

Like profit-sharing, like socialism, like trade unionism, co-operative production is based on a good deal that is true but considerably adulterated with fiction and fallacy. Frequently the good outweighs the evil. Consider the effect of co-operative production in the following cases :[1]—

Fourteen Paris piano-makers in 1848, without any means of their own, or Government aid, after great hardships and difficulties in starting, founded and carried on successfully a business which two years afterwards owned 40,000 francs' worth of property.

A co-operative association of fifteen furniture-turners started with 313 francs as their entire capital. After having at first to content themselves with wages—$87\frac{1}{2}$ cents per day—they made their enterprise a complete success.

A small association of arm-chair makers, which started in 1849 with 135 francs, made 37,000 francs of net profits, and

[1] Reports by Her Majesty's Representatives abroad on the system of Co-operation in Foreign Countries. Presented to both Houses of Parliament by command of Her Majesty, June 1886.

could afford to pay rent of 5500 francs per annum for their workshop.

An association of curriers started with only four working members : in two years, 86 members were at work.

A co-operation of filemakers, starting with fourteen members and 500 francs, acquired a capital of 150,000 francs and two houses of business—one in Paris, the other in the provinces.

A successful co-operation of boot-form makers began with two francs.

One of spectacle-makers, with 650 francs, had in 1883 a capital of over 1,270,000 francs.

Of course the difficulties with which co-operation has to deal are those which might be expected from the refusal of the workers to work in harmony and partnership with the owners of wealth. As Mr. Egerton points out in the French Report, " it has been found by experience that co-operative associations on a large scale are difficult to *start.* . . . Really good men are required at first. It is difficult to find the sums necessary to begin co-operation on a large scale. . . . Owing to the difficulty in finding sufficiently large premises, only a small number of members can generally work together at first."

The admission of the capitalist within the ranks on equal terms would solve all these difficulties. Mr. Egerton adds : " The very strict obedience to regulations exacted and enforced, and their discipline—greater far than could have been maintained by masters—are considered to be in great measure the cause of the success of these co-operative societies."

It is hardly necessary to point out that the spirit of self-help manifested in all forms of co-operation is exceedingly distasteful to the socialists. In the first workmen's congress held in Paris, in 1876, the general opinion was for co-operation, though men such as M. Isidore Finance, a house-painter by trade, and a prominent speaker at working men's meetings, expressed himself strongly against it, not so much on the ground of the many failures in 1848, and after the collapse of the *Crédit au travail* in 1868, but on account of the *selfishness* of the system, the members of co-operative societies becoming, he said, *nothing better than capitalists.*

Co-operative production as thus understood, and based on the theory that dead capital is not entitled to profits, has the support of no less an authority than J. S. Mill. Looking forward into the distant future, he is of opinion that the time will come when " owners of capital will gradually find it to their advantage, instead of maintaining the struggle of the old system with workpeople of only the worst description, to *lend* their capital to the associations—to do this at a diminishing rate of interest, and at last, perhaps, even to exchange their capital for terminable annuities. In this or some such mode the existing accumulations of capital might *honestly*, and by a kind of spontaneous process, become in the end the joint property of all who participate in their productive employment ; a transformation which, thus effected, would be the nearest approach to social justice, and the most beneficial ordering of industrial affairs for the universal good which it is possible at present to foresee." [1]   This remarkable passage shows that Mill himself did not recognise the moral right of the owner of wealth to the fruits of that wealth. Hence his denunciations of the " unearned increment " were at least consistent.

[1] *Principles of Political Economy*, by J. S. Mill.

CHAPTER VII

FINALLY, let us examine the system which may be called the Capitalisation of Labour.

In order to understand the foundations on which the system is based, it may be as well to examine the whole labour question from three distinct points of view : from the historical standpoint, the juridical standpoint, and the economic standpoint.

We may trace the history of industrialism briefly through its successive changes along with the progress of civilisation, and then, by discovering the general tendency, predict with tolerable certainty the direction which further changes are likely to take. In the earliest times of which we have any record we find the whole of the working population—that is, of those who toil with their hands, the agricultural labourers and artisans—in a state of abject slavery. Long before they emerged from that state their lot as slaves considerably improved, but still they remained slaves. We hear much of the liberty and democracy of the Greeks, but we know that at the time when Athenians were enjoying a high degree of civilisation the great majority of the people of Attica were slaves. For every freeman in Athens there must have been four or five others who were written off as mere chattels. While every citizen of full age had a voice in the affairs of the State, these poor toilers had none. So that universal suffrage in those days meant what it would mean now if the working classes were disfranchised. The slaves were of course bought and sold. Aristotle himself defines them as " animated machines." The Malthusian restraints were rigidly applied, not *by* them but *to* them, because their masters found it cheaper to buy than to rear them. They were of two classes, the bondsmen in the fields, who more nearly resembled the serfs of Norman England, inasmuch as they could not be exported or separated from their families, and the town slaves, who were chiefly barbarians, that is, foreigners and captives in war; these more nearly resembled the slaves of the American plantations of last generation. They stood on a stone in the circle, and were knocked down by auction to the highest bidder at sums ranging from half a mina to twenty or thirty minas. But these high prices were paid chiefly for courtesans and cithara players. This class of slave could not acquire property like the serfs. The miners worked in chains, and frequently died from the effects of the bad air in the ill-ventilated mines. They were sometimes kept in gangs and let out for hire, when their owners seem to have realised something like a profit of 15 per cent. Slaves were not believed on oath, but when their evidence was required they were tortured. Still, even this was an advance upon the slavery of still earlier times, for we find that it was unlawful to hurt a slave without just cause, nor could a master kill his own slave without obtaining a legal sentence against him. Moreover, slaves had certain privileges of sanctuary, and sometimes, though rarely, they were manumitted, when they were compelled to respect their former master as a patron under penalty of being again sold into slavery.

Coming down to later times we find the position of the Roman slave still further ameliorated. One law makes it penal for a master to kill his own slave: later still such an act is made murder. Again, it was enacted that when slaves were sold, the family should not be broken up. Young children could no longer be separated from their parents, nor a husband from his wife. Manumission was of far more frequent occasion than among the Greeks. From being mere domestics, mechanics, and artisans, they rose to the position of commercial agents, and were allowed to acquire property, called *peculium*, and to enforce their claims in the Courts of Law. We find also doctors, literary men, actors, and courtesans fetching high prices. Although Christianity did not condemn the institution of slavery, it is said by some to have mitigated the harshness of owners ; but the observed change may, with greater probability, be referred to the advance in morality accompanying a growing civilisation. The incursions of the northern barbarians upset the existing relations between masters and slaves, and when the clouds are again lifted we find the " Adscripti Glebæ " in the place of all the heterogeneous classes and sub-classes of Roman slaves. These " Adscripti Glebæ " were the " serfs " of the Middle Ages.

Serfdom or villeinage was at first a state in which the serf belonged to the lord of the soil like his stock or cattle. They were removable from the folk-land at the lord's pleasure. A tendency towards something like liberty is seen in the distinction between " pure villeinage " and " privileged villeinage." The first " was when a villein held land on terms of doing whatsoever was commanded of him, nor knew in the evening what was to be done in the morning." His services were undefined. Privileged villeins, on the other hand, could not be removed from their holdings so long as they performed certain definite services. Base and compulsory as these services were, it is worthy of remark that these villein-socmen were commonly described as " free." How these services came to be commuted one by one into a fixed rent in kind or in money, and finally in money only, is a long story.[1]

When the lot of the workman of to-day is unfavourably compared (as it frequently is by socialists) with the lot of the workers of four or five centuries ago, we must remember that the comparison is usually made between two different strata of society. The happy yeomen of those days (if they were so happy) are the farmers of to-day, *not* the wage-earning labourers. No doubt the small landholders of the period following upon the Black Death were in tolerably comfortable circumstances ; but when we come to examine the position of those who had no strips to plough, the case is very different. But to proceed with our short historical survey. Trade, commerce, and town life bring many changes. The rise of the great middle class in

---

[1] See Seebohm's *English Village Communities :* also *Six Centuries of Work and Wages*, by J. E. Thorold Rogers, M.P.

Europe during the fifteenth and sixteenth centuries ; its conflicts with the ancient feudal aristocracy and eventual triumph, consummated (in this country) in the great Reform Act of 1832 ; the gradual development of two new parties, employers and employed, or so-called capitalists and manual labourers, are grand historical facts which bring us down to the present day. The battle is now between employer and employed. Year by year the strife waxes hotter. We are now in the midst of it. Louder and louder roar the discontented hosts of wage earners. Inch by inch the baffled capitalists retire before the onward pressure of numbers. Masters quail ; they offer terms ; they buy off the enemy for a while ; and then again the billows swell and roll forward as before. Whither does all this tend ? See, the millions are organising : no longer a mob, they are an army. The battle cannot rage for ever with equal fortune. And which side shall win ? That is the question which some answer with hope, others with despair. It is for us to project the converging rays of the past into the future, and with that light to predict the outcome.

The workman is free at last. After centuries of struggles, of successes, and of failures, serfdom in this country is dead. The last vestige of the system perished within the memory of living men, though it was practically extinct long before. The sale of a human being in England, even though he himself be the vendor, is void. A slave landed for one moment on English soil is by law free. Even a long lease of a man (if I may use the expression) is discountenanced, and apprentices are getting rarer year by year. The question whether a contract of service intended to last during the servant's lifetime was legal, was raised for the last time, I believe, just half a century ago.[1]

The binding of even young persons for so long a period as seven years is regarded as savouring of serfdom ; and so, with all respect to the recommendations of Royal Commissioners, it is. I admit that the change brings evils in its train. Periods of transition from one régime to another invariably bristle with dangers and difficulties; but let us beware lest, in our efforts to escape from them, we magnify the good of the old order which is passing

---

[1] *Wallis* v. *Day*, 2 M. and W. 1837.

away, more than the greater good of the new order which is
surely coming. " Faith is the evidence of things not seen."
And it is a rare virtue !

And now what have we in the place of that which is
passed away ? Instead of serfdom we have wagedom. The
present system is one of labour hiring. At the bottom of the
scale we find agricultural labourers standing out for a real wage,
fair and square, without patronage or privilege : at the top we
find the men in the large mills, the factories, the iron-works,
and the mines, demanding something more than this. They
are already in the happy position to which the agricultural
labourers are aspiring, and yet they are discontent. No wonder.
They have discovered by experience that they receive no more
than is necessary to keep them in repair for the employers. ·
The evidences of increased prosperity have been worked up and
blown out by the " exploiting " class ; but the workers know
perfectly well that the accounts of their growing wealth are not
only untrue but demonstrably false *à priori*. A man will not
listen to an argument showing that he himself feels very well,
when he surely knows that he feels very ill. Nor will he
patiently listen to those who tell him he is very happy, when
he knows he is very wretched. Then what are these workers
in the advance guard of the industrial army clamouring for ?
The truth is they cannot answer definitely themselves. They
hardly know. They speak with inarticulate voice. But we ·
can see from one or two indications whither their aspirations
tend. And upon the indistinct goal of their endeavours we
must keep our eye, in order that we may be able to predict the
probable nature of the relations between employers and
employed in the near or distant future. Why have some of
them agitated for a sliding scale ? Because they feel that
they have a right to a share of the profits of the undertaking
upon which they are engaged. Therefore, they say, we
will have a sliding scale, because when the price of our product is high we shall receive a higher wage. This shows
that whatever economic doctrine they may hold in theory, they
feel in practice that they are after all worth something more
than the wages they fetch in the open market. Again, the
arbitrations between masters and men which have become such

a prominent institution of late are clearly based on a dim recognition of the same doctrine : and yet again, the establishment of large co-operative societies for the purposes of production or distribution is due to a feeling that the workers have a right to a share, if not the whole of the profits of the undertaking they contribute to. All these signs show that the working classes themselves (and, to a certain extent, their employers also) dimly perceive that they have some rights (more than those of the horses and oxen who also help to create) to the resulting compound. It is hardly remarkable that, after being long deprived of any share of the produce, they should some of them swing round to the extreme view that their share is the whole of it.

The outcome of our historical survey is not definite or precise. It amounts to this : that there is a strong feeling among the workers (and others), not perhaps amounting to a reasoned conviction, that they have a right to a share of the wealth they help to create. Will a juridical analysis of the respective rights of the workers and masters furnish the exact quantitative relations ?

I do not propose here to discuss the expediency of the institution of private property. I shall assume that it is the most economical means of equitable distribution attainable by man. Again, from time immemorial it has been admitted that the fruits of property (the so-called " unearned increment"), such as the apples that come on the owner's apple-tree, or the eggs that appear in his poultry-yard, rightly and expediently belong to the owner. Whether they ought not to belong to everybody, or to the State of which the owner is a member, or to the first finder or first taker, or to somebody else, is a question which need not be dealt with here. I shall take it ᾽for granted as an axiom that the fruits of wealth belong to the owner of that wealth. In the case of commixture or confusion of valuables belonging to different owners, where they cannot again be separated (as *e.g.* when different wines are poured into the same cask, or the wheat from two fields is stacked all together), the value of the whole so resulting is divided between the owners in proportion to the shares contributed by them respectively. In some cases one of them is regarded as the owner of the whole, and the other or others is or are said to have a lien upon it to the value of his or their shares. Such is the common-sense view of what is just in such cases. When the value of the whole is greater than the value of the several elements contributed, then the increment of value is also divided in proportion to the shares contributed by each ; as, for example, when wheat has been sown by *B* on a field belonging to *A* (the harvest may be exceptionally good); *A* is taken to have contributed the annual rent of the field (what he could have let it for in the market for one year), and *B* is taken to have contributed the original value of the seed and the value of his own services, ploughing, hoeing, reaping, etc., at the price such services would have cost in the market. The produce is then divided between *A* and *B* in proportion to the totals arrived at, or else (as in most civilised countries) the whole produce becomes the property of *A*, with the obligation attached of paying *B* the aforesaid proportion, *B* having a lien on the produce by way of security.

This certainly seems to be based on justice and convenience, and whether it is actually sound or unsound (in spite of socialistic arguments) it is the principle upon which all such-like questions are as a fact, and for centuries have been, solved. In Roman law if a man bought a mare in foal, the foal belonged to the purchaser. It is true that if he bought a female slave who was *enceinte*, without any special stipulation, the child belonged to the former master and not to the purchaser ; but that was for a particular reason, based on the relations between masters and slaves, and which need not be gone into here. As a general rule it may be affirmed that to whomsoever a thing belongs, to him belong the fruits thereof, and where things owned by different owners bear fruits in common, such fruits belong to such owners in proportion to the shares contributed by them respectively. Such was the law of Rome. Such is the law of England. For example, in the case of a riparian landowner, if the river gradually deposits another half-acre of land on to his estate (provided it cannot be shown to have been *bodily* detached from the estate of another person) it is counted as part of the fruits of his land, and belongs to him accordingly, although it has cost him nothing.

Let us use these facts to throw light on the problem of labour payment. Who is properly the owner of wealth which has been made more valuable by the expenditure upon it of labour? A cloth merchant or draper puts a quantity of cloth into the hands of a tailor with instructions to convert it into clothing. The work is done. To whom should the wearing apparel belong when it is finished? Few except lawyers could say at once to whom it actually does belong by law. In one sense (the technical and precise sense of the term ownership) it belongs to the draper. In another and looser sense, part of its value belongs to the draper and another part of its value to the tailor. And what is the just ratio of the two parts? Of course if a distinct bargain had been made beforehand, that would settle the matter. If the draper had said, " The cloth is worth £10 ; when it is ready for the market in the shape of clothing you must pay me £10 out of the proceeds of the sale," then the draper would have a *lien* (I am not using · the word in its usual technical sense) upon it to the value of £10. But he might as well have sold the cloth to the tailor at once, indeed better, for his payment is deferred without interest. Or he might have taken the interest into account and said, " You must pay me ten *guineas* out of the proceeds," in calculating which he ought to have formed some estimate of the risk he was running ; for, conceivably, the apparel might sell for less than the value of the cloth, just as most manuscript sermons sell for less than the original value of the unspoilt paper before the expenditure of the clerical labour upon it. Again, the draper might have said, " Never mind the value of the cloth. The value of *your* services is £18. I will take and sell the finished article, and you shall have a lien upon it for £18." In this case the tailor would be in a similar position to that of the draper under the first arrangement—a very foolish position. Alas ! but it is the position of the working man of the present day. Suppose the clothes, instead of selling for £28—the cost of the elements—sold for £42, owing to a keen demand, who would pocket the 50 per cent profit ? Under the last-named arrangement, of course, the draper would, and quite right too. Fools are made to be bled. But now suppose no previous bargain had been made, what would be

the equitable way of distributing the proceeds of the sale
according to the principle underlying the law of all civilised
countries? The case is one of commixture. The increment
of surplus value is £14, or 50 per cent. The value of the
whole product is £42. Clearly, the draper would take £15
and the tailor would take £27, instead of which, at the present
day, under the system of wagedom, if the tailor is a journeyman or wage-earning tailor, he gets £18 and the draper gets
£24. In other words, the draper or employer pockets £9
that ought to belong to the tailor. Of course, if workers
insist on making bad bargains, that is their own look-out.

The political economists themselves admit and even contend that unto whomsoever the capital belongs, to him
belong the profits. But they are pleased to put their own
definition or definitions on the term "capital," and out of
the dozen or so of current definitions, though they all bear
a strong family likeness to a sieve they have this one trait ᷉
in common—they all carefully exclude the right of the
manual workers to a share of the profits. Their united
testimony is valuable only as showing the influence upon
ordinary minds of the fundamental juridical principle as to the
ownership of the fruits of wealth. The question is, Who
contributes the labour in the ordinary processes of industrialism? Banish all "orthodox" dogmas about "wage funds"
and "the three agents of production" and the rest. Clearly,
if the workers are slaves, the owner contributes the labour, and
if we grant his right to his slaves we must admit his right to
the fruits of their labour. He runs all the risk. If there is
a loss he incurs it. He cannot afford to starve his slaves any
more than his horses because their labour is unproductive in a
particular venture. If their labour is continually unremunerative, if they cost more than they bring in, he must get rid of
them. He has made a bad purchase, just as though he had
bought a lame horse. Similarly, if he takes an apprentice for
seven years who turns out an incorrigible dolt, he is in the
position of one who has bought a house which he cannot let
for the interest on the purchase money. He must make the
best of a bad job. Lastly, if he hires a man by the week, or
the day, or the hour, to work for him at a pre-arranged wage,

he practically supplies the labour himself, he runs all the risk, and the temporary slave has no claim whatever on the profits.

This brings us face to face with the question whether the wage bargain is a good one for the worker, for the capitalist, or for the community. Historically and juridically the evidence seems to be strongly in the direction of a different bargain. The tendency seems to be very marked towards a system of capitalisation of labour as a substitute for the present system of labour-hiring or wagedom.

Before we can speak positively on this point we must try to ascertain what would be the numerous economic effects of so great and revolutionary a change. The capitalisation system proceeds on the assumption that labourers [1] are themselves a form of capital, because their value depends on the demand for them as an element in production. It follows that if we knew the market value of the labourers (their capital value as *slaves*), and also the market value of the capital contributed by the capitalist, we should know in what proportion the net profits on the combination ought justly to be divided. At present I have grounds for believing that the employer pockets *more than half* the workmen's just share ! To begin with, he pockets the whole of the *interest* on labourers. If we estimate this at the very low figure of $2\frac{1}{2}$ per cent on the present depreciated value, it amounts to about £375,000,000 per annum, which gives an average of about £12 a year, man, woman, and child, all over the British Isles. But figures cannot well be depended on in the absence of accurate information. Perhaps, however, even the most sceptical denouncer of civilisation will admit that, take them all round, British workmen are worth at least as much as niggers were thirty years ago in the Southern States of America. I ask for no higher

---

[1] Those who prefer it can speak of labour force, but we do not speak of engine force and horse force as articles of commerce. If one requires a portion of horse labour, he is not said to *buy* a couple of hours of horse force, but to hire the horse for a couple of hours. Such parlance is both more in accordance with usage and also more accurate. Metaphysical expressions like labour force are always best avoided. Therefore, let us rather describe a workman as letting himself out for hire by the hour than as selling so much of his labour force ; more especially as we have no means of accurately measuring that force except by time. One might as well measure the force of two different-sized locomotives in terms of working hours.

estimate.   And yet what is the worth of a civilised man, if he
would but claim his liberty and work as only a free man can ?
—not too long, not too monotonously, but intelligently and
economically, with an interest in his work, and a love for his
art or his craft ?   And what then would be the workman's
share of production ?   That he has a right to the whole profits
of his labour is the contention of the capitalisationist.   He
does not recommend the employer to " give " him a share by
way of bonus—he holds that the profits on labour belong to
the labourer by *right* and not by favour.   He believes that
the time will come when the hiring of a man will be as uncommon a transaction as the purchase of a slave is now.

But at present the bargain entered into between employer
and employed is a contract of hiring—*locatio operarum.*
Practically the transaction amounts to this : The workman says
to the capitalist, " Here I am ; you see me for yourself; I can
do such or such kind of work.   You want that kind of work
done.   You think that by the process of combining the capital
you have with my labour you will gain a profit.   I don't
know, and I don't care ; at the same time, I don't mean to run
any risk.   I reckon myself worth ninepence an hour ; give me
that, and you have me and my labour and skill for what they
are worth ; put me at profitable work, put me at unprofitable
work ; I don't care a straw which.   If you stop paying, I stop
work ; and if I stop work you can stop payment.   The
quantity and quality of my work will not be below the average,
but of course I am not fool enough to do more than that for
the sake of enriching you.   I shan't scamp any more than I
think safe, because if you find me out scamping more than the
average I shall get the sack."   To which the capitalist replies,
" All right ; ninepence an hour ; and twenty-four hours a day,
or as much of it as you can manage without food, drink, rest
or recreation.   I shall hire you by the hour, and when my
process is completed you will leave if it does not pay me to
repeat it.   I see my way to earn 20 per cent, and, if so, I
shall hire you again ; if not, you can go and hang yourself."
And so the bargain is struck.

Now the worker knows, or ought to know, that on the
average the industrial process is profitable ; the average profit

on capital is about 3 per cent. This is the reward of abstinence, and it is called interest. It is not the reward of risk. If security were *absolute* in the strictest sense of the word, even then money could not be borrowed on it for 1 per cent. Owners would rather consume than invest at less than a certain minimum. And yet the workman voluntarily foregoes his interest rather than invest his labour at a risk. He would otherwise incur the trouble of looking into the venture; he might actually incur a loss; on the whole, he prefers the happy security of the cab-horse to the responsibility of a capitalist. Whether his caution is rightly called prudence will be seen on examination. At all events, the employer hires the labourer, invests his labour, takes all risk, and pockets all profits (including interest). And quite right too, if—*if* he first offered the workman the choice of putting his labour into the concern at a venture as a capitalist.

It seems to have escaped the notice of most writers on social subjects that the ordinary employer of labour performs no less than *three* distinct functions :—

1st. He is a capitalist pure and simple; that is, one whose business is to examine every kind of investment with a view to estimating the risk thereof, and to invest his own (and in some cases his clients') capital accordingly. This process requires study, long and careful training, and vast experience. It is seen in its purest form on the Stock Exchange. It also constitutes the chief function of bankers.

2d. He is what may be called a superintending worker or manager, a position which calls for an intimate knowledge of every branch of the business in which he is engaged. Attention must be paid to the minutest economies in each department, and to the co-ordination of all—a function which is altogether apart from that of speculation, and which is in itself sufficient to absorb the energies of a lifetime.

3d. Lastly, the employer stands in a remarkable position with respect to some of those who contribute towards the process over which he presides. He actually undertakes to guarantee the labourers a certain average remuneration for their services. He is in the unenviable position of a company which should be formed for the purpose of granting an annuity

to professional men in exchange for their fluctuating incomes.
Would a doctor get up at all hours of the night if he had
compounded with such a company to hand over all his fees for
£500 a year? The work of the company would be precisely
analogous to the third function of the present employer of
labour. He has to guarantee the wages of workmen who have
no reason to care whether the work is done or not, whether the
process is profitable or not, so long as they can keep their
places, or get others equally good. The employer undertakes
these three distinct rôles—speculator, organiser, wage insurer.
And when a man undertakes to do two or three different things
at a time, he is pretty sure to do all badly. When a
carpenter sets up as doctor and horse-dealer, he is likely to
lose at all three undertakings, and to cheat and humbug his
customers besides. The employer tries to combine the distinct
operations of evaluating risk in trade, of organising and
superintending work, and of ensuring the success of other
people's investments—other people, forsooth, who have little or
no interest in the success of the investments! Is it surprising,
then, that his ventures are often hastily and foolishly calculated,
that his works are often superintended badly, and at great
expense, and that those with whom he compounds for their
labour turn out year by year less and less worth the composition?

These three functions, if undertaken at all, should be
divided among three distinct classes of persons. In some
cases this specialisation has taken place already with regard
to speculation. The professional investor (say banker) who
borrows money at interest from clients who care not to run
risk, and invests it in a hundred more or less doubtful speculations, is a useful and even necessary member of modern society.
Manufacturers who speculate least, and rely for profits on the
economic working of their own arrangements, are, as a rule,
the most successful. But as to the third function, no company
has ever yet been started with the simple object of guaranteeing
either manual workers or any other class of workers a uniform
return for their work, for the obvious reason that it could
not pay to do it except at an exorbitant rate. What the
premium is which the employer requires for undertaking the

insurance of his workpeople's earnings it is impossible to say, mixed up as it is with his profit and loss account; but we may safely affirm that, taken by itself, this part of his business is folly so far as he himself is concerned, and ruinous to his clients.

And what is the observed effect of the system of wagedom or labour-hiring on the working classes themselves? It is obvious that in many respects the interests of masters and men, so far from being identical, actually conflict.

"The minimum wage is that on which the worker can exist, however hardly. For less than this he will not work. Every shilling above this is fought over, and the wage rises and falls by competition. At every stage of their relationship there is a contest between employer and employed. If the wage is paid for a fixed day's work—as in nearly every trade—the employer tries to lengthen the day, the employed try to shorten it : the longer the day the greater the production of 'surplus value,' *i.e.* of the difference between the wage paid and the value produced. The employer tries to increase surplus value by pressing the workers to exertion ; they lessen exertion in order not to hasten the time of their discharge. The employer tries still to increase surplus value by supplanting male labour with female and child labour at lower wages. The men resist such introduction, knowing that the ultimate result is to increase the amount taken by capital and to lessen that obtained by labour."[1]

This is a perfectly truthful statement of the position, showing that the present system necessarily tends to bring employers and employed into collision.

The rate of profits in all trades varies from age to age, from year to year, and from day to day. The diurnal variations are commonly minute, and so far unimportant ; and the variations during long periods, corresponding with the rise of some trades and the decline of some others in the country or district, have their effects obscured by lapse of time ; labour is diverted into new channels before low profits have time to pinch the labourer. But what may be called the annual variations are neither too small nor too gradual to be felt, and it is with these that labourers are concerned. The sea has its tides, its waves, and its ripples, but it is the waves, and the waves only, that make us so sea-sick.

---

[1] *Westminster Review*, July 1886.

When employers are making their 20 per cent is it reasonable to expect the workman, whose toil has mainly contributed to the high profit, to sit down content with his minimum wage as he did when profits were at 5 or 6 per cent? Clearly, wages must be raised or the men strike; and what is more, are frequently backed up by public opinion and favoured by opportunity. Masters do not care to be idle in prosperous times, and the men know it, and sooner or later their demand is granted or a favourable compromise effected. Then follows a period of good fortune and tranquillity of some duration.

Meanwhile, with little or no experience of vicissitudes, our working man has married on the strength of the rise, or perhaps his children have increased in number, or he pays a higher rent for a better cottage, or his family has accustomed itself to additional comforts. And now comes the decline. The prosperity of the trade has attracted new capital, or the demand has contracted to its old limits, and profits sink again to the original level or below it. It is now the master's turn to grumble and ask for change; he very naturally determines to reduce wages. The workman as naturally resists. His scale of living has been modified to suit improved circumstances; he has become accustomed to the new rate of wages, and now he cannot well go back or retrench. Another conflict ensues, and one or other of the combatants goes to the wall. No one believes that this state of strain, this incessant struggle, is desirable; every strike entails untold misery and waste, no matter what the result may be; and yet under the present system of wagedom there does not appear to be any loophole out of the difficulty. An eternal see-saw! Pull baker, pull devil! Such is the cheerless prospect.

Trade unionism is the outcome of an organised effort to apply a remedy from the workman's point of view. It is based on the principle of the bundle of sticks—"union is strength." But men are not sticks, and the weak point in trade organisation is mutual distrust. If the men knew their strength, *and could trust one another*, the end aimed at would long ago have been attained. But what an end! Everlasting wagedom; forced reduction of the fruit of labour because it now passes into the wrong hands; restricted total production, as though overproduction were possible while there are hungry mouths to fill; and, above all, a gradual tendency in the direction of deteriorated labour; the exercise of superior strength, skill, genius, all prohibited; and the quantity and quality of work brought down to the standard of the inferior workman; in short, a levelling down of the industrial classes. Such is the end unconsciously aimed at by the trade unions.

It is clear that the solidarity of the wage earners with the object of doing as little real work as possible in a given time, and of obtaining a statutory limitation of working hours, is advocated by those who do not realise the ultimate effect of their endeavour. Of course if the effectual demand for the commodities they help to produce continued the same whether the supply was large or small, costly or cheap, their aim would be a highly meritorious one. The effect of their efforts, if successful, would be to increase the proportionate share of the worker in the total produce for distribution; that is to say, while he would individually receive no less, the wage-earning population would increase in order to fill up the deficiency in labour caused by the restricted out-put of each individual worker. In itself an increased population, without any increased pressure on the means of subsistence, is a good rather than an evil (that is, supposing that " life is worth living ").

But the actual chain of the effects of unionism, as now directed, would be this: first, there is a falling off in the supply of labour (measured by time and energy), a conscious and intentional falling off; next, the demand for the things the labourers help to produce remaining constant at present prices, the demand for labourers is stimulated; wages rise; population increases till wages are again reduced to subsistence level; and the position is the same except that there are more labourers at work supplying the old quantity of commodities at the old wage. But, since the cost of the capital remains the same, and the cost of labourers has been increased (just in proportion to the increase of workers), the price of the total production of the country must be raised to cover the extra cost, all of which extra sum goes to maintain the new population. Capital receives no more than before, but the rise in cost, and consequent rise in prices, necessarily checks the demand, *i.e.* the effectual demand. In the place of a hundred coats, or tables, or carriages, or pianos, that were asked for before, only eighty are asked for now. Some people seem to imagine that the effect of this shrinkage in the demand would be to at once lower prices again permanently. Nothing of the sort. Prices would fall at once, but not permanently. The expected reduction would not come out of profits, because profits cannot permanently fall below a certain normal percentage on capital. The effect of a fall is to drive capital out of circulation and into the absolute securities. And the reduction cannot come out of wages, because they are already at a minimum. Hence a permanent reduction in price cannot be made at all. The alternative is a restricted production. Capital flows out, and the demand for labourers correspondingly diminishes, and population must again dwindle. How? we all know. Wages cannot permanently fall below the minimum. Temporarily, no doubt, the fall does take place, and then the weakness of unionism shows itself. The strain is too much for it: a dozen men are famishing on a raft; a promise to stand by one another and to live or starve together might be binding on some few, but a terrible strain would be put on the *morale* of most by the instinct of self-preservation. This is an extreme example, but there is only a difference of degree between the case of these starving men and that of the general body of wage earners when depression in trade causes a necessary reduction in wages. All may try to live and work at something less than is needful for health, or even sometimes life, or some may break the contract and accept twice the wage for three times the amount of work. Whoever first does this sets the ball rolling. The merest rumour that out of six conspirators in prison one is going to turn informer causes a general rush. To be behindhand is to be lost. So with wage earners ; a general distrust sets in, and the union is but a name.

Meantime, what is the effect of this policy on the quality of the workers themselves ? There is no inducement to excel. Anything like superiority is ruthlessly crushed out. The labourer becomes less and less productive in proportion to the capital with which he has to co-operate, and the fruits of labour become smaller compared with the amount of labour contributed to production. Further, the increased cost of the labourer (of labour hire) in proportion to its productiveness stimulates the inventor to devise substitutes, and this again is rendered easier by the mechanical character of the work to be done. If men begin by reducing themselves to the level of unskilled labourers, they will end by being mere machines, and when that happens it is often easy to invent an iron machine to do the work as well or better and at a less cost. No one has yet invented a machine for doing work fit for a free man. Perhaps, if no other argument could be urged against wagedom, the mere fact that the whole of the gain from labour-saving machinery has fallen into the hands of the employer, instead of into the hands of the class to whose members it is almost entirely due, would suffice to condemn it.

Now it is clear that if instead of accepting wages—letting themselves out for hire by the week or the hour—the workers entered into the venture as capitalists and free men, receiving, instead of a fixed wage, a certain pre-arranged percentage of the gross produce (a percentage at first based on a calculation of the amount paid in wages over a number of years), the receipts of the hands would vary like the profits of other capitalists with the success of the venture and the state of trade. When trade was good the men would be receiving considerably more than usual, and no strike would be necessary in order to give them a fair share of the general prosperity. When trade became depressed their share would decrease proportionately with that of the other capitalists, and neither strike nor lock-out would result from a diminution in their income. The masters would have no reason to demand an arbitrary reduction in the scale of labour remuneration, as they have now. Thus the cause of strikes would be eradicated.

It has almost invariably been observed that, as matter of history, the successful strikes have been those which were based on justice or common-sense fairness and attended with public sympathy, while those strikes which have been made in response to a fair claim on the part of the "masters" to a reasonable reduction of wages have usually been unsuccessful.

If, therefore, the workpeople under the supposed new conditions should clamour to extort alms (for it would be nothing less) from their employers, in flagrant violation of contract, and in face of every reason to the contrary, a few inevitable failures would soon teach them wisdom. Public opinion could never side against employers who, in a period of depressed trade and low profits, were being called upon to *raise* their work-people's share of the receipts, and that in spite of con-tract; nor is it likely that such a demand would be made. Thus it appears, whatever the advantages or disadvantages of the capitalisation of labour, one thing is certain, and that is that strikes would completely disappear.

Another important effect of the system will be the equi-libration of supply and demand in the labour market during times of expansion and depression. It is well known that in periods of great commercial distress large manufacturers are in the habit of keeping their works going, and paying full wages, even though they may be working at a dead loss, in order to keep the hands together to be ready with the full complement in case of revival; and also in many cases for another reason, namely, as a blind to their creditors, to whom a sudden con-traction of business would be a revelation. And then, when the depression has continued too long for endurance, batch after batch of workmen and women are indiscriminately dis-missed; not those who are best qualified to obtain a livelihood in other occupations, but, if anything, rather the reverse. Under the new system, when trade is bad and profits low, the hands will suffer equally with the masters; those of them who know other crafts will prefer to change their work rather than go on at very low pay; and having thus ceased to drag at the " wage fund," will leave behind them those *least* qualified to change their occupation. Those who go will gain, and those who remain will gain.

Thus the action of the new system will resemble the action of the governor balls in a steam-engine; that is to say, it will substitute automatic equilibration for intermittent readjustment. A more perfect analogy cannot be found. A smooth continuous readjustment by infinitesimal adaptations is, all will admit, vastly better than artificial readjustments at comparatively long intervals and by rule of thumb. In the engine an accelerated pace causes the governor balls to fly out at a tangent, and by rising to shut off steam and so to slacken the pace ; which slackening of the pace causes the balls to fall, and thereby to put on steam and so accelerate the pace. So that in fact the acceleration of the pace is the cause of its slackening, and *vice versâ*. This is true equilibrium. And so in trade a falling off in profits would at once bring about a diminution in the number of the recipients of those profits, and thereby raise the average profits received by the remaining recipients. The rate of labour payment will no longer limp and hobble up and down after the rate of profits, dragged by fits and starts, as it were by an elastic chain, but will accompany it, while at the same time the number of those who divide the labour share will dwindle *pari passu* with the dwindling of the profits.

An incidental result of this self-reduction in the number of hands in response to a falling off in profits will be the consequent temporary limitation of production, an effect greatly to be desired ; an effect, too, obtained without imposing enforced idleness upon the working classes at a time when they are least anxious to be idle. This beautiful self-adjustment of the industrial machine is one of the most convincing proofs of the soundness of the system.

Again, the gradually growing perception of the manual worker that he is himself a capitalist will fairly give the death-blow to the suicidal policy of trying to injure the employer by permanently limiting production, keeping down stock, or shortening the hours of labour and the quantity of work to be done per hour. The last-named object will be brought about in another way, and with a very different effect, as will presently be shown. Finding by experience that they themselves are actually capitalists—that their own and their employers' interests are identical (which at present they are not, whatever may be said to the contrary) ; that masters and workmen are all in the same boat—they will all pull together, and do their best for the common weal ; and so will be brought to an end the great internecine war between "capital and labour." The moral effect of this change on all classes and on the stability of the State cannot be over-rated.

True morality is the result not of being preached at but of practical experience. We hear a great deal on all sides of the " improvidence of the working classes " ; but, even if true, is it very remarkable ? Under the system of wagedom the workman receives weekly a fixed sum, which he very naturally regards as practically an income to be relied on. True, a depression in trade may bring about a reduction, but not without a long notice and probably a fierce fight; or he may possibly be among those who are dismissed altogether; but this is a remote and improbable contingency, to set off against which there is the chance of a rise in wages and the possibility of promotion. On the whole then it is only reasonable that he should regard his present wage as a fixed income, up to which he may live, but which must not be exceeded. That this is the view taken by most working men is well known, and the consequences are equally well known. The day of decline comes ; the inevitable reduction is at hand ; retrenchment must be made. It is true that the labourer ought to have laid up provision against probable or possible mishap, but having jogged along for years at a fixed wage, how, in the name of reason, is providence to be learnt ? Bearing in mind that trade cycles are about ten years in length or thereabouts, it follows that a young man starting work at fifteen may never know what it is to have his income set back until he is twenty-five, with a wife and children and an accustomed standard of comfort. Is it in the nature of most men, having earned thirty-one shillings, to walk down on a Saturday to the penny-bank in order to deposit the odd shilling over and above the thirty shillings required at home, in case it may be wanted five or six years hence ? Of course it goes after the rest, just to give an extra fillip to existence—in beer, gin, tobacco, or any other article that serves to justify a little chat at the public-house. Hence it follows that a reduction of wages is sometimes tantamount to the ruin, or at least disgrace, of the workman.

Now what will be the effect of the capitalisation system ? The employer ceases to insure his workpeople ; they will have to insure themselves. One week they will receive their thirty shillings, and the next their twenty, instead of a uniform twenty-five. That is to say, they will each week (or it may be each quarter) receive the real value of their work, instead of the *average* value reckoned over a very long period. Thus they will learn providence by experience, daily experience, as their masters have done, for they will be compelled to put by the surplus on good weeks to make up for inevitable deficiences on bad weeks. No preaching will inculcate providence. Experience alone can teach it, and yet this very experience is denied to our working classes. Whether they like it or no, their average earnings are insured for them, and they are in the position of a manufacturer who should accept a fixed annuity for the profits of his business.

But further, the new system will conduce to mitigate the notorious improvidence of our labouring population in yet another way. Any recipient of a fluctuating income knows very well that he considers himself justified in living up to the *minimum* and not the *average* annual receipt. That is his standard, and all above that is regarded as so much " to the good." So that an artisan whose earnings fluctuate between twenty and thirty shillings will spend not the average twenty-five, but the minimum twenty shillings, and the balance will be put by.

Why are we always preaching " thrift " to the poor ? What is thrift as distinguished from economy ? It is the taking care of inconsiderable margins—minute balances of income over necessary expenditure. And what is the main cause of, and chief inducement to, thrift among the well-to-do classes ? I have no hesitation in saying that it is the fluctuation in their incomes. Let me explain. When a professional man whose annual expenses, according to his scale of living, are £300 a year, finds his income one year amount to £320, and another year to £280, he is compelled to save the surplus in the one year to make good the loss in the other year. He cannot tell exactly what the next year's income may be, and therefore instead of saving part of his extra savings only, he saves the whole. But if he found that his income was always exactly £305 a year, he would be sorely tempted to throw the odd £5 away in the purchase of little luxuries. This is actually the case with those annuitants who have no one to provide for but themselves. So if the workman whose household expenses are thirty shillings a week, and whose wages are thirty-one shillings, flings away the odd shilling upon any little luxuries that come in his way, he is by no means an unnatural specimen of his kind. It would take a couple of years' saving to cover a month's extra wage, and two years is a long time. Besides, there is very little inducement to put it by at all. But now suppose his income to fluctuate; he will then find it very easy, when he must put by four shillings, to put by the odd fifth shilling along with it; the shilling which now, through its very insignificance, is virtually thrown away or worse. A distinct effort of volition will be required in order to hold it back. A deliberate intention of spending so much a week in luxuries will have to take the place of a careless habit. Has any one ever attempted to estimate the enormous gain to the country which this aggregate thrift would bring about? Out . of the twenty-five millions a year and more which the revenue derives from the taxes on beer, wine, and spirits, how much is due to the odd shillings and sixpences that are spent at the public by the respectable and steady workman, merely because it is in his pocket, it is not particularly needed at home, and he has nothing better to do with it?

Money put by in a bank means a demand for capital as opposed to a demand for articles of direct consumption. It is no exaggeration to estimate the annual increase of capital in the country on the establishment of a proper system of labour payment at many millions a year.

We know enough of the effect of a joint interest in undertakings and in property to be able to predict with absolute certainty several other important effects which a just system of labour remuneration would have upon production.

To begin with, inasmuch as the workers will feel themselves to be practically partners in the concern, as in effect they will be (the legal aspect will be considered presently), each workman, finding himself a member of a great partnership, will be properly and justly jealous of the rest, and the idler will be shunned and got rid of. Dick will not work ten hours in order that Tom may work eight, both receiving the

same pay; nor will he work hard in order that Tom may
loiter. It does not matter to Dick nowadays, it does not
affect his own wages what Tom gets nor how Tom works; but
it will be a different matter when Tom's laziness diminishes
the total of which Dick takes a share. Nor will Dick make
things equal by loitering too. Not a bit of it. The tendency
will be not, as now, to level down, but to level up. The lazy
and unskilled must become industrious and skilful, or go to the
wall. The men will be jointly and severally their own
overlookers; and, little by little, an immense, cumbrous, and
costly organisation of overlookers will be dispensed with. This
is item one in diminished cost of production.

At present the workman very naturally regards his employer as a rival or an enemy—so he is; and unless he be
more than ordinarily high-principled, he scamps his work, or
at least gets as much pay as he can for as little effort as
possible. And who shall say that he is not justified in so
doing? It is the world-wide practice. And yet how much
do these few words signify: "As much pay for as little work
as possible"! Why, they mean that British industry (and
that of other countries) is the result of slave-driving, of grudged
labour, of exacted work; and this means that the work done
is less than a half of what it would be under a régime of
justice and common sense—and of incalculably inferior quality.
Hence the need for efficient overlooking. The salaries of
overlookers is an important factor in the cost of production.
And yet what can an overlooker do? You may lead your ox
to the water, but you cannot make him drink. He may
enforce the appearance of work, but not the true article. He
cannot infuse into his toiling subjects the spirit of the old
builders, whose work was a labour of love, whose soul was in
their art, and whose reward was the toil itself. Such is the
work of the independent and self-interested worker. It is not
the work of the slave, who sweats for another. Mercenaries
are not the soldiers for a forlorn hope, nor have the grandest
works of art been made to order at so much a day. Overlookers are indeed quite necessary under the present system;
but abolish them altogether, make the men their own overlookers, overlookers of greater efficiency and ubiquitous withal,

and what a saving in cost of production we have here, to say
nothing of the moral effect of the change !

But this elimination is by no means the greatest reduction
in cost of production ; for when industry is rendered coincident
with self-interest, every man will naturally and cheerfully
work as hard and as well as he can—at least it will be his
interest to do so, and not, as now, to shirk and scamp. Wherever anything approaching to this system has been tried, as in
" butty-gangs," or in piece-work, or in other modifications, as
in the slate-quarries in Wales, it has always been found to
succeed ; and even when a share of net profits has been
allotted as a bonus to overlookers, the result has been satisfactory, and this in spite of the blind attempts of the Legislature
to regulate the joint efforts with a view to gain of more than
a very few persons. The object of the men, as of the masters,
will be to make as much as possible of that quality of article
which pays best in the market—a quality which, though not
always necessarily superfine, is what it appears to be, and good
of its sort. Cheap goods are as much in demand, or more,
than dear ones, though the quality is known to be inferior.
One does not expect honeydew when one asks for shag, or
velvet when one asks for velveteen. Fifteen carat gold is as
honest as eighteen carat, and probably drives a better trade.
But the inferior quality which is to be deprecated is the
sham. Even masters are not fully awake to the difference
between a cheap article and a sham one, between butterine
sold as such, and butterine sold as butter. The scamping of
workmen has much to answer for, but it is doubtful whether
manufacturers are not the more culpable of the two. Be this
as it may, the existing tendency to scamp work will, under
the new system, diminish *pari passu* with the increased
experience of the workman ; and the imposing suite of chairs
and tables from which the castors drop off, and the veneer
begins to peel on an hour's exposure to the fire, will be a thing
of the past. In other words, the manufacturers will cease to
be deceived in the quality of the goods they manufacture, and
to this extent at least the public will benefit. The perfidity
of manufacturers has of late received a considerable and well-
merited punishment, which may prove a valuable lesson for

the future, so that an improvement in the quality of goods all round may be anticipated when the hands become partners. The more immediate effect of the change would, however, be on the quantity of work done. This has already been observed under parallel circumstances, and it is probably no exaggeration to say that, were all the labourers vitally interested in getting through as much work as possible, instead of as little as possible, the same number of hours would produce at least twice the present quantity. Any one who has watched bricklayers at work on ordinary occasions may have been struck with the remarkable, almost studied sluggishness of their movements; and if he has also observed the same men at work under the stimulus of a prize on condition of completing a promised wall within a given time, he will have been amazed at the contrast. It is confidently reiterated that the new system would more than double the amount of goods produced in this country.

Another important source of economy would be the proper apportionment of time to the quality of effort; for the labourers will admittedly be the best judges of their own hours of labour. They will wish to work as *much* as possible, but not as *long* as possible. Dr. Whewell, speaking of the value of time for the purposes of study, used to say : " Four and two make six ; six and two make four ;" meaning that the man who read eight hours a day did no better than the man who read four. Six hours, he thought, is the largest amount of time which can economically be spent in intellectual study. So it is with other branches of work. Some kinds of labour may be economically continued for ten or even twelve hours a day, whilst others cannot be wisely prolonged beyond four or five. Such differences in the nature of work do exist as all men well know except members of Parliament who persistently legislate on the assumption that no such variations exist. When, therefore, the aim of any body of working men is to get through as much work as possible, they will find out by experience what is the best length of time to work per day, taking the nature of the work into the calculation, and being guided in their decision by a proper regard to the economy of their forces. That is to say, if by working hard seven hours a day they find they can accomplish as much as by working at a necessarily reduced expenditure of force for eight hours, they will prefer seven to eight hours.

Another saving in the cost of production deserves mention. It is obvious *à priori* that men who are handling tools and machinery and materials which belong to others, and in which they have no personal interest, cannot be expected to treat them with the same care and regard for economy which they exercise over their own property. It is not in human nature to do it. Both Roman and English law make a distinction based on this observed fact in man's nature. But where all these things are the subject of the labourer's own concern, even though not his own property, it is clear *à priori* and observed as a fact that much waste and some mischief are in consequence avoided.

We have seen that the immediate and direct results of adopting the just system of capitalisation would be many and great. There would be an immensely-augmented ratio of gross produce to cost. Average profits would at first be greatly increased in proportion to outlay, and in addition to that the total outlay would be correspondingly stimulated. This would be effected in several ways. The total quantity of work done would be much greater; the value of each portion of the produce would be greater by reason of its superior quality; the cost of over-looking would be indefinitely diminished; the natural expenditure of human force in proportion not to time but to economy would result in an enormous gain. Other kinds of capital, both of those whose consumption is essential to production and of those whose consumption is merely accidental (though inevitable), would be more carefully treated, and waste and extravagance checked. The friction in trade due to class antagonism, and resulting in strikes and checks to industry of one sort and another, would be got rid of, and power now wasted would be saved by natural equilibration.

But the greatest economy of all would be made in the investment of labour. And the result would be that, although profits on other forms of capital would greatly increase, the profits on labour would increase in still greater proportion; so that not only would there be a larger total to divide, but the manual-workers' share of that larger total would also be greatly increased. And, above all, it would be permanent, and not liable to be swallowed up by increased population.

But the workman's fear lest the reward of labour should in bad times fall below its present low level is groundless. It could never even reach it in the worst periods of depression. Apart from the total amount of produce to be distributed, the greater proportionate share of the manual worker under the new system will effectually preclude such an occurrence. And then again the habits of thrift (reasonable, economic thrift) and providence will render the danger less serious, even in the worst of times. Add to which the fact that the increase of population will have no tendency to reduce labour reward to the level of means of subsistence any more than it now has to reduce the reward of professional men and investors of accumulated wealth to that level. The true *cost* of increasingly-skilled workers in every craft will regulate the pay of labour, and not the mere cost of the labourer's maintenance during the process. This is, of course, the key to the true solution of the labour question.

Of course I am prepared for the objection of the " orthodox ": " You forget that the workers must have their wages *advanced*, and *that this is why* the capitalist pockets the interest on labour." No, I do not forget it, but I do not believe it. It is a convenient fiction ; and, moreover, it is dishonest, for if it were true it would not justify the exaction. The moment a labourer has turned a handle, or stuck a spade in the ground, he has earned at least the value of his services for that second of time. To talk of giving him an advance is common chicanery.[1] Workmen convert timber into a half-finished boat, which the capitalist can *at any moment* sell for ten or twelve times the original value of his timber, and yet he has the impudence to tell them that they have no claim upon him till the boat is completed, and that any payment they may require during the process is of the nature of an advance, for which he must charge as for a loan.

---

[1] Those who would see this fallacy clearly exposed may refer to a work with which I am not in accord, viz. Mr. Henry George's *Progress and Poverty*, where they will find the trick properly shown up.

Let us examine this contention. Clearly, if the workman comes to one who has put capital into the same venture and asks for a loan to enable him to subsist till the process is complete, the position is precisely similar to what it would be if the worker applied to an outsider, to one who had not put capital into the venture. The lender would of course have a just claim to interest on the loan, but to pretend that the payment of labourers *pari passu* with the progress of their work in a transaction of this kind is trifling with common sense. The worker has *already* earned his pay. He has a just lien on the half-finished product, which he has a right to sell whenever he thinks fit. The orthodox contention is tantamount to saying that the workman is worth nothing at all—that he is a useful natural agent like the wind or the waves or the sunlight, without any value whatever; that the cost of hiring labour is, and should be, the cost of his subsistence during the process. In the words of the arch-economist himself—John Stuart Mill—" whatever things are destined to supply productive labour with the shelter, protection, tools and materials which the work requires, and to *feed and otherwise maintain the labourers* during the process, are capital." If this fallacy is not exposed by reasoning, the labourers will be justified in exposing it by an argument of another and convincing kind.

This objection being disposed of there can be no reason why the men's share should not be handed over to them at any time, weekly if necessary. The manner of making this payment will be explained presently.

Lest this should appear to some to be too sanguine a forecast, and the whole system of capitalisation merely another Utopia, let me hasten to point out, before proceeding to consider its remoter effects, certain facts which should not be lost sight of in treating of any great social change. Sound revolutions are usually slow. Rome was not built in a day, but it was burnt while Nero fiddled.[1]

[1] I do not guarantee the historical accuracy of this statement, and my reason for making this disclaimer is the fear that some hostile critic will pulverise my arguments in favour of capitalisation by pointing out either that the fire broke out before Nero began to fiddle, or that Nero stopped fiddling before the fire was extinguished. Perhaps so.

To begin with, the system cannot be introduced all along the line. Only certain classes of workers are as yet sufficiently advanced for the reform. It would probably be useless as yet to attempt to apply it to agriculture, where the labourers are only now casting off the last fetters of serfdom. Nor would it succeed at present in small concerns conducted on hand-to-mouth principles. It must have its beginning in the large coal and iron and textile fabric industries, in the cotton-mills, the foundries, and the collieries. There it is already known, or easily ascertainable, exactly what proportion of the gross receipts of the business has been paid away in wages any year these ten years. An average can be struck at once on the basis of the last year, or three years, or seven years, as may seem good to both parties, and a bargain struck. Whatever the proportion may be, let that proportion of the total receipts be paid to the hands in future, at such intervals as may suit both parties, either weekly or (as will eventually be the case) at stock-taking.

Once set on foot, the advantages to both parties would ensure its rapid spread in all directions and with increasing velocity. And the time is perhaps not far distant when the old system of wagedom will be regarded as an interesting survival, in holes and corners, of a practice once nearly universal.

I would, however, add that any attempt on the part of the Legislature to force the system upon the country would be worse than useless. Among peoples unprepared for it by long habits of self-help such a course would be positively mischievous, and it is probable that, with the exception of Great Britain and the United States of America, and the Anglo-Saxon Colonies, few nations are even yet ripe for its introduction.

A beginning is easily made. The working classes in the large industries must themselves take the lead. The masters ought not to be slow to follow, and the completion of the task may be left to time without much anxiety as to its eventual success; for, apart from the favour or disfavour with which it may be regarded in commercial circles, the capitalisation of labour is based on principles from which there is no appeal.

Approved or disapproved by masters or by men, or both, it
must assuredly come into force sooner or later. Then, and not
till then, shall we be in a position to say that the labour question has been practically solved.

The more remote effects of the new system now come into
view. One change follows on the heels of another. When
once it becomes every man's interest to work as hard as he
can, and, what is more, to see that his fellows do the same, it
will soon become evident that the best mode of obtaining new
hands is by letting the old ones elect them. It will clearly be
their interest to elect the best workers, and at the same time
to elect those who will come for a reasonable share. For it is
obvious that where the labourers as a body receive such or
such a share of the gross returns, each individual's share must
needs vary inversely as the sum of the shares of the others.
Hence every workman will be interested in keeping down the
share of his fellows to its fair limit. This mode of election
of new hands will bring into existence something like regular
meetings of the men and the election of officers and a president;
and it will soon appear natural and expedient to the employer
to pay over the whole of the labourer's share in a lump to the
workmen's president, to be distributed amongst them in their
own way, and as they, in council assembled, shall from time to
time assess and decree. Not only the differences in the values
of labour in the several branches and departments in every
manufacture, but also the differences in the values of the workmanship of individual members of the body, are difficult to
appreciate, and they never are accurately appreciated at all by
employers, who indeed ignore the latter inequalities altogether.
Quite otherwise will this be when the matter is left in the
hands of the men themselves, who will evaluate with the finest
distinctions and utmost care the work upon which they will
have to adjudicate. It will be each man's care to see that he
himself is not underpaid, nor his fellow-workers overpaid, and
the conflict of opinion and free discussion will result in a fair
valuation.

It has already been remarked that some men can, as a
matter of mere strength, work longer than others, and that,
with a true regard to economy, such inequalities should be

taken into consideration. There are other limits besides that of simple endurance which may well deserve attention. Under the present system of fixed hours the labourer is unable to choose his own holidays, to shorten his time in case of indisposition, to attend to other passing duties, or, in short, to dispose of his own time like a free man. Beyond giving notice, or running the risk of getting the sack, his liberty is of the scantiest. It is undeniable that at certain times, such as the gardening or haymaking season, it would suit some artisans to quit their daily toil and to change their employment. It would pay them better, and it would do them good in body and mind. So again, those whose wives keep lodging-houses sometimes might well dispose of their time in helping at home ; but such a thing is out of the question under the present rigorous system. When the hands are the guardians of the work-time, when each sees that his fellows are paid according to the work they do, not according to the time they spend, nor even according to the efforts they put forth, it will be easy and practicable to allow of a freer and more independent arrangement as to hours of work than is possible at present. Each man would mark down on the board, in the presence of his comrades, or their appointed delegate, the time of his entrance and the time of his departure, and his aptitude being well known and recognised, his due pay would be reckoned at once.

Thus we have a glimpse of flourishing companies of workpeople, all partners from the highest to the lowest, from the employer who supplies the capital to the smallest boy that sweeps the floor. Each is working for his own direct benefit, and not merely to increase his employer's profits, and each works as hard as he can and keeps an eye on the industry of his comrades. Paid in a lump they save the employer the trouble and expense of distributing their wages. What overlookers or managers of departments are needed for organising purposes they elect from their own number, so that efficiency and popularity will be secured at once, and at a reasonable and fair share by way of remuneration.

In time even the head manager will come to be similarly elected, for the men will not tolerate the frittering away of their profits by an incompetent management.

Even the capitalist employer, unless himself risen from the ranks, or otherwise well qualified to manage, will perceive the expediency of leaving the management of the concern in the hands of his workpeople, who will elect the most competent head in his place; for he may rest assured that his capital is safe in the keeping of those whose whole livelihood depends upon its preservation and increase. Here, with all the advantages—such as they are—of co-operative companies of working men, or rather with all the supposed, or anticipated, or theoretical advantages of such companies, we have an ample supply of all kinds of capital: of land, buildings, machinery, fuel, raw material, and hard money. Though not their own property—the scraping together of their own small earnings—as in existing co-operative manufactories, yet they exercise the fullest control over it, harassed by no meddlesome or speculating employer.

The great flaw in existing systems of co-operative production is, as I have pointed out, the hopeless attempt to divorce labour from other forms of capital ready to hand. It seems to be part of the creed of "co-operators" that capitalists have not in reality any claim to profits, and yet they inconsistently aim at making those who co-operate into capitalists themselves. , Past failures of these attempts may nearly always be ascribed to the fact that the "hives" have been capital starved. Even recent promoters of those institutions, who accept the help of rich capitalists, do so rather grudgingly, and as though forced to implore help, rather than on terms of businesslike equality. This is to swing to the opposite extreme. Capitalists have as much right to the whole fruits of their capital as manual workers have to the whole fruits of their labour. The two rights rest on the same principle.

Mr. Morris has drawn some fascinating pictures of the factory as it *ought* to be. If he would devote some of the same ability to a picture of the factory as it *will* be when we have emerged from this transitional period of wagedom into that of industrial freedom, the work would certainly be not less valuable. Fact is often not only stranger but infinitely more beautiful than fiction.

I have said that the workers of England, or at least a large section of them, are ready to embark on the system of the future.   If not, let them consider their present position.   They have had ample and bitter experience of " business principles." Do they really believe that the workman gets the whole fruits of his labour under existing arrangements ?   Do they really suppose that their salaries or wages can be guaranteed without something like a heavy discount being charged by the guarantor ? Do they actually believe that he runs all their risk for nothing ? Is he in other respects so generous and self-denying ?   Let it then be reiterated that it is the fault of the labourers themselves if they allow this sort of patronage to be accorded them. Are they incapable of taking care of their own pounds, shillings, and pence, that their fair incomes must be doled out by the week, and taken care of by a guardian ?   Let them assume the *toga virilis.*   It is high time to sever the apron-strings and to proclaim the freedom of the working classes.   But it will not be done for them ; it must be done by them.   Let them cease to agitate for State regulation of work hours, for bank holidays, for high minimum of wages, for State emigration, for this, that, and the other restriction on their liberty.   Let them throw off the shackles of wagedom, and the rest will follow to the full !   And so farewell to the much-harassed employer of labour.   The elected manager, raised from the ranks, will take his place as superintendent ; and in nine cases out of ten will occupy it far more competently.   The workpeople will take care of their own earnings, and the capitalist of non-human capital will be relegated to his right province, and become the recipient of profits varying with the risk of his investments.

The effect produced by the new system in the course of time upon the social standing of those who work with their hands will be of the nature of a revolution.   Being one of the more indirect consequences, it is perhaps somewhat difficult of explanation.

Time was when bankers were goldsmiths, and goldsmiths were common folk to be cuffed and kicked by gentlemen, to cringe and flatter and be useful.   Between the days of Shylock and the days of the Rothschilds much has happened.   Again, the civil engineer of to-day was in old times a kind of master navvy.   He helped to dig, to wheel, and to carry.   Engineering now ranks with the learned professions, so that bankers and engineers, as such, are socially held to be in no way inferior, setting aside the separate question of titles of distinction, to any in the land.   A master carpenter still continues to work with his hands along with his workpeople.   A master builder seems at present to stand in an intermediate position ; showing that there are graduated stages in the social standing of the trades and professions from that of a sweep to that of a Lord Chief-Justice.   Amongst actual manual workers this is at first sight less obvious.   Yet when we compare a working watch-maker or a compositor with a navvy or chimney-sweep we see that there are well-marked degrees of social elevation among them.

A working man under the present régime is said to have raised himself when he has accumulated enough to retire from his handiwork, to become a master or an idler.   One can hardly picture a gentleman going down daily to his forge and his anvil and hammering away all day at the glowing iron. Even a poor gentleman must do work of the scribbling order. The pen, and not the hammer or the spade, must be his tool, even though the pay be less, the atmosphere unwholesome, the work distasteful, and the hours longer.   How many poor curates, needy tutors, pallid clerks, and sub-editors have been heard to envy the lot of the rubicund Hodge, whose outdoor work, with pay almost equal to their own, seems like a con-tinuous holiday.   But it cannot be; there is a rigidity in custom which cannot be overcome.   The question now presents itself, Why cannot true gentlemen become blacksmiths, carpenters, glass-blowers, potters, house-decorators, etc. etc.? and why cannot, or why should not, the blacksmiths and carpenters become gentlemen ?   Why should the son of a barrister, who has made a fortune at the bar, follow in his father's shoes, and this, too, with pride, while the son of a man who has made money as a labourer, or even in most trades, is ashamed of his origin, and does his best to succeed at some more dignified occupation ?

The reason usually alleged is that it always has been, and still is, regarded as servile to work with the hands ; that in the olden times the dominant classes were of the military order, and the tilling of the soil and manufacture of goods were performed exclusively by the despised classes. But granting the survival of the sentiment, though in point of fact it is almost extinct, it yet fails to account for certain exceptional cases which throw much light on the subject. The first is the case of painters and sculptors and other workers in fine art, whose labour is manual; and the second is the case of engineers and bankers above alluded to, whose occupations have soared above the region of contempt. The explanation is simple. It is not the accident of its being manual that renders work undignified. Artists have always been held in esteem. Nor is it the historical associations; for banking was surpassed by no other branch of industry in meanness of origin and the abject circumstances of its early history. At the bottom of the whole matter lies the ineradicable admiration for intellectual power which is inherent in human nature, whether that power be manifested in military genius, in forensic skill, in inventive talent, in philosophic insight, or in artistic subtlety. Any one with a hale body can dig and wheel, but only a Lesseps can carry out a canal across the Suez isthmus. Any one with eyesight can paint a housefront or a deal box, but only a Millais the portrait of Gladstone in the Academy Exhibition of 1879. Any Hebrew usurer can lend money at sixty per cent to needy gentlemen with expectations, but only the man of a rare combination of talents can borrow at a low rate of interest, invest discreetly, and found a bank of stability and repute. The very poorest quality of human nature can be moulded pretty quickly into a mason capable of chipping stone evenly and in an average manner, but it is not every mason who has it in him to be a William of Wykeham or a Pugin. Ordinary mortals are fit to do the correspondence of a mercantile firm, but those who can write a *Hamlet* or a *Locksley Hall* take their seats among the gods.

Now therefore if this is the true rendering, it is asked, is there no room in wrought-iron workmanship for a blacksmith to exercise his imagination and his powers of artistic manipulation? What of those beautiful gates in the Kensington Museum? Does ancient pottery support the belief that there

is no room for the exercise of the higher powers in the manufacture of earthenware ?   How is it we never find any evidence
of the labour of love among the carvings over our gateways,
among our tables and chairs, among our carpets, our books (their
bindings, that is to say), our garden railings or walls, our cups
and saucers—anywhere ?

The answer is summed up in a single word, *wagedom*.   The
builders of our old abbeys were not wage receivers.   Upon
each minutest portion of the work there is the impress
of an individual mind.   The carvings, the frescoes, the stained-
glass designs, the mosaics, everything down to the little
conceits in oak-work as seen in Ely Cathedral, recall an age
when art was not sold by the yard.   In these degenerate days
(and it is no falsification of history to style them degenerate
in this respect) all our decoration is worked out at the least
expenditure of force by the soulless and indifferent worker.
Nor is there any expression of individuality ; there is a regulation pattern and all the designs are as if run in the same mould.
This has been pointed out so frequently before, and with such
force and ability by John Ruskin and others, that it is only
necessary to mention it in order to call to mind the cause to
which it is usually attributed.   We are told that it is the
introduction of machinery which has thus swept all the poetry
out of our surroundings ; that a machine having no soul can
infuse no true art into its productions.   But this is fallacious
and sophistical.   As well say that a painter must paint without
a brush ; for behind every machine there is a thinking mind.
Besides, what do we find where there is no machine ?   Precisely the same monotonous heartlessness.   In the industrial
arts there is a certain dead level of dulness and apathy.   The
art is all in the design and none in the execution.   The artisan
lavishes no last loving touches on his handiwork ere it leaves
his affectionate care, as the workers in fine art do.   The explanation is *wagedom*.

Let us now take a glimpse into the future : Here is a firm
of iron-workers.   The hands are self-elected and autonomous.
The company has made a name, and the returns are high and
increasing.   A *place* in the factory is a vested interest.   The
original 20 per cent paid to the workpeople's president still

remains 20 per cent, but the returns have quadrupled, and with them the 20 per cent. It is difficult to be elected a workman in such a concern. When a vacancy occurs, mindful of the reputation of the firm for fine workmanship, merit is the qualification for election—artistic talent in iron-work design or skill in execution (as the case may be) combined with a good character. The mere fact of working in this foundry is amongst metal-workers equivalent to the much-coveted membership of the Royal Academy in the present English world of fine art. So with the other industrial arts. Let the quality of workmanship once rise above the dead level of wage work, and competition will soon accomplish the rest.

And, as has been already observed, the true key to the respect and homage of our fellow-men is power. It is not the horny hand that degrades the labourer, it is the absence of any need for intellectual power in his calling ; it is the fact that his profession is open to all, too difficult for none. It is merely a matter of drudgery. Efficiency is a question not of ability, of genius, but of time and industry.

An artist has the status of a gentleman. He is sought after and honoured, be he rough or smooth in his manners. A house-painter may or may not be a gentleman, probably not ; but most certainly he has not the status of one, by reason of his class. When house-painters shall be true artists, they will be gentlemen. In the distant future the *élite* of the land (strange as it may seem) will include blacksmiths and carpenters ; not the masters and employers of many hands, but the *bonâ-fide* hammerman himself. There is nothing in . all this of the morbid *fraternité* of the Frenchman. It is only a following up of the lines of history in order to " dip into the future far as human eye can see," and form a juster estimate of the workman's destiny than can be arrived at by any other route.

But the whole question of the indirect effects of the new system on art and on society is too wide for present treatment. Perhaps it would have been more prudent to have passed over in silence these indirect effects of the introduction of a logical system of labour payment, as tending to derogate from the

practical character of the proposal advocated. But to those
who do not care to peer too far down the vistas of the future,
it is quite competent to confine their attention entirely to the
more immediate and direct effects, treating the remoter consequences as too problematical for practical consideration. Those
who anticipate great social changes must, however, guard
themselves against misunderstanding. It is not to be expected
that all branches of handicraft will simultaneously rise in status ;
that gentlefolk will flock into all the now-despised occupations.
The duke and his younger brother the chimney-sweep will
never walk arm-in-arm in Pall Mall. It will be with labour
as it has been with trade. Some branches will outstrip the
rest. Some will come to the front as handicrafts of honour,
just as engineering and banking have done in trade. Those
departments which have in them the most room for intellectual
or artistic cultivation will leave the rest behind; and those
which have least will never rise into a higher social stratum
at all. Blacksmith and butcher will not visit.

Serfdom, Wagedom, Freedom—these are the three stages
in the evolution of Industrialism. To-day we are still mostly
in the second stage. At one end of the labour ladder we have
the agricultural labourer striving to throw off the last vestiges
of serfdom, demanding higher fixed wages in lieu of a low wage,
increased by gratuities and perquisites. At the other end we
have workers in the coal and iron trades demanding wages
varying with employer's profits. The first represents the
transition (now nearly completed in this country) from serfdom
to wagedom ; the second, the transition from wagedom to
freedom. Thus we find that the same progress is not made
all along the line, for we have one wing ready to advance into
the third stage of development before the other wing is well
out of the first. We must keep our eye on the advanced
guard if we would learn the direction the campaign is likely
to take.

We are frequently met with the objection that the present
system is perfect because it is based on free contract ; that
employer and employed freely bargain together as to the work
to be done and the wage to be paid ; and that if a workman
does not like the terms offered, he is under no compulsion to

accept them. But what is the history of contract? Do not contracts themselves tend to become modified in course of time? I think nomological analysis will show us that they tend to be modified in three distinct ways. They tend to become: first, more and more free; second, more and more definite; third, more and more simplex.

Without going into the vexed question as to where direct compulsion ends and indirect compulsion begins—whether, for instance, the traveller who voluntarily hands over his purse to the highwayman in exchange for his life does it in pursuance of free contract with the robber—it will be admitted that the relations subsisting between master and wage earner are freer than those subsisting between lord and serf. The change from serfdom to wagedom was a change in the direction of *freedom* of contract. I will not demand an answer to the question whether a labourer who has the choice between subsistence wages and starvation is altogether a free agent, because this again raises a deeper question, into which we need not go here. But it will hardly be denied that the man who agrees to receive the full value of the work he actually does, instead of so much an hour for the time he stands over his work on the tacit understanding that he will apply himself with average diligence, has at all events entered into a more definite contract.

But it is in respect of the third tendency of contracts—to become more and more simplex or separate—that the system of capitalisation will show itself especially conformable. Instead of containing a bundle of distinguishable engagements, contracts tend to become fewer and fewer, and eventually the fewest possible. In this respect we may compare the fasciculus of heterogeneous duties undertaken by domestic servants, most of them rather tacitly understood than expressed, with the comparatively simplex duties of a factory operative. The contract entered into by the free worker will be even less complex. He will agree with his fellow-workers to put labour into the crucible and to take out a share of the proceeds in proportion to what he put in. The capitalist, again, who contributes non-human capital, will cease to insure a fixed return to his labouring partners. He also will take out of the crucible a share proportionate to the value of what he put into it. In fine, the history of industrialism illustrates the three-fold tendency of contracts towards increasing freedom, definiteness, and simplicity.

It may have occurred to some that all the advantages of the new system would be more than neutralised by the great and manifold inconveniences arising out of the partnership questions which would be eternally springing up between masters and their partners, the men. Many forms of robbery would cease to be felonious in the eye of the law, and, moreover, men and masters would be mutually liable for one another's debts in connection with the business. Besides, it may be said that a partnership of more than some twenty persons must by law be registered as a joint-stock company, which would necessitate the application of the Joint-Stock Companies Acts to every large manufactory.

It is not proposed in this place to enter into a criticism of the existing law of partnership in this or other countries. Suffice it to observe that the law is not slow to adapt itself to new institutions and customs, though it is not likely to take the initiative. Moreover, a careful analysis of the juridical idea of partnership reveals a definition of the term which is not the definition received in authorised legal treatises, or even in the law courts. To state the matter briefly and dogmatically, the essence of partnership is not the sharing of profit and loss, or either or both, whether alone or in conjunction with other conditions; it is simply guaranty. That persons who trade in common, sharing profits and losses, do as a rule guarantee each other so far as the debts of the firm are concerned, even though that rule may have no exception, is no reason for confounding essentials and accidentals, but it is a very simple explanation of the existing confusion. Even now, the tendency in the courts is in the direction of recognising only those partnerships which have been openly admitted by the parties, instead of arguing from community of profit and loss. And no doubt when working men have established their undoubted claim to such community of profit and loss, some way will be discovered of escaping from all the difficulties and inconveniences inseparable from the present muddled notions of mutual liabilities. The only question is, whether the present disgraceful state of the law with respect to joint-stock companies will not bring the old definition of partnership into contempt, before the correct interpretation has been forced upon the Legislature by the independent action of the labouring classes. Meantime, there is no cause for misgiving on account of the effect of the law of partnership on the working of the system.

I suppose that no measures of legislative interference have been so mischievous and so costly to the country (not even excepting the Factory Acts) as the Acts relating to joint-stock companies. It would be impossible to estimate in hundreds of millions the enormous quantity of wealth which has been diverted from productive channels by these contemptible Acts alone. Designed, doubtless, as safeguards for the innocent and simple, they have served as snares and traps, of which the cunning and unscrupulous have taken ample advantage. Perfect freedom, untrammelled private enterprise, would long ere this have rendered joint-stock adventure as safe on the average as the 3 per cents, instead of which capital has been scared off and found an outlet in foreign loans, Egyptian, Peruvian, Turkish, Spanish, and the like.

If the return to the lines of individualism in trade, which the capitalisation of labour will render necessary, were to be the only result of the introduction of that system, the country would even then be amply rewarded. Not only will a vastly larger proportion of wealth be devoted to production, bringing in larger incomes to those who invest in trade instead of Government and foreign stocks, but, owing to increased security, investors will be content with smaller profits on the turnover, made up for by quicker returns ; so that although the gross outcome of industry will be larger, and although the total receipts of the contributors of non-human capital will also be larger, yet the average reward of risk will be less, and consequently the ratio of risk reward to labour reward will be a constantly diminishing one. The working classes will receive a larger share of a larger whole. While all will benefit, they will gain the most. And what is quite as important, the inequalities in the distribution of wealth (though inequalities must always exist, corresponding to the inequalities in human nature) will be less glaring and more evenly graduated from top to bottom. The income curve, which is a sure test of social stability, will, in mathematical language, tend to approach more and more nearly to a right line.

A few words as to the morality of wagedom. The term fraud is extremely difficult to define. For our present purpose it may serve to distinguish between two classes of bargain, in both of which the knowledge of the facts possessed by one of the contracting parties is deficient; but in the one case, owing to false representations knowingly made by one party, and in the other case, owing to any other cause. The first may be called a fraudulent bargain, but not the second.

Consider the following illustration of the second case: You make the acquaintance of your groom's nephew, a poor lad living in an obscure part of the town. You, having a good knowledge of drawing and painting, find his chalk sketches on the stable walls full of merit and genius, while they are unappreciated by the grooms and stable-boys. Estimating their marketable value, you engage to buy all the lad's productions on paper at a price which, though remunerative to him, is altogether disproportionate to their true worth, and you pocket the difference. Your advantage is gained without the use of brute force, without the use of stealth, without the use of fraud. Thus in every sense of the phrase it is a voluntary contract. Yet from a moral point of view, higher than that from which modern society expects us to regard these matters, is there not an element of unfairness in the arrangement? Do we not feel that the lad ought to have all the proceeds of the sale of his drawings?

Surely this sentiment may be examined as a sign of a future restriction (no matter how sanctioned) upon the use of superior knowledge. Why should not this higher form of intellectual superiority follow the lower forms which have already been disallowed? Why should it not follow fraud as fraud followed stealth, and as stealth followed brute force? When this shall happen, if ever, the profits of an undertaking will be distributed exactly according to the value of the original contribution of each contributor, whether it consist of

inorganic or organic material, of hand labour, of superintendence, of foresight, or of any other ingredient. That is to say,
profits will be divided in proportion to the new increment of
value imparted by each contributor. At present there are two
sources of gain in business. The one consists in increasing
the value of purchased commodities while in possession of
them, and afterwards selling them at that increased value.
The other consists in buying an article at less than its real
value, or in selling it at more than its real value, or in both,
without in any way adding to its value. Is it not conceivable
that the manufacturers and traders of the future will discard
the second mode of gain ?

This mode of obtaining advantage over those ignorant of
the facts is most clearly exemplified in the case of bargains
made between the employer and employed, that is to say,
between the wage-paying and wage-receiving classes. In the
absence of open books it is clearly impossible for the workpeople to ascertain how much of the profit obtained in the
business is due to their exertions and how much to the capital
in conjunction with which they labour. Taking advantage of
their ignorance, the master is in a position to contract with
them so as to compound for their services at a valuation which
is necessarily below their true value.

When the manual labourer is deprived by force of the
fair portion of profit due to his labour, we have a system of
slavery or serfdom. Compulsion is necessary in order to
make the workman toil. When he is deprived of his fair
rights by concealment of fact, whether by fraud or by mere
suppression of the truth, or in any way by which he is kept
in ignorance of his real worth, his labour may be said to be
compounded for, and we have a system of wagedom. When,
again, the ascertained value of his contribution in the form of
work is the measure of his remuneration, he may be said to
labour freely and openly in the full light of knowledge, and we
have a system of freedom.

There may be nothing illegal in bargaining with an
individual, or with whole classes of the population, to pay any
sum which he or they will accept for their work ; but illegal
or not, it is surely immoral. It would be immoral to demand

a large sum of money from a drowning man as a condition of helping him into your boat. It would be a voluntary bargain. He would gain by promising any sum whatever, but surely it would be an unfair bargain. So it is with a hungry population a most unfair and immoral practice to pay them one penny less than the true value of their labour.

There is no intention in this place of confounding morals with law. How far a man may be legally justified in palming off upon another an article for more than it is actually worth; how far, that is to say, the law should deal with such transactions at all, is a juridical question which in no way affects the ethical one. *Caveat emptor* may be an excellent legal maxim without in any way conferring a moral justification on such dealings. It is all very well to say that every man must look after himself, that superior knowledge ought to have its reward, and so forth; but, notwithstanding, there remains the feeling (it may be mere sentiment) that there is something mean, something morally wrong in such transactions, that a stigma attaches to them. But then it ceases to be immoral so far as employers are concerned when the workers are awake to the true position and continue to insist upon the arrangement.

The question may be asked, How can we expect employers to enter into a fair contract with their workpeople ? Is there no balance to redress ? Is not the employer compelled to guarantee the workman against accidents, by the Employers' Liability Act ? to educate his children, by the Education Acts ? to provide for his unfortunate relations, by the Poor Law ? to carry him by rail at under cost price, by the Cheap Trains Act ? to supply him with water at less than cost of delivery ? to provide him with books, baths, wash-houses, parks, picture galleries, etc. etc. ? and finally to lodge him at a dead loss ? All this may be very good and humane. Perhaps not to do it would be cruelty. Besides, it would not pay to let the "proletariat" starve ! But why will the workers of England persist in claiming to be treated like first-class slaves ? Even if they obtained all they asked (which is impossible), what would it profit them without freedom ?

Again, whether we blame the employer or not, we must admit that if the wage earner does not realise his position it is mostly his own fault.   Might not the employer argue thus?— " If I were to sell myself to a sugar-planter for a thousand dollars, to invest the money for the benefit of my children, and then to pass into perpetual bondage, all of my own free will, would you call the planter a tyrant and a villain, or would you call me a fool, and add—serve you right?   Well, that is exactly what the wage-receiving classes of this country are doing to-day, and if they do not like the arrangement they have no one to blame for it but themselves, and this insensate howl against capitalists is an unmanly attempt to lay the blame on to the shoulders of any but those who are really responsible for the situation.   A man cannot in this country sell himself out and out, but he can let himself out for hire like an ox or an ass, at so much a day or a week, and this is just what he does.   To let one's self out for hire is the same thing as to sell one's services for a limited period out and out.   To turn round and complain after this transaction that the employer pockets the whole of the net profits of the work is childish and contemptible.   You might as well sell a man your pig and then complain that he sold it again for a profit without offering you a share.   I say it is an unworthy wail."

There is something in this plea.   Just so long as population goes on increasing at a greater rate than the means of subsistence, and men and women go on letting themselves out for hire instead of working for their own hand, so long will the rate of wages equal on the average the cost of keeping the human machine in fair working order, and no more.

There is no doubt the working classes have one excellent reason for preferring to remain under the system of wagedom rather than to enter upon a régime of freedom.   Under the present system they have no care or trouble for the future; they are guaranteed so much by the employer.   Come sun, come storm, it is all the same to them.   It is the capitalist's look-out; why need they bother themselves?   This is the happy-go-lucky irresponsible life which some of them truly prefer.   They would not for the world alter it if they could. On the contrary, even the wage system is a little too responsible; the golden age for the labourer, we are told, was in the glorious days of serfdom when, come what might, the serf was well cared for by his lord. There is a pleasing English ring about this: to be well cared for, fattened up, and kept in good condition like an ox is a truly noble ambition, and yet Mr. Hyndman and his friends tell us to look back to the fourteenth century for a picture of a happy and prosperous people, for what we ought, if possible, to bring back. " O ! the happy days of serfdom, the freedom from care, the jolly irresponsibility." A lofty refrain truly. But were these serfs so happy and comfortable after all? The merry England of the good old times is mostly immortalised, I imagine, in the traditions of knights and barons, while the opinions of the villeins and the cottiers of those days were not much noticed or committed to writing. Here is one genuine working man's view of his position, many centuries old, and now preserved in the British Museum :—

"' What sayest thou, Plowman? How dost thou thy work ?'—'Oh, my lord, hard do I work. I go out at daybreak driving the oxen to field, and I yoke them to the plough. Nor is it ever so hard winter that I dare loiter at home for fear of my lord ; but, the oxen yoked and the ploughshare and coulter fastened to the plough, every day must I plough a full acre or more.'—' Hast thou any fellow ?'—' I have a boy driving the oxen with an iron goad, who also is hoarse with cold and shouting. Verily, then, I do more. I must fill the bin of the oxen with hay, and water them, and carry out the dung. Ah me ! hard work it is, hard work it is, *because I am not free.*' " [1]

I suppose this sentiment is hardly intelligible to some modern ears. Their ambition is not to be free, it is to be fat ; we have had enough freedom. It is even the fashion nowadays to run it down. It is quite a common thing to hear men denouncing what they contemptuously call your vaunted freedom of contract. Doubtless bitter experience of such freedom as wagedom brings is calculated to lower very considerably the fervour with which an appeal to the love of liberty is received. That is but natural. And yet the immorality of wagedom is probably exemplified, more than in

---

[1] Quoted from Seebohm's *English Village Communities*, a work which should be read twice by those who wish to understand the land question, and once by those who do not.

anything else, in the waning self-respect of our working classes, as witnessed by their slavish appeals for aid and alms from the very classes whom they persistently abuse, and in their lack of enterprise and self-reliance. And the ranks of those who decry freedom and applaud those who would confer the same favours on the deserving and the undeserving—who would apportion satisfaction not according to efforts but according to needs—are swelled by those whose real aim is not equal opportunities of work, but equal opportunities of gain, of support and luxury at the expense of their more industrious and capable fellow-citizens. But be it clearly understood that capitalisation has nothing to offer to the lazy, the dissolute, the criminal, and the vagabond classes. Under such a system (there is no use blinking matters) these classes will go to the wall, and the sooner the better. For them there is nothing but pity and good advice. Socialism has many good things to offer to these classes, and I for one have no hesitation in advising them to embrace that fascinating doctrine with all speed. There are but these alternatives for them : either work and individualism, or socialism and idleness.

But whatever conclusion we arrive at as to the morality of the existing system of labour payment, with respect to employers or employed, there can be little room for doubt that a nation which tolerates a distribution of wealth so glaringly disproportionate to intelligent individual effort as the present system entails is guilty of a national sin. On this one point at least socialists and individualists can agree. Something must be done, and done quickly, to rectify the anomaly, and the question of the day is, What ? Socialism says, Smash up the existing social fabric and start a new one. Individualism says, No ; first try the effect of liberty—more liberty.

CHAPTER VIII

A WORD FOR ANARCHY [1]

I suppose that most of us enjoy a whitebait dinner without pausing to reflect that scores of lives are sacrificed in order to provide us with a single dish. Yet have not these tiny animals an equal right to life with ourselves ? What peculiar virtue does human nature possess that the happiness and freedom of fellow-creatures should be ruthlessly sacrificed for the transient gratification of man ? The usual answer to this question is an amused smile, or " Yes, it does seem odd, doesn't it ? " ; but when the converse question is asked in another direction, namely, Why on earth should the strong and the clever refrain from making themselves comfortable at the expense of the weak and dull ? an outcry is at once raised about the equal rights of men. Why men ? To theologians, no doubt, the phrase conveys a clear idea ; but to an evolutionist who cannot admit the existence of any distinct line of demarcation between man and his ancestors, the puzzle is to find out when those equal rights arose. I can quite understand men drawing the line at men ; it is natural ; but what I cannot understand is how they deduce the doctrine from the principle of Eternal Justice. If the greatest happiness of the greatest number (whatever that may mean) is the true guiding principle of conduct, what have the whitebait done that their happiness should be left out of account ? But perhaps it is argued that the pleasure derived by the gourmet from the dinner is greater than the total pleasures of life possible to such

---

[1] This chapter was originally read before the Fabian Society, consisting chiefly of socialists, revolutionary anarchists, and other very advanced political thinkers. It was intended partly as an answer to those State socialists who attack individualism as necessarily ending in anarchy ; partly as a *reductio ad absurdum* of the teachings of those revolutionists who would break up existing institutions, in the belief that a better order could be erected on their ruins. I reprint it here (though in smaller type) without the slightest alteration, because I believe that it meets a difficulty which may already have occurred to readers of the foregoing chapters. The extreme doctrine here enunciated will be found duly qualified in the chapter which follows. Should any critic open the book at this place, I have only to ask that he will read it in the light of this explanation.

humbly organised sentient beings as whitebait. Then there is an end of the virtue in numbers.

To apply these reflections to the political questions of the day, we may cordially accept the maxim *Vox populi, vox Dei*, and yet deny that the voice of the people is necessarily the howl of the greatest number ! If ten fools knock me down, tie my hands behind me, and otherwise work their will upon me, I bow to their superior force—brute force. I conform to their wishes rather than take the consequences of disobedience. But I claim no virtue in so doing. I have the choice of evils, and I take the less. Similarly, if the majority of persons in this or any other country can enforce their will upon the numerically fewer, by all means let them do so. I may have my doubts as to their ability, but I certainly do not for a moment dispute their right. I should as soon think of disputing the right of the wild cat to the bird he has caught. The very notion is absurd.

But if, on the other hand, the numerical majority cannot succeed in enforcing their will upon the minority, by what argument are the stronger, though they happen to be also the fewer, to be induced to forego the advantage of their superior strength for the benefit of others, who have nothing particular to recommend them except that they swarm like whitebait ?

That the effective majority (not necessarily the numerical majority) will have its own way, may be laid down as a truism. Thus the question of interest for us is not whether numbers have the right to rule, but whether the numerical majority is likely to become the effective majority as society evolves.

After which the further question must be met, whether, assuming that the tendency discernible throughout history is democratic, mankind is to be congratulated on the fact or not.

In a multitude of counsellors there is wisdom. Very likely ; but it is on the principle of the survival of the fittest. Certainly it is not true of the result obtained by taking the opinion of the majority. If all the clowns in Europe had gathered together they would never have hit on the theory of gravitation as an explanation of the movements of the heavenly bodies. One man did what a million men could not do. Is then the science of sociology so much simpler than that of mechanics ? Rather the reverse. Repetition of incredible nonsense can never make sense, though it sometimes produces conviction. Neither can the mere multiplication of folly convert it into wisdom.

Somebody says that the land of England would, if properly cultivated, support a hundred and forty millions of people. What of it ? *Cui bono ?* One would suppose that the end and aim of the race was to consist of as many units as possible, irrespective of their quality. I feel disposed to describe this as the Daniel Lambert view of the *salus populi*. What would be thought of an individual man who set before himself as the goal of his ambition, the aim of his life, to attain to the greatest possible weight or size ? Possibly the land would support a thousand times that number of flies, if we all agreed to cut our throats ; and what

a gain that would be.   And again I ask, Why Man ?   He is an ugly
beast at best, taking the majority for a pattern (as in democratic duty
bound), something, thought Carlyle, like a split carrot.   And if he does
happen to be distinguished from his fellow animals by his ability to lie
and get drunk, what then ?   Of course that or any other peculiarity
justifies him in appropriating to his own use the wealth of nature, *if he
can*, but not otherwise.   Meantime the particular species which has got
hold of the land at present is similarly justified in sticking to it as long
as possible.   In the days to come when the land shall fall into the hands
of the Daniel Lambert school, whose views of the *salus populi* is ever
increasing numbers, we may yet see a hundred and forty millions of
human beings swarming over the surface of the country ; a veritable Age
Saturnian — or shall we say Saturnine ?   What a field for the district
visitor and the missionary !   What happy hunting grounds for the quack
with his patent pills !   Fortunately this golden age still lies in the dim
and distant future.

   How far does the will of the numerical majority represent the will of
the people ?   Doubtless those who are ready to accept the *ipse dixit* of
the Catholic Church in matters theological ; those who are prepared to
swallow the dicta of Mrs. Grundy on matters social ; all such may logically take as inspired the utterance of the myriad-mouthed.   But trite as
the observation is, it cannot be too often repeated, that throughout all
history, truth, liberty, and justice have been advocated by the few and
opposed by the many.   It is true, remarkable changes sometimes take
place in the characters of men, and the same may hold good of societies
and classes.   If so, it is possible that the many, who poisoned Socrates,
who crucified Jesus, who burnt Bruno, and who but recently betrayed
Gordon, may suddenly be converted like King Hal into defenders of the
true faith.   Let us hope so.

   After these prefatory remarks, I may now proclaim myself an uncompromising democrat ; but by democracy I mean not the government of
the many as opposed to that of the few, but the government of all.

   If I have to choose between the government of the many and that of
the few, I do not hesitate to choose the latter !   I have too firm a faith in
the selfishness of human nature to expect altruism from either ; but I
know that my own interests would be better attended to, or at any rate
less impeded, by the selfish rule of culture than by the equally selfish
rule of ignorance.

   I confess to complete scepticism as to the overlauded virtue and intelligence of the self-styled proletariat.   (By the way, if I or any one else
had dubbed them with that contemptuous title what an uproar there
would have been.   I have no wish to quarrel with the term, if it is
popular ; and it certainly does connote a remarkable if not the most interesting attribute of the impecunious strata of society.)   The question I
ask myself, with the selfishness common to humanity, is this, Where do I
come in ?   On the lists of the few I fear my name would not appear ;
therefore I am against the rule of the few.   The many would not admit
me among them because they are a well-defined class, having, as they sup-

pose, interests diverse from the rest of the community, by reason of the peculiar nature and system of their work ; therefore I am against the rule of the many. But in a government of all I may be able to make my voice heard and my will counted for something ; therefore I am for the government of the people by the people—not some of the people, be they many or few, but all the people.

"What's everybody's business is nobody's business." So it is said. If so, then the government of all by all would be tantamount in the end to the government of the country by nobody, which thing is anarchy. And not a bad thing either. In my opinion a people which should begin *de novo* with complete anarchy would not get far wrong. In reply to that it is usually urged that too much liberty is as bad as too little, if not worse. It involves the liberty of the wolf to devour the lamb, and the equal liberty of the lamb to devour the wolf ; a mutual liberty to which somehow the lamb objects. But is this really a valid objection ? I doubt it. What happens in such cases ? Voluntary associations spring into existence for mutual protection against the brute force of powerful individuals. And if these prove beneficial to the people adopting them, they tend to become coextensive with the whole population. In other words, under a truly anarchic system, we should have exactly what we have now, a police system to which by hypothesis no one could effectively object. There would, however, be this difference ; the unwilling would not be coerced into joining the association or helping to maintain the system. And why should they ? A man who thinks himself strong enough to meet all probable risks and dangers from the violence of fellow-men may justly consider himself hardly treated if he is compelled to maintain a force for the protection of those who are too weak or too quarrelsome to care to run that risk. Again, one who has all his property in a strong house surrounded with a moat and practically unassailable may reasonably object to have to contribute to the protection of the property of those whose treasures are lying about at the mercy of the ill-disposed. So, one who has no property to lose may rebel against being compelled to join an association for the mutual defence of property.

The difference between Anarchy and the present system is just the difference between Voluntary Co-operation and Compulsory Co-operation, —between Individualism and Socialism. The history of civilisation is the story of the transition of society from a socialistic to an anarchic state. The prevalent notion of anarchy which precludes the combination of individuals for a common end is of course a ridiculous one. To suppose that under an anarchic system, a strong man would be allowed to cut up a weak one in the market-place while others looked on, is of course a caricature of the régime. Voluntary association would practically effect what the State does now in all that is necessary, and therefore good ; whereas it would not interfere, as the State does now, in matters which are better left to private management. The cardinal error of Socialism seems to be that combination is regarded as useless unless everybody can be brought into it. Trade unionism is good ; but the black side of its history is that which describes the miserable bullying to which non-unionists have been subjected. Leave those who will not join out in the cold. If the bond of union is good, sooner or later most will be drawn in. But if bad, then no matter what amount of coercion is used, the cause will fail and the combination collapse.

It is a mistake to suppose that anarchy is lawless. Nothing of the kind ; in fact lawlessness amongst intelligent persons is almost unthinkable. Where there is no ruling body, where there is no governmental authority, as in San Francisco within the memory of many of us, what happens ? Did the marauders and pests of society carry all before them ? Not a bit of it : those who had inherited the habits of a social and methodical mode of life, owing to its greater average economy, banded themselves together and straightway lynched those who were desirous of violating the principles of order and method which centuries of experience . have shown to be conducive to the possible existence on a given area of a considerable population in a superior state of comfort. Of course the orderly were not going to submit to the disorderly without a struggle ; and being the stronger party, though possibly composed of the weaker individuals, they voluntarily combined, and shoved the refractory element to the wall. This was anarchy.

We have now reached this position : that I and those who think with me are democrats because we expect some good from democracy. And what is that good ? Why nothing more nor less than our liberty. We support democracy because it leads straight to anarchy. For the greater the number of persons with a voice in the affairs of the nation, the more difficult will it become to carry coercive measures. Each one of us may be willing and anxious to coerce our neighbours in all manner of concerns, but we shall most surely find ourselves in a minority on some question of supreme importance to ourselves ; and then we shall begin to realise how coercion loses its charm when we are ourselves among the coerced. Therefore the larger the number of diverse interests represented in Parliament the nigher is the advent of true anarchy.

Anarchy ! The word has a dreadful ring about it. Why, it is opposed to property ; so it is urged. Not at all. The maxim of the anarchist is, " Let him take who hath the power ; let him keep who can." That is property is it not ? " But what is to prevent the strong from robbing the weak ? Suppose the many, finding themselves poor, take it into their heads to expropriate the few, what then ?" Why not ? If it can be shown that the robbery of the rich can be effected, and effected with advantage to the poor, I cannot see for the life of me why it should not be done. It is contrary to morality ? But unfortunately, high-falutin abstractions " butter no parsnips." Besides I deny it. Morality is co-extensive with self-interest. If anybody disputes that, he is wrong. It is rude and dogmatic of me to say so ; but it is a short answer, and I am not going to discuss the first principles of ethics here. I repeat emphatically, if the poor and many can see their way to dispossessing the rich and few, and to reap advantage from the process, then they have a right and a duty to do it.

But now arise the two previous questions : Can they do it ? And would it be to their advantage to do it if they could ? To the first I answer without hesitation, No ; if they could, they would have done it long ago ; for I believe they are no better, take them all round, than myself, in spite of the glowing colours in which it pleases modern candidates for parliamentary honours to paint them. I was once told by an Oriental who knew nothing of the British workman but what he had read of him in political speeches, that when he first came to this country he expected to see the "masses" winged and feathered.

But surely the many, if they will but organise and stand together, *can* overcome the few ? No ; the man who cannot overcome the temptation to a glass of grog when his wife and children have to pay for it with their dinner, is not the man to refuse the gold of the rich to stab his fellow-worker in the back. They cannot do it ; it is a physical impossibility. Or, not to put it too strongly, it is any odds against them. They may boil over in an incoherent way for a few short weeks or months, as indeed they have done once or twice in the world's history ; but the ebullition is merely temporary, and what is more significant, there are always members of another class behind, making use of them for sinister purposes of their own.

But now supposing they could effect this object—supposing the many could dispossess the few—would it be a wise course to adopt, even for the poor themselves ? To this question I again reply, No, certainly not. It is useless for me to recapitulate here all the whole chain of reasoning which goes to show that if the spur to industry were once removed, industry would cease, and I should be one of the first to strike. The consequences would be that it would be necessary to take stock of our existing wealth, and see how long it would last at a universally comfortable scale of living. The total value of all the wealth of Great Britain at the present moment, including the value of the whole population at slave prices, is just about thirty thousand million pounds. That gives us something like a thousand pounds apiece, or forty pounds a year on the condition of working like niggers. Forty pounds a year on condition of good honest work ! But would that work be done ? Who would do it ? Not I. Why should I work ten hours a day for my neighbour to fool away his time in the adjoining public ? It would soon become passing clear, either that we must prepare for a short life and a merry one (say about two years' jollification), or else we must discover some method of inducing people to work. The best method that I could bethink myself of, if my opinion were asked, would be the system of private property. To every man the fruits of his labour. If this view were adopted, a state of things would arise exactly like what we have now, with this one point of unlikeness—that confidence would have been diminished, interest would be higher, credit harder, wages lower. The many cannot oust the few ; and if they could, they had best not.

CHAPTER IX

THE chain of economic reasoning, of which the first few links were wrought a hundred years ago by Adam Smith, leads us irresistibly to two main conclusions from which there seems to be no appeal. The first of these is the law of wages, as formulated by Ricardo, and which in the hands of Ferdinand Lassalle becomes the " iron law of wages " (a phrase of ominous connotation). The second is the doctrine of *laissez-faire*, as taught by Bastiat and the Manchester school — a doctrine which in practice involves the minimisation of State inter-ference.

Between these two issues there is theoretically no antagonism whatever; but it is more than difficult to realise the existence of a democracy based on the eternal serfdom of the great majority of the citizens—the so-called working classes. Hence it is necessary to subject both these doctrines to a searching re-examination. The immediate object of the present chapter is to dissect the arguments underlying the doctrine of absolute individualism as set forth by its ablest exponents, and notably by Mr. Herbert Spencer, who, in *The Man v. the State*, has gathered into a focus all that is to be found scattered throughout his works bearing on the subject. The principles of personal liberty therein enunciated have been carried to their extreme expression by certain of Mr. Spencer's disciples, notably Mr. Auberon Herbert, with a thoroughness and a temerity equalled only by that of the English successors of Lassalle and Marx in their exposition of the creed of socialism.

But Mr. Spencer himself does not descend to details, and in meeting him it is not sufficient to point to the results of applying his principles to the concrete ; it is necessary to meet him on ground which he has himself chosen, and to test his own conclusions by his own methods.

Mr. Spencer begins with the dogmatic assertion that " the great political superstition of the past was the divine right of kings." He continues : " The great political superstition of the present is the divine right of parliaments. The oil of anointing seems unawares to have dripped from the head of the one on to the heads of the many, and given sacredness to them also and to their decrees." Whatever interpretation our fathers may have placed on the earlier doctrine, otherwise expressed in the maxim " The king can do no wrong," it is certain that there is no general acceptance of the later doctrine in the literal sense. Indeed Mr. Spencer himself admits this by redefining the political superstition in a form less open to misconstruction, as the belief that Government power is subject to no restraint.

Now, in one sense this is not a superstition, but a solid truth. That the group—society regarded as an organism— can through the effective majority (not necessarily the greatest number) do whatever it chooses, so far as the resistance of the minority is concerned, is a stubborn fact, whether it attains its ends through the medium of a despotism or through that of a representative Parliament elected by universal or any other suffrage. In another sense it is not true; but then neither is it a superstition, for no one believes it. That the group cannot act incompatibly with its own welfare is of course untrue. So says Austin ; the writings of Bentham imply it ; so do those of Hobbes. No one disputes it to-day —not even the most extreme socialist.

The question at issue between Mr. Spencer and his opponents is simply this, Have minorities, in the sense of . the weaker party, any rights which are valid against the community ? The answer depends upon the definition of the term " rights." If we accept the practical and intelligible definition of Austin, the question stands thus, Are there any claims for the defence of which the minority can successfully appeal to the group or State against the superior force of the effective majority ?   Considering that the will of the group is known only through the act of the effective majority, the question resolves into an absurdity.   And if the " rights " of the minority means the power to appeal successfully to a higher tribunal than the group itself, the answer must again be in the negative, for to admit the existence of such superior authority is to deny the existence of the group itself as an independent State.

But does Mr. Spencer mean to say that the opinion of the larger number should sometimes give way to that of the smaller—that even the effective majority should sometimes defer to the wishes of the weaker party, and that this not only conduces to the welfare of the group, but is constantly done ? In that case no one denies the proposition.   Every party compromise testifies to the fact.   To say that there is a moral law or a code of indefinite moral laws by which groups regulate their conduct, is simply to say that the conduct of societies is not arbitrary, which is obvious.   But to contend that the State, when it has once made up its mind rightly or wrongly to act in such or such a way, is subject to restraints, is to say that which has no meaning.   The group-will, once made up, necessarily manifests itself in action, and it is no more subject to restraints from within than is the will of a single human being.   So that the proposition which Mr. Spencer regards as the great superstition turns out to be a great undeniable truth, or an absurdity believed by none.   In neither case can it be called a superstition.

What is the element of untruth contained in the theory of a social pact as the foundation and justification of government ? It is not the mere fact that no such gathering and agreement ever took place, for even Rousseau only regarded it as a tacit contract ; and writers of a very different school have based the duty of obedience to the law on the ground that all members of a community have tacitly and virtually agreed to be bound by the laws.   This then is not the element of untruth contained in the hypothesis, or rather formula.   It is that the formula does not represent the fact.   The group-will is not the sum of the wills of the individuals composing it ; the two are incommensurable. Supposing that we knew the wish of every man living at the imaginary date of the *contrat social*, we should be utterly unable to predict the will of the group. It is not even the resultant of the wills of the units, but the resultant of those and many other forces acting in many other directions. It is the neglect of this fact, or rather ignorance of it, which vitiates all the social philosophy of those who build upon the foundation of a real or hypothetical social compact. Hobbes, Rousseau, and Bentham, and after them Mr. Spencer, commit the error of confounding the group-will with the sum of the wills of the units—an error pardonable enough in the first three. The following startling passage furnishes the key to the chain of strange sophistry which goes to make up the essay entitled "The great Political Superstition," and which is happily so unfamiliar to readers of Mr. Spencer's works. After admitting the indefensibility of the assumption that, in order to escape the evil of chronic conflict, the members of a community enter into a pact or covenant by which they all bind themselves to surrender their primitive freedom of action, and subordinate themselves to the will of a ruling power agreed upon—after deriding the hypothesis and its authors in language neither generous nor just, Mr. Spencer proceeds to present his own alternative hypothesis.

"Further consideration reveals a solution of the difficulty ; for, if dismissing all thought of any hypothetical agreement to co-operate, heretofore made, we ask what would be the agreement into which citizens would now enter with practical unanimity, we get a sufficiently clear justification for the rule of the majority inside a certain sphere, but not outside that sphere."

So that, after all, the outcome of Mr. Spencer's criticism of Hobbes and Austin results in the substitution of a hypothetical social compact made to-day for a hypothetical social compact made a long time ago. Of the two, that of Hobbes is preferable. His supposition is considerably more intelligible than Mr. Spencer's solution. That at an indefinitely remote period wild people, hitherto living in a state of anarchy, came together, hit upon the plan of co-operation, and there and then agreed to conform to the will of the effective majority, may not be a historical fact ; but nevertheless it is a fact that somehow men formerly in a state of anarchy did come little by little to subordinate their wills to that of the effective majority, consciously or unconsciously ; in other words, the supremacy of the State came to be recognised as a fact. What men come to do, they may be said in a sense to agree to do. And if Hobbes had expressed his pact in terms to the effect that men agreed to abide by the decision of the effective majority—the State-will —he would have been very near the mark. The social compact and the divine right of kings or of parliaments are after all merely two ways of expressing a stubborn fact—namely, the fact that right is transfigured might.

But Mr. Spencer's social compact is a sort of chronic plebiscitum. The justification for each new Act of Parliament is to be found by the process of wondering what would be the result if the people were polled. This is of course the "referendum." Carried out in practice instead of imagination its effect is to make every citizen a legislator in spite of the admitted fact that "there can be no fitness for legislative functions without wide knowledge of those legislative experiences which the past has bequeathed."

But perhaps Mr. Spencer would not go the length of taking a poll of the people in order to justify each new piece of proposed legislation. ˙ He would rather work the question out on paper ; he would ask himself—not the people—whether they would "agree to co-operate for the teaching of religion ? " and he would answer himself with "a very emphatic No." " In like manner, if " (to take an actual question of the day) "people were polled to ascertain whether, in respect of the beverages they drank, they would accept the decision of the greater number, certainly half, and probably more than half, would be unwilling." Now this is just what local-optionists deny. It is just what many others want to know. Mr. Spencer settles it offhand by intuition. But why should the majority be unwilling to abide by the decision of the majority ? Is it that the majority has no confidence in its own judgment or rectitude ? The self-regard of majorities is usually considered unimpeachable. But the strangest feature in this intuition is its marvellous precision. " Certainly half," he says, " and probably more than half," would be unwilling. Surely, if we may be certain of fifteen millions out of thirty, we might venture to be certain of fifteen millions and one. This recalls the scrupulousness of the American gentleman who solemnly swore to having brought down ninety-nine pigeons at a shot, but refused to imperil his immortal soul by setting the figure at a hundred.

"Manifestly then," says Mr. Spencer, "had social co-operation to be commenced by ourselves, and had its purposes to be specified before consent to co-operate could be obtained, there would be large parts of human conduct in respect of which co-operation would be declined, and in respect of which, consequently, no authority by the majority over the minority could be rightfully exercised."

This extraordinary passage and the superstructure built upon it are so unpractical, so unreal, and so visionary, that the conclusion can hardly be resisted that the whole essay containing it and developing it has been exhumed from a half-forgotten heap of the author's early writings, and published without re-examination. It must be obvious to Mr. Spencer and to everybody else that in the main those would agree to co-operate who believed their own views on the question at issue to be in a majority. Others would of course decline.

Nor does the prospect brighten when we come to the converse question, For what ends would men agree to co-operate? To which the ready answer is, "None will deny that for resisting invasion the agreement would be practically unanimous." Indeed! Many will deny it most emphatically. Besides, supposing that only one person held aloof, would the rest be justified in coercing that one to co-operate? If so, on what principle? Mr. Spencer himself excepts the Quakers, whom, however, he dismisses with a compliment and annihilation. "Excepting the Quakers only, who having done highly useful work in their time, are now dying out, all would unite for defensive war—not however for offensive war." This must be another of those intuitions which only a poll of the people can verify or disprove. It is at least as probable that a majority would vote the other way. Much would depend on the definition given to "invasion" and "defensive." Nearly every civilised nation that has gone to war in the present century has believed itself to be acting on the defensive. Onlookers might be able to inform the belligerents in the Franco-German war of 1870 as to which of them was waging a defensive war, but both sides distinctly claimed that justification. More recently, M. Ferry justified the operations in Ton-king on the ground that the French were acting on the defensive! Again, as to rebellions, were the English on the defensive when they ineffectually endeavoured to suppress the Boer rising? Were they on the defensive a century ago, when they successfully suppressed the Irish rising? Were the British the other day defending Egypt against the threatened invasion of the dervishes, or were the Soudanese fighting in defence of hearth and home? Then again as to the term "invasion," those modern Englishmen (or rather dwellers in England) who are smitten with the insular craze may define "invasion," so far as they themselves are concerned, as the entry of a foreign force *vi et armis* upon the soil of England, Scotland, and Wales—and perhaps Ireland. Whether a German occupation of Heligoland, a Spanish seizure of Gibraltar, or an Italian attack on Malta would fall within the definition, only the late lamented Anti-Aggression League can say. It would be even more interesting to know whether a Russian advance upon India would fall within the category of invasions which Mr. Spencer would himself co-operate to repel, and at what point in the onward march the invasion might be said to begin. Putting aside the question of British frontiers, as exceptionally simple or exceptionally complicated, according as we take an insular or an imperial view of them, let us ask whether a French occupation of Alsace would be an invasion of Germany in the above sense?

But why should "invasion" be construed as territorial invasion only? May not British interests and rights be invaded which are not territorial? Was not the tearing up of the Treaty of Paris by Russia in 1870 an invasion of England in the wider sense of the term? England, at great cost of blood and treasure, had obtained a certain negative right in the Black Sea—a certain safeguard against a definite danger. May not the German occupation of Angra Pepueña similarly be described as an invasion of British interests? The district had for many years been treated as the property of Englishmen, and under the protection of England; it is contiguous to regions in which Englishmen almost alone are interested; and the conflict of jurisdiction in those regions is calculated to injure trade to the detriment of the English people. Is it an invasion?

Further, we are not told whether there would be any limit to the subordination of individuals to the State in those matters in which they, "with practical unanimity," "almost unanimously," "omitting criminals," "excepting Quakers," agreed to co-operate. Take the agreement to co-operate for defensive war, and suppose that means something definite. Would the citizens thereby bind themselves to conform to the will of the majority in respect of measures directed to that end—all measures? Might not a citizen be willing to contribute money towards the expenses of the war without being willing to submit to conscription? Might he not accept conscription with power of substitution without being willing to serve? Or, assuming in the face of a growing party of sincere socialists that, "omitting criminals, all must wish to have person and property adequately protected," is it equally certain that all would be willing to accept the decision of the majority in respect of the measures needful for that end? And what is "property"? Mr. Spencer glides over this as a phantom ship might glide over sunken rocks. Surely people will not agree to protect property until they know what it is they are pledging themselves to protect. A thief steals a watch, and sells it to a *bond-fide* purchaser for its full value. Whose property is it that the State has to protect? A journeyman tailor agrees to make a quantity of army clothing out of cloth supplied to him by a cloth merchant, who before delivery fails for ten times the amount of his assets. Whose property is the clothing? Of course it is not difficult to say what would be a fair way of treating the claims of the different parties, or what is the existing law here and elsewhere; but the question is, Whose is the property? Whose is the property in a row of houses built by a lessee under a ninety-nine years' lease? Or in the case of "emphyteusis" under the Roman law? Or in a chest of gold coins dug up by a labourer in a field occupied by one man, owned by another, mortgaged to a third, and sold to a fourth

under the Settled Estates Act—and before completion of conveyance ?

It is when we come to the land question that we find
ourselves involved in the most inextricable maze. " In one
other co-operation all are interested—use of the territory
they inhabit." What territory does any individual inhabit, or
any determinate number of individuals ? Or, if indeterminate,
do the English people inhabit Ireland or India ? Do Lon-
doners inhabit Yorkshire ? In what sense is it true that one
is more *interested* in one's neighbour's field than in his cattle ?
The one supplies corn, the other beef. " But," it is urged, " we
must have some security for the food of the people. If
landowners conspired to grow no corn, the people would starve,
and such a state of things cannot be tolerated even as a bare
possibility." Likewise, if the owners of cattle conspired to
destroy them, the people would have no beef. If capitalists
conspired to smash up all machinery, rails, ships, tools,
furnaces, and mills in the country, the nation would be ruined
and the people destroyed. In short, if the race went mad, it
would possibly commit suicide. Practically landowners, like
capitalists in general, having interests coincident with those of
the whole people, refrain as a class from exercising their rights
to the detriment of society, and they are never likely to do so.
" But we must have room to move about; in this respect land
is *sui generis;* man is material, and space is essential to his
existence, and if all space in sea and earth and air is
appropriated (*cujus est solum, ejus est usque ad cœlum*) those
who own no space are ' in danger of being elbowed out of
existence." Quite so: then would it not be as well to find
out what kind of " use " it is which the public are vitally
interested in, and whether it is correctly described as a " use "
at all ? What kind of power the State does as a fact tend to
reserve to itself, while recognising the proprietary rights of
individuals, is ascertained more readily by a reference to the
land laws and customs of all countries, than by a guess as to
what a majority of the people in its wisdom would in this or
any other country agree to do. In all civilised countries we
find that as a fact the State dispossesses the proprietor whenever
such dispossession is expedient in the general interest. We

have railway concessions, new roads are made and new streets
cut through congested districts, without any more concern for
intervening proprietary claims than is involved in allowing full
compensation—that is, such compensation as satisfies the
national conscience. But what is Mr. Spencer's practical
conclusion from the premises that all are interested in the use
of the territory they inhabit ? " The implication is," says he,
" that the will of the majority is valid respecting the modes in
which, and conditions under which, parts of the surface or sub-
surface may be utilised, involving certain agreements made on
behalf of the public with private persons and companies." It
would take too long in this place to analyse in nomological
terms this remarkably opaque utterance. To some it might
seem to have been drafted in order to fit in with whatever
view of the land question should eventually turn out to be
correct. Others might be pardoned for regarding it as a pillar
of cloud for the purpose of veiling the transition from the
writer's doctrine of land nationalisation, as set forth in
Social Statics (and since repudiated), to the later doctrine of
individualism as advocated in *Political Institutions*. To me it
appears as an arrangement of words neither having any
particular meaning nor intended to have any.

At this point, in order to disarm criticism apparently, we
are reminded that " details are not needful here." Why not ?
In other places Mr. Spencer is most painstaking himself, and
most exacting in his demands upon others, as to attention to
details. " Nor is it needful," he continues, " to discuss that
border region lying between these classes of cases "—that
border region which, as Mill pointed out, is of all regions the
most fruitful in supplying crucial tests and essential differences.

" It is sufficient," we are told, " to recognise the undeniable
truth that there are numerous kinds of actions in respect of
which men would not, if they were asked, agree with anything
like unanimity to be bound by the will of the majority ; while
there are some kinds of actions in respect of which they would
unanimously agree to be thus bound. Here then we find a
definite warrant for enforcing the will of the majority within
certain limits, and a definite warrant for denying the authority
of its will beyond those limits."

To which the reply is that, if it is sufficient for the philosopher to recognise the said "undeniable truth," it is certainly not sufficient for the statesman, who wants to know not only that there are numerous kinds of such actions, but also what those kinds of actions are; and he will not (if he be wise) rest content with the *ipse dixit* of any one who evolves the answer out of his own inner consciousness; and furthermore, he may not feel satisfied that the mere process of counting noses, even in imagination, will solve the question as to the morality of such actions.

From the position here taken up by Mr. Spencer it is but a short and easy step to "abstract rights." After a brief and, as it will seem to most, in every way unsatisfactory analysis of the "untenable" opinion of Bentham and his disciples, we are led straight back to what modern jurists fondly hoped was the exploded doctrine of natural rights; "for sundry groups of social phenomena unite to prove that this doctrine is well warranted, and the doctrine they set against it unwarranted." We are then told that various savage races are controlled by "long-acknowledged customs," by "ancient usages," by "primordial usages or tacit conventions," by "universally-recognised customs." "So sacred are immemorial customs with the primitive man, that he never dreams of questioning their authority, and when government arises, its power is limited by them." Now, premising that no one denies, or ever did deny, that State laws grew out of customs (they must have grown out of something), what are we to infer from this long string of social phenomena, many of which, being gleanings from travellers' tales, are open to doubt, while others are false on the face of them? Are we seriously asked to believe that the quaint and often ludicrous customs of savages are themselves the germs of the laws by which natural rights are sanctioned? Are we to understand that when Government arises, its power is limited by them in any other sense than that in which the will of a man is limited by his own desires and habits? If so, how?

The truth is, Mr. Spencer is confounding three distinct classes of so-called rights: the rights which he himself would sanction if he were the arbitrator; the rights which the claimant's fellow-citizens would individually recognise as morally just; and the rights which are as a matter of fact actually sanctioned by the law of the land. The first may be called "natural rights," or rights as they ought to be in the opinion of their advocate; the second may be called moral rights, or rights as they would be under a code of laws deduced from the morals of the day; and the third may be called legal rights, or rights which are as a fact recognised by the State, and which are a natural development.

It is perfectly true that, as the leaders of the German school of jurists assert, the State laws which are actually carried out are not in all cases and in all respects identical with the State laws as they are expressed, whether embodied in a code or in a heterogeneous heap of statutes, or in authorised or received commentaries on the law. The invariable sequences which actually tend to hold good at any given time in any country, may be called the statical laws or internal group-morals of that particular State at that stage of its development. The laws as expressed are necessarily but imperfect and often distorted reflections of these true laws, the distortion being due not only to imperfect expression and inadequacy of language but more especially to the false generalisation of legislators or law-makers of one sort or another. Now, it is approximately the former class, the statical laws, which the German school style "Naturrecht." There is another sense in which the term may be used, and that is, to denote the law as it tends to be but for disturbing causes; or, assuming those disturbing causes to be more or less evanescent, the laws as they tend to become. In neither of these senses is there any resemblance to the natural rights championed by Mr. Spencer, who is of course aware that although "recht" may be translated by "droit" or "jus," it cannot be translated into English by the term "right" or "rights" or any other single word; and furthermore, that although "recht" and "droit" are fairly synonymous, "Naturrecht," on the other hand, cannot be rendered into French as "droit naturel." Mr. Spencer's "natural rights" are the "droit naturel" of Rousseau, the "jus naturale" of Ulpian, the "inalienable right of every man born into the world" of Mr.

Henry George; but not the "Naturrecht" of Savigny. So that the appeal to the "root-idea of German jurisprudence" (which is, above all, historical in method) to shore up the justly discredited card-castle of "natural rights," is, to say the least of it, unfortunate.

Mr. Spencer does not usually allow himself to be a slave to words, but his singular criticism of Hobbes's explanation of the origin of justice seems to show that for once he has fallen into this condition. "The definition of injustice," says Hobbes, " is none other than the not performing of covenants " (including the tacit compact entered into by the members of a society, upon which Government, according to him, is based); " therefore, before the names of just and unjust can have place, there must be some coercive power to compel men equally to the performance of their covenants."

Hence it is clear that by "injustice" Hobbes meant to denote the breach of legal duties. Ignoring this definition, Mr. Spencer substitutes his own, and naïvely remarks that among his own friends he could name half a dozen over whom the requirements of justice would be as imperative in the absence of a coercive power as in its presence. Possibly! The majority of Mr. Spencer's friends will hardly feel flattered by the limitation. But the question is, Could Mr. Spencer find half a dozen friends so law-abiding that they would obey the law even against their conscience without the terror of some punishment?

The truth is, Mr. Spencer is himself under the blinding influence of a great superstition—a superstition he has out-lived in other departments of thought. He still believes in abstract justice, as something anterior to society or even to man—something immutable and absolute. He still holds, as he held in 1851, that the elimination of the mentally and morally inferior is in accordance with "the decrees of a large far-seeing benevolence." He has since emancipated himself from the anthropomorphic belief involved, and declines to be held "committed to such teleological implications" as the passage cited contains; but, to use his own illustration, just as " Carlyle, who, in his student days, giving up, as he thought, the creed of his fathers, rejected its shell only, keeping the contents," so his own mind is still under the sway of the metaphysical abstraction Justice. The laws, to have any validity (whatever that means), must conform to this test. He regards the laws solely as a means to an end, rather than as the products of evolution, the resultant of diverse forces acting in various directions through countless ages. His standpoint in viewing State laws is precisely that of Dr. Paley viewing the marvellous adaptations of organic forms to their surroundings. A giraffe with a short neck, argued Paley, would assuredly perish of starvation ; hence his long neck is evidence of the far-seeing benevolence of his Creator. Honesty is the best policy, argues Mr. Spencer ; the just tend to survive and the unjust to perish ; hence the sufficient cause of good laws in Justice. Is it not remarkable that Hobbes, writing more than two centuries ago, should have examined nomological phenomena in a more positive spirit than the great philosopher of the nineteenth century ? Hobbes argued, there are certain classes of actions which tend to conduce to the well-being of society. Experience has taught us what in the concrete these are ; they are detailed in the expressed laws. We find by induction they may be classified under certain heads in accordance with certain practical middle principles ; there is no general principle under which they can all be subsumed ; but their common trait appears to be conformity with the group-welfare. Let us denote them by the term Just. The connotation of the term we cannot tell. This is not the language of Hobbes's day, but it describes with fairness the method he adopted. He then inquired what it could be which counteracted the antagonistic efforts of individuals actuated not by group-welfare but by self-welfare ; and he saw that it was none other than the power of the State. He did not attempt to resolve that force into its elements in terms of individual force ; there it was as a fact. That was sufficient. He might have asked himself how far the State force represented the will of the greater number of men, women, and children in the society ; whether the will of a strong man went for more than that of a weak man ; of a rich than of a poor man ; of a clever than of a weak-minded man ; whether the wills of half a dozen children contributed as much to the State will as the will of one man or two women.   But he was neither curious nor dog-matic on these points.   The fact was there, and he accepted it as a datum.   In his day he found that the channel through which this State force operated was that of monarchical govern-ment, and he lived to see the so-called republic develop into a monarchy in all but the name, and later still to see the old monarchy restored.   It is absolutely misleading to say that "Hobbes argued in the interests of absolute monarchy;" such an assertion is as unjust and as unfounded as would be the more plausible one that Mr. Spencer argues in the interests of the Liberal party.   Hobbes was, and Mr. Spencer is, far above arguing in any interests.   Hobbes was unquestionably the pro-foundest thinker of his age—the age of Shakespeare and Bacon ; and many Englishmen who cherish his name will bitterly resent this imputation.   We have already referred to Mr. Spencer's sneer at Carlyle.   Here is what he has to say of the founder of the English school of jurisprudence, probably the acutest logician of the century : "Austin was originally in the army, and it has been truly remarked that the permanent traces left may be seen in his *Province of Jurisprudence.* When undeterred by the exasperating pedantries—the endless distinctions and definitions and repetitions—which serve but to hide his essential doctrines, we ascertain what these are, it becomes manifest that he assimilates civil authority to military authority."   It is difficult to deal patiently with this passage. It is useful as showing up in a strong light the fundamental error which underlies and vitiates the whole of Mr. Spencer's political doctrines ; an error he unconsciously adopted from his precursor Comte.   That Austin was once in the army we know, but beyond this statement of fact, this criticism of the great jurist is as untrue as it is ungenerous.   Those who attended Austin's lectures testify that, so far from having anything of the drill-sergeant about him, he was exceptionally modest and conversational in his method of teaching ; he would listen attentively to all doubts, and ask the opinions of his hearers on points where he felt himself weak.   But if we are to look for the traces of his army discipline in his conclusions, it is only necessary to repeat that it is Mr. Spencer himself who, after Comte, mistakes for a difference in kind what

T

Austin clearly saw to be merely a difference in degree; the difference, namely, between the "military and industrial régimes." As to exasperating pedantries, Austin himself attributes his own peculiarities of diction to a scrupulous anxiety to express each idea by a suitable word, and to use invariably that word to express the idea. His aim was to be not an elegant but a precise writer. From the expression "endless" distinctions, it may be inferred that the complainant has never got to the end of them; those who have, only regret that poor Austin did not possess the health and strength to add to them, containing as they do some of the finest master-pieces of logical analysis. The repetitions which are a blemish on the published editions of his works are, as Mr. Spencer might have ascertained, the necessary result of delivering several lectures on the same subject to different audiences in different places; and the able editors of his lectures and posthumous papers have probably acted wisely in publishing them as they stand. For it is seldom that science can be caught, so to speak, in a state of growth in a great mind, as it is presented to us in Austin's wrestling writings. While, as for the definitions that glitter like crystals throughout his works, and which so vex the soul of his critic, it is enough to say that an accurate acquaintance with even one of them (the wonderful definition of property) would have saVed the author of *The Man v. the State* pages of useless writing, the whole of the fifteenth chapter of *Political Institutions*, and hours and days of anxious thought. There is nothing in the whole range of juristic literature comparable with Austin's final definition of property and the chain of masterly analysis which leads up to it. Mr. Spencer writes in complete ignorance of it.

Austin and all his works having been thus contemptuously thrust aside, the search is continued for a justification of the supremacy assumed by the sovereign body, or, as it has been styled, the effective majority. " The true question is, Whence the sovereignty ? What is the assignable warrant for this unqualified supremacy assumed by one, or by a small number, or by a large number over the rest ?" Does any one really believe that any community is or ever was subject to the arbitrary caprice of one or of any determinate number of its

members? Does Mr. Spencer believe that this country is
governed in accordance with the will of a numerical majority,
or that any such government is even conceivable? Is it not
clear that the forms of individual force which go to make up
the group-force are of very various kinds? Possibly brute
force or muscular force contributes the least to the result.
Force in the form of wealth, intellectual force, moral force, and
many other and derivative and combined forms, pour into the
common stream, all operating in countless directions, like the
sensations and ideas and emotions in the mind of a man, and
the resultant of these and other forces is the group-will. To
ask for any higher warrant for the authority of the group over
its units, is to rake up in a fresh place the threadbare controversy about freewill. "How comes it," asks the befogged
controversialist, "that a man often refrains from doing what
he wills to do? that something within him at the last moment
whispers 'Don't do it,' with the effect of dissuading him?"
Mr. Spencer would answer him, "My dear sir, go home and
learn the meaning of the words you use." He certainly would
not set about to think why the body does not move in the
direction of least resistance, or why the lesser force should
overcome the greater; or if not, by what peculiar virtue or
authority, or warrant, or justification, the greater overcomes
the less. And yet when the subject of the inquiry is not the
organism a human being, but the organism a society, he
searches everywhere for "an assignable warrant," and bitterly
complains that Austin while admitting that a government is
actuated by group-morality furnishes none. "What we have
to seek is some higher warrant for the subordination of the
minority to the majority than that arising from inability to
resist physical coercion." "We have to find, not a physical
justification, but a moral justification for the supposed absolute
power of the majority." But what is meant by the majority?
Does any one suppose that the numerical majority, as such,
either exercises absolute power, or ought to exercise it? All
that Hobbes and Austin contend is, that what the group wills
it does, and that those members of the community who happen
to be in line with the group-act may be called the effective
majority. No one pretends that any determinate person, or

number of persons, ever did have or could have the making of the group-will.

If Mr. Spencer will recast his question, and ask, " What is the test of the goodness or badness of group-acts ?" we can cordially join in the quest. Bentham's answer was simple : " The greatest happiness of the greatest number ; " but it was not true, and it was not definite. The greatest number of whom ? Of living persons ? or of the countless millions to come ? If of the former, it is far from certain that a socialistic redistribution of wealth, accompanied by wholesale infanticide, would not be the readiest path. If of the latter (assuming that the two interests may be antagonistic), then we have to ask, " Why should the living sacrifice themselves for the sake of the unborn ? " Sympathy with the unborn ? A frail motor ! Though Mr. Spencer evidently has faith in it. " If," says he, " we adopt the meliorist view " (not the optimist), " that life is on the way to become such that it will yield more pleasure than pain, then those actions by which life is maintained are justified." Not at all : no act is morally justified which does not conduce to the ultimate welfare of the agent. This is what Mr. Sidgwick would call Egoistic Hedonism, but it is also common sense. Evidently Bentham's answer is unsatisfactory in theory and utterly unworkable in practice. To expect the legislator to measure the million and one effects of a proposed law with his " hedonometer," to say nothing of the remote effects, is preposterous. What, then, is the test of which we are in search ? To any one who has once grasped the conception of the group as an organism—as a whole not to be expressed in terms of its component parts, any more than a man can be expressed in terms of the cells of which he is composed—the answer is clear enough : the welfare of the group. This is the warrant, this the justification.

When we seek for the motive of a law, we must not look for it in the minds of individuals conforming to that law. The motive is to be found in the group-mind. This is delicate ground. Group-psychology cannot be studied subjectively. The group-will can only be known objectively, by its acts. Hence we are not called upon to ascertain what the group may *think* of contemplated actions and their results ; we must

assume that it approves those actions of which the results conduce to the group-welfare. We have no other course ; but it
is sufficient. Our conclusions in individual ethics are for the
most part similarly based on observation of the results of
conduct.

We are not even bound to show that all the units of the
group are benefited by the operation of the law ; nor that the
majority of the individuals are benefited ; nor that *any* of the
individuals are benefited. It is true there are powerful forces
tending to bring about coincidence between the will of states
and the wills of their component units, but this may be
regarded for the present purpose as accidental. Certainly
there are laws, good laws, operating in civilised communities,
of which the advantages to the citizens are undiscernible, if
not altogether non-existent. Nor is it necessary even to prove
that future generations will be benefited by the observance of
the law in question, although it is difficult to show the gain to
the race without at the same time showing that at all events
some members of it share the gain individually. It is enough
if we distinguish between the essential and the accidental.

It is for us, after having observed the invariable sequence
(the law), to verify it by showing its bearing on the group-
welfare. That is the only proof open to us beyond the mere
induction. And without deductive proof, inductions in so
complex a science as sociology are extremely untrustworthy.
Hence no science of law can be firmly based which does not
furnish this verification. And it is disregard of this branch of
the science which is a blemish on the work of the historical
school of jurisprudence.

But we must not fall into the mistake of confounding the
explanation of a law with the explanation of its origin. The
cause of the origin of a nomological law and the cause of its
persistence are two different things. Illustrations of this
distinction in the department of biological study will readily
recur to the mind. No moth every consciously tried to mimic
a butterfly, and yet such is the result of conforming to their
own little desires that whole species of moths have so completely imitated certain species of butterflies that even the
practised eye of the naturalist can hardly distinguish between

them.   And—what is more important from the moths' point of view—neither can the birds.

We have then to look for the origin of justice (using the term, after Hobbes, as connoting that which is common to the enduring laws) in the conduct of individual men or animals which are not yet members of an organic group or state.   Its germ or germs must be sought for in the anarchic stage of development.   At the risk of repetition this should be clearly understood ; the group-welfare is not the origin of the laws, but it is the cause of their survival—of their present existence.   The strong man who first deferred to the wish of a weak man was not actuated by solicitude for the wellbeing of his race.   But it was the compatibility of such acts with the wellbeing of his race which preserved and rendered organic the habit of such acts.   Tribes practising such acts predominated by elbowing other tribes out of existence, and by perpetuating a race of men actuated as a rule by like promptings, whatever they may have been.   What those feelings were—why one of superior strength should form a habit of yielding in certain classes of cases to one who could not otherwise prevail against him, is the question we have now to answer.

The result of our inquiry will prove somewhat startling. Justice has two distinct origins.   Nay, they are not only distinct, but even antagonistic.   Justice then has two connotations.   In one sense, justice enjoins a certain line of conduct ; in another sense, justice enjoins an opposite line of conduct under precisely similar conditions.   No wonder there has always been great confusion in this domain of thought.   But let us set to work and trace the notion back to its double source.

Those who have watched the behaviour of dogs will have observed that a strong dog will seldom attempt to deprive a weak dog of a bone.   Though stronger, he hesitates to attack the dog in possession.   A fortiori, a little dog will not dare to attack a big dog in possession, though he will put on all his best military airs before yielding up his own bone.   In this instance there are two minds to dissect.   There is the mental attitude of the little dog, and there is the mental attitude of the big dog. Action is the end of will, or, in other words, the resultant of motives. The strongest motive actuating the little dog is the idea of enjoying the bone in the very near future. This future is so near, and the associations engendered by the smell and feel of the bone so intensify this idea, that it borders on realisation, and we have what is called an intense expectation. Hence, so far as the idea of gnawing a bone is capable of stimulating to action, we have it in its strongest form. And what is the mental attitude of the strongest dog ? First, he also pictures to himself the pleasure of gnawing the bone which he sees before him; but the idea is far less intense than that of the possessor ; he neither feels nor smells the bone, and the contemplated time of enjoyment is more remote. Moreover, experience has taught him (or instinct, the experience of his forefathers) that the little dog will most probably make a fight of it, in which case even though victory be with the strong, it will not be unalloyed with pain and trouble. In short, his expectation will be nothing like so intense as that of the possessor. It is unnecessary to go farther into the psychology of the position : it is enough to show that a custom will tend to develop of respecting possession. But it will be based upon fear, and, among the lower animals, eventually inherited habit, rather than upon any sense of possessory right.

Here is no recognition of the expediency of proportioning satisfaction to effort, but a recognition of the inexpediency of gratifying a desire at an expense in pain or risk which more than counterbalances the probable gain. The resulting habit is called the spirit of compromise. A boy with an apple in his hand has a better chance of eating it than a man a hundred yards off. The latter must give chase ; he must then struggle for the apple, and may, even though successful, get a blow or a kick, and moreover, the apple may be eaten or thrown away before he can get it. The boy's *right*, his well-warranted expectation of enjoyment, is recognised without any extraneous interference. Again, here is a weary hunter sitting alongside a stag he has captured. One who is fresh, and perhaps stronger, comes up, impelled by hunger. Here are the elements of a fierce conflict. Both expect pleasure and both expect pain as the result of the fight. Now, both parties argue thus: A little with peace is better than the chance of much with the certainty of bruised limbs and the possibility of getting nothing. Why not share the prize in some proportion? The question, What proportion? is not settled by any reference to the efforts of the hunter, but by a rough calculation as to the least amount of blackmail which will induce the stronger man to keep the peace. Compromise is the germ of justice.

It is obvious that, on the average, force is greatly economised by compromise. This force, which, on the average, is wasted to no purpose on internal conflicts, might be turned to better account by the group for purposes of external defence or aggression. And moreover, on the average, individuals would not lose by the arrangement. The State would therefore be impelled by self-interest to recognise all such compromises; the State whose members practised the rule would tend to survive; and the habit would be hardened into what we call instinct in the "lower animals," and conscience in man.

But justice has another and a very different origin. This also is to be found in the patriarchal stage of social development. We need not go farther back in our search than the stage in which already there is recognition of offspring, and what is called parental love. Nor need we analyse that sentiment. Parental love is a fact which nomology accepts as a datum.

A parent, without perhaps being able to assign a better reason for it than sympathy, will not permit an elder child always to take advantage of his superior strength in his dealings with a younger. An arbitrary State interference takes place. And here is the second germ of justice. Why it is not just, parents do not trouble to inquire, but for some reason or other, based on sympathy with weakness, the possessor of superior muscular force is arbitrarily debarred from reaping the natural advantages of that superiority. Here is no question of fore-casting the probable result of a trial of strength, no compromise based on average economy. On the contrary, there is no doubt of the victory of the stronger if uninterfered with; and, moreover, the adjustment is not a voluntary one, but compulsory. It is imposed from without.

When the "gens" takes the place of the family as the political unit, the head of the house is no longer swayed by quite such immediate sympathy with the weaker members. In the meantime, his decisions have come to be based on principles of a more general character. Again, as these compound groups are recompounded, and the gens gives place to the tribe, personal sympathies are still further weakened, and judicial decisions are based on still wider generalisations—all of them, be it remembered, the outcome of experience, and not severally deduced from any high moral principle of abstract justice. When at last we reach the stage in which we see nations, each containing many tribes, all welded together into an organic state with its *corpus juris civilis*, the ruler can have but little, if any, personal knowledge of the citizens, and he (or those to whom the judicial function is delegated) must be guided in his decisions by rules of high generality which are popularly believed to be based on what is termed justice ; though what that is, not even the shrewdest of ancient or modern jurists has been able to tell us. What is connoted we do not know ; but we are now in a position to define "just," in this its second sense, as denoting those group interferences between individual citizens, which aim at more or less equalising the *conditions* of the competition. Here is no question of ascertaining by a rough forecast what the result of conflict would be, and arranging the matter accordingly, without recourse to force. Nor is the arrangement a voluntary one, based on the good sense of the two parties concerned—their reason, conscience, or inherited habit. It is an external interference by third parties for reasons based on sympathy with inferiority. This is accomplished by prohibiting the exercise of certain faculties (as a general prohibition) which, in a state of anarchy (or nature, as some wrongly call it), would give a decided advantage to one of the contending parties. Thus, on the plea of justice, forms of superior force came to be one by one eliminated. Stealth was, as a matter of history, long tolerated by the State when violence was deprecated. Later on, when stealth ceased to be allowed, low cunning was admired and permitted free play, just as nowadays sharp practice is winked at by many who would recoil from fraud; while even among those who are accounted high-minded among us, it is regarded as a laudable exercise of intellectual superiority to buy cheap from one who is ignorant of the true value of an article, and to sell dear to another who is also ignorant of it. Similarly the State permits what all honest men regard as blameworthy, while it ruthlessly puts its foot down on what appears hardly more culpable. Where the line will eventually be drawn it is impossible to say. The Roman law allowed one who had sold a thing far below its true value to come upon the purchaser for an account: we do not. Which is just?

I wish to lay special stress on the double origin of what is popularly regarded as justice. One is socialism: the other is individualism. The one is based originally on parental sympathy, which slowly expands from the family to humanity; the other is based on selfish compromise, and tends finally to absorb the whole field of law. Altruism tends to become wholly voluntary and law to become wholly based on average individual advantage and implied voluntary contract. Thus scientific anarchy is shown to be the end towards which society is moving. That is to say, we are approaching a state in which law, based on the rights of the selfish, will be tempered not by paternal despotism and compulsory *charity* (a contradiction in terms), but by true voluntary altruism.

At the same time the individualist is bound to recognise the organic nature of social groups, and to remember that to artificially and arbitrarily impose a more advanced form on an organism not yet ripe for it is not to hasten but to retard its development. To uproot the poor-law system, to abolish the system of State police, to leave prosecution for murder to the initiative of the murdered man's friends, or the Union to which he voluntarily affiliated himself, to leave the defence of territory to those who cared to defend it—such an extension of the principle at the present time in any existing country would be about as prudent and scientific a course as to impose free institutions, a representative system, and trial by jury on the Fijians. A wise gardener does not open a rosebud with an oyster knife. Hence I must not be understood as advocating the immediate practical application of principles which apply to future civilisations. I prefer to regard them as tendencies, and therefore as finger-posts to direct us on the line of least resistance. The ideal in all things is that towards which we may ever strive but which we may never reach.

It now remains for us to decide whether by the term " rights " we mean moral rights or legal rights. The definition is optional. Usage justifies either. But having chosen, let us beware of employing the word in one sense in the major premiss, and in the other sense in the minor premiss, or the conclusion. Austin chose to define rights as legal rights; he was quite justified in doing this ; and having done it, he never swerved to the right hand nor to the left. Mr. Spencer chooses to put the other interpretation on the term as used by Austin, and thus makes him appear to say that which is ridiculous. Austin knew perfectly well that usage precedes law, but he also knew that rights could not precede government in the sense in which he employed the terms, which is obvious.

It is clear from argument based on economy of force that the State would tend in many classes of cases to sanction pre-existing moral rights ; but the " justification " or " warrant " for this course would be not the moral rights themselves, but the gain to the group. Hundreds of instances will readily occur to the mind wherein the State has, so to speak, ridden roughshod over moral rights, and wisely so too. Lazarus at the gate of the rich man had a moral right (in the opinion of the narrator's countrymen) to some part of the other's wealth ; but the State did not sanction that claim, and it is currently admitted that it would be inexpedient for any state to sanction such a claim. Here we have a moral right which does not tend to grow into a legal right. It is unnecessary to ascertain the basis of the moral right ; it is enough to show that if law is to be based, as Mr. Spencer thinks, on " natural rights," by which he seems to mean some kind of moral rights, then we shall have group-morality (law) which is not based on group-welfare, which is absurd.

Let us turn to the evolution of law. What is a law in the nomological sense ? It is the statement of an invariable sequence of which the antecedent is the act of an individual citizen or individual citizens, and the consequent is the act of the group or state. No amount of enacting or legislating makes a law ; it is the carrying out of the enactment, or an invariable tendency to carry it out, in the absence of disturbing causes, such as ignorance, false evidence, escape of wrongdoer, etc., which justifies the statement and verifies the law. Of course there are many so-called State laws (statutes, etc.) which are not as a fact carried out in practice. Some are obsolete, others unworkable, and others uncongenial to the conscience of the age. All such are but distorted reflections or mendacious mis-statements of the true law (Naturrecht), which as a fact obtains. Such so-called State laws, statutes, decrees, edicts, etc., must continue to be called laws out of deference to popular usage ; but the true laws in the scientific sense—statical laws—are the statements of invariable sequences, by whomsoever promulged. It is the province of the legislator to discover these laws ; and more—to divine by a study of history and his own time the changes which are in course of being worked out ; to discover by some process not only the law as it is, but the law as it tends to become. The laws of the change and development of statical laws may in Comtist phraseology be termed dynamical nomological laws. And the first question for the nomologist to decide is, as to the method to be adopted in the search. Transcendental jurists, it is needless to observe, adopt the method which, oddly enough, Mr. Spencer has followed and defended. The laws as they ought to be, must, they say, be deduced, like the propositions of Euclid, from one or a few fundamental principles, of which the chief is *fiat justitia*.

The empirical school of jurists, on the other hand, contend that there are no known truths of the highest generality, and that each law must be tested on its merits by its fitness to conduce to the wellbeing of the people, or some of them. And they proceed to find this out in each case by observation, experiment, or calculation—an heroic task, which does more credit to their patience than to their appreciation of the vastness of the subject. All seem alike to overlook the suitability of the method adopted in the other inductive sciences — that of making inductions from the minor social rules which have stood the test of time ; of casting the conclusion into the form of a more general rule ; of extracting, when possible, that which is common to this rule, and other general rules arrived at by a similar process, and so of arriving at a rule of higher generality. As in other departments of science, the inquirer is then in possession of many laws of various degrees of generality, which he must verify by applying them to new or unconsidered or hypothetical cases. This process of exhaustive subsumption will either strengthen the probability of his original conclusion, or show up the weak point in it; in which latter case he will be in a position to qualify it in accordance with his widened experience. The third part of the process which is conveniently carried on concurrently with the others, is that of making deductions from the general laws reached by induction. As in other branches of inquiry, some of the greatest and most valuable truths will be brought to light by this process; but it need hardly be said that the value of a deduction depends not only on the correctness of the logic, but on the truth of the premiss. Hence it is that most of the deductions hitherto contributed to ethics and jurisprudence, being deductions not from general-isations based on the actual sequences observed in the actions of men and of groups of men, but on meaningless dogmas as to Duty, Justice, Virtue, Right, and the like, have little or no value whatsoever.

The historical source of law has already been indicated, and it is evident that State laws are not, and never have been, deductions from the highest moral truths, or supposed truths. They took their rise from the generalisations which were of necessity made when questions became too numerous and too complicated to be decided, each, from beginning to end, on its merits. Precedents were cited; the *ratio decidendi* was extracted, correctly or erroneously, and the result was a State law.

In making these generalisations, either consciously or unconsciously, the law-makers or judges of old naturally made imperfect inductions, just as our lawyers do now. They seized upon some accidental feature common to a number of cases which seemed similar, instead of upon the essential feature. This accidental feature they took as the basis of the new generalisation or State law. To take a modern instance of this fallacy. Of thousands of partnership cases tried in this country, community of profit and loss seems to be a common feature. Hence lawyers of high repute (see Lindley on "Partnership") have seized upon this trait as the distinctive mark of partnership; thus confounding the accidental with the essential, and entailing great injustice and hardship. The essential element in partnership is not community of profit and loss, but reciprocal guaranty. It may be said that nearly all bad State laws which are not the result of erroneous beliefs are due to false generalisations. Nearly all the confusions, the complications, and the injustice of the English laws relating to liens, to mortgages, to debts of priority, to consideration, to bankruptcy, etc. etc., are due to blundering generalisations. Lien, for example, has never yet been correctly defined in any legal authority, simple and beautiful as the connotation is. Consequently, many true liens are unrecognised by law, whilst others are sanctioned which have no proper existence, to the great injury of the actual owner. Like remarks apply to such elementary legal conceptions as debt and security. In many cases the false generalisation is too wide; it covers cases which bear only a superficial resemblance; but in others it frequently fails to cover cases to which the correct *ratio decidendi* applies.

Some State laws are repealed, or cease to be operative; others persist through centuries of social development. What is the reason for the survival of some laws and the extinction of others ? Tribes whose laws conduce to the wellbeing of the race necessarily outlive and thrust out of existence those tribes whose laws, however apparently reasonable or just, do not conduce to the group - welfare. This becomes more obvious when we reflect that in some times and places laws are operative and conducive to group-welfare which in other countries or in other ages would clearly lead to disintegration. No one pretends that monogamy, for example, would be a desirable institution in a poultry-yard. Few would condemn polygamy among nomad tribes in a thinly-populated area. Is there a hint as to its immorality or inexpediency in the Old Testament ? Again, infanticide was legally practised by Greeks and Romans, and to-day it is recognised in China. Even stealing is said to have been lawful in Sparta; and duelling is allowed and encouraged in several European countries to-day. We have only to refer to Montesquieu for numerous instances of laws and customs in vogue among peoples separated from us by space and time, which, if introduced into nineteenth-century England, would probably ruin the country. We shall easily satisfy ourselves that the fitness of a law is not to be tested by any reference to a supposed standard of justice or virtue, but by its effect on the eventual welfare of the race adopting it. If it is not conducive to the group-welfare one of two things will happen: either the law will be dropped, or the group will perish. Thus the just and the unjust laws (regarded from any arbitrary standpoint) will survive together where they are conducive to the welfare of the group; they will perish together where they are not conducive. And so it befalls that many good laws are not just, if judged by the common sense of a so-called just man. (For that justice has a connotation, though undiscovered, there can be little doubt; and that, in the absence of a true definition, there is no better clue to the connotation of the term than the instinctive feeling of the multitude in applying it to the concrete, is also tenable.) Indeed since the widest-ranging laws are but generalisations from laws of less generality, and since every step of the process opens the door to fallacies which may become ingrained in the law, it follows that in a highly civilised and complex society hardly any of the laws, whether written or unwritten, can be regarded as just. The most that can be shown in their favour is that any alternative laws which might be proposed would probably result in even greater injustice—in a larger number of cases of hardship than the existing laws; which in many cases is not saying much. But such is the force of habit that we seem to see justice in a law of undoubted expediency in which there is not a tittle, in any sense of the term, which has ever been suggested. This habit blinds us to the immense differentiation which has taken place in morals and laws. He who would deduce laws as they ought to be (*i.e.* as they tend to be) from morals, must be capable of calculating the present position of the geological strata from a knowledge of the antecedent physical conditions of the globe.

From a very early stage we find the moral and the legal rights in collision. For instance, how came it that when the weaker child tried to take possession of a thing which the elder and stronger was using, the parent refrained from equalising the conditions ? Brute force was allowed to predominate. Here the sympathy with intensity of expectation overpowered the sympathy with physical weakness. And so at the present day proprietary right prevails over sympathy with the hardships and disadvantageous position of the poor. It is in accordance with the group-welfare. It is only when man enters upon the scene that sympathy with intense disappointment after intense expectation and antipathy for the cause of the disappointment are manifested. From the moment when the family as a whole, through the patriarch, interferes on behalf of the holder or possessor of a thing and against the would-be despoiler, from that moment we have the recognition of possessory right.

Let us follow up the development of this recognised right. We have seen how it would come about that one who had gathered a cocoa-nut would be left in undisputed enjoyment, or that otherwise the State would interfere to ensure that result. Now suppose he had captured a stag, and could not eat the whole of it at one meal. Four courses would lie open to him : he could carry about with him as much of the carcase as he could lift, and relinquish the rest ; or he could sit down alongside of it until he was again hungry ; or he might hand over to a friend as much as he could not eat ; or lastly, he could inform all and sundry that the carcase was his own, that he claimed it, that he could, if he chose, remain with it and so get his claim respected, and that to compel him to do so would be a restriction on his liberty. Probably this fourth course would be the last to be adopted, but it would necessarily come into use, for the simple reason that it would be a saving of the common time—an economy of group-force. And not until the recognition of this right over a thing not in actual possession came to be assured, could the right of property in its fullest sense be said to have reached maturity. From the third course, which would be based on the possessory right of intensity of expectation, would of course spring the right of gift, transfer, or alienation.

The right to things within the grip or within the power of immediate resumption has widened into a right to things not within the grip; this presently and necessarily extends to prescriptive ownership. The claim to ownership, once put forward without dispute, lasts indefinitely. Then the right of gift develops irresistibly into a right to transfer, from donor to donee, a thing out of reach by word of mouth. And since it takes time to obtain possession of a thing at a distance, it clearly comes to pass that a future gift is regarded as valid. Meanwhile mutual gifts or exchanges have become frequent, and gifts in exchange for future services have developed into conditional future gifts, or rather conditional promises to give. It is clear that from this would arise in the most natural manner the recognition of gift contingent on the death of the donor, or, in other words, of testamentary bequest; which is the key-stone of the present system of civilisation— property in perpetuity. Temporary rights over things held by others would tend to come into existence without blurring or weakening the proprietary or permanent right of the true owner; and thus the State would come to sanction the rights of hirers and lenders. It is quite needless in this place to trace the gradual growth from the original germ—possessory right—of the innumerable forms of rights over things now sanctioned by the modern State.

Thus from absolute liberty, common to man and the lower animals, tempered by sympathies and antipathies in harmony with group-welfare, spring first possession by tacit understanding, then right of possession sanctioned by patriarchal power, which is the incipient State; this extends to recognised possession of things not within the grip or immediate resumption. (No hard-and-fast line can be drawn between these stages of possessory right.) Then come prescriptive ownership, together with uses to alien property, sub-uses of several degrees; *condominium,* which tends to split up into property in the narrow sense, and lien (not even yet fully differentiated); and finally, property in ideas and other more complex proprietary rights.

To sum up. If " rights " is a term with two meanings, " justice," which is used to connote that unknown principle common to all rights, must also have two meanings. Justice may be that which is common to all moral rights, or that which is common to all legal rights; and if it is the one it cannot be the other. It is not a case of the greater including the less; the two principles are disparate. Most moderns employ the term in its ethical sense. Hobbes, as we have seen, employed the term in its nomological sense, just as Austin employed the term rights; and (so far as Mr. Spencer's criticism is concerned) with the same result, namely, that of laying himself open to misrepresentation by one who does not take the trouble to ascertain beforehand in what sense the term is used. Common usage hardly justifies Hobbes's use of the word, which, at all events nowadays, is used to express a moral abstraction ; and it will be well to confine it to this purpose. To contend that the true laws (those actually carried out as an invariable rule) cannot be unjust, would be paradoxical to modern ears. That they cannot be illegal is a safer proposition, and a truism withal.

We have seen that there was a time when justice was non-existent, and by what process of evolution it was eventually brought about that certain classes of actions came to be regarded as just and others as unjust. Nothing now remains to be done but by a survey of just actions (as generally admitted at any time and place) to extract the essential common peculiarity, and the result is the connotation of justice. The definition will never be reached by laboured arguments on the model of a geometrical theorem, as may be seen from an examination of Mr. Sidgwick's able analysis of the conception in his *Methods of Ethics*—a work of great negative value, but absolutely barren of positive results. With ethics, as a so-called practical science—as a science of that which ought to be, in contradistinction from that which is—we have nothing to do ; neither, similarly, with jurisprudence as vulgarly defined. It is in all probability the visionary and unpractical conclusions reached by jurists which have rendered that branch of inquiry so unpopular with lawyers—that is to say, with those who may be supposed to be more than other people practically acquainted with the problems contemplated. It is not jurisprudence as hitherto treated which is the necessary preliminary to the fruit-ful study of politics, but rather what may be termed nomology,

or the inductive science of law.   Before proceeding farther, it
may be as well to restate what has so far been stated only by
implication as to the nature and method of this science.

Nomology then is the scientific study of certain of the
relations subsisting between the organised group and the units
or individuals of which it is composed ; or, in other words, of
those sequences of which the consequent is a willed act of the
group following upon an antecedent act or situation of one or
some of its units.   This definition of the subject is no doubt
technical, and at first sight not very intelligible ; but it is
accurate, and strictly in harmony with the definitions of other
branches of science.   For the scientific study of things (which
term rightly includes relations) means an inquiry into their
origin, growth, development past and future, and decay ; and it
is well, before making use of colloquial or slipshod language, to
be sure that it truly represents a clear and precise idea.   At
the same time, a translation of the technical into homely
English is also desirable in order to avoid pedantry of diction
throughout, and to dispense with circumlocution.   Vulgar
parlance, in fine, often serves as a short formula, and combines
brevity with apparent simplicity—an appearance due, however,
rather to use than to logical exactness.   In plain language
then, nomology treats of those acts of the State which are
voluntary and which are caused by the contemplation of
situations or doings of individual members of it.   And indeed
we may without much danger cut out the term " situation,"
for by far the greater proportion of State acts are performed in
response to the *acts* of individuals ; while those due to the
contemplation of their unchanged situation are at all times few,
and in the case of developed societies almost entirely absent.
Thus in this country at the present day the State punishes no
man on account of his position, as, for instance, because he is
deformed, or dark complexioned, or unfit for military service,
or even leprous or otherwise loathsome.   Nor does the State
reward or compensate men otherwise than for a change in their
position, except in case of extreme poverty, and even the poor-
laws may be said to be rather a safety-valve against rebellion
than a tribute to pity.   Be that as it may, it is certain that
the enormous majority of State acts follow upon a change :

that change is brought about either by so-called natural causes (accident), or by the act of a member or members of the State. Thus, on the one hand, your house may be struck by lightning, or you may be kicked by a horse ; or, on the other hand, your watch may be taken by a thief, or your ribs broken by a garotter.   In the first of these cases the deplorable change in your situation will not induce the active sympathy of the State ; but in the latter cases, where the change is due to the act of another person, then the State is moved to action.   So that we may eliminate, as the causes of State action, not only unchanging situations, but also changes caused by accident or nature (in which terms are included all causes other than the acts of fellow-members of the State).   Again, those acts of members of a state which are virtuous and worthy of approbation do not in a highly-developed society entail any regular recognition by the State, such as a reward.   Where rewards for virtue or for public service are made, it is not according to law or regular rule, but according to the feeling of the moment.   So that we may also eliminate such acts of the citizen as do not so arouse the anger or antipathy of the State as to entail State action.   And this leaves us with no cause worth much consideration but the hateful acts of members of the community.

These group-acts being voluntary and following on the contemplation of the acts of members, it is clear that such contemplation must arouse feelings of pleasure and pain sufficient to serve as motives.   When produced by regarding the sufferings or pleasures of others, these feelings are called sympathy or antipathy according as they are like or unlike the feelings regarded.   Thus we may sympathise with one who is either in pain or in pleasure ; so similarly we may antipathise (so to speak) with one in either situation.   It is absolutely essential to conceive of the group or state as acting in accordance with the motives of sympathy and antipathy ; such acts taking the form of charity, compensation, or reward, in the one case, and of spoliation, compulsory restitution, or punishment, in the other.   It will be objected that this arrangement leaves no room for the whole important class of legal rights.   And this is in fact so.   But it will be remembered that we are at present considering the antecedents or causes of State acts, and

not the effects of such acts (which may of course be regarded
as included in such acts), and it will become apparent that a
legal right, as such, cannot rouse the State to action. How
should it ? A legal right has by implication been defined as a
liberty or power which owes its existence to the recognition
and guaranty of the State. So long as that right exists, the
power is or may be exercised; but when the power ceases to
be exercised or exercisable, that right is *ispo facto* dead.
There no longer is any such power, whether guaranteed by the
State or not. Therefore a legal right cannot serve as a cause
of State action.

But the change in the situation may arouse the sympathy
of the State; and if that change has been caused by the act of
a citizen, then such act may arouse the antipathy of the State.
Or both sentiments may be aroused simultaneously. Thus the
wrong may be an antecedent of State action; and the change in
the situation of the injured party may likewise so serve. And,
as has already been hinted, it is only, or almost only, when
the misfortune is regarded as connected with the reprehensible
conduct of another, that the State as a fact does take
action, and then probably as much for the sake of hurting the
wrong-doer as of benefiting the sufferer.

It is impossible in this brief sketch to enter upon the
keenly-debated question of the nature of the difference between
crime and injury, involving, as it does, the definition of crime.
It may therefore be pardonable to express dogmatically the
view that crimes are those acts ·of individual citizens which
arouse the antipathy of the State for the wrong-doer sufficiently to bring about a State act of the nature of punishment; while a civil injury is an act which, without necessarily
arousing any State antipathy for the agent, arouses State
sympathy with another citizen who is hurt by it. The
resulting group-act has for its end, not the punishment of the
doer, but the rehabilitation of the sufferer; though for reasons
connected with group competition, the restitution or compensation or reparation resulting from the State act does, as a rule,
also operate as a punishment on the doer of the injury. For
example, if one who carelessly breaks a shop-window is made
to pay for a new one, it is not because his act is regarded by

the State with positive antipathy, but because sympathy with the owner of the window is sufficient to entail State action on his behalf. At the same time, it is clearly a painful thing (virtually a punishment) for the injurer to be compelled to pay.

A fundamental division in the study of the law is that which is based on this difference between crime and injury. And one of the first dynamical laws which the study of nomology will bring to light, is that which relates to the gradual absorption of the law of crimes into the law of civil injuries.

Seeing that both classes of laws tend to restrain rather than to impel, it is clear that the law as a whole may be regarded as restraint on liberty. In order to understand liberty, we must first understand law. Liberty is the complement of law. When we know the angle, we know its complement.

And now let us reconsider the whole question from the opposite point of view. What is liberty? We are told that in a state of nature we are all free; there is too much liberty. Take the case of the wolf and the lamb. Here we have a " state of nature "—a state of absolute liberty. The wolf is at liberty to devour the lamb; and similarly, the lamb is at liberty to devour the wolf—if it can. The poor Indian, bound to a tree to be shot at by his neighbours, is living in a state of perfect liberty—equal liberty; for he was free to tie his neighbours to the tree and take shots at them. A state of full liberty then, is one in which the strong are free to rob the weak, and the weak are free to rob the strong. Clearly this is an unenviable state of things for the weak. The strong may call it liberty, but the weak call it anarchy. The two are identical. Then why all this outcry for liberty, and never a word for anarchy? We all know that in order to éscape from the evils of liberty, men banded themselves together in groups not consciously or suddenly, but by a slow process of evolution which can be explained; and virtually agreed to suppress by united action certain forms of force. In short, the actions of individuals were brought more or less under the control of the group—Society, the State. Once created and set in motion, this club or state tended from various causes to encroach more and more on the freedom of the individuals composing it, until the restraints, the exactions, and the meddlings of the governing body at last brought about a reaction in favour of a partial return to anarchy—liberty. Certain matters and things were removed from the domain of State control, and men were no worse, but all the better for the change. The State, for various reasons connected with the structure of the ruling body, brought itself into disrepute ; and each deliverance from its arbitrary interference was hailed as a clear gain to the liberties of the people. In some cases the change was for the better. In others it was again found necessary to revert to the system of State control. The reason why certain matters can safely be left to the free action of individuals, whereas others can not, may be shown in detail ; but no general statement has yet been framed by which we can see at a glance beforehand whether a particular matter should be controlled by the State, or may safely be left to the unfettered action of the units. Civil liberty then may be accurately defined as the greatest possible freedom of the individual from State interference, compatible with the well-being of the social organism.

But to set up this definition as a practical rule of action is vain. It is like telling one who asks for moral guidance to keep to the path of virtue. What he wants to know is, which is the path of virtue. Similarly, the practical statesman wants to know which are the matters wherein the State must here and now exercise some kind of control in order to secure the stability of society, and which are the matters to be safely left to individual caprice.

Is it not unphilosophical, without the strongest reason, to contend that what at one time led to the elevation of mankind, namely the substitution of organised social control for antagonistic and competitive individual free efforts, at another time leads to its deterioration ?—that what was once a factor in social integration, is now a factor in social disintegration ? And yet this is the position taken up by the worshippers of liberty pure and simple, like Mr. Spencer and Mr. Auberon Herbert. Government is the cement which binds the units together into a complex whole. Moreover, the study of history shows us unmistakably that the increasing tendency has been and is in the direction of rendering the Government stronger and'stronger in proportion to the individual forces opposed to it. Crime is followed by punishment more speedily and more certainly than it was of old. It is not the weakening but the strengthening of the State to which we must look for the amelioration of society—the subordination of the will of each to the welfare of all. And this is called socialism. Yet we do not find that even the most pronounced socialists aim at supplanting freedom of thought by the religion of the majority, or of any ruling body ; nor do they aim at reviving any of the ancient laws by which the dress and food of the various classes of persons were prescribed by Government. Just as the extremest individualist would shrink from destroying Government altogether, and repealing the whole of the criminal law, so would the extremest socialist shrink from subordinating the will of the units in all matters to State control. Hence we are again driven to the conclusion that "a line must be drawn somewhere." And the question still is, Where ? Mr. Auberon Herbert draws it at the elimination of brute force, or what he calls " direct compulsion." But on his own showing he is driven to some strange shifts in order to show how certain actions, which he and all men agree should be forbidden and punished by the State, are but forms of brute force. If one pours noxious vapours into the air, he is " constraining the faculties of those who are obliged to breathe the poisoned air against their own consent." If one falsely libels his neighbour, he has "taken his own actions from him, and substituted other actions for them ; " and so on. It is fair to say that Mr. Herbert has misgivings as to the soundness of these explanations. What is " direct compulsion " as distinct from indirect ? Two monkeys in an apple-tree are apt to fall out—especially if the apples are few. Two hungry hyænas in presence of a fat carcase are apt to fight. Sheep on a barren hill-side, on the other hand, eat away as hard as they can, and starve each other to death, indirectly, as it were. They do not seem to have arrived at a perception of the elementary truth, that the simplest way to get the better of a rival is to " remove " him. Perhaps the Carnivora find

themselves better armed for the fray; and besides, if successful, they are immediately rewarded with a ready-made
repast. Sheep do not care for mutton. But there is another
reason for their peaceful behaviour. If the weaker, or more
cowardly, or more peaceable of the two hyænas, glaring at the
dead turkey, could see a few lean birds lying about all round,
perhaps he would leave his bigger rival in undisputed
possession of the turkey. But he does not, and he is very
hungry. He must fight, or starve a little longer. Now, when
a strong sheep finds a weaker one browsing luxuriously on a
well-covered hillock, he quietly hustles him out of the way
and takes his place, while the weaker brother retires to some
neighbouring spot where the herbage is short and brown.
Why the stronger do not pommel the weaker out of existence
once for all, is a question of sheep sociology which is not the
subject of the present inquiry.

What should be pointed out is, that savage man in the
hunting stage did rise, and does rise, to the far-seeing standpoint of the tiger, and, consciously or unconsciously, discerns
the expedience, as an economy of force, of fighting and killing
his rivals at once, rather than putting himself to the trouble
of continually outstripping them in the chase day after day
and year after year. One of these modes is direct, the other
is indirect. In what way is the one more justifiable than the
other? At all events they do fight and eliminate one another
to an extent unsurpassed even by the Carnivora, so that, as a
fact, few if any of them die of starvation after the manner of
their more peaceable descendants. But presently again, without any very clear consciousness of what they are aiming at, they
begin to discover that although it is in the main a good thing
to decimate their fellow-men, it is just as well to tolerate the
competition of a few of them, with a view to co-operation against
more distant rivals. There can be little doubt that the germ
of co-operation is to be found in the instincts of gregarious
animals. Here the instinct of competition comes into conflict
with the instinct of co-operation, and thus at this early stage
a line has to be drawn in practice, if not in theory, between
the one province and the other. During the course of social
development, when co-operation becomes conscious, organised,

and compulsory, we have the State.   Some classes of actions
pass in and out of the domain of State control many times in
the course of history, and it is only after centuries of experiment that the consensus of society finally settles down (perhaps
for no clearly assignable reason) in favour of leaving them
permanently in one province or the other.   Thus, what may
be called the group-opinion in this country seems now to be
settling down in favour of allowing the expression of religious
and scientific beliefs to be left free from State interference.   In
the matter of the marriage relation, the group-opinion seems
for the present pretty well settled in the opposite way.   Now
this group-opinion is tolerably clear and steady long before the
advent of majorities to direct control of legislation, and it must
therefore have a basis, a *raison d'être*, though not necessarily a
consciously recognised one.   And that basis is surely the wellbeing of the group as a whole.   So that, although we may not
be able to tell beforehand whether any particular class of
actions should or should not be brought within the domain of
State control at any particular stage of social development, we
can say that, whatever the group-will may be on the subject,
it is actuated, consciously or unconsciously, by a striving after
the welfare of that particular society as a whole.   The group may
be mistaken, just as an individual may err in honestly doing
what he believes to be best for himself in the long run ; but it
is surely better and safer to trust to the group-instinct, and
to have faith in the forward tendency of society, though its gait
be a little zigzag, than to put it into a strait-jacket whenever
its action does not seem to fit in with some preconceived theory
of group-morals.

     But though liberty thus turns out to be a word without
any positive meaning, it is clear that certain forms of liberty
are good and other forms are bad.   And the distinction between
them at any stage of development is between the individual
liberty which is compatible with the group-welfare, and that
which is not.   Names are of little consequence ; but the latter
may be called license, and the former civil liberty.   It may
fairly be doubted whether there has ever been a restraint put
upon individuals by even the most despotic of governments,
which may not at one time or another have been a necessary

and beneficent concomitant of social evolution. The power of life and death exercised by the old Roman paterfamilias over his children and slaves was probably at one time an unmixed good. And the like power of the King of the Ashantees is or was probably conducive to the group-welfare.

Is there then no discoverable rule for our practical guidance ? Is there no observable tendency, no law of social development, upon which we can build up a practical working maxim of legislation ? I believe there is ; but it is not embodied in the formula " No Government."

The first requisite for social integration was a strong central power which should effectually suppress all forms of individual activity calculated to injure the group as a whole. Tribes which developed this form of organisation waxed strong, while tribes which consisted of undisciplined and *disorderly* numbers were crushed out in the struggle for existence. Thus the tendency to centralise was brought about necessarily, and to a certain extent unconsciously, just as the gregarious habits of sheep and deer have been developed without that clear prevision for group-defence which the habits seem to imply.

And just as in getting copper out of the earth we get with it many other things which are worse than useless, so in obtaining control of certain of the actions of its component members, the group got control of many other classes of actions which could not at the time be easily distinguished or dis-entangled. Having got our copper-ore and its surrounding rubbish to the surface, succeeding operations consist of disengaging the useless from the useful. Some of the substances, like sulphur, are very persistent, but in time the metal shines forth pure and bright. So it is with political institutions. The whole history of civilisation is one long series of operations for the disentangling of the metal from the dross. That which is good and necessary in the law—State prevention or elimination of certain classes of actions, such as murder and assault, stealing and breach of contract, nuisance and indecence, etc. etc.— becomes more and more marked, stronger and more popular. Good citizens do not chafe under it—it even ceases to be re-garded as a restraint upon liberty ; while that which is bad and unnecessary is from time to time expelled from the body of the law, or, as the saying is, the people wrest from their rulers one liberty after another. To take a recent instance : it is only a generation ago that the English people wrested from the Government the liberty to buy what they wanted in the cheapest markets. To-day they are struggling to throw off the last remaining fetters in the matter of full religious liberty.

This then is the observed fact, that as civilisation advances the State tends to throw off one claim after another to interfere with the free action of its members, while at the same time it becomes stronger, more regular, speedier, and more certain in performing the functions that remain to it. Where it interferes it interferes thoroughly.

At the present time the tendency is one of throwing off certain forms of State control. Therefore when we see an agitation got up for the purpose of adding to the duties of the State, we may reasonably conclude *primâ facie* that it is an agitation in the wrong direction. This is one practical rule. And when we see the State interfering in matters having little in common with what is becoming more and more clearly marked out as its normal province, and much in common with what has long ago been relegated to the domain of private enterprise, we are again logically justified in presuming that such matters ought to be removed from the domain of State control. Upon those who maintain a contrary opinion must rest the *onus probandi*, the burden of showing why these matters should be under control, while those are left to individual freedom. This then is the ground upon which individualists can take their stand. If they aim at more they are in danger of drifting into circular arguments about rights and liberty, and the like metaphysical and casuistical shallows, where their adversaries will have them at advantage.

But if this is the position to be taken up by those individual thinkers whose study of sociology has led them to perceive that the tendency is in the direction of the widest liberty compatible with social stability, while others have reached the opposite conclusion, namely, that the State is a great machine for doing things better than individual enterprise

—what is to be the attitude of the bulk of non-thinkers towards these two parties? It is hardly to be expected that each labourer, before recording his vote for a parliamentary candidate, will make himself acquainted with the principles of sociology, nor is it likely that he will arrive by intuition at a more correct view of political questions than those who, even after some study, have embraced the doctrine of socialism. Even if he entrust his political conscience and his vote to a better-educated man than himself, is there any reason to hope that he will choose an individualist as his mentor rather than a State socialist? Not the least. What then is the *form* of government which both parties should concur in regarding as best calculated to lead in the end to that political system which they respectively regard as the best system? Probably every one believes in the one-man form of government, provided he himself is the one man. If individualists could get hold of the tiller, assuming always that they are on the right tack and in advance of the age, no doubt they would realise the ideal of good government more quickly than by trusting to the resultant of conflicting forces in a democratic society. But putting that on one side as out of the question, can they refuse to lend their support to a system of civil equality, a system towards which we are gradually approximating? In the conflict of opposing efforts that which is fittest will survive. To deny this is to despair of the race. If we have not faith in the ultimate emergence of our struggling fellow-countrymen from darkness into light, then we are trying to bring about by artificial means what will not come by nature. Those who lack faith in the destiny of the race must do what they can to keep afloat, so long as may be, by a process of patching and tinkering, and of a judicious drawing upon the group-capital for the requirements of the present generation. But those who have that faith must learn to look without dread on the temporary aberrations of the people. They must bear in mind that throughout history it has marched steadily forward, not indeed without turnings and backslidings, but still, in the long run, forward on the path of civilisation ; and that there is ingrained in the very nature of civilised man an inherited love of fairness, and an instinctive belief in the wisdom of proportioning satisfaction to intelligent effort, which will not easily be eradicated. It is this belief which underlies respect for property, and not any sublimated *à priori* " warrant " whatsoever. Thus every man who has faith in the race must ascertain by observation the tendencies in the structural development of the State, and instead of struggling against those tendencies—instead of stemming the advancing tide with his mop—he must welcome such reforms as history points to, in the confident expectation that any temporary concomitant ills will be more than counterbalanced by future gains. If his own ideal conclusions on matters political, scientific, or æsthetic are correct, they will be realised by trusting to the unimpeded advance of the democracy. If they are wrong, he will rejoice to think that his efforts will be cancelled by those of better men. Be he individualist or socialist he will loyally accept the verdict of the people.

Personal liberty is the final outcome of social evolution, and not the cause. The wider the area, the greater the number and diversity of conflicting interests, the nigher will be the advent of individualism. As each class and each individual fights for his own hand, he will find that the lowest price at which he can obtain his own greatest freedom is the granting of equal liberty to others in certain departments of activity which experience, and experience alone, can demarcate.

Whether we regard the question from a positive or a negative point of view—as the science of law or the science of liberty—we shall find that, in order to be of any value, our work must take the form of an inductive science ; and it must deal with the facts of social organisation, and not with high-sounding sentiments, however sublimely conceived—with the " Natur-recht " of the school of Savigny, not with the " droit naturel " of the school of Rousseau. Until this is conceded, we can have no stable foundation on which to base a sound and progressive individualism.

Since liberty is the complement of law, it is impossible to understand liberty without understanding law. If the actions of individuals were so controlled and subordinated to the group as to leave no liberty whatever, we should have a state of absolute socialism. This is actually the case with the individual cells or groups of cells which together constitute the human body. The cells have, so to speak, "lost their identity." The welfare of the human being, or other highly-developed animal, is alone the end consciously aimed at and unconsciously approached, without reference to the separate interests of the cells of which he is made up. This is absolute socialism, and we must therefore beware of reasoning too much concerning social matters by analogy. If, on the other hand, the welfare of the group as a whole is absolutely ignored, and there is no combined or organised action to interfere with the separate interests of the individuals composing it, then we have absolute anarchy. This is precisely the case with many races of wild animals, especially the Carnivora. The welfare of the race as a group or whole is ignored, and the units alone are considered. Thus we may take a tiger as representing in his person absolute socialism and absolute anarchy—socialism in his internal relations, anarchy in his external relations. If we take tiger-kind as the whole, and tigers as the units of which it is made up, we see that there is an anarchic relation between the whole and the parts. If we take a tiger as the whole and the cells (which in the remote past were individuals having separate feelings and interests) as the units of which it is made up, we see that there is a socialistic relation between the whole and the parts.

The whole history of civilisation is the history of a struggle to establish a relation between society and its units, between the whole and its parts, which is neither absolute socialism nor absolute anarchy; but a state in which, by action and reaction of each upon each, such an adaptation shall take place, that the welfare of the whole and that of the units shall eventually become coincident and not antagonistic. Such is the problem of civilisation, of the development of the hyper-organism; integration without impairing the individuality of the component units. The final result to which we shall ever approximate, but never attain, will be perfect civil liberty, or the greatest liberty which is compatible with the utmost wellbeing of society as a whole; and perfect law, or such subordination of the individual will to that of society as may be compatible with the utmost wellbeing of the individual.

The outcome of these reflections seems to be, that just as from parental sympathy springs State interference, which when developed casts off every shred of sympathy and antipathy, even to the extent of awarding to Shylock his pound of flesh, so from special interference, through a long process of generalisation and friction, springs law, which in its final development is as incommensurable in terms of justice as is an oak-tree in terms of gravitation and molecular repulsion. Growing out of justice, as the living, thinking animal grows (or grew) out of inorganic matter, it cannot be resolved by man into its component elements. And the process is going on around us to-day.

While then we may say that the law is a fairly coherent body of rules prohibiting the exercise of certain kinds of force (superior faculties) in certain classes of cases, it is not possible to say offhand, or to discover on paper, what those kinds of force are, or what are the classes of cases in which their exercise is prohibited. This can only be done by a careful and exhaustive examination of the laws themselves, by subjecting them to a searching analysis, by a scientific instead of a popular and superficial classification of their matter, and in short by a process of rigid reduction.

Thus are we brought to a position the very opposite of that taken up by those who would test every law by the standard of justice. We have reached the standpoint of Bentham, who cared nothing for vapourings about justice, but who would test every law by its effects on the welfare of society. (It is true he substituted the welfare of the greatest number for the welfare of the group; but this is immaterial here.) We are in the same boat with those who, rejecting the appeal to abstract virtue as a test of the goodness or fitness of their actions, substitute the ultimate welfare of the individual. A practical test is as far from view as when we started. Hence the persistence with which the need should be insisted on for the thorough study of law in the concrete, and *the discovery*, not the manufacture, of the true statical laws which are actually operative in societies ; of their tendency, and of the dynamical laws of their change and development. It is by the discovery of these laws that we shall find ourselves in possession of true and useful practical guides through the labyrinth of legislation and politics. We shall arrive at rules which are neither so simple as that enjoining an equal deal at cards, nor so vague and inapplicable as that which requires us to follow the effects of an action, down through its million ramifications, to the utmost ends of time.

The art of politics is the application of the science of nomology to the concrete; just as engineering is the application to human wants of the science of mechanics, and as navigation is one of the arts based on the science of astronomy. Until we have mastered the science we shall make but little progress with the corresponding art. Till Adam Smith laid the foundations of modern economics the fiscal policy of the Government was a game of perpetual see-saw between rival crotcheteers. All was rule of thumb. So is it to-day with the great question of liberty and law. Yesterday we were all free-traders and advocates of "let be"; to-day we are on the highroad to socialism; to-morrow the Fates only know where we shall be. The only cure for this policy of drift is a patient and intelligent study of nomology, whereby middle principles of practical application will be brought to light, and the absurd fallacies of social doctrinaires put to flight for ever.

x

IT is easier to diagnose a disease than to prescribe a remedy. Most persons admit that the land law of this country is not what it should be. But it does not in the least follow that the cure proposed by each of the army of quacks ready to prescribe for the malady is the best, or even a wholesome treatment. At the same time it is a mistake to speak of land-law reformers as if the term denoted a number of persons with a common aim. They detest the present system, and there their agreement ends. It is impossible to deal with them as a single body with definite plans, because as a rule they disagree among themselves on almost every point of the program. Furthermore, they seldom set forth their views as a whole ; and to pick out one proposal from one reformer and another from another would be manifestly unfair to both. Consequently in our endeavour to ascertain the opinions of this somewhat motley crew it is necessary to deal with them separately. I propose in this chapter to discuss the suggestions of a gentleman who has put himself prominently before the public in connection with what is called the Free Land League, and whose views on land-law reform are pretty clearly sketched in a lecture on the land question delivered some few years ago at the Oxford Reform Club, and since published with the sanction and approval of a cabinet minister who has since passed out of public notice. At the time of the delivery of the lecture, Mr. C. A. Fyffe described himself as the Liberal candidate for the city of Oxford, and although the election has since taken place, he is still in a position (so far as I know) to sustain that rôle. Commenting upon the plans set forth in the lecture, Sir Charles Dilke was not ashamed to write : "What may we expect with regard to the treatment of the land question in the next Parliament ? On this subject I will commend to notice a pamphlet which has been written by Mr. Fyffe, who is Liberal candidate for the city of Oxford, and who I hope will represent the city of Oxford. Mr. Fyffe in his pamphlet has discussed in a thoroughly practical way the difficulties of the agricultural interest in this country at the present time, and has shown methods for their solution which are deserving of much attention." I think Mr. Fyffe's views, though not altogether clear and definite, are shared by a considerable number of neo-radicals at the present time, and I am therefore of opinion that a careful examination of his proposed alteration of the law is not by any means a mere waste of time.[1]

Before prescribing a remedy, our social physician must needs diagnose the disease, and this he does through the mouth of an imaginary "intelligent foreigner." Unfortunately for the correctness of his diagnosis, the intelligence of the created cannot exceed that of his creator, and the foreigner is consequently a very unintelligent foreigner indeed. He expresses surprise at seeing the condition of a great manufacturing country unlike that of his own. He cannot understand large farming and its effects ; still less the necessary results of the introduction of machinery. Let him speak for himself : " I see substantial farmhouses with good useful buildings, and often with immense cornricks about them ; but . . . I do not see the little houses scattered about, that one might expect, or the frequent large villages that would be met with in any equally rich district on the mainland. . . . And when I go from your lonely country districts into your towns, I observe enormous over-crowding and over-competition." Mr. Fyffe and his foreigner are unable to see the economy of concentration in the case of manufacture as opposed to the impossibility of concentration in the case of agriculture. His

---

[1] What follows was originally written for and adopted by the Parliamentary Committee of the Liberty and Property Defence League, and was published by them under the title of *Land*, 1885.

foreigner is equally surprised to find that a population which exports millions of pounds' worth of manufactured goods should be obliged to import provisions. " I find," says he, " that you pay to the French and other nations annually the following sums: For butter, £12,000,000; for cheese, £5,000,000; for potatoes and vegetables, £4,000,000; for poultry and eggs £3,000,000. And I am not surprised that under such circumstances the English people, conservative as they are, are now asking themselves whether there is not something in their land system which needs a good deal of amendment."

The intelligent foreigner having pointed out the evils in a land system which, acre for acre, produces more food from the soil than is produced by any other system from the soil of any other country in the world, calls in the physician, Mr. C. A. Fyffe, whose " own ideas, such as they are, have been gathered in the course of some years' superintendence of corporate estates amounting to about seven thousand acres," and who has so far bungled his own affairs that he has now " the misfortune to be personally interested in a small landed property, of which," says he, " I have at present one hundred and fifty acres on my hands ; so that I address you to-night in the character of a distressed agriculturist."

What a spectacle for the gods ! The distressed agriculturist, after hopelessly collapsing under the load of one hundred and fifty acres, boldly comes forward and volunteers to undertake the management of the whole land of the country. But then, what city clerk does not know exactly how to smash the Mahdi, or to drive the Russians back beyond Sarakhs ? The only difference in the cases is that somehow the city clerk does not succeed in propounding his views from the shoulders of a cabinet minister, that is all.

However, Mr. Fyffe begins well. It was doubtless a revelation to the reformers to learn that " there *is* no law of primogeniture, except when a man dies without a will." The previous belief may be inferred, namely, that every landowner is by law compelled to leave the whole of his realty to his eldest son. Another disillusion awaited them when the news was to be announced that perpetual entail was also a bogey of the reformer's imagination, having been practically knocked on

the head as far back as the days of the Red and White Roses.
Surely the reformers' occupation was gone !

At the same time, while admitting that the custom of
primogeniture is an arguable question, it is possible to differ
from Mr. Fyffe on the wisdom of altering the law in case of
intestacy. In all such cases law should follow custom, otherwise great injustice may be done. For example, out of a
hundred landowners one forgets or neglects to make his will,
or by some accident or fraud the will cannot be found.
Meantime he has made careful provision for all his younger
sons and daughters, setting some up in business at great
expense and settling large sums on others at marriage—all
with the intention of leaving the land to his eldest son.
Such is the belief of all, such the expectation of all. Is it
just to disappoint these expectations and to leave the eldest
son not the richest but the poorest of the family ? No ; the
excellence of all laws relating to intestacy depends on their
strict observance of the prevalent customs. In the words of
Mr. Justice Stephen : " Laws ought to be adjusted to the habits
of society, and not to aim at remoulding them. . . . If the
law deviates from these guiding principles it becomes a
nuisance." Alter the custom if you can, Mr. Fyffe, but in
the name of justice and common sense leave the law alone.
As to family settlements, if there is nothing more to be urged
against them than the lame economic arguments brought by
the lecturer, they may safely be left to take care of themselves.
Perhaps, however, this is the place to remind the great school
of reform by State interference, that whatever of evil (and of
good) there may be in the present curious system of limited
entails, by means of disentailing assurances and resettlements,
it is mostly due to the action of the State in standing virtually
as trustee for or protector of a non-existent person. And before
proposing any new law for doing away with the effect of this
abnormality (be it good.or bad) it might be more consistent to
remove the cause. The idea of a non-existent owner is not
altogether natural, and whether it might not be dispensed
with is an open and an arguable question.

But Mr. Fyffe's cure is far more drastic, if less intelligible.
He trusts that " the simple course will be taken of abolishing

family settlements altogether." Until the meaning of this is made clearer it is useless to offer any observation on it. Will Mr. Fyffe tell us how he proposes to make the proprietorship of land everywhere ownership in fee simple ? Is he also prepared to abolish trusts altogether ?

When we are told that all mortgages and charges on land "ought to be made public, and to be registered in some Court open to public inspection," we readily assent ; but are at once met with the warning that to cede an inch is to lose an ell. "It is an open question whether in the public interest all mortgages and charges whatsoever on land should not be made null and void." If so, the sooner the question is closed again the better. Firstly, it is an impossibility. Whoever holds a valuable property can borrow on it, whatever the law may be as to the precise nature of the transaction. Secondly, if there is one form of credit which is open to fewer objections than any other, it is that highly expedient and useful arrangement for tiding over an emergency, by borrowing at a low rate of interest on what is practically absolute security. How many manufacturers have been saved from collapse in periods of depression and commercial crisis by the accident of holding estates which were never bought with such a view ? As for simplification of transfer, Mr. Fyffe has nothing to say to it, except that the abstract of title would be cheaper and less bulky if it were not for these charges and mortgages.

So far there is nothing either very startling or very original in all these suggestions. Indeed the whole subject of land ownership is a difficult one, not to be dealt with by rule of thumb or by uninstructed persons. Instead of raking up and refurbishing the rusty old weapons of Owenite law-tinkers, Mr. Fyffe might do better service if he would rummage in the dustiest corners of Oxford libraries and contrive to unearth some of the lectures delivered there seven hundred and fifty years ago, in which abundant evidence will be found that the foundations of law lie beneath the surface, and that in the learned discussions of the glossators and scholastic jurists are more likely to be found the true solutions of these problems than in the amateur superficialities of nineteenth century demagogues.

To do our author justice, he is not satisfied to follow in

the footsteps of the land reformers of the last generation.
That is not enough for him. He opens up a prospect of
changes based, not upon freedom or its semblance, but on
State interference. In plain words, Mr. Fyffe is a State
socialist. " After all," he says, " we are great communists in
this country ; " from which fact (melancholy or the reverse)
the inference is drawn, why not let us be more communistic ?
Possibly this argument has weight with some who would
shrink from drawing a parallel inference from the allegation
that after all we are to a certain extent dishonest people in
this country. Anyhow, whether in other matters communism
is good or bad, there can be no doubt that it must be good in
the matter of land, which we cannot surely bring ourselves to
believe to be a " purely commercial object." Phraseology of
this sort is invincible. How can any one prove or even argue
that land is a " purely commercial object " ? What does it
mean ? The explanation throws no light on the subject.
" Land," we are told, " has two characteristics, which taken
together distinguish it from any other commodity. The use of
a portion of it is absolutely indispensable, and it is not capable
of being increased." One would have thought that the use of
a portion of air, water, food, clothing, and a variety of other
things (not of course including common sense) was absolutely
indispensable, and certainly as to some of these it is true that
they are not " capable of being increased." Water and air for
example. At the same time what does it signify to the wretch
to whom these said things are indispensable whether or not
they are capable of being increased, if he himself is not
capable of getting them. A man in want of a loaf derives
no consolation from being told that bread is one of those
things which are capable of being increased, or even that it
falls into Mill's third class of commodities. But is not land
capable of being increased to all practical intents and purposes ?
Land, which is rendered doubly productive, is *practically* doubled ,
in quantity. But leaving that on one side, is it not a fact that
within the last two centuries the English people have increased
their land by millions of square miles, in spite of the quaking
insular policy of those who, with punctilious respect for the
proprietary rights of Red Indians over their hunting-grounds,

evince the most callous unscrupulousness in curtailing and
even destroying the proprietary rights of their own fellow-
countrymen ?   It is true that if a man with one acre of land
wants another, he cannot have it in the same place ; he must
move : but what does it matter what form his labour takes,
whether it consists in bringing goods to himself or carrying
himself to the goods ?   That is to say, by the application of
labour land *can* be increased—and by land is meant useful
land, valuable land.   At all events at the present time there
are more acres in the world waiting to be claimed, cleared, and
utilised, than there are people anxious to claim them.   When
the planet is thickly populated with civilised people we will
undertake to reopen this discussion with Mr. Fyffe.   Just now
we must let his theory pass and turn to his practical proposals
based thereon, for he himself trusts less to his metaphysical
arguments than to the brute force of the many.   Says he :
"We know perfectly well that the accumulation of landed
property in single hands might easily reach such a degree that
the nation would not put up with it ; and I *therefore*" (not be
it observed for any speculative reasons) " make no apology for
assuming that the public interest ought even now to be the
first principle in regulating our land laws, and that private
property in land must be subject to such limitation as the
public interest dictates."   Would not this argument hold with
respect to the accumulation of corn in single hands, which
actually did take place with much effect at one time ?   And
are we not therefore to " assume that private property in corn
must be subject to, etc. ? "   Forestalling and regrating were
terms familiar to the ears of our forefathers, but we vainly
hoped we had got past those days of paternal government.

Wait a moment.   *Do* we know perfectly well that landed
property in single hands might easily reach such a degree ?   It
has not reached that point yet, and the tendency is even now
in the opposite direction.   Again, is it not a contingency
equally probable in the case of other kinds of property ?
Suppose some half-witted or misanthropic person contrived to
collect at any cost all the extant works of some great painter
with the malicious object of burning them.   Would the nation
" put up with it " ?   And if not, what course would it adopt ?

And furthermore, does this possible danger justify us in assuming (without any apology too) that "the public interest ought even now to be the first principle in regulating our laws relating to personalty of a kind strictly limited in quantity"?   After all, it would be a harmless proposition. What is meant by it ?   No one denies that property in land must be held subject to such limitation as the public interest dictates.   What one objects to is Mr. Fyffe's limitation. Even Oxford reformers must have heard of compulsory purchase of land for purposes of public utility, of railway concessions and the like.   If it can be shown to the general satisfaction that any square yard of this country could be bought by the State with advantage, there is nothing in the laws or the constitution to prevent such compulsory purchase from being effected.   The only dispute between the reformers and ordinary mortals is as to the expediency of purchasing the land against the will of the holder without any conceivable cause shown.

The whole question lies in a nutshell.   Is a system of land tenure, such as we now have, under which the holder enjoys undefined rights over the land subject to the public right of purchase at full market value—is this a good system or not ?   The reformers say no, and each reformer has a project of his own which is better.   Mr. George would tax landlords about 90 per cent, of their rent, and let them alone.   Professor Wallace would buy them out by degrees over a period of about twenty years, by which they would be robbed of the difference between the value of the freehold and that of a twenty years' lease.   Mr. Hyndman would expropriate them at once without compensation or so much as "by your leave."   But we are now concerned with Mr. Fyffe's project. His plan is not wanting in that simplicity which characterises the systems of Fourier, of Henry George, and of Prince Krapotkine.

The central idea is to empower any corporate body or single individual lacking land to take it on payment of a reasonable sum to the owner.   "I would therefore suggest," says our author, "that an individual or a company requiring land for any useful purpose, and not necessarily affecting the public at large, shall have the right of going before the local Land Court and obtaining an order for the compulsory sale of the land." It is true that the object alleged must be one that is beneficial to the neighbourhood, and that no substantial objection can be adduced by the landed proprietor, whatever a *substantial* objection may be—most certainly the objection that the land belongs to him and that he wishes to keep it will not be accepted as substantial. Why not ? Because " he who needs ground for his own occupation seems *primâ facie* to be a more suitable owner than one who lets it to another. It is not, however, necessary to dwell upon the grounds which would naturally influence the Land Courts in the exercise of their discretion." Certainly not. And now a word upon this argument of *primâ facie* suitability. Does it apply to the horses of a livery stable-keeper ? Is the person who wishes to ride one of such horses clearly a more suitable owner than he who merely lets it out for hire, and ought he therefore to have the power to purchase it at a fair figure ? Again, as to suitability, there can be no doubt that a hungry man would be a more suitable owner of a cake than the confectioner who puts it in the window for sale ; and really one fails to see why this test should not at once decide the ownership apart from any vulgar question of price, reasonable or otherwise.

The lecturer has not got quite so far as that yet, and he leans to the view that some compensation should be made to the owner. First let us see on what basis this compensation is to be calculated, and then let us follow the economic reasoning by which it is supported. Now the principle of valuation by which the Land Court is to be guided is the beautiful and elastic principle of equity. " By an equitable value, I do not mean either an agricultural value on the one side or a fancy value on the other, but such a price as an owner desiring to sell would accept from an ordinary purchaser." Now who is the thought-reader that is to find out what price one who does not want to sell would accept if he did want to sell ? One has heard too of men so desirous of realising that they have parted with really marketable things in a hurry for "an old song." Then *how* desirous of selling is the owner to be pictured by the Land Court thought-reader ? Is he to be

anxious to sell, or willing to sell, or prepared to consider a
good offer ? But before solving these problems we must learn
what it is which the landowner has to sell, or ought to be
taken as having to sell. How are we to find out, not what the
rent actually is, but what, morally speaking, it ought to be ?

"I think we ought to proceed in this way," says our teacher :
"first the labourer should be kept in decent comfort " (please
define) ; " then the landlord should have a trifling payment for,
as it were, putting the tenant in a position to use his capital."
And how much might this be we are anxious to learn ; and
here is the answer, " Say, the value of what the land would
grow uncultivated." The thought-reader is non-plussed ; we
must have recourse to the Wandering Jew this time. What
sort of land was this before a spade was stuck into it ? Was
it forest, or moor, or marsh, or barren rock, or was it perchance
under the waves of the sea ? And in any case what would
the market value of its produce have been at that time ?
Were there any inhabitants in the neighbouring country, and
did they build with timber, or burn peat, or did they graze
sheep or cattle ? " Nonsense," shriek the reformers, " nobody
asked the value of what the land *did* grow before it was
cultivated, but the value of what it would *now* grow uncultivated." Now this in no way alters the question ; for at
what point in its history is the piece of land to be supposed
to have begun to be cultivated ? And what is cultivation ?
The richest acre of golden wheat at harvest-time has not been
cultivated for weeks and months. The poorest acre on the
wooded hillside is being cultivated when the leaves fall in
autumn, or else pasture land is not cultivated at all. But wordy
speculations of this kind make such a dust that it is a relief to
get back to something definite. Mr. Fyffe is prepared to be
generous, or at least to admit that generosity might be shown.
After proceeding as aforesaid, he allows a *reasonable* percentage
to the landlord and the farmer on the actual capital they have
put on to the land, and a fair return to the farmer for his work and
superintendence ; and then, " *if* there is something over afterwards, the landlord *might* have *part* of it as purely unearned
income, over and above what he may fairly claim." What
that is we have seen. At this point one feels strongly tempted

to commend to Mr. Fyffe's careful perusal a little work written about seventy years ago by one David Ricardo, and entitled, *On the Principles of Political Economy and Taxation.* He will find therein some elementary truths simply stated which will cause him much surprise; amongst other matters he will find an explanation of rents, and how they are arrived at. He will find that the wages of the labourer are settled by circumstances over which neither landlord nor farmer has any control; he will find that after paying these wages, the normal profits of the farmer, together with the return of his outlay, are next deducted from the gross produce of the land, and finally if there is anything left over (on an average of years), it passes to the landlord as rent.

Now, this is precisely the state of things for which the heart of the candidate is yearning. He is after all in the same boat with his constituents, who are still buckling on their armour for an onslaught upon perpetual entails and compulsory primogeniture. What he is struggling to bring about is the existing custom of the country. But it is no satisfaction, they say, to live even in Paradise without knowing it.

In order to bring the new order of things about, the first requisite is of course a District Land Court. Without this it is clear there could be no means devised of giving one party to a contract the best of the bargain, and that, it need hardly be said, is the ultimate object of the reform. Having got the indispensable machine, how is it going to be worked, and what is it going to turn out? Under the heading of "necessary changes in the law between landlord and tenant" (we had no idea there was any law so situated), we find exposed to view our three old friends from Ireland, known as the three F's. There they are in all their hideous nakedness, just as might have been predicted. Manufactured for Irish consumption only, it was not to be expected that they would long be excluded from the English market.

1. Fixity of Tenure : "No tenant to be removed from his holding without the permission of a District Land Court." It is unnecessary to examine the grounds on which the court may refuse such permission, for it is enough that such requirement at once creates a dual ownership.

2. Fair Rents : " The Land Court must have the power of
fixing rents in cases of dispute and of reducing them even in
the case of existing leases." This again is plain speaking, and
requires no further elucidation or comment. But when this
interference with contract engagements is justified by the act
of " the English Court of Chancery, in interfering with and
setting aside those clauses in mortgages which gave the
mortgagee absolute rights over the mortgaged estate in case of
default of payment," we may be permitted to doubt whether
Mr. Fyffe has any clear idea of the principle on which equity
of redemption is based. Perhaps the Oxford reformers will
tell us whether the mortgagor or the mortgagee is the proprietor in the exact sense of the term. However, these
supposed analogies had better be avoided by those whose
acquaintance with legal philosophy is of so dubious a character.

3. Free Sale: " The farmer should have the right of
selling his tenancy to any one whom he chooses, subject to the
landlord's right to urge any objection to the new tenant before
the District Land Court." In support of this contention our
guide again displays an extraordinary ignorance of history.
" Of course," says he, " if the tenant is to be regarded as a sort
of feudal retainer of the landlord, it sounds shocking that he
should have the right of nominating a successor." Now this
is just the case in which the nomination of a successor, so far
from sounding " shocking," was, as a matter of fact and history,
a thing of everyday occurrence. And what is to be the
landlord's safeguard against having any sort of vagabond thrust
upon him for a tenant ? Simply this ; the incoming tenant is
to be " put upon his oath as to his means, his character, and
his qualifications." Now, supposing our author put upon his
oath as to his qualifications as a land reformer, should we be
justified in stigmatising his probable answers as perjury ? The
spectacle of the incoming tenant on his oath as to his means
would not perhaps be very striking ; but when it came to his
character, unless the whole thing is to be a mere formal farce,
there would be some interesting situations. " Are you a sober
man?"—"Mostly,your Honour; six days out of the seven,anyhow."
—" Are you strictly honest ? "—" Well I never take anything
that doesn't belong to me unless I want it very badly."—" Do

you always adhere to the truth ? "—" For choice, your Honour, when there is no harm in it."—" That will do ; you can pass ; —the next incoming tenant."

So much for the three F's, to which a fourth is added, evidently necessary to the well-working of the other three ; and this is the opinion of the lecturer, or of some equally exalted and disinterested person, on all questions of " fairness," " reasonableness " and so forth. May we venture to call this fourth F " Fyffe's opinion " ? For instance, in case of compulsory sale the landlord might not get as much as he could wish, nor yet the market value of his freehold, nor even as much as the purchaser would be willing to give for it if pressed ; but he would get as much as it is " fairly worth." Here the fourth F comes in. Who is to judge what it is fairly worth ? Apparently there is no other test than " Fyffe's opinion." Again, when the municipality of a growing town takes up the land around it, neither an agricultural value nor a fancy value is to be paid, but an *equitable* value. Now, what is the measure of this equitable value ? Apply the fourth F. There is no other course open. Yet again, before paying his rent, the farmer is to deduct a " fair return for his work and superintendence." What is a " fair return " ? Apply the fourth F. It solves at once even greater problems. What is the proper rental of the whole country ? " When landlords complain of the present bad times, I ask myself whether the good times, which they unconsciously make their standard of comparison, were not the result of injustice, and whether the rents they then received would not have been impossible if there had been anything like a *fair* distribution of the profits of agriculture." Exactly ; but then landlords do not yet understand the principle of the fourth F. They think that an article is worth what it will fetch in the open market. When they shall have mastered the four F's they will doubtless cease to bewail the agricultural depression, so far as it con- cerns themselves. They will adopt the stoical attitude of the owner of one hundred and fifty acres, who thus gives his mis- fortunes the go-by : " Therefore, in so far as the land difficulty merely means the unpleasantness of landlords not getting so large a rent as formerly" (let us pardon the style, in considera-

tion of the sentiment!) " which is what it means to a good many
representatives of the landed interest in the House of Commons,
I put it by, as a matter which may indeed excite individual
commiseration, but does not call for public attention."

Before following our public-spirited teacher from country
to town, attention should be drawn to one passage in his
lecture to the reformers which is really significant enough.
" During the last few years statistics show that nearly a million
acres have been transferred from the plough to grass. But now
comes a very striking fact, and one on which a great deal
hinges. Though a million acres have been turned into grass,
there is no increase in the number of cattle. The meaning of
this is, that the farmer's capital is gone, and that he has not
the means of getting a sufficiency of stock, even when the
land is laid down in grass. This is only one out of a multitude
of facts all pointing in one direction." True, but in which
direction? After years of "beneficent legislation," from the
Agricultural Holdings Act at the top down to the Bill for
defining a rabbit-hole at the bottom, what do we find? Why,
that the sense of insecurity brought about by all these
interferences with freedom of contract, and all these violations
of the sanctity of property, has resulted in shortness of credit
and dwindling capital. There is nothing new in all this, but
our modern reformers are just where the great thinkers left
them at the beginning of the century, and must be met with
the same old weapons.

I have already referred to Ricardo ; let me now quote
Bentham : " If the legislator find it good to take away from a
particular class of citizens a fifth part of their revenue, why
stop there ? Why not take away another fifth part, and still
another ? If the first reduction answered its end, a further
reduction will answer it in the same proportion ; and if the
measure is good in one case, why should it be bad in the
other ? Wherever we stop, it is necessary to have a reason
for stopping, but whatever reason prevents the second step will
be just as good to prevent the first. This operation is exactly
the same as diminishing rents under the pretext that the
proprietors are useless consumers, and the farmers productive
labourers. If you shake the principle of security as respects

one class of citizens *you shake it for all.* The bundle of rods is its emblem."

Though this is the language which Bentham addressed to French "reformers" of nearly a century ago, it is equally appropriate to their English imitators of to-day.

It is merely a question of time. Give but free scope to "beneficent legislation" and sooner or later every trade and interest in the country will attain to the ruined condition of British Agriculture. To take but one example, it is a fact that the Mines' Regulation Act alone threw no less than 63,000 persons out of work within less than six years of its coming into operation. In other words, while it is hard to show that it has been the means of saving ten lives a year, it is a fact that indirectly it has killed at the rate of ten thousand. But the appetite has been whetted. The blood has been tasted and the trembling capitalist shall himself be thrust aside in the rush for more.

> " Si torrida parvus
> Venit in ora cruor, rediunt rabiesque furorque ;
> Admonitaeque tument gustato sanguine fauces,
> Fervet, et a trepido vix abstinet ora magistro."

Mr. Fyffe clinches his argument in favour of the *four* F's with a little anecdote which, so far as it proves anything, shows that if you want to make extensive alterations in your farm, you had better take it on a long lease. But, as an illustration of the kind of stuff that is used in certain quarters as a substitute for argument, it is worth quoting :—

" One of the best managed farms I know is conducted by two partners, one of whom had always been a local farmer, while the other had been in business in London, and, after leaving London, took with him, I believe, a considerable capital into the country. There, instead of setting up the farming business entirely on his own account, he entered into partnership with the local man, and so combined his own capital with the skill and experience of a professional farmer. Their holding was a sort of oasis in the midst of an impoverished neighbourhood. Unfortunately, however, they were so imprudent as to be content with an annual tenancy under a peer, thinking that his lordship would never disturb them. My lord, however, found it desirable the other day to sell his land, and the result is that the partners find themselves under a new landlord, whom they cannot get on with, and they have, in consequence, to leave the place. In this case the inducement to the capitalist to put his money into the concern

was the supposed security of tenure under a peer—this proved imaginary ;
and I contend that it is necessary to make such security not imaginary
but real, and that this can most effectually be done by such changes in
the law as those which I have sketched."

This same anecdote has, no doubt, been pigeon-holed for
use as an argument for the abolition of the House of Lords, and
may do good service in many other causes. There are, however, two considerations which seem to throw some doubt on
the story ; one is the improbability that two men enjoying the
friendship and advice of our teacher should be so stupid as to
have dealings of any kind "with a peer," and the other is the
circumstance that "my lord" should have found it desirable to
sell his land. That a peer, having once held land, should,
under any conceivable pressure, have been induced to relinquish
his hold, must have struck the reformers as extremely un-
historical ; the theory being that he gradually tends to elbow
out all his neighbours and accumulate all the land in his own
hands. But let that pass. The point is that the farmer persists
in paying too much in rent, and the consequences are manifold.
To begin with, all the agricultural labourers in many villages
are old men. Whether they began life as old men, or have
been reduced to that condition by the scantiness of their wage,
we are not clearly told. Or it may be the absence of young
people that has provoked the remark ; if so, perhaps a peep
into the Board Schools would explain the matter, where the
children are still to be found, not, it is true, learning much of
their future work, but plodding steadily on in the direction of
the differential calculus. So that when we are triumphantly
asked, "Whose fault is this ?" some might answer it is the
fault of the reformers, and others might go so far as to single
out Mr. Forster or Mr. Mundella as mainly responsible. But
the true explanation, according to the pamphlet before us, is
the rent. "We come back to the real mainspring of the
whole concern—because the farmer has agreed to pay too
much in rent." The question now is, How are we to smash
this "mainspring of the whole concern"? It is partly to be
done by reducing the hours of labour, and "the reduction of the
hours of labour, I suppose, can only be accomplished by an
agricultural labourers' trades union (*sic !*) ; but the object is a

Y

right one and a possible one. It is a right one because the
social improvement of the labourer is all but hopeless if he has
to work twelve hours a day ; and it is a possible one, because
there is a margin of unearned profit in the shape of landlord's
rent, which may perfectly well be diminished without inflicting
a wrong on anybody." The attention of all property owners
and all honest men is called to the fact *not* that such stuff can
be written and is written to-day without danger of criminal
prosecution, but that it is written with the approval and
blessing of a cabinet minister, who commends it to notice,
after asking the question, " What may we expect with regard
to the treatment of the land question in the next Parliament ? "

And while all this is going on in the country, what is
going to be done in the towns, for " people have of late begun
to understand that the land question is a town question as
well as a country question " ?   And why a town question ?
One reason is, we are told, " because the action of our land
system has been to drive people unnecessarily out of the
country, and so artificially to increase the overcrowding of our
towns, and the misery resulting from over-competition." In
other words, the condition of the labourer in the country is so
dreadful that he is driven to take refuge in the towns, which
are already overcrowded and full of misery. The misery and
wretchedness of the towns is great, but that of the country is
greater ; so much greater that the towns are *relatively* gardens
of Eden, and are a positive attraction for the peasants. Now
if this is so, we should expect to find that the lot of the
working classes all round is going from bad to worse. But
without endorsing all that is urged to the contrary by Mr.
Giffen and the optimists, it may safely be asserted that the
condition of the working classes is, at any rate, no worse than
it was forty years ago. Hence we must find another reason
for the observed influx of the country population into the
towns. And that reason surely is not far to seek. Any one
with more knowledge of recent events and better powers of
observation than Mr. Fyffe's intelligent foreigner, is aware that
the economic working of great manufactures requires local
concentration. The times have altered since every village had
its hand weaver and every cottage lass was expected to " mind

her wheel"; and only persons of the type of the intelligent
Maori or Hottentot can be pardoned for lamenting that "it is
difficult to draw employers of labour away from the large
towns, and to induce them to start their works in new places."
Very difficult indeed!

Another reason why the land question has become a town
question is because of the system of building-leases, so we are
told. And this is how it operates. "Any one wanting a house
must go either to one of the ground landlords or to some
builder to whom they have let the land." That is a bad job
to begin with. Why should not the ground landlord come to
him? Then he has to pay more than the agricultural rental
of the site. Preposterous! Surely land in Lombard Street or
Cornhill ought to be let for twenty-seven shillings an acre.
As a matter of fact it fetches a trifle more in the market, but
that is on account of the rapacity of the landlord, and must be
put a stop to. For, after all, "the value of the land has
increased through the industry of the people, not usually
through the merit of the landlord." But this is not the worst.
Not only will this landlord make you pay rent during the term
of your lease, but when it is over "he will make you pay to .
renew the lease." Incredible! "Of course this is particularly
hard on tradesmen and men of business."

It is a pity the reformers could not have been left to
ruminate on the woes of the landless in general, without
having their attention distracted by the harrowing narrative of
their guide's own misfortunes. We have seen how the luckless
lecturer bungled his farm of 150 acres, to such an extent that
not one of the reformers offered at any price to take it off his
hands and set them free for the great work of land-law reform.
Well, this ill-fortune (to use a euphemism) follows him up to
town. He buys a house, the landlord of which and a speculative builder, some mortgagees, a loan company, some bankers,
and "a whole army of money-lenders and lawyers" had got so
hopelessly mixed up and tied in a knot, that when he came to
take part in the conveyance, counting "the surviving partners
of the bank and the representatives of those who were dead,
there were no less than five firms of solicitors making profits
out of the sale of the house, to say nothing of the profits made

by the bank and the loan company. Of course *somebody* must pay for all this, and that somebody is the purchaser." There it is! Alas! that *somebody* was the lecturer. No wonder the land question has become a town question. Such is Mr. Fyffe's luck, that if he went for a cruise in the Mediterranean the land question would straightway become a sea question. If he went up in a balloon, it would become an air question ; and if he went to another place, it would become a " burning question." It may be some comfort to Mr. Fyffe to learn that the unfortunate somebody who has to pay for the luxury of five firms of solicitors, is *not* the purchaser but the vendor.

Meantime the question for the reformers is, how to get rid of all these crying scandals. Fortunately it is not a difficult task. On the contrary, " the remedy as between tenant and landlord seems simple enough, namely, that proposed by Mr. Broadhurst's Bill, empowering every tenant with more than twenty years' lease unexpired, to acquire, on equitable terms " (remember the fourth F), "the fee simple of his holding." Could anything be simpler ? You hire a horse for a ride, Mr. Broadhurst gets his Bill through Parliament, and, hey, *presto !* you acquire the fee simple of the horse. Everybody would be happy. In the case of the leasehold estate "the landlord would get what his reversionary interest is *fairly worth*"—in the opinion of Mr. Fyffe ; and the tenant, " if he made the place more valuable by his industry, would get the fruits of his labour." One cannot analyse the fourth F at every turn. The reader will see that if the landlord did not value the reversion at something more than the figure based on a calculation of the rent, he would clearly have sold the premises altogether and invested the proceeds in something else. Those who have taken the trouble to wade through the Leaseholders' (Facilities of Purchase of Fee Simple) Bill will be inclined to think that its proper title would be Freeholders' Spoliation Bill. The objection has been raised to the Bill that if all the occupants in a certain respectable locality were independent freeholders, some one maliciously disposed might erect a frantic piece of architecture enough to scare the birds and make the horses shy. But we are now told that this objection " could be easily remedied by making the ownership of

each tenant subject to the same stipulations against nuisances
or annoyances which existed in his lease, and giving to other
occupants of the estate the same power of enforcing those
provisions which originally belonged to the ground landlord."
Town dwellers who know the difficulty of building a new wing
or throwing out a billiard-room or conservatory, owing to the
grumbling punctiliousness of neighbours, jealous of their rights
of light and prospect, even after the landlord's consent has
been obtained, will hardly look forward with glee to the time
when all the fellow-occupants of the estate are to have the
same power of enforcing those provisions which originally belonged to the ground landlord.   Besides, what is the bond
which is to hold these fellow-occupants together?   Is the
memory of the old estate and its boundaries to be handed
down for ever?   And if not, how is a householder to answer
himself the question, Who is my neighbour?   Perhaps on
inquiry this "simple plan" is not quite so simple as it looks
at first sight, apart from the question of its honesty.   But even
this is not enough.   "I think," says Mr. Fyffe, "that the Leasehold Enfranchisement Bill does not go far enough."   Here,
again, he is a little mixed.   There never was any such Bill
before Parliament as the one named.   Mr. Broadhurst's Bill was
entitled "Leaseholders' (Facilities of Purchase of Fee Simple)
Bill."   There was, it is true, a Bill brought in in 1884, entitled
"*Leaseholders*' Enfranchisement Bill," not indeed by Mr. Broadhurst, but by Lord Randolph Churchill.   Has Mr. Fyffe read
either?   And if so, to which does he refer when he says that
it does not go far enough?   He proceeds: "In my humble
opinion, the community, say the municipality of a growing
town, ought to have the power to take up the land round it,
just as a railway company might, at an equitable value" (fourth
F) " to be fixed by some public authority.   The community, as
it expanded, would then be its own landlord; and the increased
value in the land would fall to the benefit of those whose
activity had produced it, and not to the landlord, who has sat
still."   Now, assuming the market value to be paid to the
owner (anything less is robbery), the speculating community,
say municipality or *commune,* will either gain or lose by the
transaction.   According to Mr. Fyffe, it will always gain;

such is the inference.   This being so, why does not Mr. Fyffe get up a company for buying up all these belts or areas round growing towns ?   He need not pocket the increase.   After deducting his expenses, he can present the balance to the municipality and be put on the register of public benefactors forthwith.   Is it that there are keen men with as good an eye for a rising market as himself, that deters him from undertaking this remunerative and philanthropic task, or is it the dread that his ill-luck will follow him even here ?   When bought up, this belt of land " might then either be built upon by the municipality and let to tenants, or be sold in plots for the citizens to make their own buildings.   There would be this further advantage, that the suburbs of growing towns would then be planned and laid out by some responsible authority."   Now this " responsible authority " is just the party we wish to avoid.   We know him better by the name of "jobbing official."

Municipal bodies have quite enough to do, and as some think far too much, without launching into the land speculating and building trades.   But as if this were not enough, they are to be empowered to advance money on loan out of local funds to persons anxious to keep a cow or grow fruit and vegetables ; otherwise where is the money to come from ?   The labourer with the holding granted him by the municipality, " will want at least from £20 to £50 to make a fair start. I see nothing else for it."   And the neo-radical's goal is reached at last.

" Every Englishman is entitled in the last resort to have food, fire, and lodging provided for him in the workhouse out of the ratepayers' pockets, without the least chance of their getting anything back ; and I do not see that it is by any means so bad an application of public funds, if, instead of waiting till people are paupers, we lend, with due precautions for repayment, in order to give a start to those who, in the absence of such assistance, will certainly live upon the public rates as paupers in their old age."

Such is the outcome of the Oxford reformer's philosophy —one colossal scheme of national pauperism.

CHAPTER XI

IN a memorable speech delivered in the House of Lords on the 31st of July 1885—a speech that will live in the pages of history when most other utterances of the session are buried in well-earned oblivion—Lord Wemyss divided socialists into three classes : the socialists of the street ; the socialists of the schools ; and the socialists of the senate. The first he summarily disposed of as hardly worthy of serious consideration. " The socialism of the communist," said he, "may be treated very shortly. There are four very happy lines which I think accurately describe the communist :—

> " ' What is a communist ? One who has yearnings
> For equal division of unequal earnings :
> An idler or bungler, or both, he is willing
> To fork out his penny and pocket your shilling ! '

That I believe to be a very fair description of a communist, with the exception that I greatly doubt his readiness to fork out his penny. Nevertheless, I have a great respect for him. He knows what he means. He means business. His business is the equal division of unequal earnings. There is no theory about him. He is a thoroughly practical man ; and one respects practical men."

True ; but these are not the people with whom I here propose to deal. There are the theorists—the socialists of the schools, of whom Mr. J. L. Joynes is one of the ablest exponents in this country. Of these Lord Wemyss uses a very different language. Says he :—" I come next to the socialism of the professor—the socialism of the schools. Now we live in a time when, perhaps more than in any other, men feel for the sufferings of their fellow-creatures. It is essentially an era of humanitarianism. Philosophers and professors in their writings are casting aside the old school of political economy and *laissez-faire*, and advocating State intervention as a cure for all evils. They look to the State to protect the weak against the strong, and to equalise the conditions of life. I believe, my lords, that all these attempts will end in signal failure, and that, in the long run, it will be proved that the older school of political economy is, on the whole, sounder, ay, and more humane, than that of the modern humanitarian school of philosophy."

It is this class of political thinkers with whom I propose to discuss the social problem in the present chapter. It must not be forgotten that the doctrines underlying neo-radicalism are the self-same doctrines which are openly expressed and consistently acted upon by the leaders of the party of scientific socialism. Hence, though few neo-radicals have either the courage or the education to lay down the first principles of their own policy, it behoves us, who find ourselves opposed to them at every turn, to learn from their unacknowledged leaders what these principles are. Probably the most compact, and also the most plausible epitome of socialist principles obtainable in this country, is Mr. Joynes's *Catechism*. It is simply written, and *appears* intelligible to ordinary readers. For these reasons I propose to take it to pieces, to examine it in detail, and to expose the fallacies on which it is built up. It is contained in ten short chapters. Let us take them one by one. Chapter I. is entitled "Division of Toil." Mark the use of the word " toil." Adam Smith spoke of the division of *labour ;* others have made use of the expression division of *work ;* but Mr. Joynes chooses the word *toil ;* it rhymes with moil, and it bespeaks a poetic pity for the toilers—the horny-handed sons of toil ! I mention this only because it is one of the socialistic tricks. The middle-class tradesmen are styled *bourgeois,* which is French for burgher or townsman, but English ears are reminded of that sleek snob and fool, the *bourgeois gentilhomme.* It would be difficult to arouse antipathy amongst English audiences for the stout burgher. Then the poor are called the proletariat, because the term recalls swarms of helpless little children, born without any request on their part to fight their way through this struggling world. It is all very touching, no doubt, but *ad captandum* phrases are not logic after all.

The chapter about toil consists of fifteen short questions with the socialistic answers. With the first three it is not necessary to quarrel. But with the fourth answer begins the begging of the question. "How may these two sets of persons be roughly distinguished ? As employers and employed; idlers and workers; privileged and plundered ; or more simply still, as rich and poor." Here we have "employers," "idlers," "privileged," and "rich," used as synonymous terms. Every honest man knows that employers as a rule, so far from being idlers, work harder than their employees. Their work may be less disagreeable, and may (in some cases) occupy less time ; but taking quantity and quality together, they work far harder and do far more work. Their ability to do this has, in many cases, earned them the position of superiority which they enjoy. Then again, the poor are by no means, as a rule, addicted to work. They must earn their meals or starve, but beyond that they show, as a rule, very little taste for work. As for the allegation that the employers plunder the workers, it is simply an unfair way of describing a series of transactions which by a gross straining of language might be so put. The facts are, that the workman barters all prospective profits of his labour for a consideration in cash down. It is a foolish bargain, and the workman of course gets the worst of it. In short, he forfeits the whole fruits of his labour, but he does it voluntarily, readily, and for choice, because he has neither the courage nor the industry to use his own judgment and take his own risks. To call this plunder on the part of the employer is untrue and unjust.

That the poor are in this helpless position is due, he says, to the fact that society is at present organised solely in the interests of the rich, evidently regarding the social organism as an artificial creation. Nature is not surely accused of working "in the interests of the rich." But not only does nature,

or the human artificer who constructed the social organism
with this class partiality, place the poor in an unenviable position ; it is also necessary to arrange that they shall not find it
out until the advent of Mr. Joynes. The poor cannot, he says,
organise society on a system which will prevent their being
robbed of their own productions, because *the existing organisation itself keeps them ignorant* of its own causes, and consequently
powerless to resist its effects.

Now for the cure. This is to be based on the principle
of justice—the principle which has ever been appealed to by
each wrong-headed reformer from the days of Adam. But in
order to give justice a chance, and something to go upon,
another question must needs be begged ; and that is that the
fruits of industry are the fruits of labour. If capital contributes to the increase of wealth, clearly the capitalist has a
right to at least his proportionate share of the increase. We
must therefore pretend that capital does not contribute. Yet
the contention is absurdly false.

I cannot see why socialists are *necessarily* opposed to all
political parties as our author alleges. It is true that existing
parties are both opposed to them. That is to say, Conservatives
deny the truth of the political doctrine on which socialism is
based, while neo-radicals have neither the consistency nor the
courage to carry their principles into practice. They are
afraid of being *extreme !* But there is no necessary antagonism
between neo-radicals and socialists. Nor are we concerned to ask
why the name socialist has been bestowed on these extreme
advocates of compulsory co-operation. The reason adduced by
Mr. Joynes is certainly not the true one ; firstly, because there
are many persons quite as anxious as he is to " displace the
present system of competition for the bare means of subsistence,
and to establish in its stead the principle of associated work,"
who do not call themselves socialists, and whom nobody calls
socialists ; secondly, because the description of the socialistic
aim is utterly inadequate. The individualist believes that the
enlightened and progressive self-interest of individuals will
eventually, though gradually, bring about a higher order of
society—higher, probably, than any human being now living
could even conceive, much less plan. The socialist, on the

contrary, has no faith in this individualist evolution, or is too impatient to wait for it, and he proposes to effect a sort of artificial evolution on lines laid down by a majority in council assembled. The acts of the citizens are to be dictated by *society*. Hence the doctrine is called socialism.

The second chapter of the *Catechism* is entitled "The Capitalist System." It abounds in fallacies, and perpetuates the ridiculous notion of "use value," which is carefully distinguished from "exchange value." The whole tissue of cobwebs is extracted bodily from the works of the orthodox political economists. It is the padding which forms part of their stock-in-trade.

It will be seen that the sole source of wealth is said to be labour. Now some economists define wealth as everything which is useful to man *and* which has exchange value. But Mr. Joynes defines it very distinctly as "everything that supplies the wants of man and ministers in any way to his comfort and enjoyment," whether it has an exchange value or not. Hence air and water are wealth. When he goes on to say that all wealth is derived from labour, he says that which is absurdly untrue. Let him either adopt the old definition of wealth—which is wrong—or else give up the old Ricardian theory of the origin of wealth. His present position is untenable and ridiculous. I prefer to define wealth as all that which is useful to man; we can dispense with Mr. Joynes's rigmarole. Wealth then falls into two large classes. 1. Those useful things to which man has been adapted, as all animals are adapted to their environment by the elimination of the unfit and the survival of the fit. 2. Those useful things which man has adapted to his own use. In the former class would come air and water; in the second class would fall all kinds of tools and manufactured commodities. Man has become adapted in the wild state to the fruits and other foods around him; and the berries and nuts he gathers from the trees, though wealth, are no more the result of his labour than the sun, by whose rays he is warmed and comforted. Even Mr. Joynes would hardly go so far as to base any theory of distribution among tribes of monkeys on the ground that the apples and cocoa-nuts around are the product of their labour.

Farther on we shall see the object of this baseless contention that wealth is derived from labour; for yet another false premise must be improvised before the doctrine is of any use as the basis of socialism.

As for the term " use value," it is almost meaningless, and absolutely without either use or value as an economic expression ! It is impossible to measure the amount of pleasure which anything is capable of affording. Such amount varies with the individual enjoying it. Moreover the different kinds of pleasure enjoyed by a single individual are, *inter se*, incommensurable. How many times does the pleasure of eating cheese-cakes go into the pleasure of gazing on a lovely landscape, or listening to a grand symphony ? Let us clear our heads of all these cobwebs. The elements of plutology are not really very difficult or mysterious. Most of the dust has been kicked up by the economists themselves. Let us see. Wealth is everything which affords pleasure to man. Part of it is found ready to hand, contributed, so to speak, by nature ; and part of it is due (in part) to the labour of man. But even this latter is not, as a rule, wholly the product of labour. If the raw material had value before it was operated upon, that part of the manufactured article's value is due not to labour but to nature. The value of a thing is simply the amount (according to any standard of measurement) of other things for which it can be exchanged. And this of course varies in different localities. In London a spectroscope is *worth* a good deal more than a handful of glass beads ; on the Gold Coast, a good deal less. The expression " use value " should be abolished altogether. Then value stands for exchange value, and that alone. The following statement, therefore, amounts to nothing more than that a loaf is more useful to a hungry man than to one who is satiated. This is quite true, but not very original or profound. " Its use value to a starving man is infinitely great, as it is a question of life and death with him to obtain it ; it is nothing at all to a turtle-fed alderman, sick already with excessive eating ; but its exchange value remains the same in all cases."

We have next to learn what capital is ; and the definition given of it is just as accurate as the definition of wealth. It is the result, we are told, of past labour devoted to present productions. Of course capital is as much the result of past labour as wealth in general is the result of past labour, and no more so. Capital is, in truth, all that wealth whose value is due to the demand for it as an element of production, and not as an immediately enjoyable commodity. Nobody enjoys a file, or a saw, or a bale of flax ; but most of us enjoy a ripe peach or a basin of turtle soup. Now coals we may enjoy directly by making a good fire on a winter night; and they also serve as elements of production. They are capital or not capital according as their value is determined by the demand for them in use in furnaces and factories or for keeping us warm. Thus jet burns quite as well as coal, and would be as useful in furnaces. So do diamonds. But they are not capital because their value is due to the demand for them as directly enjoyable or useful commodities.

However, Mr. Joynes's definition is quite good enough for the purpose he has in view, as will be seen. Having fashioned his tools, he sets to work with them. He points out that the landlord secures his profit by extorting from the labourer a share of all that he produces under threat of excluding him from the land ; and that the capitalist extorts from those labourers who are excluded from the land a share of all that they produce, under threat of withholding from them the implements of production, and thus refusing to let them work at all. He then agrees, we are told, to return to them as wages about a quarter of what they have produced by their work, keeping the remaining three-quarters for himself and his class. And this is the capitalist system.

One would have supposed that even the most orthodox political economist would have been able to detect the circular form of this fallacy. How do the landlord and capitalist secure their rent and profit ? By *extorting* from the labourers, who are excluded from the land and from the ownership of capital, the greater share of what they produce, and leaving them only sufficient to keep them alive. That is the explanation with which we are supposed to put up. But why do the silly labourers permit this extortion, seeing that they far out-number the landlords and capitalists ? Oh, the landlords and capitalists, with their ill-gotten gains, hire soldiers and police-men to keep the labourers in subjection. But why do not the labourers extort from the capitalist the whole profits of his capital, and with the proceeds hire an army to hold him in subjection? Well, you see, they have to get the profits first; the capitalist has got the start of them. And how, we further ask, did he get the start? Why did not they get the start, seeing what an advantage they had in numbers? Well, the fact is, he made a bargain with them, and they got the worst of the bargain. Quite so; the whole transaction is a volun-tary one. There is no extortion, no coercion. The capitalist system merely denotes the arrangement under which each contributor to an adventure takes a share of the gross returns proportionate to the capital contributed by him.

And now from a great falsehood we come to a great truth, namely, that the amount returned to the labourer is the amount necessary to keep him and his family alive. Yes; such is the result of the iron law of wages—the terrible law which keeps the bulk of the population down close to the starvation limit. Mr. Joynes does not seem quite to understand it, or the proof of its truth, for he considers it necessary to bolster it up in a palpably superfluous way. He calls in the doctors as witnesses. Now no proof of this kind is required. The pro-position can be demonstrated deductively, and is as certain as any proposition in Euclid. Given the wage system and the postulate that population presses on means of subsistence, and then the iron law of wages follows as obviously as day follows night.

It is true the "orthodox" have woven a fabric of moon-beams wherewith to clothe the nakedness of this spectre, and they have called it "the standard of comfort." But the hideous form gleams through the unsubstantial vesture, and the victims of wagedom are devoured as before. The fiction is comforting; and as for the fact—well, that does not affect the "orthodox political economists." But the present system must be made to appear decent.

Setting aside the animus shown by the use of the words "extortion" and "threat," there is little or no fault to find with Mr. Joynes's statement of the case. It *is* true that under the wage system now in vogue, the "iron law of wages" does operate to keep down the reward of labour to the cost of "keeping body and soul together," and we need not quarrel with the manner in which the truth is brought to our notice. Neither need individuals quarrel with the remedy proposed, namely, that the labouring classes should become their own employers. By all means let the workers become their own employers. By the laws of civilised communities all persons are the owners of their own bodies; but they are permitted to let themselves out for hire, though they cannot sell themselves out and out. This system of letting themselves out for hire by time is called the wage system, and it is doubtless the cause of most of the ills affecting the working classes. But the change would not abolish idleness. Idle people (and I do not admire them any more than Mr. Joynes) would continue to flourish in idleness on the fruits of capital, which is not the fruits of the labour of living persons, but (for the most part) the fruits of the labour of persons long since dead. This curious fallacy crops up again and again.

Chapter II. concludes with the observation that the work done by a company would go on just as well if the shareholders disappeared. Possibly it would; but how would the work of the Company have progressed if there had been no share-holders to begin with? Take this case. A man, who might have been tilling the ground and growing potatoes, spends his time in making a plough. It takes him many weeks to make it. When it is finished, he lends it to his neighbour for a consideration which pays him better than if he had tilled his land. Both parties gain by the arrangement. Straightway the agriculturist says: "Very good, friend, but you are not wanted. The ploughing goes on well enough without you. Leave your plough with us, and go and improve yourself off the face of the earth." That is just what Mr. Joynes says to the shareholders. And this is socialism!

The third chapter deals with what socialists call surplus value. We shall see what is meant by this term. Meantime no objection is taken to capital as such. "The way in which it is used is attacked by socialists, not the thing itself, and it is only by means of a democratic state, acting in the interest of the producer, that it can be turned to the advantage of the labourer."

Here we see the cloven hoof, bearing out my previous contention, namely, that it is not merely co-operation which socialism denotes, but compulsory co-operation—co-operation planned and enforced by the State or organised society.   Here it is admitted.   In the description of socialism in the first chapter this feature is entirely ignored.   While admitting that under the system of wagedom, capital is not exactly used " in the interest of the labourers," we shall see whether State socialism is really the *only* scheme by which a cure can be effected ; whether individualism is not capable of evolving an industrial system workable " in the interest of the labourers," and also in the interest of the capitalists, who, after all (and despite modern cant), are worth more, and a good deal more—man for man—than the much-belauded " proletariat."

But to return to our text.   How is State socialism to work ?   " By taking into its own hands all the land and capital, or means of production, which are now used as monopolies for the benefit of the possessing class.   As the State has already taken over the Post-Office and the Telegraphs, so it might take over the Railways, Shipping, Mines, Factories, and all other industries."

The expression, " in whose interest," which frequently occurs throughout this *Catechism*, is either meaningless or misleading.   If it means that there is any conscious purpose—any design on the part of those who uphold the present industrial system—it is manifestly untrue.   If it merely means that the employers get the best of the wage bargain, it will not be denied.   The employers do receive a profit on their investments, and the wage receivers do not.   But to say that production is now carried on in anybody's interest is a most unjust insinuation, more especially when Mr. Joynes himself admits that employers are not individually responsible for the system ; for he will hardly pretend that employers have consciously entered into a sort of class compact to keep the proletariat in subjection.   That may be the *effect* of certain social causes, but it certainly is not the *purpose* of willed acts.

We are then told that the labourers produce the machinery, which is no more true than the statement that the female alone *produces* the offspring. It is apparently true, and that is all. Sometimes capital contributes less than the labourers; sometimes a great deal more. Again, to say that the employers " take it away " from them is just as fair as to say that Mr. Joynes goes and takes what he wants from the grocer's shop Of course he does—and pays for it. We are intended to gather that the employer *steals* the labourer's machinery, whereas the " taking away " is pursuant to the wage contract. When Mr. Joynes says that the cure is for the State to " take into its own hands " the land and the capital which is now private property, he might be a little more explicit and say whether he means *buy* it or *steal* it; because in the one case the community would be ruined, in the other case only the best members of the community—just at first. There is no need to quarrel with the contention that to buy these things —all the ships, mines, railways, factories, gas-works, canals, furnaces, etc.—would be just as good a stroke of business, and just as sound a policy, as the " taking over " of the post-office and telegraphs. I can bethink myself of no more improving task for socialists than to be set to work to go through the accounts of the department from its commencement down to the present year. And alas! when all is said and done, our teacher in the very next sentence admits that the workers would be no better off than before. Look at the poor postman.

Cannot the workers combine together by co-operation, it is asked, to defeat this principle of competition ? No; not unless the whole body of workers are included in one society, and that is simply socialism, says our teacher.

Here we have the grand socialist mistake of confounding voluntary co-operation with compulsory. If the whole body of workers were included in one society of their own free will and accord, that would no more be socialism than the present system. It is really time the socialists dropped this absurd contention. Trade unionism is no more socialistic than a

z

joint-stock company or a cricket club. But what is the conclusive reason adduced for discarding voluntary co-operation? Simply that it cannot get rid of competition. So much the better. It must be proved that competition is really the harmful principle in the existing system. That has never been done. It is some comfort to find the wage contract described as a "bargain." It is usually described by our teacher and his fellow-socialists as an arrangement *forced* on the labourer.

We are next introduced to "surplus value," which is defined as the difference between a bare subsistence and the fruits of labour. "Necessary labour is that which would feed and clothe and keep in comfort the nation if all took their part in performing it." It is already evident that Mr. Joynes, like all socialists, is a member of the "Daniel Lambert" school of politics. To exist is necessary; to be fat is necessary: but to be educated, cultured, something above the mere brute—that is not necessary, it is a luxury.

What do we mean by necessary labour? I mean nothing by it. I never use the expression. The labour which results in a noble work of art is in my opinion quite as *necessary* as the labour which results in a pair of corduroy trousers. Moreover, the very existence of most persons is by no means necessary in the sense of "indispensable." The world could get on very well without them. Once upon a time a thief put forward the plea of necessity—"*Mais, il faut vivre!*" But the judge quietly and pertinently replied, "*Je ne vois pas la nécessité.*" There is no necessity to keep alive a huge, ugly, and stupid population; and the labour spent in "feeding and clothing" the nation might well be more suitably, and even productively, spent in creating things which minister to the higher tastes. However, all these reflections fall under the still unanswered question, Is life worth living?

No individual employer, we are told, is responsible for the exploitation of the labourers; the blame applies to the whole class. Individual employers may be ruined, but the employing class continue to appropriate the surplus value. And the reason of this is because competition is as keen amongst the capitalists as among the labourers. It determines the division of the *spoil*; different sets of people struggling to get a share in the surplus value. It does not affect the labourers at all. It is assumed that the *plunder* is to be shared among the "upper classes," and the only question is in what proportion this shall be done. All this may be quite true without justifying the language used when we are told that that which the employers *take from* the employed is *spoil* and *plunder*. It is nothing of the sort. It is merely the fruits of a bargain which, from the labourers' point of view, is a very foolish and bad bargain. We may admit that, without accusing those who get the best of the bargain of being plunderers.

But in what follows it is not the language only which is censurable, it is the gross fallacy on which the whole socialist argument rests. "This plunder is labelled by many names, such as rent, brokerage, fees, profits, wages of superintendence, reward of abstinence, insurance against risk, but above all, interest on capital. They are all deducted from the labourers' earnings. There is no other fund from which they could possibly come, and they are simply taken for nothing, just as a thief accumulates his stolen goods." Here is the socialist fallacy in its nakedness. "There is no other fund from which they could possibly come!" *i.e.* wages of superintendence, fees for medical attendance, and legal advice and such like; as if all these payments were not for hard work and skilled work done. To say that a man who adds more to production by working with his head than perhaps one hundred men do by working with their hands is paid necessarily out of the fruits of *their* labour is simply transparent nonsense.

There is quite another explanation of the payment for interest and rent, and "abstinence" and insurance against risk. Capital, as I have said, contributes to new value, sometimes more, and sometimes less, than the labourers engaged on the work. It may be the saved result of work done a year ago, or fifty years ago. Anyhow, it has never been consumed by those who had a right to consume it. As soon as it is employed in further production it has to be destroyed. When the product emerges it may be worth less than the elements invested, or it may be worth more. As a rule, civilised man being a prudent animal, it is worth a little more, *on the average* about 3 per cent

more. This is the average profit on capital, and it is properly
called economic interest, because the element of risk may be
eliminated by spreading it over a wide area of investments.
Those who insure the interest reap the larger profits if any,
and incur the loss if any. You cannot eat your corn and sow
it ; and if you sow it, you are not satisfied to receive a like
amount at the end of the year. Is it not ridiculous to say
that the man who sows your corn in your field for you is the
sole producer of the new value next harvest ? All capital
fructifies—grows like a tree. If a sapling, eight-feet four in
height, grows three inches in a year, it fairly represents the
annual growth of capital.

Here is an interesting definition of interest. " Interest is
a fine paid by the private organiser of labour out of the
surplus value which his labourers supply, to the idle person
from whom he borrows his capital." We now see what a
particularly ridiculous conclusion we are driven to, if we
accept this theory of surplus value. Interest a fine ! Of
course the expression " surplus value " has no definite meaning
whatever. It vaguely conveys to the socialist's mind the
difference between the value of the work which has to be done
and the value of the work which he would not mind doing
without the stimulus of hunger; that is to say, the average
amount of work which would be required if everybody was
satisfied to be warm and fat, and to have plenty of sleep. It
is curious to observe that in such a sodden state of society
prevision would be weaker, a future pleasure would compare
less favourably with an equal present pleasure, and *consequently*
interest would be higher. No one will exchange a present
pleasure for a future pleasure without an extra inducement.
Mr. Joynes himself, with a peach in his hand on a hot summer
day, would not exchange it for the promise of an equally
luscious peach on the next hot day. Why should he ? But
if the would-be purchaser agreed to give him two peaches on
the next hot day, he might think it worth his while to close
the bargain. That would be 100 per cent interest ; and
yet Mr. Joynes would hardly consider he was imposing a *fine*
on the other party. A man must be a metaphysician, a
lunatic, or a political economist to understand the stuff that

has been written by the "orthodox" about interest. Thus, when we speak of interest, we must steer between Scylla and Charybdis—between the socialist contention that it is a device of the devil for enriching the rich at the expense of the poor, and the orthodox theory that it is a divine reward for the exercise of some subtle and saintly virtue called abstinence or thrift. The plain truth is (as every banker assumes in practice) that interest is the current estimate of average national profits. If, therefore, interest is a fine, profits are a fine. One cannot draw a line between two men, one of whom draws $2\frac{3}{4}$ per cent from Government securities, and the other of whom draws $3\frac{1}{2}$ per cent from Great Western preference stock. But, after allowing for these peculiarities of thought and of language, Mr. Joynes makes one very true and important admission. The share contributed to industry by the capitalist, as compared with the share contributed by the wage slave, tends to become larger and larger. And the tendency must continue so long as the workers tolerate the present wage system. True ; but socialism is not the cure or the substitute for it.

. Mr. Joynes makes it clear that he shares the neo-radical delusion that factory laws have the effect of raising wages. This is untrue. I shall not take refuge behind the argument that, owing to the ease with which laws are evaded, the expected effect in the abstract fails in the concrete. I go farther. I say that, even granting inviolable factory laws, wages would not be permanently affected. Let it be supposed that an Eight Hours' Bill is passed, prohibiting all— men, women, and children—from working more than eight hours in any one day. What is the effect? Not that of making an eight-hour day's wage equal to a ten-hour day's wage ! No ; the first effect is that the worker will get only four-fifths of his former wage. But this is *below subsistence wage*. True; but subsistence wage includes the item for a sinking fund to enable the worker to rear up children to take his place. This is the first item to be knocked off. The workers of the required kind are not reproduced ; the price of that kind of labour rises a little to meet the demand ; then the price of the goods at which they work is raised. The demand shrinks: down goes the trade, and a lower level is reached—we have a smaller population, dearer necessaries and luxuries, and (it is true) shorter hours.   Mr. Hyndman has over and over again pointed out that an Artisans' Dwellings Act would have no other effect than to put money into the pockets of employers.   If the State paid the whole of the labourer's rent the employer would be able to reduce his wages by precisely that amount.   Mr. Champion lately pointed out the same thing.   If Mr. Joynes really understands and accepts the "iron law," he should admit that he has made a mistake in speaking of degrees of exploitation, of "exploiting to the uttermost."   Wagedom *is* what socialists call "exploitation to the uttermost."   There is no deeper depth to sound.

The fourth chapter in this curious *Catechism* is characteristically entitled "Methods of Extortion."   Capital without labour is helpless, we are told.   Now, nobody ever said that capital without labour is, as a rule, productive.   Nor will Mr. Joynes pretend that labour without capital is productive. *As a rule*, both labour and capital are helpless without the other.   It is true that in certain cases capital is productive alone, as, for instance, when an owned tree of value produces fruit without any attention.   So, also, labour is occasionally productive without the aid of capital, as when a sculptor creates a work of value out of some valueless stone or clay. But, *as a rule*, Mr. Joynes is right in saying that without labour capital is helpless.   He should have added that labour without capital is helpless.   He proposes as a remedy that the State should compete with the capitalist by providing employment for the labourers, and paying them the full value of their productions.   Now, what in reason's name is meant by the State ?   And how is it going to acquire the capital necessary to enable it to employ the labourers ?   It is clear from the context that by "the full value of their production " Mr. Joynes means " the full value of the total product of industry "; that is to say, the fruits of labour *plus* the fruits of capital. If so, it is obvious that the capital held by the State would rapidly dwindle away, unless made good from some other source.   The question is, What source ?   And the only possible answer is, Taxation.

Large accumulations of wealth by individuals is an evil, says Mr. Joynes, but capital in private hands is worse. No proof, and not the smallest evidence, is given in support of this sweeping allegation. No proposition has been more keenly disputed than this. I for one certainly cannot accept Mr. Joynes's *ipse dixit* on the subject. If large accumulations of wealth in private hands is an evil, it must be for some reason. What reason ? I assert that so far from being an evil, it is an unmixed good. No one is forced to accept my dogmatic assertion, but there it is. Large accumulations of the particular kind of wealth denoted by the term "capital" is also a good in itself. At least we have been shown nothing to the contrary ; and, moreover, we see that it is an increasing tendency, and that such tendency is accompanied by a diminishing cost of production. At the same time nobody denies that good things may be abused. Wealth may be expended in drink and debauchery. And this is true of capital. At the present time capital is expended in hiring wage slaves. If it were reserved for investing in industrial undertakings in which only free men were engaged, the larger the accumulations of capital in individual hands the better. If wagedom were suppressed anyhow—by capitalisation or by socialism—then large accumulations of wealth would, we are told, not matter so much. Why not ? Because the capitalist system presupposes the existence of two factors, and is unworkable and impossible without them. First, private property in accumulated wealth ; and secondly, the presence of propertyless labourers in the market, who are forced to sell their services at cost price, that is to say, at wages that will give them a bare subsistence and enable them to work on the morrow, this being the cost of the daily reproduction of the force or power to labour which constitutes their sole property. There is a slight but important omission here. The whole of the factors are not enumerated. There is the item which goes to enable the different kinds of workers to rear up children to take their place when they are used up. When this is neglected, and the item is not paid to the wage slave, the result is that the number of hands in the trade where the omission has taken place is reduced, and wages rise till the normal proportion of hands is again reached.

Thus the employer cannot permanently shirk the payment of this item. As a rule, he does not try.

Still there is an element of truth in all this. The present wage system is one under which the labourer forfeits (there is no need to say that he is robbed) the whole of the profits of his labour. That is true ; but he does it voluntarily. The socialists propose an alternative system in which the capitalist is to forfeit the whole of the profits on his capital. This is equally unreasonable, and inasmuch as it is proposed to deprive him by force against his will, it is robbery. Why cannot capitalist and worker pull together, and agree to take each the profits on his own contribution ? The capitalisation of labour would solve the labour question without injury to any one.

Perhaps the best answer to this question is that given by Mr. Joynes himself. What has hitherto prevented the workers from combining for the overthrow of the capitalist system is ignorance, he says—ignorance due to the system itself, which compels them to spend all their lives upon monotonous toil, and leaves them no time for education.

Throughout this *Catechism* a free use is made of technical terms, both economical and legal. But the use of the term "fraud" is the most unwarrantable. What is fraud ? If a drowning man is induced to promise half his fortune before another man on the bank will throw him a rope, is the bargain a fraudulent one ? Not a bit of it. It is a shameful bargain, but there is no fraud in it. If a man sells a rare book for a mere trifle to one who knows its true value, the sale is not fraudulent. The buyer may get a book worth £200 for half-a-crown by what we should call a shabby act, but there is no fraud. Then, where is the fraud in hiring a wage slave ? It is simply nonsense to use such language. "Under the slave-owning system there was no fraud involved, but only force," says our author. "The similarity between the slave-owning and the capitalist system is complete, with the single exception that force was used in place of fraud."

Freedom of contract is next described as a farce. Now it is not altogether a farce. First of all the labourer is free to choose his master. But, beyond that, he is perfectly free to

capitalise himself if so disposed, and, by union, force the proper
system on employers, who would benefit as much as the
workers. His "freedom" is limited in this respect only by his
own ignorance and laziness—internally, not externally.

Having described freedom of contract as a farce, the
question arises in what sense is it free? The answer given is,
that the labourer is free to take what is offered or nothing.
Or, let me add, the full fruits of his labour, as ascertained after
the completion of the process. This he is fool enough, or
coward enough, to refrain from demanding, and to reject when
offered. As a class, for this reason, wage slaves deserve no
pity. Folly may be a pitiable quality, but it does not always
arouse the emotion of pity. Of course, failing this course, the
workers must, as Mr. Joynes says, accept the market value of
their services, or nothing.

"Nor has he anything to fall back upon, except that in England
Humanity has revolted against the reign of the capitalist, and provided
the workhouse as a last resource for the labourer, taxing the capitalist for
its support. But the capitalist has turned this piece of socialism to his
own ends by rendering the workhouse so unpleasant to the poor that
starvation is often thought preferable, and by insisting that no useful
work done in the workhouse shall be brought into his market, where its
presence would disturb his calculations and impair his profits. He only
allows it to exist at all because he knows that its existence may stave off
for a time the Revolution which he dreads."

Surely there is a contradiction here. Mr. Joynes has
carefully divided the population into capitalists and labourers,
rich and poor, idlers and workers. He now tells us that the
capitalist allows the workhouse to exist, " *because* he knows that
its existence may stave off for a time the revolution." He
also tells us that *Humanity* has provided the workhouse.
Who are included in the ranks of humanity? Have the
workers provided the workhouse for themselves? The fact is
Mr. Joynes has not yet made up his mind whether the workhouse is a socialistic tribute to pity, or a cunning capitalistic
safety-valve against revolution, or, as he prefers to call it, " *the*
Revolution " with a big R. Educated persons can talk about
revolutions in manners, customs, habits, morals, etc., without
feeling to tingle at their own daring. Just as salvationists

trade on the mob's well-known weakness for a good romping chorus, so the socialists trade on the taste of the young roughs for Jack Sheppard, blood and terror. It makes budding " Britons strut with courage." The orator who hints with flashing eye at deeds without a name, at hidden knives and dynamite, who menacingly reminds the Duke of Broadacres and landlords in general of the fate of Foulon ; such an one is already a hero in his own conceit, and half a hero to the buffle-heads who listen to him as children listen to ghost stories.

However, Mr. Joynes is not quite so far gone as that. By revolution he means what ordinary people mean—a complete change, a change which we all look forward to, one which will abolish all unjust privileges and differences, and will render the workers their own employers. That is what co-operationists and capitalisationists all look forward to, but they are content to spell the word with a little modest " r," and to risk·the support of the Tichbornites, the Skeleton Army, and other " thinkers of that School." But let Mr. Joynes explain himself. By revolution he means " the complete change in the conditions of society which will abolish all unjust privileges, distinctions of rank, or difference between wage payers and wage earners, and will render the workers their own employers." We are next treated to a diatribe against landlordism, " of which force is the chief element, since it labels the surplus value ' rents,' and uses all the resources of civilisation in the shape of police and soldiery to enforce their payment by the people ; but the element of fraud is present, since the labourer is told that he is free to give up his holding if he does not wish to pay rent." If our author is addressing himself to the silly rabble above mentioned, his workmanship is, on the whole, too good. It is thrown away upon them. But if he is writing for educated persons, I venture to say that this last passage is an insult to their common sense. To call the bargain between landlord and tenant a fraudulent one, *because* the tenant is told that he need not enter into it unless he likes, is trifling with the intelligence of the reader. As for the other and " chief element," it is absurdly untrue that force is used in this or any civilised country for the extortion of rents. No one is compelled to pay rent any more than he is compelled to buy a fiddle or to hire a cab.

There is practically no difference between the mode of enforcing rent and the mode of enforcing payment for the hire of other goods. If Mr. Joynes hires a horse or a threshing machine for a week he will be *forced* to pay, if he can ; and whether he can pay or not, he will be *forced* to deliver up possession of the horse or machine, however much he may sincerely believe that the act of hiring has somehow invested him with some kind of proprietary right. The element of force enters as much into one class of cases as it does into the other. There is no appeal to police and soldiery in the one case more than in the other. When one man takes or retains what belongs to another, he must be made to surrender it—by force if necessary. Where the fraud comes in it is hard to see.

But there is another egregious fallacy herein contained. The man who pays rent and then takes the whole profits of his industry is not a wage slave at all, but a free man, more especially when his bargain with the landowner is of the nature of a lease, calculated on the average productiveness of like land. Whether he pays his rent in the shape of money or of services makes no difference whatever as to the honesty of the bargain.

I have so little criticism of a substantial kind to pass upon the gist of Mr. Joynes's fifth chapter, entitled " Machines and their Uses," that I am almost tempted to reprint it without comment as a fair statement of the capitalisationist view of the subject. But the tone of the answers is so unsatisfactory that I could not adopt that course without compromising myself, and moreover, the first and last portions spoil the effect of the whole. " Labour-saving machinery is used, as its name indicates, to reduce the cost of production, and by cost of production we mean the amount of human labour necessary to produce useful things." I mean nothing of the sort. It is true that the employment of machinery is one way of reducing cost of production, but it is only one way. Neither does the term " labour saving " cover all the methods of reducing the cost of production. Nor is it correct to describe machinery as reducing cost of production solely through the reduction in the amount of human labour required to produce useful things. To begin with, locomotive engines save horse labour, which is not human. Furthermore, machinery effects a great saving not only in labour, but also in capital. For example, the wool-combing machine saved the whole of the noil which used to pass away with the waste. To such an extent was this the case, that whereas hand - combers were charging fourpence a pound, machine-combers were able *to comb for nothing* at a profit until competition compelled the whole trade to adopt the machine. So brick-making machines and certain mineral oil processes enable us to utilise materials which were formerly so much refuse.

I have already dwelt upon the persistent socialist fallacy —shared, it is true, by the orthodox school of political economy —that the cost of production is the amount of human labour required to produce. First of all, it is not even literally true, because nature supplies some valuables without labour. But the main flaw in the statement is that it overlooks the *successive processes* in production, and in practice attributes the value of the product to the labour consumed in the latest process, or, at all events, in the last few processes. Having premised this, I am in complete accord with the rest of this chapter, which states very fairly and very clearly the precise position of wage receivers with respect to machinery. Labour has not benefited as it should have done through the introduction of machinery. " It is questionable," says John Stuart Mill, " if all the improvements in machinery have lightened the day's toil of a single man." Unfortunately this is by no means the worst of it. In addition to these occasional and transitory evils, there is a great and growing evil resulting from the increasing introduction of machinery. The resulting division of labour so specialises the work of the several classes of workers that there is less and less need for the exercise of intelligence. Their work tends to become more monotonous, easier, and consequently sustainable for longer hours than formerly. They are becoming less like men and more like automatons day by day. People do not make boots or shirts now ; they make tops or button-holes.

"Their employer, it is true, saves their labour in the sense of getting
the same work done by the machine without having to pay their wages.
But this is not a permanent advantage to him individually. As long as
he has a monopoly of the machine, it is a great advantage to him, but
other capitalists soon introduce it also, and compel him to share the spoil
with them. The owners of the machines try to undersell each other,
with a view to keeping the production in their own hands; and competition beats down prices until the normal level of capitalist profits is
reached, below which they all decline to go."

All this is very true, and altogether at variance with the
teachings of the orthodox school. Nor need we quarrel with
the succeeding portion, except as to the absurd and ideal
division of society into two classes, idlers and workers. This
is, of course, a piece of socialist stock-in-trade; but if for
workers and idlers we read wage receivers and wage payers,
Mr. Joynes's contentions are not very wide of the mark. He
very properly exposes the orthodox fallacy which vitiates every
argument of the economists, and that is the assumption that
the labourers have no right to complain so long as the
employers are content with taking only the normal rate of
profits as their share of the surplus value. It is well that this
fallacy should be pointed out and insisted upon. I have often
been met, when advocating capitalisation, with the argument—
No room for improvement. The "orthodox" shakes his head.
"You admit," says he, "that profits cannot fall below their
normal level. Where then, under *any* system, is an improvement in labour remuneration to come from ? Clearly, it must
come out of the consumer's pocket, or not at all."

Again, he is right in pointing out that cheapness of
production is only an apparent, not a real benefit to the
workers. "It would be real if all who consumed were also
workers. As it is, the working class get all the disadvantage
of the low wages, and of the adulteration, which has been
described as a form of competition."

All this again is true. At the same time the manual
workers do not suffer so much from adulteration as might at
first sight appear. Few articles consumed by the wage receivers
are adulterated with substances injurious to health; and
cheap substitutes for expensive articles do not, in the end,
bring extra profits to the manufacturer. Competition brings

down the profits on the sham to the normal level. The
calico-maker who puts 40 per cent of China clay into his goods
gets in the long run 40 per cent less for them. Consumers
who like these cheap goods, irrespective of their quality, get
articles *more* than 40 per cent worse. The consumer is the
chief offender and the chief sufferer; serve him right. But
the workman who buys (as a rule) the best quality of goods
he can, cannot long be cheated out of his money's worth.
Competition does it.

" What makes the reduction of cost appear advantageous to the wage
earners is the fact that their wages are paid in money. The money price
of all articles has risen enormously during the last three centuries owing
to the increased abundance of gold. The money wages have risen also,
but not in anything like the same proportion. Again, the cheapening of
bread and other necessaries is shown to have been an empty boon to the
workers, because it has been proved again and again on the highest
authority that the labourers, as a body, at present obtain so bare a subsistence that it does not suffice to keep them in health ; therefore they
could not at any time have lived on half the amount. Similarly if bread
became twice as dear, wages would necessarily rise. A Wiltshire farm-
labourer could not maintain his family on half their present food ; and
though capital cares nothing about individuals, it takes good care that the
labourers shall not starve in a body."

Here, again, the first effect of a general fall in wages is lost
sight of. The population of the workers whose wage is below
the normal subsistence level ceases to increase. It is not a
case of wholesale death by starvation. The capitalist, so far
from taking care that the thing shall not occur, watches it
with indifference every day. He cannot help it. Indeed, it
may be said that it is no business of his. It all goes on in
accordance with " the laws of supply and demand "—laws
which have a real existence, in spite of the fact that they have
never yet been stated by political economists, who are content
to refer to them as immutable but mysterious decrees, located
somewhere, and sanctifying the existing state of mundane
affairs, more especially the extravagances of the rich and the
sufferings of the poor.

But in spite of all the evils resulting from machinery Mr.
Joynes would not advise the workers to destroy the machinery.
To destroy what they have themselves produced merely because

it is at present stolen from them, would be absurd. The right
course to pursue, he says, is to organise their ranks; demand
restitution of their property; keep it under their control; and
work it for their own benefit.

Here again we meet with the altogether unjustifiable word
"stolen." Mr. Joynes himself would never accuse an individual employer of stealing. The term has a moral connotation, and this should be borne in mind. I quite agree that
that which, under a better system, would have passed into the
pockets of workmen has, under the existing wage system,
passed into the pockets of capitalists. It is to be regretted,
because it tends to keep whole strata of society down at the
level of cost of subsistence. There can be no reasonable doubt
that if British wage receivers had been free workers—had
broken down the wage system—at the beginning of the
present century, the many, many millions of pounds' worth
of produce due to machinery would now be their property.
The future is likely to be quite as prolific in inventions, and
it is not too late to mend. But to pretend that because
labourers of one sort or another have been too indolent or
too stupid to take care of their own investments, therefore
they have been robbed by their employers, is the height of
folly and untruth.

In disputing some of Mr. Joynes's propositions it is
necessary to be very cautious for fear of doing an injustice,
because terms are used in a sense which is unusual with
political economists, or, at least, which ought to be. For
instance, "cost of production" is employed to mean the labour
expended in the process. Ordinary people use the term as
meaning the united values of the labour and capital consumed
in the process. But now the question arises whether the
prices of articles would be raised if the community were
organised on socialist principles? Mr. Joynes thinks not—
"not necessarily, nor in most cases; but in some this would
certainly be the result." But surely, if the labourer received
more for the same amount of work, either the price of the
product would be higher, or else the difference would have to
come out of somebody else's pocket. Now I am far from
denying that under a better industrial system the manual

workers would receive a larger share of the proceeds of industry. I think they would. I also agree that in the present state of improved communications a large number of the middlemen are unnecessary, and consequently a useless element in cost of production. This is the case with many retail shopkeepers. If the reduction made in the cost of middlemen went into the pockets of artisans, etc., it is evident that total cost of production would remain the same, and prices would remain the same.

Substituting proper language for such words in the *Catechism* as "theft" and "stolen" it is true that the poorest class of workers do actually give their labour away, or very nearly so. But this can be remedied without adopting socialism. Some of us cannot roast a sucking-pig nowadays without burning the house down! And who, now, are these dreadful people—these middlemen who are to be so ruthlessly swept away? We ought to sympathise with individuals who have been reared to perform services which are no longer required. If cheap, safe, and rapid transport have rendered a good many distributors superfluous, they will have to learn new trades, or do as best they can. Such was the case when railways pushed on one side those who only knew the coaching business. When machinery supersedes hand-workers, the socialists proclaim unbounded pity for them. Then why anathematise the unfortunate superfluous retailers? Simply because with them are confounded in the socialist imagination a host of others, with whom they have absolutely nothing in common.

Who are the middlemen who intercept and share the surplus value produced by the labourer? They are, says our guide, the unnecessary agents and distributors, the holders of stock, bonds, and shares of every description, and all those who are supported by the wealth producers either in idleness or in useless labour, of which latter class of persons flunkeys are a conspicuous example.

Here we have the unfortunate distributors jumbled up with shareholders—that is, simple capitalists who may or may not be workers—and with flunkeys, who, poor fellows! work hard enough in all conscience. To stand and sit about for

hours with tight stockings, cold feet, and "powdered" (that is
whitewashed) hair is a form of martyrdom which most workmen would fly from, even though the factory or the workhouse
were the alternative. This passage alone testifies to a hopeless
confusion in the mind of Mr. Joynes, which goes far to explain
his strange attitude toward many classes of useful public
citizens. Where does Mr. Joynes draw the line between the
flunkey, the private gardener, the piano manufacturer, and the
lacemaker?

"But the rich," it seems, "do not even support their own
flunkeys, and maintain in comfort those who produce luxuries
for them. These people are maintained entirely by the
workers, though the maintenance is passed through the
hands of the rich, who therefore imagine that they produce it."

This statement is absolutely false. Flunkeys (under which
carefully chosen term of opprobrium Mr. Joynes probably includes all classes of domestic servants) are maintained entirely
out of the fairly acquired property of those who employ them.
And by this I mean, of course, not that thieves do not sometimes acquire property unfairly, and even employ domestics
with their ill-gotten gains, but that honest masters and mis-
tresses pay their servants out of the fruits of capital without
inflicting the smallest injury or loss on other classes of workers.
If John and William by diligence and ability acquire more
than enough to keep themselves in ordinary comfort, they are
justified in resting from their labours and spending their superfluous gains in luxuries. John buys horses and carriages and
works of fine art; William hires singers and dancers and
"flunkeys" to wait upon him and amuse him. In what way
does William rob or injure those who are obliged to go on
earning their daily bread any more than John? Surely even
socialists must see that this is a distinction without a difference.
This conclusion in nowise precludes us from giving a hearty
assent to the contention that expenditure on luxuries is not
good for trade or beneficial to the workers.

It is clear that if rich people had better taste than they
seem to have, less would be spent on "luxuries" which are
not luxuries, on things which utterly fail to give the pleasure

2 A

which is expected from them. The money which is spent on Brummagem trinketry, on hideous female apparel, on florid gingerbread architecture, on meretricious painting, and on gorgeous equipages and retinues, will in time to come, when the taste of mankind is elevated, be devoted to the production of things from which more true, lasting, and proportionate pleasure can be derived by educated minds. Meantime, while human nature is what it unfortunately is, we must remember that everything which affords pleasure—even to the unrefined —is useful. Economically there is no other definition of "useful" but "that which gives pleasure directly or indirectly." Flies are useful to spiders, thistles to donkeys, glass beads to Hottentots, and sham jewellery to factory girls. A hundred-weight of each would be of very little use to Mr. Joynes, except to sell to those who appreciate them. Nobody pretends that money spent on "flunkeys" benefits anybody except those who enjoy, or think they must needs enjoy, the services of the "flunkeys"; just as nobody is benefited by a like expenditure on pine-apples or expensive cigars except those who eat and smoke them. At the same time it is a matter that concerns the spenders only. If they demanded even what in our opinion are more useful things, nobody else would benefit, un-less, of course, they happened to be public-spirited, and were pleased to spend their surplus wealth on the gratification of their fellows. But then the question of altruism enters here, and no one has a *right* to complain because his neighbour is not generous. One who lays out a public pleasure-ground is a better citizen than one who lays down a cellar of port for his own drinking. Granted; but we have no right to coerce a rich man to "enjoy" his own wealth in our own way.

There is a lamentable absence of definitions all throughout this *Catechism*, and indeed throughout all socialist works. What *is* waste ? What is useful ? One cannot understand in what sense the terms are employed here. By "useful" I mean all that affords pleasure. The barrel-organgrinder is very useful in an East-end alley, but not at all useful in a West-end square. "Flunkeys" are useful to those who take a real pleasure (no matter how indirectly caused) in their ser-vices. And even the most cultured person finds domestic

servants useful in doing necessary work, which he would otherwise have to perform himself—such as cooking and laundry
work. Socialists cannot honestly believe that the world would
be better if Mr. Herbert Spencer and Lord Tennyson blacked
their own boots. Then by waste I mean the expenditure of
wealth without a corresponding or proportionate attainment of
pleasure. It is wasteful to use seasoned oak for fuel, because
the pleasure effect is small—out of all proportion to the outlay. But socialists regard everything as wasted which does
not go into a poor man's belly. It is all a question of
definition.

All this is meant to lead up to the grand conclusion, the
irrepressible socialist fallacy, that people who earn wealth on
Monday cannot rest and spend it on Tuesday without robbing
those who are working on Tuesday. That is the whole contention in a nutshell. It ought, say they, to be obvious that
a man cannot rest and eat without being indebted to those
who produce the food he eats. But why do the " workers "
supply the " idlers " with food and also with luxuries ? Simply
because the " idlers," that is the *resters*, give them in exchange some of the wealth for which they or their fathers
worked in days gone by. The thing is simple enough, and
yet it is strangely ignored.

And then follows the socialist cure for all this, namely,
compulsory work. But what again *is* work ? M'Culloch
described bubble-blowing and turtle-eating as productive labour.
Mr. Joynes would not dignify these occupations with the title
of work. Then where would he draw the line ? Is dog-training
work ? angling ? scene-painting ? If scene-painting is work,
then acting must also be work, and probably ballet-dancing ; for
work is defined by its *end*. Poets and composers and philosophers
would cease to exist except as amateurs who dabbled in these
studies after work hours, unless the State undertook to define
poetry and music and philosophy, and to recognise some specimens as work. It would then be necessary to declare how many
lines of epic (say, the *Idylls of the King*) should go for an
hour's work in a smithy, or an hour's fishing on the Dogger
Bank. Would all work be measured by time ? Then it would
be necessary to measure the philosopher's work by the time he

took to write out the conclusions he had reached, or else to allow him for thinking ; and the State would have to take precautions to see that when he was apparently sitting still and doing nothing, he was, in fact, *thinking.* And then, if the outcome of his thinking was Mr. Joynes's *Catechism,* the State would have to decide whether it would rank as good work alongside of boot-making or as waste time alongside bubble-blowing. What an absurd slough this socialism lands us into ! Then follow the exceptions in favour of the " old," for which one can see no justification except on the ground that, as a rule, they may be taken to have done their work in the world. And this is just my case for the rich, when once it is admitted that a lawful and moral way of enjoying one's wealth is to make one's children happy. As for Mr. Joynes's exception in favour of the children of the State, I fail to see how they are a " perfectly just charge " upon those who are not responsible for their existence, and who do not happen to care very much about them. We may pass over " the infirm " till we know who they are. Are born idiots included, or confirmed drunkards, or persons ruined by vice, or persons injured by accidents in the course of their work, or in the hunting-field ? Further and better particulars, please, Mr. Joynes. It is already passing clear that under a socialist system the workers would not get the full fruits of their labour. Our mentor glides very swiftly over " certain other deductions for measures of public utility." Which be they ? An army ? A navy ? Courts of justice ? Inspectors ? Paid legislators ? State instructors of youth ? A post-office ? Harbours and lighthouses ? What else ?

   " Theories of Profit " is the title of the next chapter of the *Catechism.* It is a pity that Mr. Joynes enshrouds the problem with which he has to deal with the " money fog." He could have explained his position (the socialist position) without dragging in this political economist's dust-cloud. *Money* has nothing whatever to do with it. We are introduced to the crooked ways of those who make money by gambling either on the race-course or on the stock-exchange, in which case one gambler's gain is another's loss. " But another form of exchange prevails, that of those who, not being workers, produce no goods, but yet have command of money. They exchange their money for goods, and those goods back again into money."

I have not the pleasure of the acquaintance of any of these lunatics. It seems to be an innocent form of amusement; but one cannot help thinking that Mr. Joynes must be unintentionally misrepresenting them. If, at the end of the double process, these amiable persons turn out to have, *as a rule*, more money than they began with, one would suppose they must have done something in addition to what Mr. Joynes has been able to see. No wonder he asks the innocent question, " Then what is the use of the process if they only get money at the end, when they had money at the beginning ? " What indeed ? He thinks it may be that at the second exchange they get more money than they gave at the first. " This fact has been explained by economists by the mere statement that the money-monger either gave less money than the goods were worth at the first exchange or got more than they were worth at the second. But they omit to note the fact that these same money-mongers are in the market both as buyers and sellers, and that without a miracle they cannot all gain on both transactions, but must lose in selling precisely the amount they gain in buying." The economists, then, are represented as saying that " the other fellow " is the lunatic. According to them, there is a class of persons who spend their time in exchanging goods for money, and in buying with that money other goods which are worth *less* than the goods they had to start with. Now Mr. Joynes is unable to credit the existence of this class. Neither does he believe in miracles. Hence he is driven to search for another explanation. The first that he comes across is that decaying old survival from anti-machinery days ; but it is fair to remark that he dismisses it as altogether inadequate to account for all the profits of capitalists who do not work. Indeed it is too small, he says, " to account for a tithe of it."

" Does not this add exchange value to his productions ? Not unless he has a monopoly of the machine, and can thus fear no competition except that of hand labour ; otherwise the exchange value of his goods sinks in proportion to the increased rapidity of their production. If he can make two yards of cloth in the time which he formerly devoted to one, and all other weavers can do the same, the price, or exchange value of

two yards, sinks to the former price of one ; though of course the use
value of two is always greater than that of one.

"Are not monopolies frequent ?   No individual capitalist can keep a
monopoly for any great length of time, as all inventions become common
property at last ; and although it is true that the capitalists as a body
have a monopoly of machinery as against the workers, which adds a
fictitious value to machine-made goods, and will continue to do so until
the workers take control of the machinery, yet this extra value is too
small to account for a tithe of the profits of the money-mongers."

All this seems to show that, reluctantly enough, socialists
recognise that capital of, at all events, one kind has the
" power of creating exchange value in excess of its own cost."
Mr. Joynes prefers to say that labour is itself rendered more
productive by being placed in juxtaposition with this kind of
capital ; just as we might say (with perfect truth) that when
coals are thrown into the fire-box, it is not the coals which
have the power of creating more motive-power ; it is the
engine which accelerates its speed and increases its productiveness, owing to the fact that the coals are there.   Mr. Joynes
would argue that the owner of the engine should have all the
resulting gains, and the owner of the coals none.   Let that
pass ; another explanation has to be found, and this time it is
to a certain extent a substantial explanation.   It is not
sufficient, because it does not explain nearly all the profit of
the capitalist ; but it is true, because it does explain a great
part of it.

" There must be one thing needful which they must be able to buy
in the market in order to make these profits, something which shall itself
have the power of creating exchange value largely in excess of its own
cost, in order that, at the end of the transaction, they may have secured
more money than they have expended.   There is only one thing with
this power, and that is the labourer himself, who offers his labour force
on the market.   Competition compels him to be content with its cost
price, namely, subsistence wages—that is, enough to keep himself and his
family from starvation."

This is the great truth contained in socialism—the jewel
in the dungheap.   There is a soul of truth in almost all false
doctrines, and this is the truth which almost justifies the
existence of socialism.   Too much stress cannot be laid upon
it.   The orthodox political economists not only ignore it, but

flatly deny it. Wage receivers do not receive more and never can receive more, permanently, than subsistence wages, all the fallacious arguments of the economists to the contrary notwithstanding. I sincerely trust that thorough and consistent socialism will spread and prosper until this truth is firmly grasped and acted upon by the manual workers of this and other countries. " The bargain between him and the capitalist requires him to give ten hours or more of work for the cost price of two or three ; and he enters into it because, in spite of all so-called freedom of contract, he has no other choice." To contend that the majority of citizens in a free country have no choice but to put up with a bad bargain is the height of absurdity. I am quite ready to admit that a part of the profit which goes to the capitalist should properly go to the manual worker ; and it *would* go to the manual worker if he had the courage and energy to ask for it. Instead of that he *compels* the capitalist to hire him by time or by the piece, come luck, come loss ; and for this insurance surely the employer must charge. Why should he run a risk for nothing ? If Mr. Joynes ran his own omnibus from Bow to Brixton he would expect to get a profit on his outlay. If, in addition, he also ran my omnibus over the same line, at a hire of £3 a week, payable to me for 'bus and horses—win or lose—he would also expect to make a profit on that. So the employer of wage receivers expects not only a profit on his own capital, but also a profit on his workpeople. He pockets the profits which they forego ; but then they incur no risk of loss. And the effect of their cowardly policy is just this—that they forfeit all along the line the average profits of trade in the country in which they work. In other words, they give away the interest on that valuable property—their own selves. Perhaps some blame does attach to employers as a class for not exerting themselves to enlighten their employees as to their true interest ; but the chief blame rests with the workers themselves, who voluntarily submit to wagedom when the times are ripe for a higher form of industrial organisation. It must be obvious that by shirking their share of risk, wage receivers seriously impair their own efficiency, and thereby again diminish their gains. They will wake up some day without any assistance from socialism or from mawkish philanthropy.

" Has the capitalist no conscience ? " asks the catechist. " Individuals cannot alter the system, even if they would, and the capitalist is now often represented by a company, which, if it had a conscience, could not pay its 5 per cent. After the labourer has produced the price of his own wages, he goes on to produce exchange value, for which he is not paid at all, for the benefit of the capitalist." And this, says he, is surplus value.

Mr. Joynes is very angry with the capitalist. What does he do with the surplus value ? he asks. " He keeps as much as he can for himself under the name of profits of his business." And quite right, too. He keeps *all* the profits on his raw materials and tools, his land and plant, his machinery and horses, and slaves (if any) and wage slaves, and everything else which he has to buy or hire, and for the investment of which he is himself responsible. Mr. Joynes seems to think he does not keep it *all*, but he does, every penny of it. Of course he has to buy his raw materials and plant, and to feed his horses and find fuel for his engines ; to pay rent for the "loan " of the land he uses (if it is not his own property), and wages or rent for the loan of the labourers he uses (if they are not his own property), and so forth. It matters little what we *call* these payments. He has to pay them, and he expects his profit, and, as a rule, he gets it; and when he gets it he sticks to it. Mr. Joynes thinks he does not keep quite all, because out of it he has to pay landlords, other capitalists from whom he has borrowed capital, bankers and brokers who have effected these loans for him, middlemen who sell his wares to the public, and finally, the public, in order to induce them to buy from him instead of from rival manufacturers. " And he tries to justify this appropriation of surplus value by his class on the ground that capital has the power of breeding and producing interest by as natural a process as the reproduction of animals."

Yes, so far as the profits on his own capital are concerned, he does so persuade himself, if he thinks at all. Some do not. He has seen apples grow on an apple-tree without any human assistance whatever, and he has seen a windmill working away without any more than the smallest help from man ; he has seen machinery producing wealth out of all proportion to the labour which is expended in attending to it.   He fails to see anything absolutely inconceivable in the idea of a monster engine worked by concentrated solar heat or tidal action which, without any assistance from living men, shall produce, continuously, articles of use to a lazy generation.   He regards this as highly improbable, even in the distant future; but inasmuch as it is not inconceivable, it completely knocks the bottom out of the socialist notion that only the living workers have a right to the products of industry.

It is odd, thinks our author, that the capitalist can find any dupes to believe in so absurd a theory, but he instils a genuine belief into himself and others that this is the case.   " From which the inference is, that the labourer ought to be grateful to the capitalist for furnishing him with employment.   Whereas, the labourers really have to thank the capitalist for defrauding them of three-quarters of the fruits of their toil, and rendering leisure, education, and natural enjoyment almost impossible for them to attain."   I am glad to be among the " dupes," and am much obliged to Mr. Joynes for giving some of us credit for a *genuine* belief.   But the inference as to the labourer's gratitude does not follow.   No thanks are due either way. Each does the best he can for himself, and asks for no testimonials.

The eighth chapter of the *Catechism* deals with " objections "; but that title would not be enough.   Mr. Joynes must knock his antagonist down before shaking hands; so the chapter is entitled " Inadequate Objections."   Most people would prefer to prove the inadequacy of the objections before stigmatising them; but socialists will be socialists.   If socialists happen to be poor, he says, they are described as interested schemers for the overthrow of an excellent society in order that, being themselves idle and destitute, they may be able to seize upon the wealth accumulated by more industrious people.   If rich, they must obviously be insincere in their socialism, or they would at once give away all their capital, instead of denouncing what they themselves possess.   The charge of interested motives is invariably brought by socialists against all who uphold existing institutions.   And how should individualists meet the charge ? With contempt. The idea that those who prosper under the present just system have no right to uphold it because they are gainers by it, is too absurd to require refutation. Persons who fling this charge about on either side may safely be left out of calculation. But the charge against the rich socialists requires a little more attention.

" In a capitalist society, the mere purchasing of an article in the market involves the exploitation of the labourers who produced it ; and this is not in any way remedied or atoned for by giving away the article afterwards to somebody else. The owner of capital cannot prevent it from exploiting the labourers by giving it away. It cannot be used as socialism enjoins, except under an organised system of socialism. The wealthy socialist can mitigate the severity of competition in all his personal relations. Beyond that he could do nothing except use his wealth in helping on the socialist cause."

There is an element of truth in all this ; but it is not quite accurate. It is correct to say that the wealthy capitalist with socialist leanings cannot, *after* making his profits by wagedom, remedy or atone for it by giving it away to somebody else, but there are two things he might do : he might give back his profits, not to somebody else, but to the workpeople who earned it for him ; or, secondly, he could refrain from employing wage earners at all, and insist on co-operating with free labourers for the production of new wealth. Of course I do not recommend either expedient, but I say that they are both open to honest and wealthy socialists.

Clearly, if a capitalist adopted the first course, namely, that of returning the interest on labour to the labourers, he would be running all their risk for nothing, while they would have lacked all the stimulus to industry which such risk (and corresponding chance of gain) affords. If he adopted the second course, which at some future time will be a prudent course, he would have to spend most of his time in looking round for thrifty, provident, honest, and industrious co-workers, who know their own value, and are willing to invest their labours and take the risks. Such men are not easy to find to-day, because our manual workers have hardly yet emerged from the wagedom stage of industrialism. Just as slaves could not be converted into wage earners in a generation, so neither can

wage earners be transmuted at once into free workers. They
lack *mutual trust.*

How may socialists reply to the taunt that their scheme
is impracticable ? " By quoting the opinion of J. S. Mill that the
difficulties of socialism are greatly over-rated ; and they should
declare that, so far from being an impracticable Utopian
scheme, it is the necessary and inevitable result of the historical
evolution of society." Now the quotation from Mill merely
shows either that Mill himself *under-rated* the difficulties of
socialism, or that he used the term in a sense different from
that in which it is nowadays understood. For the second retort,
namely, that socialism is inevitable, I cannot give Mr. Joynes
much credit. I might with equal eloquence rejoin, " It isn't."

And now we are introduced to a remarkable confusion
of ideas, with which socialists invariably try to cajole the
advocates of any form of co-operation—the pretence that all
co-operation is socialistic. As though there were no difference
between voluntary co-operation and compulsory co-operation.
This is exactly the *whole* difference between socialism and individualism ; for both look forward to increased co-ordination
of industry. It is therefore no proof of advancing socialism
to point out the fact of an increasing tendency towards co-
operative production.

And here we come to a compromising and even damning
admission. Individualism has, we are told, prepared the way
and rendered socialism practicable. Socialists are to take
advantage of the good which individualism has done. But if
the results of individualism up to the present are satisfactory,
and even essential to further progress, one may be excused for
suggesting that it might be as well to let it alone, and trust to
its further development. A system which has worked well
from the year one down to to-day may surely be tried a little
longer before being condemned. " Cut it down ; why cumbereth
it the ground?" is not a wise sentence, even in the case of a tree
which produces no fruit : still less of one which admittedly
produces good fruit.

It is not necessary to dispute the proposition that if the
State were to "take into its own hands," that is, to *steal* (Mr.
Joynes is sometimes very fond of that word !) the capital of

capitalists, and to divide its proceeds among the workers only, the workers would gain by the arrangement, pecuniarily, for a few years. Similarly, if the railways were taken away from those who own them and given to the shipowners or the omnibus conductors, the latter would be gainers. I am superstitious enough to hold that stolen riches never bring lasting prosperity; but I admit the recipients would temporarily be wealthier for the "transaction." There is no better illustration of the inefficiency of State trading than that adduced by Mr. Joynes himself—the post-office. Is he really ignorant of the reason why private capitalists cannot compete with the State ? Is he not aware that the State rigidly enforces its monoply in the most tyrannical and overbearing manner, and that, but for this, it would long ago have been so far out-distanced by private enterprise as to be a laughing-stock and an eyesore ? The same precaution might, it is true, be taken in the case of State railways ; and then, surely enough, private enterprise would be unable to compete. But remove the heavy hand of the State, and I will give Mr. Joynes the whole of the existing capital of the country to start with (without compensation), and undertake to leave him and his state miles behind in the race in half a dozen years. I fear he has never studied the history of the railway system in India, or compared the progress of railways on the Continent and in England. I would also commend to his notice the writings of Lysander Spooner on State letter-carrying.

And now the question arises, Would the expropriated capitalists be entitled to compensation ? The reply is noteworthy. " As a matter of principle it is unjust to compensate the holders of stolen goods out of the pockets of those who have suffered the theft ; but it might be expedient to grant some compensation in the shape of annuities." No. Injustice is never expedient. If capitalists have really stolen their wealth, it cannot be expedient to compensate them for restoring it to the rightful owners. Here we must be more uncompromising than the socialists themselves. But first show how a man who has refrained from at once consuming the produce of his labour can be said to have stolen it when an interval of time has elapsed between its production and its

consumption. This plunder part of his program is evidently
very distasteful to Mr. Joynes himself. He glides quickly over
it. He proposes a compromise and compensation. And he
passes rapidly on to a more congenial topic—the tendency of
the evolution of society. It tends, we are told, always towards
more complex organisation, and to a greater interdependence
of all men upon each other; each individual becoming more
and more helpless by himself, but more and more powerful as
part of a mightier society. And yet, says he, it is not true
that individuality would be crushed by socialism. On the
contrary, it is crushed by the present state of society, and
would then alone be fairly developed.

Yes, individuality is sorely crippled by wagedom; but it
would be altogether paralysed by socialism. Freedom is a
slow development. It must be worked out on the present
lines without any breach of continuity or artificial cataclysm.
The increasing dependence of man upon his fellows—upon
society as an organism—is an undeniable fact, which individualists recognise as readily as socialists:—

> "Knowledge comes, but wisdom lingers, and I linger on the shore,
> And the individual withers, and the world is more and more."

The whole history of civilisation is the history of a struggle
to establish a relation between society and its units, which is
neither absolute socialism nor absolute anarchy (in the old and
absurd sense of the absence of co-ordination and voluntary
regulation), but a state in which, by action and reaction of
each upon each, such an adaptation shall take place that the
welfare of the whole, and that of the units, shall eventually
become coincident and not antagonistic.

No class of persons, as a rule, speak so contemptuously of
authority as socialists. It is therefore surprising what delight
they always manifest when they can exhume any passage from
the works of leading political economists which can be twisted
into something like an approval of their theories. Mr. Joynes
quotes Mill and Fawcett. Mill says: "The restraints of
communism would be freedom in comparison with the present
condition of the majority of the human race. The generality
of labourers in this and most other countries have as little

choice of occupation or freedom of locomotion—are practically as dependent on fixed rules and on the will of others—as they could be in any system short of actual slavery." Fawcett is cited as saying that there is no choice of work or possibility of change for the factory hand, and that the boy who is brought up to the plough must remain at the plough-tail to the end of his days. There is nothing in this with which individualists quarrel. Every capitalisationist affirms the evil of wagedom quite as emphatically as Mill himself, or the socialists. Two medical men may agree about a disease without for a moment concurring as to the proper cure.

But let us see what these witnesses have to say about the proposed cure. Mill's essay " On Liberty " is too well known to need quotation. It is one long indictment of socialism. Take this passage from the fifth chapter: " If the roads, the railways, the banks, the insurance offices, the great joint-stock companies, the universities, and the public charities were all of them branches of the Government; if, in addition, the municipal corporations and local boards, with all that now devolves on them, became departments of the central administration ; if the employees of all these different enterprises were appointed and paid by the Government, and looked to the Government for every rise in life, not all the freedom of the Press and popular constitution of the Legislature would make this or any other country free otherwise than in name. And the evil would be greater, the more efficiently and scientifically the administrative machinery was constructed, the more skilful the arrangements for obtaining the best qualified hands and heads with which to work it." Mr. Fawcett's pamphlet on State Socialism is less known. He ends it by saying: " The conclusion which, above all, we desire to enforce is that any scheme, however well-intentioned it may be, will indefinitely increase every evil it seeks to alleviate if it lessens individual responsibility by encouraging the people to rely less upon themselves and more upon the State." If these are the authorities Mr. Joynes puts forward on behalf of socialism, he is welcome to the support he obtains. But of course the case is not left to rest on authority. It has been urged against socialism that it will take away all the incentives to exertion, and induce universal idleness in consequence. "On the contrary," says our author, "it will apply the strongest *incentive* to all alike, for all must work if they wish to eat, while at present large classes are exempted by the accident of birth from the necessity of working at all." And to the objection that socialism will destroy culture and refinement by *compelling* the leisured classes who have a monopoly of them to do some honest work, he replies that on the contrary it will bring the opportunity of culture and refinement to all by putting an end to the wearisome labour that continues all day long; while the leisured class will learn by experience that work is a necessity for perfect culture.

Mr. Joynes has not yet mastered the moral of the fable of the Sun and the Wind. He does not distinguish between persuasion and force. He jumbles up together as incentives to industry the love of knowledge and the ambition of the scholar with the birch rod of the pedagogue. In a sense these may all be said to be *incentives* to work. But those which socialism would relax are the internal incentives; those which socialism would substitute for them are external—coercion. It would certainly be better for everybody if those among the leisured classes who, having enough to live on, prefer to idle away their time, could be induced or persuaded to work at something useful to mankind. It would also be better for themselves. Most of their class do. But to coerce those who do not choose to work would be to place the liberties of one set of citizens in the keeping of another set. Possibly Mr. Joynes would make an excellent task-master. I believe he has had some experience in furnishing incentives to industry to leisured specimens of the rising generation. I do not wish to be understood as implying that Mr. Joynes would not make the best task-master procurable. My contention is that liberty is better than any task-master; and that in the long run it will bring about the best quality and most desirable quantity of work. "Wearisome labour that continues all day long" is inefficient labour. The best quality of labour is that which cannot be continued all day long. Slovenly, shirking, scamping drudgery can hardly be dignified with the title of labour at all. The *incentives* of the stick and the sack do not stimulate to the highest quality of industry. The best work is even now done by the leisured class under a short-hours' system. And if, as Mr. Joynes contends, " work is a necessity for perfect culture " (which I admit), so culture is a necessity for perfect work. We have a great field before us in trying to reform the *tastes* of all classes. Labour is wasted in supplying that for which there may indeed be an effectual demand, but which affords an absurdly small amount of gratification in proportion to its labour cost. This cannot be changed by State action.

When we urge that State management would give rise to jobbery and corruption, he replies by pointing to the present State organisation of the police and the post-office, in neither of which are jobbery and corruption conspicuous features. It is odd to find a leading socialist proclaiming the purity of the police. Perhaps I may refer to the socialist organs for a refutation of this amiable contention. A Radical member of Parliament lately declared that, to his knowledge, nearly all the unfortunate women in his neighbourhood paid black-mail to the police. Mr. Joynes might find corroborative evidence of this if he would make a tour of the public-houses and ascertain the conditions of their freedom from police espionage and interference. As for the post-office, I will refer not to the organs of socialism, but to the organs of individualism for the proofs of official purity or the reverse. A few questions have in the present Parliament been asked of Mr. Raikes about some singular promotions in the post-office. But apart from corruption, what about the more crushing charge of inefficiency and incapacity? Take the telegraph department or the parcels post. Or compare the success of a private firm of letter-carriers in America with that of the State department, even when the former was handicapped to the extent of 60 per cent! If no better examples of State action can be adduced on behalf of the State socialism of the future than the police and the post-office, the less said the better. Socialists would do well to rely on the magnificence of the unknown.

Having demolished these objections to his own satisfaction, Mr. Joynes proceeds to pulverise another, which it is not my business to sustain—the cuckoo cry—that if you make all men equal to-day they will all be unequal to-morrow, because of their different natural capabilities. But, says he, what socialists aim at is equality of opportunities, not of natural powers. There are scores of unnoticed objections to socialism besides the "cuckoo cry," which no individualist ever puts forward, except in reply to some of the cruder proposals of ignorant communists, to whom it is neither necessary nor wise to reply at all. If the "cuckoo cry" has ever been raised by an interlocutor to the "scientific socialism" advocated by the author of the *Catechism*, it must be that such interlocutor was a bad advocate of a good cause, and not worth powder and shot.

Mr. Joynes proceeds to expound the doctrine that those who are especially gifted by nature owe a larger return to the community than those who are less naturally gifted. But why should we repay to the community what we owe to nature? Why pay B what A has lent us?

"But capitalists, instead of acknowledging this debt, *arrange*," says our teacher, "that persons of extra industry and talent shall have every opportunity of enslaving their less fortunate neighbours, thus adding an inequality of conditions to the natural inequality of talent."

"Capitalists *arrange!*" How can capitalists arrange to enslave their fellow-citizens? Are they strong enough to resist a combination of their less fortunate neighbours, if those neighbours refuse to fall into the arrangement? If so, Mr. Joynes may as well stop his preaching. He and the "less fortunate neighbours" will have to do as they are told. The strong· will have their way. But if the "less fortunate neighbours" are capable of putting a stop to this one-sided "arrangement," why do they not do it? There is no need for socialism. Those who are capable of inaugurating a socialistic régime are equally capable of breaking up the present *arrangement* by which certain persons (presumably weaker than themselves) pocket the proceeds of their work. Mr. Joynes does not tell us how the weak can arrange to despoil the strong. Nor, on the other hand, if the despoilers are the strong, how the weak are going to shear them of their Samson locks by the mere process of talking socialism.

We have now reached the ninth chapter, entitled " Gluts and their Results." It should be carefully read and considered by all. It is well and clearly put, and, but for a few hints at the cure for the evil, might have been written by a capitalisationist. It may be divided into two parts, which, unfortunately, are inextricably woven together. The one part describes the evil to be remedied, and points out the futility of the proposals of " reformers," and is, in the main, admirably done. The other part sets forth the remedy proposed by socialism. This part is clearly and ably written, but embodies some fundamental fallacies, and would, if accepted, result in national disaster— the very first to suffer being the wage receivers, in whose interest it is put forward. The chapter now under consideration belongs for the most part to the pathological division of the subject, and demands very little adverse criticism, except in so far as it attributes the evils to the wilful malfeasance of a particular class of persons.

The periodical depression of trade, with its accompanying distress among the labourers, is said to be due to the fact that individualist capitalists are striving to enrich themselves alone, instead of co-operating to supply the needs of the community. " During a period of activity, when prices are high and the markets for goods are not overstocked, a great competition goes on among capitalists, who wish to take advantage of the high prices and produce more quickly the goods which can command them. And the effect of this competition is that all the available labourers are employed ; all the machinery is set going ; and no effort is spared by the manufacturers to produce the utmost quantities of the goods which are in demand on the market."

Truly, the love of money is the root of much evil ; but under a system of capitalisation, that is, of free labour, capitalists would not receive such abnormally enhanced profits (by " capitalists " I here mean the owners of non-human capital), and the workers would be less likely to push a rising market to extremes. And what, it is asked, is the inevitable result ? A glut is shortly created of these goods. Far more than were wanted have been made. All the store-houses are full and no more purchasers are to be found. The capitalists soon get tired of heaping up what they cannot sell, and wish to stop production. They turn off all their extra hands, and propose such a reduction of wages that the rest agree to strike rather than accept it. Production is stopped for a time, and the capitalists are not obliged to pay wages, or else agree to pay only for half time until the glut has gradually disappeared as the goods are absorbed by the public. A fresh demand arises. The workers are all employed again, and the glut recurs with the utmost regularity. Now there is not the smallest necessity, says Mr. Joynes, for this periodical distress.

In the main this is true, but as a statement it is surely a little dogmatic. Will it be denied that slavery itself was necessary at an earlier stage of industrial evolution? Wage-dom is necessary now ; but whether the day is not nigh when it will no longer be necessary, with all its concomitant gluts and strikes and distress, is the question we want to find the answer to.

Here is a queer passage which seems to show the cloven hoof of despotism, always to be found under the garments of socialism. Mr. Joynes must be taken to aim at the enthrone-ment of some High Priest of Humanity who knows better than his fellow-creatures what is good for them, and who is endowed with powers to compel them to make what he thinks useful or desirable instead of what they themselves choose to make : " That which vitiates the whole system of production at present is the prevailing idea that goods are not to be produced for the sake of their usefulness, but for the sake of making a profit for capitalists and giving employment to labourers." But surely it is the demand of the general consumer which causes things to be made ; the profit of capitalists is merely the intermediate cause. Of course if there were no effectual demand for *apparently* useless things, there would be no profit in making them. If a tawdry chromo gives more pleasure to the frequenters of an inn-parlour than one of Meissonier's finest masterpieces, the chromo is actually the more useful of the two for the inn-keeper's purpose. Mr. Joynes wants a high priest to forbid the creation of works of bad art. Individualists may regret the prevalence of bad taste in all things, but they hold that the consumer is the only judge of what is useful. If "cheap and nasty" wares drive dear and sound wares out of the market, that is the fault of the consumer—of the people themselves, whose tastes are imperfectly educated. Besides, the State has no right to call things nasty if they please those who demand them. Mr. Joynes may call them nasty, and we may agree with him, but to the State nothing is nasty except that which the people dislike. Adulteration is not bad when the purchaser prefers a cheap and adulterated article. Fifteen carat gold is no nastier than eighteen carat. Some men would prefer three shoddy coats of different cut and colour to one broadcloth coat which would outwear the whole three, provided the three coats cost altogether no more than the one coat. In that case the shoddy coats are more useful than the broadcloth.

When fraud comes in, the case is altered. But large profits are not the cause of fraudulent adulteration. The consumer is again to blame. His foible is cheapness in disregard of quality. And the manual workers are the greatest sinners in this respect. I have no wish to make light of adulteration. Union is the cure for fraudulent adulteration. For open adulteration there is no cure but steady reform of the people's taste. There is no more hideous sight on this disfigured earth than a party of workpeople in their "Sunday clothes." And surely the abominations which do duty for "ornaments" in their houses cannot be set down to poverty. A cultured person would find it both cheaper and pleasanter to be without such ornaments.

Mr. Joynes is justly wroth with those well-meaning reformers who do not understand the labour question, but who are constantly calling on the workers to be sober and thrifty.

"As addressed to the individual struggling against his neighbours under the capitalist system, this advice is excellent. It may enable him to rise into the capitalist class, that is, to exchange his position in the ranks of the oppressed for one in those of the oppressors. But as a panacea for the wrongs of the system, or as a cure for the sufferings of the labourers *as a class*, it is inadequate, because a general improvement in intelligence, thrift, and sobriety, if shared by the whole class of labourers, merely supplies the capitalist class with a better instrument for the production of surplus value."

Such also is the result of improvement in the ability of the workers under the present system. It is not easy to improve upon all this. So long as the workers accept wages it is useless to hope for a general improvement in their condition. Individually they may become better instruments of production, in which case a larger number of them may be enabled to exist on the planet. Some people would define civilisation itself by this feature. For example, M. Eugène Simon, in his work on China, says: "We speak of that state as most *civilised* in which on a given area the largest possible number of human beings are able to procure and distribute most equally among themselves the greatest amount of wealth, liberty, justice and security." It is true that this trait is, as a rule, an accompaniment of high civilisation, but it is not the essential attribute of it. If life is in itself a good, then the more the merrier. Let us have a well-packed planet:

> " But what is life ?
> 'Tis not to stalk about and draw fresh air
> From time to time, or gaze upon the sun ;
> 'Tis to be free. When liberty is gone,
> Life grows insipid, and has lost its relish."

It is hard to see of what use a large population is, unless the life is a happier and more beautiful life than that now lived in " civilised countries " by the great bulk of the people. Doubtless thrift, sobriety, hard work, and above all " Malthusianism," give those who practise them an advantage in competing with other individual workpeople similarly situated. And to this extent the advice is sound ; but it should not be overlooked that while thrift and parsimony, if general, would increase population, the Malthusian practise would not tend to diminish it. The richer classes invariably adopt the plan of late marriages, and middle-class people of moderate means adopt other prudential restraints ; and it is sensible advice to the still poorer classes to follow their example. But from a Race point of view the advice must be justified (if at all) on very different grounds from those usually adduced. Is it wise to check the increase of wise people while that of the imprudent goes on with increased facility by reason of the gap left by their more provident fellows ? And yet self-control brings unforeseen blessings in its train.

Mr. Joynes excuses social reformers on the ground that they seem incapable of understanding either the inefficiency in one way or the efficacy in another of their well-meant advice to the labourers as a class. I am not disposed to credit "social reformers" with the degree of incapacity necessary to justify them in preaching the doctrines they do. There is something a little worse than incapacity about the sleek preacher who goes up to men living on subsistence wages, or, perhaps, altogether out of work, and recommends them to try "thrift." At the same time thrift falls into the category of the self-regarding virtues, and does not deserve all the hard things said of it by those who see that it is of no use as a class panacea.

Our author rejects the Malthusian doctrine. He says it is perfectly true that a limited space of land cannot support an unlimited number of people, but as even England, to say nothing of the world, has not reached that limit to population, it has at present no bearing on the case. The Chinese seem to have recognised this truth. "In regard to population," says M. Simon,[1] "the Chinese far exceed us (the French), and while we complain of the excess of ours, which we endeavour to restrain by wars, celibacy, and voluntary sterilisation, the Chinese continue to multiply as if the earth were without limits. Correctly enough; they have no fear of the result, for the fertility of the land depends not upon its extent but upon the quantity of labour applied to it."

It is perfectly true, say the socialists, that in the present capitalist system the man who has no children at all is in a better pecuniary position than the man with a large family, since, just as in actual warfare, children in the modern competitive battle-field are an encumbrance where every man has to fight for his living, and maintain his family as best he may. But the standpoint of the Malthusians differs from that of the socialists, inasmuch as the former accept the basis of the capitalist society—namely, the existence of two distinct classes of wage payers and wage earners—and merely advise the workers to attempt to secure a larger wage. Now this

---

[1] *China: its Social, Political and Religious Life.* By G. Eug. Simon. Sampson Low, 1887.

result would not be attained by following the advice of the Malthusians, except, as I have said, by individuals. The wage-earning *class* would gain nothing by it, except the satisfaction of being more productive instruments for the creation of wealth.

Apart from the political or social aspect of this question, there is an economic criticism on the above treatment of Malthusianism which ought to be made. Mr. Joynes makes the somewhat shallow " Georgian " observation that England has not yet reached the population limit, and that therefore Malthus's law does not apply. We may perhaps attribute this remark to carelessness; for it is obvious that all peoples, civilised and savage, have reached the limit. Possibly there are rare occasions (though it would be difficult to point to them) in which the population of a tribe or nation has doubled every twelve and a half years. This is the rate (according to Euler) at which Europeans tend to increase under a system of unlimited supply of necessaries and absolute freedom from plagues, wars, etc. If wheat and meat could be had for nothing in the British Isles, the population would be just about eighty millions at the end of this century.

The chapter closes with the usual socialistic appeal to brute force. It is a pity socialists make such a display of *drapeau rouge*. Every reform rests ultimately on the will of the strong. Socialism has no monopoly of democratic stability. Neither is there any reason (beyond its own inherent logical rottenness) why this doctrine should not be accepted by the effective majority in this country and put into practice without any appeal to force. It might lose its attractions for some of its supporters. Stripped of its fireworks and barricades and trumpets and little red caps, it might appear too humdrum and commonplace for the bulk of the party, but it would gain considerably in the respect of sensible men and women who have grown out of the heroic age. " The workers' claim is likely to be attended to as soon as ever the majority of the workers really understand their own position, and consequently become convinced of the advantages of socialism ; and as for the capitalists, though appeals to justice may make isolated conversions of individual capitalists, nothing short of a display of organised force will enable the idlers, as a body, to perceive the advantage of taking their due share in the necessary work of society under a just system of socialism." It is a pity to cast a damper on all this ardour. Many of us also look forward to the day when all classes of workers will rebel against wagedom. When they do this they will receive the full fruits of their labour, neither more nor less. At present they forfeit the whole of the profits on their labour, with the indirect effect of reducing their own efficiency and removing the natural incentives to healthy and happy work. The prospect at the far end of the vista opened by capitalisation is quite as ravishing as, and more " realistic " than that painted (in lovely colours, it is true) by William Morris. It wants an equal artist. It is not the pictures in the socialist gallery, but the men at the door that shatter our nerves with the splitting trumpet and deafening drum. If only for ten minutes, please, Mr. Joynes, *con sordini*.

We have now reached the tenth and last chapter of this singular production. It is hardly necessary to mention the title. No work on socialism would be in order without a chapter entitled " Revolution ! " To be orthodox, it ought to be printed in blood-colour, but we are fain to put up with black in a penny pamphlet printed in small type on flimsy paper. Unfortunately the good sense which characterises the *Catechism* throughout the other nine chapters (though interlaced with fallacies) is entirely absent in this final effort. It must be admitted that it is difficult for a sane man to write anything readable on such a silly theme as revolution. It is absolutely necessary to intentionally jumble up two distinct meanings of the term. All social changes, when complete, are styled revolutions. We constantly hear of the revolution brought about by the invention of the steam-engine, of revolutions in manners and in tastes, and in social habits and customs. But in another and a narrower sense the word is understood to signify the upheaval of the governed classes against their rulers—a successful rebellion. The attempt to confound the revolution of printing with the democratic irruption under Oliver Cromwell is simply to play upon words—to make a heavy joke at the expense of the gaping fat-heads who usually do duty for the advance guard of socialism. Mr. Joynes stoops to perpetrate this antic, as we shall see ; but he begins by pointing out a real evil in competition. It tends to retard the evolution of altruism. No one disputes it. There is never a rose without a thorn, as the lying proverb truly says. It must be shown that the evil outweighs the good before it can be held to condemn the source of both. And as for saying that Man rises superior to Nature, and that he is not subject to natural laws, no one's *ipse dixit* is enough to sustain such a contention. Men can alter their surroundings, while lower animals cannot, we are told. But if some men not only can, but do alter their surroundings for the better, and maintain the change, then it surely follows that such men were and are the fittest. If Mr. Joynes believes that it is the destiny of man to live in filth, foul air, and squalor, it is his duty to bring men into harmony with such conditions with the greatest possible expedition and the least friction. It is cruel to keep up a class of men hostile to their destiny and artificially cultured against their nature. If he does not take this low view of humanity he should be content to remove all hindrances of an artificial kind to the operation of natural laws, among which is that of natural selection.

" Capitalists defend the principle of competition on the ground that it brings into play a man's best qualities ; this is occasionally its result ; but it also brings out its worst qualities by stimulating him to struggle with his fellows for the relative improvement of his own position, rather than for the absolute advancement of the interests of all. Because in ordinary competition one man's gain is another's loss. The theory of the survival of the fittest is that the class of persons who are most fitted to live and propagate their race in the conditions with which it is surrounded is certain to survive the rest ; but such are the existing social conditions that they favour the survival of the most valueless."

This question of the ultimate result of the survival of the fittest has been much debated, alike in the zoological and in the social world. The common fly of the window-pane seems to be gradually exterminating his more able-bodied relative, the blue-bottle. The fine old black rat of our ancestors is as dead as Diana of the Ephesians ; and his successor is as inferior to him in physique as a Cockney counter-jumper is inferior to a mailed warrior of feudal England. Can we then put our trust in natural selection ? Or shall we follow the socialists, and pin our faith to artificial selection ? Much has been done by that process among domestic animals and plants, and much more will be done. But we must bear in mind that in all such cases there is a selected type fixed upon by a higher mind—that of man. Is man prepared to decide the future type of humanity ? He must be a bold man or a fool who undertakes the task. Selection is either natural or artificial. Socialists professing evolutionism advocate artificial selection ; whereas individualists prefer to put their trust in natural selection, because, while the good results of artificial selection are *limited by human prescience*, those of natural selection are unlimited.

" The final result of such conditions and surroundings as the filth, foul air, and squalor of a town rookery is the crushing out of those who are least able to adapt themselves to these surroundings, and the consequent survival of those who are most fit for filth, but least for decent social life ; and the law of the survival of the fittest does not affect men in the same way as it affects the lower animals, because it is possible for men to alter their surroundings, while other animals must simply adapt themselves to them, whatever they may be."

But then we are confronted with the question, What is the end of life ? Is it better that there should be one living being supremely happy, or a million fairly comfortable, or a thousand millions whose pains outweigh their pleasures ? Is consciousness itself an evil ? Would it not be *better* (whatever that may mean) if there were no human beings ? We cannot tell. But assuming that life is worth living—as we must if politics are worth discussing—then that social system which enables the largest population to get subsistence out of a given area is *primâ facie* the best system. And the system of unlimited competition seems to satisfy that requirement. At all events, nobody has shown, or pretended to show, that any other system will produce a *better* result— using the word *better* in the sense of " productive of a larger sum-total of pleasure-feeling sentient beings." This weighing of happiness by the ton of flesh seems a coarse proceeding, but it is also the only mode of comparison available. However,

Mr. Joynes does not dwell long on this aspect of the subject : he flies off to his orthodox socialist joke :

"What is the revolution for which socialists strive ? It is a Revolution in the methods of the distribution of wealth corresponding to that which has already taken place in the means of its production. For wealth is now almost entirely produced by great numbers of men working in concert, instead of by individual effort, as in former times ; while individuals still possess command of its distribution, and use their power in their own interests. Now, forms of government are changed so as to readjust them to the economical changes in the forms of production which have been silently evolving in the body of society by means of Revolutions ; for instance, the French Revolution of 1789."

Here we have it—the revolution, " which has already taken place in the means of production," is thrown into the same category with the French Revolution of 1789. The word Revolution occurs seven times in this chapter, and each time it is spelt with a big R. The word " change " is spelt with a small " c "; words like " feudalism," and " capitalism," and " aristocracy," are not printed with capital letters. Then why is this absurd distinction conferred upon the word revolution ? It is a small matter, but it is very significant. It is part and parcel of that rather ridiculous habit that socialists have contracted of tricking themselves out as heroes and swash-bucklers. It reminds one of little boys making themselves paper helmets; and there is not the slightest evidence to show that, like some of those valiant urchins, they would not run screaming away if the cat jumped out of the cupboard.

Leaving Mr. Joynes in the proud possession of his big R and his paper helmet, let us see what ground there is for saying that the structures of states are adapted to their functions, as a general rule, by revolutions. The " cataclysm " theory is abandoned even in geology. " Sudden appearances upon the planet " of vegetable and animal species are not now spoken of except by very ill-educated persons, and those who are paid to disseminate untruth. Then how is it that the pioneers of a new political system should be found planting their foundations on the old-fashioned doctrine of " jumps " ? The only instance furnished by Mr. Joynes is the locally-circumscribed though dramatically-thrilling *bouleversement* which took place in

France just a century ago.   We are asked to regard this irruption as the cause of the demolition of feudalism.   Doubtless it did accompany the consummation of that historic change in that part of Europe; but how is it that feudalism disappeared in other parts of Europe?   This sort of stuff reminds one of the old palæontology.   The Tigris and Euphrates have more than once overflowed their banks, but that does not quite explain the existence of "stone cockles" on the Great Orme's Head.   We should have more faith in "scientific socialism," if its form and method were more in line with latter-day science.

That the French Revolution failed to attain its objects is admitted:

"But its objects were not those at which socialists aim.   It was merely the political expression of the fact that feudalism was demolished, and the reign of capitalism established on its ruins.   It ended in the overthrow of the political supremacy of the landed aristocracy, and the establishment of a bourgeois plutocracy; that is, putting the political power into the hands of the merchants and money-lords of the middle class.   The change in the forms of production which rendered this inevitable was the fact that the possession of agricultural land had ceased to be the chief means to the attainment of wealth.   The possession of capital and the use of machinery had taken its place."

To be more accurate than Mr. Joynes, agriculture had declined relatively to other forms of industry.   Trade and manufacture absorbed a larger proportion of the world's capital.   The contrast between aristocracy and plutocracy is altogether misleading.   When the landowners were the richest class of the community they were the plutocrats.   When the manufacturers and traders take a predominant part in the Government, so long as they are comparatively few, we have an aristocracy.   Mr. Joynes uses the terms as though "blue blood" had not lost its fascination for him.   The change which took place was simply a change from the rule of a few to the rule of a few more.   And as time moves on, more and more are added to the number of the ruling class; till now, in this country and in France and America we have completed the change properly described as the democratic revolution. And I use the term without a palpitating heart or a flashing eye or a big R, for I have no wish to infringe the socialists' monopoly.

Finally, we reach the grand consummation. There is something very lofty in the purity and abnegation of the classes who are next going to snatch at the tiller. There is no selfish greed about them. The "bourgeois" rebels grasped at power for their own " bourgeois " ends. They cared nothing for the poor " prolétaire." Socialists are not as other men ; they do not aim at the supremacy of their class at the expense of other sections. No ; they will force other sections to adopt their views, to do as they are bid, and to fall into the socialist section, and so all will be happy. " We don't wish to persecute those who differ from us in opinion, therefore let them be quick and adopt our opinion, or take the consequences." That is the gist of the following argument.

" The French Revolution was a selfish struggle, because after the displacement of the upper by the middle class in political and social supremacy, the latter established its own power irrespectively of the rights of any other class. But the struggle which precedes and heralds the Social Revolution is not one of selfish class interests in the same way, for socialists do not aim at the supremacy of a class or section of the community at the expense of other sections. True ; they wish the workers to control the State, but this is not the supremacy of a class, for they insist that every able-bodied person of sound mind should do a fair share of necessary work. When all are workers, the workers will be no longer a class, but a nation. Selfishness will then become public spirit, when the motives which formerly led men to work for the interests and advancement of themselves alone operate for the benefit of the whole human race with which their class has become identified."

We shall all be Czars then, and there will be no more serfs. That is the end of socialism—and of the *Catechism*.

CHAPTER XII

SINCE sociology is an inductive science; since Society is an organism which has by no means reached its highest and final development; it is clear that a system of politics based on *à priori* reasoning is necessarily inapplicable to the concrete at any given stage of social evolution. When a friend asks, " What ought I to do under these difficult circumstances ? " one does not answer, " Do right," or " Choose the path of virtue." Similarly when a practical statesman seeks for guiding principles of action, it seems a mockery to say, " Study the greatest happiness of the greatest number," or " So act as to ensure the greatest liberty of each compatible with the equal liberty of all." And yet these and the like are the only rules of action furnished by the absolutist schools, be they socialist or individualist. Anarchy may and probably does supply a sound leading idea of perfection towards which we may strive, but it cannot furnish the working drawings from which we must construct our governmental machine under existing circumstances. In order to emphasise this distinction, I have thought it well in conclusion to subjoin the following letter addressed to Mr. Auberon Herbert on the principles under-lying his treatise on *Compulsion by the State.*[1]

To the Hon. Auberon Herbert.

MY DEAR SIR—I have been reading over, very carefully for the third or fourth time, your booklet on *Compulsion by the State*, with a view

---

[1] Mr. Herbert has promised to reply to this letter, but pressure of work has, I believe, prevented his doing so up to the present. When circumstances allow of the fulfilment of his promise, my readers will receive a printed copy of Mr. Herbert's reply on application to my publishers.—W. D.

to finding out the fundamental cause of our extreme divergence of opinion on certain political questions. I think you will admit that we are both what some people would call *extreme* individualists; and yet, "having offered my allegiance to liberty, prepared to follow her frankly and faithfully wherever she leads," I do *not* find that I am "irresistibly drawn step by step to the same conclusions" as those set forth in your program (*Compulsion*, p. 59). To me it seems that some of them are not only arbitrary but false. And I am therefore driven to conclude either that your logic is faulty, or that the principle upon which you build your superstructure is in some way defective.

We agree, as you know, on so many points regarding internal legislation and administration, that I need but glance at them in the order in which you mention them.

Class A.—The abolition and reduction of State departments and officials seems to be rather the necessary result of narrowing the State functions than a deduction from the principle of liberty. So, again, the abolition of perpetual pensions is merely a question of political expediency. It cannot much matter to any one whether the State pays a deserving servant £20,000 in cash down, or a perpetual pension of £600 a year, except that by adopting the latter alternative it constitutes itself the trustee for his successors, instead of leaving them free to squander the capital at their pleasure. But my reason for taking exception to your proposition as it stands is that it is open to the construction—a construction sure to be put upon it by the "people"—that you are prepared to rob the present holders of perpetual pensions, whereas what you really mean is to buy them out for a lump sum at the usual actuarial computation.

The next point is Free-Trade, the full scope of which you hardly, perhaps, in this place explain with sufficient clearness as meaning free trade in all things, as well internal as external, in which, of course, I cordially concur.

With you I should like to see the National Debt paid off as quickly as is compatible with the convenience of the tax-payers; also, as far as possible, to make a beginning out of the proceeds of the sale of such national property as is not required for the efficient working of Government. I suppose you would sell the British Museum and National Gallery, but not the Houses of Parliament nor Knightsbridge Barracks ? But beyond making a start and getting rid of a few encumbrances, I am afraid you would make but a small hole in the debt when all was sold, after which what would remain to be mortgaged, as you suggest ? When you speak of selling such ecclesiastical property as may be adjudged to belong equitably to the nation, I should first want to know who is to sit as judge. If the House of Commons, then I protest against having questions of fact as to title decided by a legislative body.

Class B.—By all means abolish legislation creating a monopoly in the drink traffic. Throw open the professions of law and medicine, but straiten the law as to practising either under false pretences. Remove legal impediments restraining the free sale of land by its owner, but specify what those impediments now are. Get out of the postal and telegraph business with as little loss as possible. And by all means let us devote a little careful study to the law of libel, mindful of the fact that it should not always be permissible to injure another even by telling the truth.

Class C.—Agreed, without qualification. Do away with State education, State religion, and poor laws ; also with State inspection and regulation of factories, mines, railways, ships, etc. etc. Nothing could be better.

Class D.—There is little disagreement between us as to the matters comprised under this heading. Repeal laws enforcing vaccination and compulsory notification of disease ; repeal laws imposing oaths ; laws imposing special observance of Sunday or any other day ; laws suppressing brothels, not otherwise nuisances (if any) ; laws empowering the police to arrest prostitutes, not otherwise nuisances ; all laws worrying persons of an inquiring turn of mind as to the future or the unknowable, such as fortune-tellers, spiritualists, and expounders of " revelations " ; laws forbidding vivisection ; laws interfering with the stage and the amusements of the people ; laws restricting the liquor traffic, and all other laws having similar objects.

But I do not quite see how you can well deprive Government of the power to take property compulsorily, provided full compensation is paid.

And I do not see what the State has got to do with either sanctioning or preventing marriage or divorce, except in so far as it is the duty of the State to enforce the fulfilment of a contract, or the payment of reasonable damages for the breach thereof. When a prepossessing woman marries young on the terms of a life-partnership, and is put away at the age of fifty, and the partnership dissolved against her will, her capital (so to speak) having in the meantime been exhausted for the good of the firm, it seems but just that, as her youth and beauty cannot be returned to her, some compensation should be made for breach of contract.

As to vivisection, I suppose you would hardly repeal the Cruelty to Animals Acts, and the common law relating to such cruelty. It seems to me that here we have a case in which it is hard to draw a hard-and-fast line. Cruelty to animals is a crime in the most accurate sense of the term, and it is impossible for the law of civil injury to take cognisance of it. In this respect it is on all-fours with murder ; for neither a living dog nor a dead man can sue for redress of any kind.

Class E.—Let us certainly do away, as you propose, with the thrusting of so-called " special " contracts upon contracting parties ; such as those required by the Employers' Liability Act, the Agricultural Holdings Act, and many others.

So far, we are very much in accord ; and I should not have thought of troubling you with my points of disagreement, but that as soon as we come to classes F, G, and H, I find myself almost in complete antagonism.

Class F.—I fail to see how the abolition of a House of Lords is a necessary deduction from the principle of liberty. If you had said "abolish the hereditary principle," that would be quite another matter ;

but surely a second chamber of notables, whom, for past services, the people delight to honour, is an excellent part of our constitution, and has even in its present state, of late years, amply justified its existence.

Neither do I see how the ballot can be defended on the plea of liberty. The exercise of my vote is either a right or a duty. If it is a right, you cannot justly prevent me from selling it for what it will fetch. If it is a duty, then the ballot is simply a cloak to enable me to shirk my duty by voting secretly against my conscience or against my professions.

Again, the "referendum" appears to me to be opposed to all the principles of differentiation. It operates so as to make all citizens legislators instead of judges of legislation and choosers of legislators. It is like making all of us bootmakers, instead of allowing us to judge of the boots made by rival makers and to choose our bootmakers accordingly. It is, moreover, an admission of that pestilent heresy that members of Parliament should be not representatives but delegates—mere mouthpieces. I do not see where liberty comes in there.

Separation of the Indian and Home armies—apart from my humble opinion that it would be a move in the wrong direction and a gross blunder—seems to me to be a very arbitrary kind of deduction from the principle; and the steps of the logical process are not indicated. The same remark applies to the abolition of military life in barracks; a proposal, I suppose, intended to be directed against militaryism as a system. But surely, so long as soldiers are necessary, so long as antagonistic races and nations quarrel and fight, it is better to differentiate the special arm, and avoid as much as possible the leavening of society with the tastes and habits of military life. The great development of the volunteer system strikes me as an almost unqualified evil. It has had much to do with the decay of our regular army, and with the development of the "Jingo" spirit, and the spread of quasi-military weaknesses in all ranks of society. Vivisectors are necessary; so in a lower walk of life are butchers; but do not let us encourage every man to do a little amateur butchering and vivisecting. Let us rather withdraw State recognition altogether from the volunteers—leave them alone, in fact; and abolish short service in the regular army, with its rusty reserve and its first line of incapables; and bring back the good and natural old system under which a man enters the profession as a life-work on which he can rely, and to which he can devote himself. This, however, is merely opinion, but I wish to point out my inability to deduce your program hereon from the great principle of liberty.

Class G.—Why should Ireland choose its own form of Government any more than Wales, or even Anglesey? And if there is any good ethnographical reason, then why in the name of reason should the north-east part be allowed, as you propose, to federate with a foreign country against the wish of the whole of Ireland? For precisely the same reason Cumberland might elect to join Ireland and break with England. Cumberland men are mostly of Celtic descent, and they would be sorely tempted to embrace the Irish land system in preference to their own. Certainly the people of the West of Scotland would welcome the change.

And why not ? I am bound to say that all this seems to be based on no principle at all ; and if anybody else had proposed it, I should say it was a bid for the Irish vote. As for your loan to buy out the landowners, it would half-ruin every tradesman in Ireland, and be an act of gross injustice and tyranny.· Besides, who, on your own principle, would contribute to the taxes for interest ?

Class H.—Ruling India with a view to its own "approaching self-government," and allowing Egypt to choose her own form of government, seem to me to be based on a mistaken view of foreign and colonial policy, and of the evolution of liberty. The problem surely is, how to extend the Anglo-Saxon social system with the least possible cruelty to the existing members of the races whose political systems, sooner or later, must melt away before it—whether Red Indians, Chinese, or Celts.

I cannot see what local or municipal governments have got to do with the defence of person and property any more than the Stock Exchange or the Jockey Club ; but, on the other hand, I fail to see how municipalities could get on at all without general or occasional powers of compulsorily taking land at the full market value, with compensation for disturbance. How else could they cut new streets through congested districts, etc. ? I quite agree with what you say against compelling any person to take water or gas provided by a particular body, though I am not clear how we are to dispense altogether with the levying of a uniform rate for defraying such general expenses as road-making, repairing, and cleansing. At the same time, I fully recognise the truth and importance of what you say (p. 45) as to the mischief and iniquity of compulsory taxation. I am, as I think you know, in favour of voluntary taxation, though not precisely of the kind or extent you advocate, which would, I think, be to maintain the stingy at the cost of the generous.

I have now run through the main points of your program, with much of which I am by no means in complete accord. Of course I am ready to admit that where all is matter of opinion (as in some of the questions raised) my own opinion may be a mistaken one. What, therefore, I wish to emphasise is the fact that extreme individualists may, and do, differ upon many of these important questions, and that, consequently, they are not "irresistibly drawn to the same or (even) very similar conclusions" from apparently identical premises. This being so it seems to me some-what dangerous to run the risk of weakening the position and thinning the numbers of the party of individual liberty by, as it were, pledging them to views which are outside the true province of individualism. Granting that your foreign policy and theory of State structure may be sound, still many good individualists may consistently decline to accept them.

I think the weakness of your theoretical position is most apparent when you set forth the normal functions of the State (pp. 35-38). I do not wish to lay stress on the almost sophistical reasoning by which you endeavour to deduce your conclusion from a hard-and-fast moral principle of respect for the free choice and free action of others, because you your-self admit your distrust of, and dissatisfaction with, the argument. If we can defend a law of libel, or even a law prohibiting certain very indirect forms of nuisance, on the ground that such acts or omissions are a constraining of the will and faculties of others, it is impossible to see where we shall stop. The man who (on· p. 36) destroys your lettuces might have effected his purpose by diverting the stream in his own field, which formerly watered your garden. Now this question might fall under the Roman law of real servitude, and in England a question of prescription would arise ; and in either case very complicated issues might be involved, according as the stream took its rise in his land or elsewhere, according as the bed of the stream was natural or artificial, according to the time during which you had benefited by it, and a great variety of other considerations.

In fine, the question could not be justly solved by any appeal to so simple a principle as your theory seems to imply. Let us take a much simpler question, that of acquiring something which is the portable property of another—say, a valuable ruby. You may acquire this ruby legally or illegally, morally or immorally. And, if possible, you may draw the line between the two (or either of the two) at the employment of direct or indirect coercion.

A.—I meet Smith in the desert ; he is in possession of a splendid ruby worth £10,000. I knock him down, tie his hands, rifle his pockets, and carry off the ruby.

B.—Conditions the same. I hold a pistol to his head, and demand the ruby ; he hands it to me of his own freewill and accord, and I carry it off.

C.—Conditions the same. Smith is dying of thirst ; I have a skin of water ; I threaten to leave him to perish unless he gives me the ruby ; he hands it to me, and I ride off with the ruby and the water also, and leave him to fate.

D.—Conditions the same. The same bargain as in C. I carry off the ruby, but give him the water as agreed on.

E.—Conditions the same. I give myself out as an expert lapidary ; I satisfy Smith that his ruby is only a fine but common form of amethyst, worth about £10 ; I buy it for that price, and sell it for £10,000.

F.—I meet Smith in London ; he cannot find a purchaser for his ruby at a high price ; meanwhile, I have learnt that Jones is willing to give £10,000 for such a ruby ; I keep the secret, and offer Smith £1000, which he accepts, whereupon I sell the ruby to Jones for the full price.

G.—I meet Smith in London ; I do not know of any likely purchaser, but I believe the ruby to be worth £10,000 ; I offer him £5000, which he accepts, and I carry off the ruby, and eventually sell it for £10,000.

Query.—At what point does direct coercion end and indirect begin ? At what point does my conduct cease to be immoral ? At what point is it and ought it to be regarded as illegal ?

I know that A is a case of direct coercion ; I know that it is immoral, and I know that it is and ought to be illegal. I know that G is not a case of direct coercion ; I think it is not immoral, and I know that under the English law it is not illegal, though the Roman law provided a

388 INDIVIDUALISM: A SYSTEM OF POLITICS CHAP.

remedy, and I *think* the Roman law was wrong, and the transaction ought legally to stand. With respect to B, I know it is immoral and illegal, but I am not quite sure about direct coercion. With respect to C, D, E, and F, I cannot regard them as cases of direct coercion. I consider C immoral and illegal ; I consider D immoral, but doubt whether it should be illegal ; I consider E immoral, and I think it should probably be illegal ; I think F should not be illegal, and I am doubtful of its immorality. And between any two of these roughly-graduated instances scores of delicate shades of unfairness could be drawn, concerning which it would be impossible for the subtlest casuist to generalise. If this is the case in so simple a matter as acquiring a ruby from its possessor, how can we expect to be able to deduce any general rules as to private morals or State functions from a single principle *à priori?* I regard the attempt as futile ; and I hold that only by the experience of generations can any rough, practical working rules be arrived at—that is to say, by a process of careful induction and verification.

And now to go a little deeper. Let us examine the first principle which you borrow from Mr. Spencer without, as it seems to me, sufficient analysis. According to him, it is the duty and eventual tendency of society to allow the widest liberty to each of its component individual members compatible with the equal liberty of all. Now there is here no form of liberty excluded, not even the exercise of brute force ; unless the exclusion of the exercise of brute force is involved in the term liberty. But is it ? And if so, are any other forms of force excluded—*i.e.* cunning, fraud, undue influence, etc. ? Again, if so, can all these excluded forms be generalised under some such class name as direct coercion ?

If not, the liberty of each, limited alone by the like liberty of all, is a precise description of absolute anarchy. Says the anarchist, You are free to do whatever you can do ; you are free to kill me ; I am free to kill you. Your liberty to take my goods is limited only by my liberty to keep them. All is freedom—equal freedom.

But perhaps the formula is intended to mean that you are at liberty to do whatever you please, so long as you do not thereby prevent me from doing just what it would have pleased me to do had you not been there. This is all very well so long as we keep out of each other's way. You do as you please within your ring-fence ; I do as I please within mine ; but we must not trespass on each other's preserves. Good ! But when numbers increase till the ring-fences touch and press one against the other, and tend to overlap, what then ? What shape are the fences going to assume ? "Give and take ?" Good again ! But what are we respectively to give and take ? "You may hunt in my domain and I in yours ; but you must not gather the fruits on my trees, and I may not gather the fruits on yours." It is observed, however, that there is plenty of game in my forest, and very little in yours ; whereas the proportion is reversed in the case of the fruits. I protest against the arrangement ; it looks well on paper, but it works out badly in practice. Where is the necessary and immutable fitness of it ? Or in terms of modern life, you may starve me out of existence, but I may not shoot you out of existence. Why not ?

Because one is direct coercion and the other indirect. And what then ? I prefer to make use of the direct ; it is at least more "natural." It is a custom common to all "God's creatures," and I decline to conform to your new-fangled arrangement, of which the final aim seems singularly fitted to your requirements, if not to mine. You are a crack shot, and I a good swordsman ; swords, therefore, are not fair.

But if your underlying principle is nothing more than a definition of anarchy, your defence of Government serves equally well as a defence of socialism. There is nothing whatever, either in the rule or the exception, to furnish us with the slightest clue where to draw the line. And the same remark applies to Mr. Spencer's *Man v. the State.* There is nothing in it from one end to the other which gives the smallest help to a practical lawmaker, municipal or imperial. My neighbour may not keep pigs in his own back-garden ; but he may keep an ashpit full of malodorous refuse. Why ? Ought we to allow both, or to forbid both ; or one and not the other ? and if so, which, and why ? These are trivial matters ; but trivial matters make up the whole body of law, and neither your teaching nor Mr. Spencer's seems to throw the faintest light on the problems. And until something is done to rectify this omission, I am afraid our enemies are within their logical rights in stigmatising us as doctrinaires and hobbyriders. Let our theory be such as to answer simple questions like these : Why should the State enforce contract ? Why should it enforce the fulfilment of one class of promises and not of another ? Should I be forced to compensate my neighbour for injury caused by me accidentally ? Should a bankrupt who has paid over every shilling's worth of property he possesses outside his own skin be still treated as a debtor ? Should a man be entitled to receive money damages for an insult ? If so, on what basis should they be calculated ? Should a millionaire receive heavier damages from a railway company for a broken leg than a farm-labourer ? If so, why ? And again, should a railway company be liable at all for pure accidents ? And what is an accident ? Who is really the owner of a mortgaged estate ? And who is the owner of a pawned watch ? And upon what theory of liberty should the mortgagee and the pawnbroker have priority over other creditors ? What is the basis of a prescriptive right ? To what extent should a principal be responsible for the act of his agent ? Thousands of difficult questions could be asked one after another, to the solution of which I find no guidance, either in your book or in Mr. Spencer's. And the reason is, as I have said before, that you have built on foundations of sand. The problem cannot be worked out *à priori*, but only by rigid induction. Why should the limit of individual liberty be a simple figure when even a bee's cell has eighteen sides ? In applying the deductive method to the concrete, disturbing causes very soon take us out of our reckonings. In calculating the velocity of sound, one is apt to overlook the generation of heat. In working out the direction of rays of light, a child would certainly overlook the phenomena of refraction. How much more likely are we to overlook some of the countless factors in a complex problem like that of the liberty limit ?

Let us take an extremely simple illustration. Suppose a number of men were set down on a prairie, each with a given length of wire-fencing, each with instructions to enclose as much land as possible within his wire. What shape of field would be adopted? Would they vary? And what shape ought to be adopted? Some would mark out squares, others triangles, and only those who had some little knowledge of mathematics would properly mark out circles. Now let us suppose that they all come at last to adopt the circular field; and suppose that their numbers increase till the circles press one upon another and it becomes necessary to close the interstices. What will the shape be now? Here again a little knowledge of geometry will teach us that not squares, nor triangles, but hexagons will give the largest area of land at the least expenditure of wire-fencing. But now, suppose the injustice of allowing a new-born babe an equal share with full-grown men is recognised; it is also perceived that a large man requires more than a small spare man, and it is consequently agreed that the length of each man's wire shall vary directly as his weight; what will the shape tend to become on that understanding? Here we are already out of depth. The result must be ascertained by experiment. But let us take an actual illustration. Here is a number of equal soft spheres. If they are all squeezed together till there are no spaces left between them, what will be their shape? Will they be dodecahedrons, or hexagonal prisms, or what? Well, this was the problem the bees had to solve, and any one can find out the solution by examining a honeycomb. Having done so, he can go off to a mathematician and quarrel over the answer. Their solution will differ for this reason, that the bees had to take into consideration a factor which the mathematician had not, namely, the gravity of the bee. Now if a mathematician, working out so simple a matter as the shape of a bee's cell, is liable to overlook one of the few factors in the calculation, how much the more are we certain to overlook some of the countless factors in calculating the shape of that cell which may be called " the Empire of the Individual"? We must discard all attempts to derive just laws from a single high moral principle. The attempt is as vain as that of Descartes to recreate the universe out of a single physical principle.

Moreover, whence sprang this grand moral principle that " a man has inalienable rights over himself, over his own faculties and possessions"? This, even if true now, was not always true. It is meaningless when applied to " bears and lions," and also when applied to man's remote ancestors. It is an ethical statement, and is therefore highly complex. The very term " rights" shows this. But *ex nihilo nihil fit!* From what then sprang these rights inalienable? There must have been something capable of giving them birth in the days before morality. What was that something? Surely it is obvious that right sprang out of might. A right is nothing more even now than transfigured might. The force is no longer contained in a single right arm, but it *is force;* and it is spread over a considerable surface, and is highly complex. It appears as the force of law or of public opinion. It is none the less physical force when analysed.

We must get at the bottom of this liberty. We are not to be put off with a poetical phrase. If a man is rightly, or, as a fact, the owner of his own faculties, it is for some better reason than "by virtue of that wonderful self which is in him." It is hardly courageous, at this point of the inquiry, to call in a *deus ex machina.* It is easy to say that "the freedom of a man to use either his faculties or his possessions as he himself wills, is the great moral fact that exists in independence of every form of government." Such freedom may be a right ; but surely it is not a fact. If it is a right—if it ought to be a fact—let us prove it by reasoning, and not by asserting that some great mind, which we "neither know nor understand," has placed it as the foundation of human society. I prefer to regard my rights, not as a legacy from a great mind, but as liberties which I exercise through the restraints which society in its wisdom places on the liberties of others ; out of consideration not for my welfare, but for its own. If it should hereafter appear that my exercise of proprietary right, for example, is incompatible with the lasting wellbeing of society, then my right ceases, and I have not even "a right to complain" ; for I have hitherto exercised that proprietary right not by my own strength but through that of the group which was at the back of me.

When you ask, "By what title do men exercise power over each other ?" I answer simply enough, By the title of superior strength—*force majeure*—not necessarily muscular force, but force for all that ; and what is more, physical force, by which expression I wish to exclude that which is metaphysical or supernatural. And every title, every right, can be resolved by analysis into physical force. There is no other. I regret that you have complicated matters by dragging in altogether superfluous causation. If evolution will not explain morals and rights, then I think we had better take a deep draught of Fichte's *Destiny of Man,* and tie ourselves to the apron-strings of Blind Faith. I have no doubt Leo XIII is quite ready with a cut-and-dried explanation of the origin of all rights. I ask again, Is it prudent, is it fair, at this time, when men of science have tacitly agreed to drop the antiquated appeal to an indescribable account-for-anything sort of First Cause, to rake up the mud and raise the interminable controversy anew, as the prelude to the science of law ? Is it not clear that whether we manufacture our own premisses in the form of an intelligent artificer, or of a code of "natural rights," we close the door to reason and leave it open to the dogmas of the Rousseaus, the Paines, and their modern successors ? The following paragraph from your book (p. 22) is surely a mere paraphrase of some of Mr. Henry George's writings : "I see that each man is by virtue of that wonderful self which is in him, the owner of certain faculties and energies. I see that he and none other has the rightful direction and control of these faculties and energies. They are vested in him as an inseparable inalienable part of himself ; and I can see no true way in which they can be taken forcibly from him and owned by another. But I see that the exercise of these energies and faculties depends upon the observance of the universal law that no man shall by force restrain another man in the use of his faculties."

An budge.An budge.

"And I see," says Mr. George, "that every man has an equal and an inalienable right to a share of that land which is God's gift to His creatures. I see that it is impossible for one man to be born into the world with a rightful share in that land, while another is born without it. God is just to His children. I see that none can rightfully dispossess his brother of his natural heritage." And so forth. And who shall say unto which of us "it is given" to see most clearly? Above all, let us refuse to rest until we have laid the foundations of a science of law on something more solid than natural rights of which each man must be his own judge.

An incidental evil of this substitute for reasoning is the necessity it places us in of regarding rights as something absolute, and holding good for all times and for all societies. If every Red Indian has a "right" to fish in the rivers of his country, so has every Welshman in his. If a Hindu has a "right" to maintenance by his family or clan, so has an Englishman. If every Scotchman has a "right" to a parliamentary vote, so has every Turk. This is to exclude law from the domain of evolution. But what ground have we for this? Now that the animal and vegetable kingdom have been brought within that domain, now that human institutions, customs, habits, and even beliefs have been shown to be subject to general laws of development, what conceivable ground can we have for leaving ethics and nomology out in the cold, to be expounded on the ancient methods of dogmatism and supernaturalism? Why should "rights" alone, of all things in nature, be absolute, immutable, and eternal? This strange superstition must follow the others. Doubtless it has its origin deep down in the instinct of self-preservation. It is difficult and terrible to realise the fact that *oneself* is outside the circle of the "fittest," who only shall survive. There must be some reason why *we* should not succumb. And so we clutch at the first straw held out to us—the Right to Live. Presently follow the train of other rights with a like foundation, ending with "the inalienable right of every babe born into the world to a box at the opera." Whether we create our own Creator, and endow him with our own feelings and beliefs and sentiments, or draft a code of "natural laws" which are but the embodiment of our own notions of what ought to be, we do but make the ultimate appeal to our own selves. The creator which each moralist worships and calls in as arbiter is his own ideal creator, and by no means in perfect accord with the creator appealed to by his brother moralist. The mere affirmation of the existence of an interfering providence, or its denial, is not the point in question. Nor is it necessary to quarrel with the moralist who maintains that whatever eventually turns out to be the right view concerning conduct is the view taken by the Deity. Such assertions in no way vitiate the process of scientific inquiry. Such an attitude was adopted by Buckle without any prejudicial effect on the value of his conclusions. It is not the First Cause (intelligent or otherwise) towards which science is hostile. It is the wooden idol, the god made by each baffled investigator out of his own head, against which her denunciations are directed.

Some time ago the following appeared in *Justice*, the organ of the Social Democratic Federation (August 29, 1885): "What is the ideal towards which the spirit of the age is tending—the ideal to which the best and bravest throughout the world aspire? It is the principle of equal justice to each and all, in all the relations of life, and through all the ramifications of society. It is equal liberty, equal opportunities for growth, for progress, for every human being, not excepting even one. The principle of justice is eternal, immutable, unchangeable. It is not one thing to-day and another to-morrow—not one thing in Europe and something else in Asia or Africa. Man existed long before society, as society existed long before Government. The rights of the individual are sacred. They can neither be alienated nor abdicated nor transferred. Society is but an aggregation of individuals, and it is sacred only in virtue of the sacredness of the rights of the individuals of which it is composed. The only legitimate basis of society is that of free association for equal advantage, for the mutual benefit of all its members. The violation of the rights of a single individual is an act of treason—is an act of war against humanity."

I suppose there is hardly a word in this which might not have consistently appeared in *Compulsion by the State;* but what is the conclusion which the writer draws from these lofty premisses? "Let then the good and true of every class and of every nation grasp hands in the name of the Social Revolution, and let their cry be, Down with Landlordism! Down with Usury! and the reconstruction of society on a socialistic basis."

Does not this bear out my contention, that from vague premisses anything may be apparently deduced which suits the fancy of the manipulator?

Every word in the above applies with equal force to much that is contained in Mr. Spencer's essay on "The Great Political Superstition," after which admission you will be justified in replying to me in the few but forcible words, *Mallem mehercule errare cum Platone.*

However, in spite of all this "captious" criticism, I do not hesitate to say that I know of no book the extensive circulation of which is, in my opinion, calculated to do more unqualified good than your *Compulsion.* My quarrel is *mainly* with the speculative foundations on which you base your principles.—I am, my dear sir, yours truly,

WORDSWORTH DONISTHORPE.

THE END

Printed by R. & R. CLARK, *Edinburgh*

Messrs. MACMILLAN & CO.'S PUBLICATIONS.

The American Commonwealth. By JAMES BRYCE, M.P., D.C.L., Regius Professor of Civil Law in the University of Oxford, Author of "The Holy Roman Empire." Three Vols. Demy 8vo. 54s.

PART I.—The National Government.	PART IV.—Public Opinion.
PART II.—The State Governments.	PART V.—Illustrations & Reflections.
PART III.—The Party System.	PART VI.—Social Institutions.

Library Edition. Uniform with "The American Commonwealth."

The Holy Roman Empire. By JAMES BRYCE, M.P., D.C.L. Eighth Edition. Library Edition. Demy 8vo. 14s. Popular Edition. Cr. 8vo. 7s. 6d.

By JOHN RICHARD GREEN, M.A., LL.D., late Honorary Fellow of Jesus' College, Oxford.

A Short History of the English People. New and Thoroughly Revised Edition. With Coloured Maps, Genealogical Tables, and Chronological Annals. Crown 8vo. 8s. 6d. 148th Thousand.

History of the English People. In 4 vols. 8vo. With Maps. 16s. each.

The Making of England. With Maps. 8vo. 16s.

The Conquest of England. With Maps and Portrait. 8vo. 18s.

The Swiss Confederation. By SIR FRANCIS OTTIWELL ADAMS K.C.M.G., C.B., late Her Majesty's Envoy Extraordinary and Minister Plenipotentiary at Bern, and C. D. CUNNINGHAM. 8vo. 14s.

Reports on Elementary Schools, 1852-1882. By MATTHEW ARNOLD, D.C.L., one of H.M.'s Inspectors of Schools. Edited by the Right Hon. Sir FRANCIS SANDFORD, K.C.B. Crown 8vo. 7s. 6d.

By A. V. DICEY, B.C.L., of the Inner Temple; Barrister-at-Law; Vinerian Professor of English Law in the University of Oxford; Fellow of All Soul's College; Hon. LL.D. Glasgow.

Lectures Introductory to the Study of the Law of the Constitution. Third Edition. Demy 8vo. 12s. 6d.

Letters on Unionist Delusions. Crown 8vo. 2s. 6d.

The Privy Council. Crown 8vo. 3s. 6d.

By the Right Honourable JOHN BRIGHT, M.P.

Speeches on Questions of Public Policy. Edited by Professor THOROLD ROGERS. Second Edition. 2 vols. 8vo. 25s. With Portrait. *Author's Popular Edition.* New Edition. Extra fcap. 8vo. 3s. 6d.

Public Addresses. Edited by Prof. THOROLD ROGERS. 8vo. 14s.

Richard Cobden's Speeches on Questions of Public Policy. Edited by the Right Hon. JOHN BRIGHT, M.P., and JAMES E. THOROLD ROGERS. Extra fcap. 8vo. 3s. 6d.

Edmund Burke's Letters, Tracts, and Speeches on Irish Affairs. Arranged and Edited by MATTHEW ARNOLD, with a Preface. Crown 8vo. 6s.

MR. JOHN MORLEY'S COLLECTED WRITINGS.

A New Edition. In 10 vols. Globe 8vo. 5s. each.

Voltaire. 1 Vol.	On Compromise. 1 Vol.
Rousseau. 2 Vols. [2 Vols.	Miscellanies. 3 Vols.
Diderot and the Encyclopædists.	Burke. 1 Vol.

By JOHN FISKE, formerly Lecturer on Philosophy at Harvard University.

The Critical Period in American History, 1783-1789. Extra Crown 8vo. 10s. 6d.

The Beginnings of New England; or, The Puritan Theocracy in its Relations to Civil and Religious Liberty. Crown 8vo. 7s. 6d.

American Political Ideas viewed from the Standpoint of Universal History. Three Lectures delivered at the Royal Institution of Great Britain. Crown 8vo. 4s.

MACMILLAN AND CO., LONDON.

Messrs. MACMILLAN & CO.'S PUBLICATIONS.

By E. A. FREEMAN, D.C.L., LL.D., Regius Professor of Modern History in the University of Oxford, Fellow of Oriel College, and Hon. Fellow of Trinity College, Oxford.

Old English History. With Five Coloured Maps. Ninth Edition, revised. Extra fcap. 8vo. 6s.

Historical Essays. First Series. 8vo. 10s. 6d. Second Series. 10s. 6d. Third Series. 12s.

The Growth of the English Constitution from the Earliest Times. Fifth Edition. Crown 8vo. 5s.

General Sketch of European History. New Edition. Enlarged, with Maps, etc. 18mo. 3s. 6d.

Comparative Politics. Lectures at the Royal Institution. To which is added "The Unity of History." 8vo. 14s.

Historical and Architectural Sketches; chiefly Italian. Illustrated by the Author. Crown 8vo. 10s. 6d.

Subject and Neighbour Lands of Venice. Being a Companion Volume to "Historical and Architectural Sketches." With Illustrations. Crown 8vo. 10s. 6d.

English Towns and Districts. A Series of Addresses and Essays. With Illustrations and a Map. 8vo. 14s.

The Methods of Historical Study. Eight Lectures read in the University of Oxford in Michaelmas Term, 1884, with the Inaugural Lecture on "The Office of the Historical Professor." 8vo. 10s. 6d.

The Chief Periods of European History. Six Lectures read in the University of Oxford in Trinity Term, 1885, with an Essay on "Greek Cities under Roman Rule." 8vo. 10s. 6d.

By J. R. SEELEY, M.A., Regius Professor of Modern History in the University of Cambridge.

Lectures and Essays. 8vo. 10s. 6d.

The Expansion of England. Two Courses of Lectures. Crown 8vo. 4s. 6d.

Our Colonial Expansion. Extracts from "The Expansion of England." Crown 8vo. 1s.

Annals of our Time. A Diurnal of Events, Social and Political, Home and Foreign, from the Accession of Queen Victoria down to Jubilee Day, being the first Fifty Years of Her Majesty's Reign. By JOSEPH IRVING. 2 vols. 8vo. 18s. each. Volume I.—June 20, 1837, to Feb. 28, 1871. Volume II.—Feb. 24, 1871, to June 24, 1887.

** The Second Volume may also be had in three parts. Part I.—Feb. 24, 1871, to March 19, 1874. 4s. 6d. Part II.—March 2, 1874, to July 22, 1878. 4s. 6d. Part III.—July 23, 1878, to June 24, 1887. 9s.

TWENTY-SIXTH YEAR OF PUBLICATION (Revised after Official Returns) of the

Statesman's Year-Book: A Statistical and Historical Annual of the States of the Civilised World. For the year 1889. Edited by J. SCOTT KELTIE, Librarian to the Royal Geographical Society. Crown 8vo. 10s. 6d.

THIRD AND POPULAR EDITION, PRICE TWO SHILLINGS.

The Parnell Commission. The Opening Speech for the Defence, delivered by Sir CHARLES RUSSELL, Q.C., M.P. Carefully revised by the Author. Demy 8vo. LIBRARY EDITION, 10s. 6d. POPULAR EDITION paper covers, 2s.

Profit-Sharing between Employer and Employee ; A Study in the Evolution of the Wages System. By NICHOLAS PAINE GILMAN. Crown 8vo. 7s. 6d.

MACMILLAN AND CO., LONDON.

www.ingramcontent.com/pod-product-compliance
Lightning Source LLC
Chambersburg PA
CBHW032340280326
41935CB00008B/390